DONNA KOOLER'S

encyclopedia *of* knitting

A LEISURE ARTS PUBLICATION

DONNA KOOLER'S

encyclopedia
of
knitting

A LEISURE ARTS PUBLICATION

Library of Congress Cataloging-in-Publication Data
    Kooler, Donna
    Donna Kooler's Encyclopedia of Knitting
    "A Leisure Arts Publication"

ISBN: 1 - 5 7 4 8 6 - 2 8 3 - 9

contributors

produced by

published by

If you have questions or comments
please contact:

LEISURE ARTS CUSTOMER SERVICE
5701 RANCH DRIVE
LITTLE ROCK, AR 72223-9633
www.leisurearts.com

KOOLER DESIGN STUDIO, INC.
399 TAYLOR BLVD., SUITE 104
PLEASANT HILL, CA 94523
kds@koolerdesign.com

PRINTED IN CHINA BY
R.R. DONNELLEY & SONS, CO.

creative director
DONNA KOOLER

editor in chief
JUDY SWAGER

encyclopedia editor & project manager
MARSHA HINKSON

writers
TEXT: SHELLEY CARDA
PATTERN GALLERY: NANCY NEHRING

editors
PROJECTS: LEISURE ARTS
TEXT & PATTERN GALLERY: SHELLEY CARDA
PATTERN GALLERY: NANCY NEHRING

technical advisor
EVIE ROSEN

proofreader
MU'AFRIDA BELL

indexer
FRANCES BOWLES

book design & production
NANCY WONG SPINDLER

illustrators
JO LYNN TAYLOR, JESSICA MAIN

project designers
LILY CHIN, EVELYN CLARK, JOANNE CLARK,
LISA DANIELS, JANE DAVIS, NICKY EPSTEIN,
BEV GALESKAS, DEB GEMMELL, MARSHA HINKSON,
KATHLEEN POWER JOHNSON
PHILOSOPHER'S WOOL CO., COY ROBERTS

photography/color separator
DIANNE WOODS, BERKELEY, CA

photo stylist
BASHA KOOLER HANNER

models
MISSY MITCHELL, ANDREA MITCHELL,
MICHAEL HENDRY, EMERY LOW, JENNIFER FOYE,
COURTNEY THOMPSON, GRACE RHOADS,
THEA DORA HANNER

knitters
PROJECTS: JOYCE TOBENKIN
PATTERN GALLERY: CINDY HAUSMAN

foreword

My mother, an avid knitter, taught me to knit when I was about five years old. I loved her long, brightly colored plastic needles; it was fun to see how far I could bend them before they broke. She did not find this fun, and thus I found myself with a pair of silver aluminum needles and some purple yarn, knitting a pair of mittens. I was quite proud of them, even though one was much larger than the other. I didn't know then that those mittens were the beginning of a life-long love affair with yarn and needles. That purple yarn probably came from the dime store, and certainly bore no resemblance to the gorgeous yarns we knitters are blessed with today. Much of the impetus for the resurgence of interest in knitting is due to those fabulous, textured, wonderfully colored yarns, as well as to fashion trends.

As an almost life-long knitter, and a constant reader of books about knitting, I thought I already knew just about everything there is to know about the subject. I was wrong. In this wonderful book Donna Kooler, one of the needlework industry's most talented and respected designers, authors, and publishers, has shown me a lot of things that I didn't know I didn't know about knitting! For example, I had never heard about Baltic knitting, an intriguing method of braided knitting. I never knew that "lace knitting" and "knitted lace" were two different things. I didn't know there is a way to make the knit stitch truly square. And there was a lot I didn't know about the fascinating history of knitting.

In this book are the best instructions I've ever seen for felting and knitting with beads. You'll find complete guides for entrelac, jacquard, Fair Isle, and intarsia—all traditional methods for working with color. The variety of stitches, shown in both diagram form and written, will make you want to drop everything and try them. And of course there are projects, some classic and some just plain "wow." And this wonderful book is all wrapped up in colorful photos that can't help but stir up your creative juices.

Thank you, Donna, your great staff, and contributing designers for this must-have book. I recommend you do not lend it even to your closest friend, as you will probably never get it back!

Jean Leinhauser

acknowledgements

For me, this is the best part of producing books. After a year and a half of intense work, I get a chance to thank and acknowledge the talented group of experts who made this encyclopedia a treasure trove of information and creativity. My heartfelt thanks to Marsha Hinkson, for her extraordinary patience, talent, and dedication to this project, and to Shelley Carda for allowing us to share her knowledge and love of knitting, past and present. Shelley's use of the English language is a delight for the mind and eye. I want to thank the talented designers for their wonderful projects, and the knitters who lovingly brought them to life—stitch by stitch. Thanks to Nancy Nehring for her imaginative pattern gallery and to Cindy Hausman for stitching and proofing each and every one of the pattern gallery samples. My thanks to Jo Lynn Taylor for the intricate and informative charts and diagrams she so expertly created, Nancy Wong Spindler for her great book design, and Dianne Woods for her beautifully photographed images. Also a thank you to Meg Swansen at Schoolhouse Press for her heroic search for out-of-print books and her generosity in allowing us to photograph her unusual knitting implements.

I am forever grateful to Basha Kooler Hanner for her beautiful photo styling, the entire staff of Kooler Design Studio, and Judy Swager for supporting this project with their talent, encouragement, and hard work. And to countless others who have contributed their time, talent, encouragement, and resources to make this the beautiful, informative, and enjoyable book that it is, I thank you!

This book is dedicated to Doug Kooler, who has been my support, my partner, my husband and best friend for most of my life.

Donna Kooler

contents

beginnings

knitting basics

beyond the basics

projects

pattern gallery

for your information

FOR CENTURIES knitting provided warm clothing in cold climates. But since mass production took over the drudgery, knitting has become a beloved pastime for producing beautiful, one-of-a-kind clothing—and much, much more.

Hard to imagine that the task of yesteryear is now the diversion of movie stars, top executives, and busy young homemakers? It is relaxing and practical, of course. But when you see ingenious and streamlined basics combined with a wealth of decorative techniques, you'll wonder what happened to the knitting you thought you knew. Dust off your imagination and your knitting needles. Welcome to the 21st century.

Are you looking for a lot of style with your basics? We serve up traditional knitting techniques from all corners of the world and with a healthy dollop of avant garde. Projects from today's brightest designers inspire you as they teach you the latest tricks of the knitting trade. Once you understand how knitting works, you will be able to turn your warmest, woolliest dreams into reality. If you dream beyond wool, we include beads, ribbons, spangles, lace, flourishes, trims, and curlicues.

Spend the weekend "curled up with a good *knitting* book," and Monday morning will find you brimming with creativity and accomplishment. This is the reason people the world over keep the knitting tradition alive and well. Come join us!

WHERE KNITTING COMES FROM

Imagine getting up and pulling on pantyhose made of ripstop nylon, or wrapping strips of wool gabardine from toe to knee before stepping into loafers. Imagine a world where all is woven, a world without nylons, socks, tee shirts, stretchy lingerie, sweaters, and sweatshirts. Unlike woven cloth, knitted fabric adjusts to a body in motion. Knits make our lives flexible.

Generations of people have worn woven clothing that did not move or stretch with them. Knights in armor wore woven woolen hose with seams that ran from crotch to toe, and were cranky enough to wage war for a century.[1] (Riding breeches are still cut like deflated beach balls because woven fabric does not stretch as you straddle a horse.) Ladies have suffered through fitted linen slips that required corsets, brassieres like rocket nose cones, and panties the size of pillowcases.

Still, the question is not "Why didn't someone invent knitting sooner?" but rather, "How did anyone figure it out at all?" Weaving was on the scene in the stone age, tens of thousands of years before knitting, because in the course of observing nature, lots of things lead you to think of weaving. Weaving is in bird nests and spider webs. Look at your folded hands, with fingers interlaced and palms down; you have before your eyes the inspiration for a tabby or a twill pattern. Perhaps you are sitting by the fire one prehistoric night, playing with a piece of sinew from dinner. You wrap it over and under the fingers of one hand and have weaving.

Knitting, on the other hand, mimics nothing in nature. There must first be loops on a stick, then a second stick to draw a new loop through each loop just before you drop it, creating a flat fabric structure that is flexible in every direction. This is genius, plain and simple. No wonder it took millennia to figure out; we are lucky to have it at all. But where did it come from?

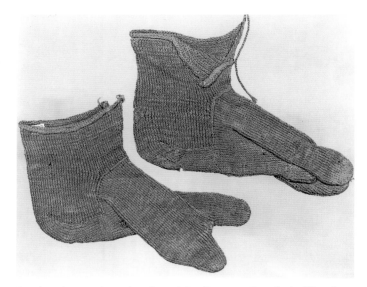

Oxyrhynchus socks, 4th–5th c. A.D. (Romano-Egyptian) (Victoria & Albert Museum)

UNRAVELING THE MYSTERY

Though we see examples of sophisticated woven cloth even before the Neolithic period, about 6000 B.C., nothing even resembles knitting until the late Iron Age (c. 400 B.C.–1 B.C.) with a fragment of a needle technique for netting, most commonly known as nålbinding.

Nålbinding is a stretchy, looped fabric made by sewing loops of yarn through each other with a blunt needle. The basic nålbinding stitch is formed around the thumb and twisted during construction, so the stitches look like stitches knitted through the back loop. Each loop is sewn through one other free loop. This differs from offset meshes of regular netting, in which the ends of each mesh are looped around the threads of two separate meshes.

Tenth century woolen sock from Coppergate made using the nålbinding technique. (Property of York Archaelogical Trust.)

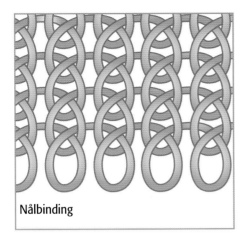

Nålbinding

Nålbinding is technically a knitted fabric, odd though the manufacture may be. On closer inspection it differs from modern knitting at increases and decreases. Some things possible in nålbinding are unwieldy or impossible with knitting, so it is possible to distinguish shaped garments made by the two techniques. Ancient nålbinded items found include small bags, and garments that need to stretch and bend around odd shapes—usually feet and hands. Because such garments receive hard wear, the technique may be much older than the oldest extant examples. Nålbinding is generally considered the precursor to modern knitting and still plays a limited role in garment making, usually in a folk context.

There are examples of nålbinding from the 3rd century found in excavations of the city of Dura-Europos (destroyed in A.D. 247) which was at that time a Roman outpost. The fact that Roman officers wore sock-like garments under their boots[2] suggests that soldiers in this Roman outpost could have availed themselves of this functional garment. There are also pre-Islamic Egyptian nålbinded socks from the 4th–6th centuries, indicating that the technique did not die at Dura-Europos.

A 3rd century mitten of nålbinding also exists from Åsle, Västergötland, Sweden,[3] as well as later examples of nålbinded garments from Scandinavian and Baltic countries. Norse invasions into England introduced the technique there, too, as seen in a 10th century A.D. sock found in the excavations at Jorvik, a Norse settlement that became York. The Roman presence in Dura-Europos, Germany, and England establishes a connection by which Romans could have introduced nålbinding to northern Europe, but the invention of nålbinding in the two widely separate regions may be independent of each other.

Nålbinding could also have developed from weaving. Twining (looping) a separate, colored thread around the warp (lengthwise) threads, one by one, formed a design while cloth was being woven. Nålbinding is a similar concept: a strand of yarn looped through other loops. The invention of rigid heddle looms allowed decorative threads to be laid between whole sections of threads at once, but it limited artistic spontaneity, so fiber artists did not abandon the old techniques when they

adopted the new ones. Twined weaving was widely used in the Egyptian period, and is still used today. In any case, since the earliest evidence of knitting in Scandinavian countries is from the 16th century,[4] it is more likely that knitting developed from Egyptian than from Scandinavian nålbinding.

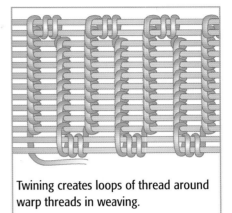

Twining creates loops of thread around warp threads in weaving.

FOOT NOTES

Weaving was remarkably sophisticated even in Neolithic times. As early as 3000 B.C. the Egyptians were picking up loops of warp or weft (crosswise) thread on sticks as they wove, making decorative raised-loop designs on fabrics. Bedspreads are often made this way even now. This shows that the basis for knitting—a row of loops on a stick—was a familiar technique in ancient Egypt.[5] The next step of picking up a loop through each loop on the stick might not occur for 4000 years, but the first step was established.

Egyptian nålbinded socks have moderate-looking stitch gauges, such as you might obtain using a slim knitting needle. It seems likely that a thin rod (rather than the thumb) was used as a gauge when forming stitches. Early connections between nålbinding and weaving might have made differences between "woven" and "knitted" less significant in ancient times than the way we view them today.

There is evidence of knitting worked on rods (modern knitting) in the Islamic period in Egypt, which began c. A.D. 639. One fabric fragment (now lost) from the collection of textile expert Fritz Iklé (d.1946)[6] was dated 7th–9th century A.D., though the stitches were twisted. Egyptian fragments and stockings, done with untwisted stitches and characteristic knitted (rather than nålbinded) shaping, exist from c. A.D. 1200–1500. At least some of these examples of multicolored knitting were done in the round for clothing.

Exotic goods from the farthest reaches of Roman power and beyond,[7] anything novel in dress or fashion, was of great interest in wealthy, luxury-loving, Imperial Rome. Egypt became a tributary to Rome in the first century A.D. when Cleopatra, Julius Caesar, and Marc Anthony had their disastrous romp. Had knitting been a significant, or even insignificant, craft while Rome was the dominant power in Egypt, it would have aroused interest in Rome simply because it was

II

Knitted blue and white Islamic stocking, c. A.D. 1200–1500. (Textile Museum, Washington, D.C.)

new and different. There is no evidence that it did.

Even when the Roman empire became the Byzantine empire in A.D. 330, with Emperor Constantine's new capital city of Constantinople (now Istanbul, Turkey) conveniently linking the Eastern and Western Roman Empire, knitting did not show up in the West until well into the Islamic period. There is no reason to believe that knitting did not originate in the Middle East and linger there for a while in relative obscurity.

From Islamic North Africa it is but a short jump to southern Spain, where knitting appears next. The craft was already highly developed by the last quarter of the 13th century, from which period we find a beautiful knitted pillow in the tomb of Spanish royalty. Fernando de la Cerda, Infante of Spain, was buried circa 1275 with a silk cushion knitted in two colors, gold and brown (or faded red). One side has a pattern of alternating fleurs-de-lys and eagles in a lattice pattern, and on the other side is an even more complex pattern.[8]

Socks and funerary cushions are very different objects. Socks pragmatically exploit the stretchy qualities of knitting to permit a wide range of motion to an oddly shaped appendage. But the Spanish funerary cushion is an unshaped bag, stuffed and stationary. The knit-like qualities of knitting are completely ignored while multicolored brocade qualities are the focus. This is a contrary use of knitting if you see it as knitting, but not very surprising if you see it only as fabric. There was no functional reason for cushions to be knitted rather than woven brocade, which suggests that the knitted textile was chosen for its beauty or novelty as a textile rather than for its knit characteristics. The fine gauge of 20 stitches per inch is finer than most modern socks, but not particularly fine compared to woven fabric, especially the silks, damasks, and brocades of the East; the Arabic inscription around the cushion links the craftsman with the Islamic world.[9] A blurring of the distinction between knitting and decorative weaving would not be exceptional if knitting were originally perceived as being merely a variant of weaving, with socks being either functional offspring or even the surprised parent of a new use for loops picked up on rods.

Vitale degli Equi called da Bolognia 1309 ca. 1361–1361
The Virgin of Humility with Saint Catherine of Alexandria and
a Martyr Saint (Museo Poldi Pezzoli, Milan, Italy)

ON THE OTHER...

The hand is as irregular as the foot and even harder to cover, especially if you want the fingers to be separated. Bishops' gloves were part of their liturgical regalia, and did not see hard use. This explains the numerous preserved gloves from the early medieval period, throughout Europe and England. Liturgical regalia was luxury knitting, outranking even royal luxuries, and would demonstrate the best technical achievements of the times.

Knitters had contrived to produce gloves by the 13th century. The Cathedral of St. Sernin in Toulouse, France, houses a pair of plain white knitted gloves.[10] Fragments of gloves from Bonn, Germany, interred with Bishop Siegfried von Westerburg in 1297, were made with stranded color knitting, similar to that found on the Spanish funerary cushion.[11] The level of knitting was quite good for the high classes of society, but what about the lower classes?

Peasants and craftsmen were the basic classes that created the technology,[12] including all the techniques to make gloves with fingers. But we haven't seen knitting in the context of the medieval European worker, probably because a knitted object was worn out by the owner, or passed along to heirs and worn out. Still, there is pictorial evidence of who used knitting.

13

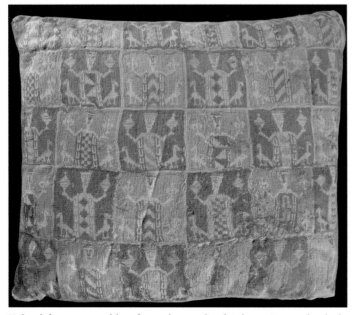

Knitted funerary cushion from the tomb of Infante Fernando de la Cerda, c. A.D. 1275. (copyright © Patriomonio Nacional, Madrid, Spain)

Back of funerary cushion.

Holy Family, attributed to Ambrogio Lorenzetti (c. 1349) of Siena.
Photo: Abegg-Stiftung, Riggisberg (Christoph von Virag)

BABY CLOTHES

Paintings of the Virgin Mary knitting, sometimes called "knitting Madonnas," attest to the knowledge of knitting in Italy by the first half of the 14th century. These paintings show the Virgin knitting as she tends the Christ Child, watched by angels, other saints, or St. Joseph, her husband. (Knitting still draws spectators.) The Virgin knits in the round, sometimes with multiple colors, showing that the technology used for Egyptian socks was already associated with women's work, at least in the painters' minds.

The earliest of these compositions, from the 14th century by Vitale of Bologna,[13] has strongly Byzantine characteristics. Itinerant Byzantine artisans traveled between North Africa, Asia Minor, and Europe in the seven centuries between the rise of Islam and the fall of the Byzantine Empire,[14] and were well placed to become acquainted with other craftsmen. Knitting is certainly more portable than weaving, an obvious advantage to itinerant artisans (and their families), who could have brought both knitting and Byzantine stylistic influences into Italy simultaneously.

A second knitting Madonna, by Ambrogio Lorenzetti, c. 1349, is interesting because Lorenzetti is noted for having been quite radical in depicting the Virgin with the humanity of the commoners, rather than the honor due to queens, throughout his career.[15] In this painting the Virgin is sitting on the floor, like a peasant, knitting while the Christ Child clings to her knee, and St. Joseph, sitting on a stool, watches. Knitting was one of the activities of peasant women at this time.

It is unlikely that reverent altarpieces of the Madonna and Christ Child would introduce a revolutionary theme of the Madonna usurping a male-dominated trade, so we may assume the sight of a woman knitting for her child was unchallenging, even sweetly domestic. If knitting was unknown in the regions where the paintings were painted, observant local women would have been quick to learn the extremely practical needlework that the Virgin Mary did at home. So would their children.

ON TOP OF IT

Sons who learned to knit at their mothers' knees were well equipped to expand knitting into manufacturing and lucrative new trades. Hats were worn by all levels of society, what with lice and no shampoo and all the other medieval inconveniences. Usually hats were made of felt: wool or hair fibers pounded together into a shaped whole. But if you knitted yarn into the shape you wanted first, then shrank the structure into a felted whole, the shaping process was more controlled and more variable. Enterprising cap makers added another specialty to their long-established trade. In Paris the hat makers' guild (Corps de la Bonneterie) chose St. Fiacra as their patron saint because he was already the patron saint of the cotton-hat makers,[16] but he has become, by logical confusion, the patron saint of knitters. No matter, the real patron saint of hat makers is changing fashion. Hats grew tall like sugar loaves, then they became flat like accordions; they became pancakes with small brims, then with broad, floppy brims. Knitting the shape first, with increases and decreases, made it easier to control the areas of folding, brim flare, and all the other changes that fashion could dream up.

England trailed behind its European neighbors in acquiring knitting, though knit hats were manufactured in England at least as early as 1465.[17] There are some remnants of skullcaps, and pancake-like bonnets have survived miraculously since the 16th century. In one of these the gauge is 1 stitch per centimeter,[18] or about 1 stitch per ½ inch, similar to modern hats knitted with thick yarn. This is not fine knitting for royal tombs, but common knitting for utilitarian garments. Though used in a skilled trade, coarse knitting suitable for caps could be done at home by women and children. Protected knitters' guilds were not formed in England as they were on the conti-

Daniel Hopler, *Landsknecht and Wife,* 1510–1530. (Print Collection, Miriam and Ira D. Wallach Divison of Art, Prints and Photographs, The New York Public Library, Astor, Lenox and Tilden Foundations)

nent,[19] which set the stage for the cottage industry that sprang up later. In the meantime, socks were made for English children, with rudimentary heel shaping in garter stitch.[20]

Even early knitted fashion had its odd moments. In 1477, in a decisive battle between Swiss and Burgundian soldiers at Nancy, France, the Burgundian Charles the Bold was killed. Swiss soldiers ransacked his tent for spoils, hacking his extensive wardrobe and luxurious textiles into bits to stuff the holes of their ragged clothing. When the victorious soldiers returned home, admiring Swiss civilians adopted this bizarre fashion of slashed hose with different colored underlayers puffing out of the slashes.[21] Swiss mercenaries spread and exaggerated this fashion as a mark of professional pride, and the fashion continued into the mid-16th century in Germany, Italy, and wherever folly allowed.[22] Fashionable men of the time slashed their long hose and allowed a second, bright layer of hose to show through beneath. If they could not afford two layers, hairy

thigh showed through.[23] While distasteful, this does not differ significantly from modern mesh gym clothes.

Not content with having their hose divided only at the crotch, men's long hose were divided yet again, this time at the knee. Now in quarters, the upper pieces became trunk hose and the lower pieces became nether hose. Trunk hose could be knitted with long buttonholes instead of slashes, solving the problem of snipping holes in expensive fabric, which bothered the fashionable nouveau riche.[24] Perhaps mercifully, knitting usually disguised itself as underwear and no one saw it or talked about it.

Knitted underwear crept up the social ladder. In 1499 Princess Margaret Tudor (Henry VIII's sister) listed "two pairs of hosen, knit"[25] among her possessions. In 1509 Henry VIII married the Spanish princess Catherine of Aragon. Despite the knitted artifacts in royal Spanish tombs, we know that knit stockings were not introduced by Queen Catherine because of the interesting comment that "Henry VIII commonly wore cloth hose, except that there came from Spain by great chance, a pair of knit silk stockings."[26] If the rare knit stockings were to Henry's taste, his divorce of Queen Catherine and the resulting insult to Spain dried up any more such gifts. Perhaps if one of his last five wives had been French or Italian he would have had a source. The oldest known guild of stocking knitters was formed in Paris in 1557,[27] and silk hose knitting businesses in Venice and Milan by 1539.[28]

By 1560 in England, Queen Elizabeth I wore only silk knitted stockings and made her preference known. Her Scottish rival, Mary Queen of Scots, also wore knitted stockings, which she may have become accustomed to in France. European royalty were all wearing knitted silk stockings by the end of the 16th century. Once the royals were wearing knitted stockings, the nobility realized how much better knitted stockings were than woven ones. They all wanted knitted stockings, too, and they didn't intend to make those stockings themselves. Knitting guilds on the continent flourished.

Stockings were being knit in the city of Nottingham by 1519,[29] but stocking knitters' guilds never formed because there was little fashionable demand for stockings for another 40 years.[30] Guilds formed only when tradesmen organized to protect the trade secrets and promote commerce. Once knitting became fashionable enough to spur the development of a full-blown trade it was too late to protect the trade secrets of knitting.[31] Then the bourgeoisie wanted luxurious knitted stockings, too, but they wanted to haggle over the price.

British merchants undercut European guild stocking knitters by going directly to rural British peasants and getting them to knit for almost nothing, then sold stockings dirt-cheap at home and abroad. Everyone loved the high quality, low cost stockings knitted by British farm families, and the farm families were glad to oblige. Knitting for pittance kept impoverished rural folk off the parish dole with a respectable, if scant, subsistence. Queen Elizabeth I is said to have denied William Lee a patent for a knitting frame because "To enjoy the privilege of making stockings for the whole of my subjects is too important to be granted to any individual…I have too much love for my poor people who gain their bread by the employment of knitting to give my money to forward an invention that will tend to their ruin by depriving them of employment and making them beggars."[32] Lee took his invention to France.[33] The French continued to import cheap, well-made English stockings.

Finally in 1657 a Framework Knitters' Guild was allowed to incorporate in England.[34] High tech knitting began, though it didn't overtake hand knitting for 200 years, in part because frame knitting was not that much more productive than hand knitters. Hand knitters could work anytime, anywhere, in any light, while frame knitters could only work at their frames in daylight.[35] The other factor was that frame-knit stockings did not have the exquisite shaping of hand-knitted stockings. Decent women didn't show their legs, but men in knee breeches depended upon elegant legs for their fashion status, and baggy stockings were a disaster. Cheap won out sometimes, but not often enough to eliminate the preference for hand knitted stockings. Not until the French Revolution, anyway, when the knee breeches of the aristocracy were abandoned in favor of the long trousers of the triumphant proletarians.[36] If you were not wearing calf-revealing breeches, who cares how your stockings fit?[37] Thus died the international hand-knitted stocking trade, a slave to crass fashion. This led to renewed rural poverty and emigration.

Where does all this talk of stockings lead? It seems interminable, and in many ways it was, because for most of its history knitting was stockings or underwear. If you were lucky enough to be rich, someone else knitted it for you. There were occasions when even underwear got its moment in the sun. At the execution of King Charles I in 1649, the doomed monarch stripped to his undershirt, which was sky blue silk, knitted in geometric knit/purl brocade patterns, and declared before he was beheaded that, "A subject and his sovereign are clean different things."[38] This showed what kings and their underwear were made of. Afterwards the king's physician kept the garment, which still exists at the London Museum.[39]

CASTING OFF FOR NEW LANDS

Puritans who left to colonize New England took along knitting because it discouraged wicked idleness, not because they preferred fashionable knitted stockings. Woven ones "are much more serviceable than knit ones."[40] Still, an enormous amount of idle time was made profitable by knitting, a skill that all the girls in the new land mastered before marriage and used perpetually thereafter. Orphan girls or daughters of indigent parents were taught to knit and sew so that they could support themselves when they were older. Women with large households or purses took on maids to help with sewing and knitting. Young girls were customarily "bound out," much as boys were apprenticed, to households where they were taught the skills of housewifery, knitting first of all.

Widows made a living by running "dame schools," where very young children were taught the alphabet and girls were taught knitting. This was often the only formal education girls received. Women in truly dire financial straits mended and washed stockings.[41] Knitting was, then as now, much more pleasurable than laundry.

At first yarn was imported by the new colonies because getting enough food took too much time to make spinning economically feasible. As land was broken and food became more plentiful, spinning wheels were imported and the production of wool yarn and linen thread were transferred to colonial soil. This did not become a matter of dispute until England, wishing to refill its war-depleted coffers, began to demand that the colonies buy only English-made yarn and thread, rather than producing their own. This led to hard feelings, the Revolutionary War, and American independence.

Time passed and America became more wealthy. Education became an increasingly available luxury. Reading, writing, needlework, and knitting were taught to girls in day or boarding schools. The population, growing in literacy and wealth, was a perfect market for publishing businesses, which brought out books of morality, household hints, and needlework patterns. These early books are a wonderful view into which skills were basic education and which ones weren't. The earliest books have patterns for knitted items, some decorative stitches, but not instructions on how to knit, so we know that in the 1840s knitting was not learned from books. The items in the earliest books are stockings or accessories or baby clothes, not outer garments, which was nothing new. Garments were made of woven cloth, and why shouldn't they be? Women and men wore corsets to set their figures into the acceptable shape. When inner clothing admits no real movement there is no reason to wear stretchy outer garments. Miss Lambert was sufficiently radical in 1857 when she included a pattern for a knitted spencer,[42] which was a short jacket, sometimes worn under the dress for warmth. They are still popular underwear in Australia and New Zealand, where central heat is not the norm.

THE WILD COLONIALS

America was not the only land colonized by knitters. From the 17th century on, colonization was one of Europe's leading industries. The earliest emigrants couldn't get along at home for economic differences (poverty), or moral differences (criminal behavior). Such people were exported to distant lands that needed the civilizing touch.[43]

Canada, New Zealand, and Australia all became knitting societies because colonists soon discovered that there were no handy peasants or factories to do the knitting. New Zealand emigrant lists of the 1840s recommended to working class male emigrants that they take knitted guernseys (pullovers), while "neither shoes nor stockings are at all necessary."[44] Work shirts of woven fabric sufficed when the guernseys wore out, and knitting skills were abandoned by women who no longer needed stockings for their families, a blessing when you are trying to make your living in a new land. At the same time, gentlemen emigrants were advised to take with them 60 pairs of stockings.[45] When those stockings were gone, where would new stockings come from? Sometimes working class immigrants refused to knit in the new land because knitting was still, to them, the work of peasants.[46] Gentlemen's imported stockings were slow to arrive and expensive, so the wives of gentlemen had to learn to knit.

All immigrants to Canada still needed warm knitted stockings to keep from freezing.[47] Ladies traded essentials or money for these when they could, but sometimes there was no other choice but to learn to knit.

Knitting might be learned from a former peasant (often an emigrant from the chaos of industrialization) who had knitted back home, or it could be learned from a book. The degradation of taking up knitting wore off with the first pair of warm socks, if not sooner, and new knitters wrote home of their daring exploits with yarn and needles. The upper class families that had spawned wild colonials learned that knitting could be enjoyable.

CHANGING PLACES

In England factories knitted the interminable stockings, so women did not need to knit. They bought stockings instead. As functional knitting became identified with factories, knitting gradually lost the "peasant" stigma.

Knitting is really very enjoyable when it is not the grinding work of poverty. Knitting non-essentials[48] soon became a parlor activity.[49] Buying a book to learn a pleasant parlor diversion was not the same thing as taking up subsistence work. To allay any hesitation a newly middle class housewife might have about taking up a pastime only recently the work of peasants, many books refer to noble or even royal knitters.[50] The middle class English housewife is assured that in the best circles of European society, ladies on their balconies after dinner take out delicate knitting.[51]

There were also garments for babies, a perfect target for the unreliably sized and styled garments of the early design industry. Turning idle tedium to charitable[52] use by knitting for the poor was a noble upending of the knitting pyramid, also supported by royalty,[53] and knitting book publishers exploited this. Many of the early patterns were for silk purses, hardly a gift for the wretched poor, but purse patterns were practical from the publisher's point of view. Stitch gauge was a concept as yet unknown,[54] but a bag is a bag, large or small.

Knitting publications developed better instructions and more practical designs, spurred on by yarn manufacturers. Soon pattern books recommended specific brands of needles and yarns—their own products, by coincidence. By 1896 there was even a collection of patterns for working men's garments in tough, cheap, charity-grade wools.[55]

The earliest publications describe techniques that are only now being rediscovered, or re-rediscovered. Miss Lambert mentions "raised knitting,"[56] which uses one large needle and one small needle, and was published in the 1980s as the latest thing—"condo knitting." Another is double knitting, or tubular knitting on two needles, which was published by Mary Thomas in the 1930s and by Beverly Royce in the 1990s. Everything old is new again.

PLAYING AT WORK

To make sure there was no mistaking the charitable parlor knitter for the peasant knitter, knitting needles were held differently in parlors. Antique photographs show Cornish women holding the needles under their palms as they knit fishermen's sweaters in between stints of gutting fish. Lest parlor knitters be associated with fishwives, various books advised ladies to hold their needles in a graceful[57] manner, German style, with the yarn coming over the left fingers,[58] so that the ladies might present an attractive pose to the men watching them knit odious little comforts. Others preferred to hold the needles like pencils, as inefficient a position as exists, but efficiency and ease of motion were absolutely not the point.

"On no occasion does a lady seem more lovely than when half occupied with some feminine art which keeps her fingers employed, and gives an excuse for downcast eyes and gentle pre-occupation. This sort of playing at work and working at play, sheds a home feeling around the guests which no studied effort at hospitality can produce ..."[59]

Besides turning knitting postures into decorative poses, parlor knitting ended quite a lot of functional folk knitting traditions and banished useful tools from polite knitting bags. Round knitting (except for the totally plebian sock)[60] was replaced with flat knitting on two needles. Knitting belts and knitting sticks, used by production hand knitters in the outer British Isles, vanished because only small, flat items were being made.[61]

But knitting was not just decorative. It was a pastime that kept women out of trouble. Even if the knitting fit no one (as was common with vague instructions and no gauge), knitting helped "otherwise idle women find occupation for fingers and thought in employments that if not always profitable, are at least innocent and inexpensive."[62] No small task in the wild colonial days.

EXPANSION VS. CORSETS

Expanding empires required merchant ships to supply goods to colonists and collect the rewards of colonization, and large navies to protect the merchant ships. Fishermen joined the navies and brought with them tough hand-knitted sweaters (called guernseys or "ganseys"), which inspired what may be the first frame knitted "knock-offs." Sailors required warm, close-fitting clothing that allowed freedom to clamber up the rigging, but before 1857 the navy didn't provide uniforms. After 1805 sailors bought their own jackets, trousers, and knitted underwear from the enterprising Nottingham frame knitters.[63] French sailors had been wearing the same type of knitted clothing, too, for about as long,[64] possibly supplied by the same Nottingham knitters. Even officers wore knitted clothing under their tailored coats. When a battle broke out, the coats were off and everyone was free to move. Finally the British Admiralty ordered that knitted clothing be issued to the sailors, but not to the officers. Gentlemen still didn't dress like the working class, at least officially.

Fashion facilitated climbing, too—social climbing. The fashionable silhouette, for man or woman, had always been dependent on boning, wiring, and lacing up—hardly conducive to freedom of motion. Knitting didn't change this.[65] For as long as knitting had been worn by royalty, clothing had been as stiff as a post. The corset market didn't slump and the upper class still wore woven underwear, but the working class wore knitted inner garments. Besides warmth, women wore them to permit freedom from bunching under restrictive women's clothing. Double-knitted petticoats,[66] spencers (camisoles), and knickers not only stretched better than woven fabric, they contracted better, too. Knitting provided a modicum of comfort under a corset.

Society was also rippling beneath the surface. Once scorned, grubby Industrial Revolution money made "in trade" was now all that it took to climb the social ranks, buying titles and filling government coffers depleted by colonial expansion's territorial disputes. Newly wealthy working men preferred games and sports that did not involve wearing corsets and shooting things for dinner. By the last quarter of the 19th century pulling an oar, swinging a tennis racquet, or breaking a golf club were the entertainments rich men took up. They soon discovered that if they couldn't move they couldn't win, or even enjoy themselves very much. Since cash was the coin of the realm and a gentleman's pleasure was a close second, fashion had to loosen up a bit. It did.

Long knitted stockings and pullovers (jumpers in British terminology) allowed the active gentleman to swat and swing without splitting a seam. The moneyed world became accustomed to wearing comfortable, knitted, working class-inspired garments for conspicuously nonworking activities. Business suits became tailored to a snobbish nicety to offset the indulgences of comfort in quest of sport. But young men at elite schools such as Eton wore brightly striped, frame-knitted pullovers for their sports. Ironically, Paton's publication of charity garments for working men also contained the pattern for a brightly striped sporting pullover.[67] Other publications were even more adventurous, including patterns for bicycling outfits and "a disturbingly unreliable-looking pair of gentleman's bathing drawers."[68]

Working class comfort entered the real world, too. New Zealand's volunteers for the 1899 Boer War in South Africa had no intention of putting on constricting woven uniforms for Queen and Country. They demanded and got the stretchy pullovers that British seamen had been wearing for a century.[69] English officers, gentlemen of active habit, were already acquainted with the advantages of knits, but it took colonial regiments to introduce the quintessential working man's garment into war, the original home of metal clothing. Knits challenged the woven world and expanded their empire.

Knits freed men for the sporting avocation. In the 20th century this meant conquering brutally cold territories like the Antarctic, Mt. Everest, and the moon. Scott's tragic Terra Nova expedition to Antarctica in 1910–1913 was outfitted with knitted garments,[70] and succumbed to starvation rather than hypothermia; it is a sad distinction. Amundsen reached the South Pole wearing knitted garments, and lived to tell of it.

LOOSEN UP!

There had long been a desire to get women out of their corsets. Clothing reformers wore comfortable, if peculiar, garments and were mocked or ignored, depending on how genteelly they behaved. Comfort and health were insufficient to free women from the clutches of fashion. Liberation required a higher purpose—upper class pleasure.

Wives of wealthy industrialists liked to play golf and tennis. Some refined boarding schools were hotbeds of social insurrection, with girls shamelessly walking around the playing fields in sweaters.[71] In any case, knocking a golf ball to kingdom come was impossible in a corset, so the corset went.

Knitting publications began tentatively to introduce sporting garment patterns for ladies, usually golf sweaters or shooting jackets, also perfect for young women experiencing the freedom of travel on bicycles. Early designs for outer garments tended to follow the fitted shape of traditional tailored clothing, though they gradually assumed a more relaxed, natural shape.[72] American ladies also set aside corsets both as a matter of practicality and as a matter of belief: belief if they had a reforming type of nature, and practicality if they liked sports and comfort. But these two motivations were not themselves sufficient to overthrow the whole of women's fashion. It took the horrors of the First World War to shake off everything inessential. Women serving in hospitals and medical units in the trenches needed to move freely and stay warm just like the soldiers, and they abandoned corsets and donned knitted outer garments in one of the few totally sane acts of that entire period. Unrestrictive undergarments; warm, flexible outer clothing; everything that men had used for play clothes became the real clothing of postwar man—and woman. No one who returned from the war was unchanged, and sensible clothing was a permanent change for everyone, even civilians who had stayed home knitting. Women, children, and even grown men who had never touched a skein of yarn learned to knit, and some of them didn't stop after the war was over.

When peace again reigned many knitters put aside their needles and patterns and took up their previous tasks. Some never knitted again, but many enjoyed the sustained, creative process, and continued to knit for pleasure. Yarn manufacturers, freed from the restraints of khaki, worked to meet the postwar knitting demand with colorful yarns and designs. While they were expert at yarns, the commercial fashion design trade was in its infancy. Designs were "curiously primitive garter stitch jerseys and jackets for men, women, and children",[73] minimally shaped and easy to work. The garter stitch aspect may be explained by recalling that most wartime knitters made simple garments in the round, primarily using knit stitch. To keep pleasure knitters in their comfortable rut, designers translated round knitting to flat, resulting in the garter stitch. A less charitable interpretation is that "garments were ideal for inexperienced knitters and, as in more recent times, the designers themselves probably had limited knitting skills."[74]

The first knitting scholars and scholar-designers, such as Mary Thomas, Heinz Kiewe, Christine Duchrow, and Marianne Kinzel, wrote precise books that systematically laid out advanced techniques and regional secrets for pleasure knitters around the world.

NEW EYES

Despite the slow spread of knitting, once people see knitting they immediately find a use for it, sometimes along the same lines and sometimes in vastly different ways. When knitting was in its infancy it was adapted to bags and other useful articles, but never really lost its chief use as clothing, and then assumed the role of fashion.

Scandinavian, Latvian, Turkish, Maori, Aleut, or any of the multitude of societies that have adopted knitting have expanded its artistic possibilities to suit their cultural requirements, adding patterns, figurative decoration, textural stitches, and garment shapes to appropriately carry the art. Hundreds of groups have developed identifiable styles of decorative knits that have become sought after for their beauty alone. Sometimes the styles grew slowly, through generations of daily life, like Norwegian ski sweaters, Latvian mittens, and Turkish socks. Others, such as the Bohus knits of Sweden, were invented quickly, to provide support in desperately hard economic times, and were beautiful enough to succeed for generations despite the harsh inspiration. Knitting has lent itself to innumerable trends and aesthetics, many of which are revived time and again, far from home, because they are simply too beautiful to lose.

PEACETIME AND BEYOND

When men to go war, women pick up their knitting needles to knit warm comforts for their loved ones in danger, to cope with fabric rationing, and to keep from going mad with anxiety. Until the last quarter of the 20th century, knitting for wartime was an economic necessity to keep the forces in socks and other garments. This is no secret to the yarn industry, which fought to keep peacetime knitting the major force it was during wartimes.

It is not necessary to knit now because of the enormous growth of the knitted clothing industry, which grew according to the demands of modern life. Movement and comfort are motivating forces, and society has matured to the point where it occasionally says "pooh" to the demands of fashion. How many woven slips or circle stitch bras are in the modern lingerie drawer? Even the modern fantasy corset is made with light, knitted fabric between the boning.

Ever since Coco Chanel bought surplus knitted underwear yardage to create her first collection in the war-wracked France of 1916,[75] fashion has seen the potential of knits. A young lady's first formal gown may be as lithe and supple as she is, for knit gowns that cling like a whisper compete with the stiff fabrics of yesterday's ballroom. Money can't buy the beauty of a vest that you knit on a brisk autumn weekend because knitting is a mood, not just a fabric. Knits snuggle against our skin; they are intimate.

The technical world has also recognized the value of knitting. Space suits, industrial filters, surgical mesh, garden hoses, and life-saving bandages for burn patients all utilize the brilliant innovation that was first disguised as a humble Egyptian stocking. Now factory workers wear protective gauntlets knitted of light, flexible wire. After a thousand years the dream of knights is finally achieved for the working man.

Nevertheless, machine knitting denies the pleasure of knitting with your own two hands, the sensation of beautiful yarns running through your fingers, the power to make something from the first stitch to the last. Aside from the warmth and comfort of knitted garments, the value of knitting is in the endlessly satisfying creativity it puts within our grasp. Creation is our natural inheritance, and something is lost when we abandon timeless urges and skills and let a machine dictate our choices. Stretch out your fingers and knit something beautiful.

knitting
basics

BASIC SKILLS OF KNITTING—casting on, knitting and purling, binding off—are basic because they are the heart of knitting. What you do with them need not be basic. The most festive, glamorous, comfortable, or classic garments are made with basic techniques.

Despite the wealth of knitting techniques, you can make a perfectly magnificent sweater with nothing but the basics! And the more exotic the yarn, the better it is suited to basic techniques. There are techniques for different needs, such as extra-stretchy cast-on, invisible bind-off, and knitting for people who prefer left- or right-hand yarn control. We have included only our favorite techniques because they give great results easily. Ease is part of the pleasure of knitting, and we rely on it. Find your favorite techniques and dive in.

Why stop at your favorites? After you have completed a few projects, the techniques that seemed tricky will be child's play, and lead you into new knitting vistas.

There seems to be so much to learn. You have only two hands to control two needles and a strand of yarn, and only two eyes to watch this and read instructions. But knitting has been popular for centuries because the pleasure comes quickly. Soon each hand does its job, the yarn cooperates, and your eyes feast on the satisfying length of knitting in your lap. You can relax, knit, and turn dreams into reality.

Your dreams are too precious to be machine-made, and are so easily made real with knitting. If you dream of a cashmere sweater, you can have it—in the shade you want, perfect from neck to fingertips, and you did it yourself. No wonder people long to "get back to the basics."

21

FREQUENTLY USED ABBREVIATIONS

beg begin
bo bind off
cn cable needle
co cast on
dec(s) decrease(s)
dpn double pointed needle
inc(s) increase(s)
k knit
k2tog knit 2 together
kwise knitwise
lp(s) loop(s)
M make 1
p purl
p2sso pass 2 slipped stitches over
p2tog purl 2 together
pnso pass next stitch over
psso pass slipped stitch over
pwise purlwise
rnd round
rs right side
s2kp slip 2 together knitwise, knit1, pass 2 slipped stitches over
sk2p slip 1, knit 2 together, pass slipped stitch over
skp slip 1, knit 1, pass slipped stitch over
s or sl slip
ssk slip, slip, knit these 2 stitches together
sssk slip, slip, slip, knit 3 stitches together
St st stockinette stitch
st(s) stitch(es)
tbl through back loop
tog together
ws wrong side
wyib with yarn in back
wyif with yarn in front
yo yarn over

ABBREVIATIONS USED IN THIS BOOK

approx. approximately
beg begin
bo bind off
cc contrasting color
ch chain
cm centimeters
cn cable needle
co cast on
dec(s) decrease(s) or knit 2 stitches together
dpn double pointed needle
inc(s) increase(s)
k knit
kb knit through back loop, pushing bead into stitch
k2tog knit 2 together
k3tog knit 3 together
kwise knitwise
lc left cross
lckp left cross - knit, purl
lcpk left cross - purl, knit
lcpp left cross - purl, purl
lh left hand
lp(s) loop(s)
M or m1 make 1
mc main color
mm millimeters
p purl
patt pattern
pb purl stitch, pushing bead into stitch
p2sso pass 2 slipped stitches over
p2tog purl 2 together
pm place marker
pnso pass next stitch over
psso pass slipped stitch over

pwise purlwise
rc right cross
rckp right cross – knit, purl
rcpk right cross – purl knit
rem remaining
rep repeat
rnd(s) round(s)
rs right side
s2kp slip 2 together knitwise, knit 1, pass 2 slipped stitches over
sc single crochet
sk2p slip 1, knit 2 together, pass slipped stitch over
skp slip 1, knit 1, pass slipped stitch over
s or sl slip
ssk slip, slip, knit 2 stitches together
ssp slip, slip, purl
sssk slip, slip, slip, knit 3 stitches together
St st stockinette stitch
st(s) stitch(es)
tbl through back loop
tog together
ws wrong side
wyib with yarn in back
wyif with yarn in front
yo yarn over
* repeat instructions between *s
( ) repeat instructions between parentheses specified number of times
w&t wrap and turn

CHART SYMBOLS FOR KNIT PATTERNS

General

	empty space
	(rs) knit; (ws) purl
	(rs) knit; (ws) purl pattern repeat
—	(rs) purl; (ws) knit
X	(rs) knit 1 through back loop; (ws) purl 1 through back loop
X	(rs) purl 1 through back loop; (ws) knit 1 through back loop
•	slip 1 knitwise
⚊	slip 1 purlwise
⊙	with yarn in front slip 1 knitwise
⊙	with yarn in front slip 1 purlwise
Ջ	cast on
⅄	bind off
▲	stitch remaining after bind off

Specialty Stitches

●	bobble, knob, knot, peppercorn, tuft
⦂	bobble over multiple rows
⋀	pick up slipped strand(s) from below and knit
⸦	knit in next stitch through stitch in previous row
—	pulled stitch
≡	wrapped thread
		drop stitch and unravel
⋈	multiple threaded stitch
V	pull up loop through row below
■	special yarn over

Increases

ⴸ	one stitch right slant increase*
ⴺ	one stitch left slant increase*
ⴸ₂	two stitch right slant increase*
₂ⴺ	two stitch left slant increase*
M	(make 1) insert source needle front to back lifting thread between stitch just worked and next stitch; knit lifted thread through back loop.
O	yo yarn over
②	yo yarn over (number indicated)
V	knit in front and back of same stitch
▽	purl in front and back of same stitch
Ⴅ	knit 1, yarn over, knit 1 in same stitch
⋎	knit 1, purl 1, knit 1

There are dozens of decorative increases. To keep the charts readable, only the slant direction is indicated. Specific instructions are noted in the key below the chart.

Decreases

╱	(rs) knit 2 together; (ws) purl 2 together
╲	slip 1 knitwise, slip 1 knitwise, knit 2 stitches together through back loop
╲	(rs) purl 2 together; (ws) knit 2 together
╲	slip 1, knit 1, pass slipped stitch over
⋀	(rs) slip 1 knitwise, knit 2 stitches together, pass 2 slipped stitches over; (ws) slip 2 knitwise, knit 1, pass 2 slipped stitches over
╱₃	(rs) knit 3 together; (ws) purl 3 together
₃╲	(rs) purl 3 together; (ws) knit 3 together
╱₄	(rs) knit 4 together; (ws) purl 4 together
₄╲	(rs) purl 4 together; (ws) knit 4 together
╱₅	(rs) knit 5 together; (ws) purl 5 together
₅╲	(rs) purl 5 together; (ws) knit 5 together

Crossed and Cable

⌐	lc (left cross) skip first stitch, knit second stitch through back loop, knit skipped stitch
⌐	(rs) rc (right cross) skip first stitch on source needle, knit second stitch, knit skipped stitch, slip both stitches to working needle; (ws) lcpp (left cross purl-purl) skip first stitch on source needle, purl into front of second stitch, purl into fro
⌐	lcpk (left cross, purl, knit)
⌐	rckp (right cross, knit, purl)
⌐	3 stitch left knit cable
⌐	3 stitch right knit cable
⌐	3 stitch left purl-knit cable
⌐	3 stitch right knit-purl cable
⌐	4 stitch left knit cable
⌐	4 stitch right knit cable
⌐	4 stitch left purl-knit cable
⌐	4 stitch right knit-purl cable
⌐	4 stitch left cable
⌐	4 stitch right cable
⌐	6-stitch left knit cable
⌐	6-stitch right knit cable
⌐	8-stitch left knit cable
⌐	8-stitch right knit cable
⌐	10-stitch left knit cable
⌐	10-stitch right knit cable

READING INSTRUCTIONS AND SYMBOLS

Skill in reading directions and symbols will contribute enormously to your satisfaction in knitting. International symbol versions of patterns now give us access to gorgeous foreign designs, so it is well worth your while to learn the international symbols. Symbols are not standardized, but if you are unsure as to any specifics, check the legend or key for clarification. (Some color patterns are also printed in symbols rather than in color. This may or may not be mixed with shaping symbols.)

Many instructions provide both written and symbol versions. They are equally useful, even if you prefer one over the other. Written instructions assume you knit from right to left. This is not a problem in charted designs. If you come to a confusing part in your preferred version of the instructions, look at the other for clarification.

When reading a chart, remember that a purl on one side is a knit on the other. Charts are read from the front, that is, the right side of the knitting. When you turn knitting, the symbols are understood to be the opposite of what is on the right side of the fabric. Sometimes knitting in the round is done inside out, with the purled side of the fabric facing out. If it will be clearer, write out a new symbol key and fasten it to the chart.

A CHARTED PATTERN allows you to see on paper the design that you will be knitting. This is often far easier than trying to read instructions written as phrases and sentences, especially when they are written in a foreign language. Knowing how to read a charted knitting pattern will take you beyond the limits of language (see Chart Symbols, page 23).

DECORATIVE KNITTING is easily described on graph paper, with knit and purl stitches drawn in as they appear from the right (front) side of the work. Symbols are not standardized, but once you understand how charted patterns work you should be able to decipher most systems. Each square equals one stitch, and the symbol in the square indicates whether it is knitted or purled. There are symbols to show shaping—increases and decreases—including the direction they slant on the right side of the work.

SHAPING SYMBOLS will slant to the left or right, perhaps with an indication of how many stitches are involved. For lace knitting, increases and decreases with holes are incorporated into the design. Because a "yarn over" hole is larger than a stitch, there may be blank squares (white or tinted) that allow you to see the lace design as it will look when knitted. Just ignore the blank squares as you knit.

You can also see shaping on a chart. A small garment may be completely shown in a graph. A larger garment may not need to be charted, but is often shown in a schematic drawing with measurements at strategic points, such as the outline of a sweater with the hem, chest, shoulder, and length measurements shown. A sweater knit in stockinette stitch with a multi-color band across the chest may simply show one repeat of the color chart and where it is placed on the body of the sweater. Shoulder shaping, waist shaping, and neckline shaping may be shown on the schematic, or with individual smaller charts.

WRITTEN INSTRUCTIONS are not the gibberish they seem when you first read them. They use a shorthand to indicate stitches or actions. (See Abbreviations, page 22.) Abbreviations and punctuation symbols define logical groups, either repeated operations or small groups of stitches that make up a whole. Minimal writing saves space and keeps instructions clear and methodical. The abbreviations are defined at the beginning of each pattern or each book of patterns. Any special techniques will also be explained there.

Repeated groups of instructions are given working names used throughout the instructions, e.g., "buttonhole." These may also be explained the first time they appear in the text, and then referred to by working names thereafter. If no specific explanation of how the buttonhole is worked appears in the text, choose your favorite method.

PATTERN STITCHES, used for an overall patterned fabric, are given so that you can work swatches. These are usually given with their repeat numbers, e.g., the number of stitches it takes to completely reproduce the pattern once. This is written as "Multiple of 8+2." If you wish to make a swatch that repeats the pattern 4 times to check your stitch gauge (see page 25), multiply the number of repeats you want times the first number in the repeat number: (4 repeats x 8 stitches=32). Then add two more stitches (the +2 part), to keep the pattern lined up. (4 repeats x 8 stitches=32) +2=34. So when you make your pattern swatch, you will need to cast on 34 stitches.

BRACKETS AND PARENTHESES group related information. They indicate alternate measurements to be substituted according to the size garment you are working: "Sizes S (M, L, XL); 10 (15, 20, 25) sts; 2 (4, 6, 8) inches."

They group a series of instructions that are to be repeated as a whole:

(Knit 2, yarn over, slip 1, knit 1, psso) 3 times, k 2.

Brackets and parentheses can be used separately, to indicate grouped steps, or they can be used within each other to separate subsets of instructions, where each group is being repeated within the context of a whole piece: [(A series of buttonholes) worked while you are also shaping the center front] of the left side of a cardigan.

Brackets and parentheses can also contain explanations needed at that point.

Stars ☆, asterisks *, or any other symbol serve the same basic function as brackets and parentheses: to set apart a group of stitches or actions, which will be repeated as a whole. Generally these symbols define repeats for the row, rather than the whole piece.

Gauge swatch

GAUGE

Pay attention to this: Correct gauge is the difference between a favorite sweater and a charitable donation. The correct size of your finished project depends on gauge. Gauge depends on the size of the needles, the size of the yarn, and how tightly you knit.

Make a decent-sized gauge swatch—4 inches x 4 inches (or 20 stitches x 20 rows) is reasonable. The number of stitches for a swatch may be recommended in the instructions, on the yarn label, or may be determined by the pattern repeat number.

THE NEEDLE SIZE suggested for a pattern is just a place to start. You may work more tightly or loosely than the person who wrote the pattern. You need to work at exactly the gauge the pattern requires in order to reproduce it accurately.

Do not be lazy. Work at least a 4-inch square of whatever pattern stitches are called for by the pattern, then block the swatch and measure the stitches precisely. Partial stitches matter: a half-stitch per inch multiplied by 30 inches is a disaster.

Make swatches until your stitch gauge is correct. Change needles until you find the size that allows you to make the gauge. If you can't make gauge with your usual brand of needle, try another brand or material. Tiny things like weight and finish make a difference. When working at the correct gauge you should be able to insert the needle in a stitch comfortably. If you can't, try different needles.

THE ROW GAUGE is important, but if you repeatedly obtain the stitch gauge and never quite get the row gauge, you can adjust lengths in a garment as you make it.

Pull out enough yarn at the beginning of a row to complete the row. Having to constantly tug on the yarn will make your knitting uneven. Constant tension will stretch the yarn as you work, making the gauge incorrect. Pulling out 4 times the width of the row should be enough.

Stress shows up in your work. After a hard day check the gauge as you knit to make sure you aren't working more tightly than usual. Check the gauge frequently on a long or complicated project, and change needles when your gauge is off. If you always have a hard day at work, start your knitting on a project that requires a lot of tension. Once you relax, switch to a project that is knit more loosely.

Buy an extra ball of yarn to work swatches. Don't pull out your test swatch and use the yarn in your project from misguided motives of thrift. Your swatch is a test run. Use it to check your gauge, but don't stop there. Work a couple of swatches to learn any new pattern stitches that will be in your project. Work a swatch to see which buttonhole suits the yarn. Throw a test swatch in the washer if the finished project is washable. You will never regret taking the time to learn about the yarn you think you want. Use old swatches as reference squares in your knitting archives, as afghan squares, or for random patch pockets. Partial balls of yarn are great for small projects or donations to charitable programs, such as *Caps for Kids*. You can even carry spare thrift shop needles and partial balls of yarn to teach your friends to knit when they say it looks interesting (or soothing, or fun).

BAD LANGUAGE

The older your books of pattern stitches, the less uniform the abbreviations will be. For example, when a stitch is slipped the yarn is carried in front or in back of the stitches. This has several different names and abbreviations in written patterns: With Yarn in Back (wyib), With Yarn in Front (wyif), With Thread in Back (wtib), Yarn in Back (yib), Yarn in Front (yif), Yarn to Front (ytf), Yarn to Back (ytb), Wool in Back (wib), and Wool Forward (wf or wfwd), etc.

There is a subtle trend to standardized terminology in written knitting patterns, but different publishers still do what makes sense to them. Don't we all. There are as many ways to state something as there are to understand it. Generally speaking, anything indicating yarn or thread in the back or front means that you simply shift the yarn from one side of the work to the other.

On the other hand, some pattern stitches require adding or subtracting stitches. Terms for these include Yarn Over Needle (yon), Yarn Over (yo), Over (o), Make 1 Stitch (m1), Narrow 1 (n1), Decrease 1 stitch (dec1), etc. Do not confuse a Yarn Over (increase in number of stitches) with a Yarn Forward (shifting the placement of the working strand), or you will see your knitting fan out like a peacock on display.

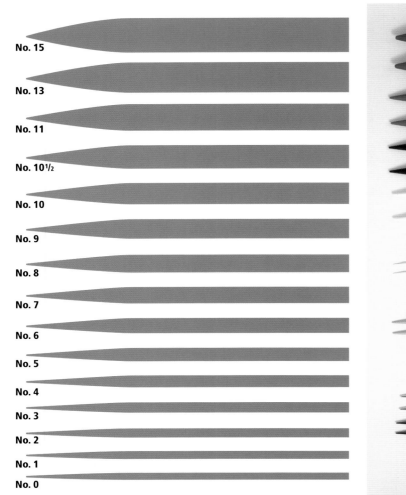

No. 15
No. 13
No. 11
No. 10½
No. 10
No. 9
No. 8
No. 7
No. 6
No. 5
No. 4
No. 3
No. 2
No. 1
No. 0

Straight needles No. 0 (2 mm) through No. 15 (10 mm).

Single pointed plastic knitting needles in various sizes.

TOOLS

NEEDLES

Needles come in a vast array of types, materials, and sizes. They are categorized by diameter (size), length, and type (the number of points). Check the points and shafts when buying needles to make sure that they are smooth and well polished. Rough spots will make knitting a trial rather than a pleasure.

Dropping a needle can damage the point. Polish away small nicks with a nail buffing chamois and a little red jeweler's rouge. If that doesn't work, try ultra-fine garnet paper, or ask a friendly jewelry repair shop to buff a point. Sometimes there is no saving a worn or damaged needle.

SIZES are not completely standardized, but there is a trend towards it. Most manufacturers list the actual diameter in millimeters and the company's sizing (if they differ)—generally speaking, the larger the diameter, the higher the size number. Older British needles are sized in reverse order, so very fine lace needles are sizes 12–16. With a metric needle gauge you can measure whatever kind of needles you have, since most modern patterns come with recommended metric needle sizes. In the end, all that matters is whether or not your stitch gauge is correct: if it is, the garment size will be accurate.

It may be that your needles do not exactly match any size, but that is not all bad. There are advantages and disadvantages to standardized sizes. If you are having trouble matching your gauge to the required gauge of a pattern, try a different brand or material of needles. The weight and finish of a needle can change your gauge. For this reason it is best not to switch needles during the course of a project unless it is required by the pattern, or to work a ribbing.

NEEDLE SIZES

The size of a stitch is determined by the diameter of a knitting needle and the diameter of the yarn. The size of the needle influences the size of yarn you can use and vice versa. Knitting a very bulky yarn on very small needles is tiring and produces a stiff, tight knit that does not drape well. Knitting a very fine yarn on very large needles will make a lacy fabric, possibly too open and limp.

STRAIGHT NEEDLES come in single point and double point.

SINGLE POINT are the familiar needles sold in pairs. They have a point on the one end and a button on the other end of the shaft to keep stitches from sliding off. Single point needles are for back-and-forth knitting only. They come in lengths from 8" to 14", and in sizes from 0 (2 mm) to 15 (10 mm), and sometimes 17 (12 mm) or 19 (15 mm). There are a few brands of single point needles with cables on the button end. These are for working very wide projects. If the brand you want does not come with a flex-cable, consider using a circular needle.

DOUBLE POINT NEEDLES (in sets of 4 or 5) are used for knitting in the round, for cables, and sometimes for fine straight lace. They range in size from 000000 (.75 mm) to 19 (15 mm). Most common in 8" lengths, you can sometimes find 4" or 5" sets for glove fingers. Also, 10" double point needles are sometimes available, but very long, fine, double-pointed needles (called "wires") are available only from Scottish sources, since they are used mostly for Shetland lace knitting.

CIRCULAR NEEDLES have a flexible cable with a point at each end, and are used for knitting in the round or for back-and-forth knitting on very wide pieces. There are both fixed-length needles and needles with interchangeable points and cables, so that as a garment changes circumference you can switch cable lengths, or you can switch point sizes for ribbings, etc. Circular needles are available in sizes 000 (1.5 mm) to size 35 (20 mm), and in lengths from 12" to 60". Knitting with circular needles shorter than 15" may be less comfortable than using double pointed needles.

NEEDLE MATERIALS can accommodate any yarn, slick to sticky, and any hand, hot, cold, or arthritic.

METAL needles come in aluminum, steel, and brass, and are available in the widest range of diameters, from 000000 for the finest laces, to size 11 or 13 for quick-knit bulky weight yarns. They also come in the widest variety of types—single and double points, as well as circular.

Early circular needles are entirely metal, from point to cable, but modern ones have plastic cables. Check the joins of points to cable, making certain there are no snags and that the stitches can slide easily onto the point. In very damp climates it may be necessary to use a very light machine oil or beeswax on steel needles to keep them from corroding. It is not wise to store pairs held together with rubber bands since this can cause corrosion or stickiness.

If you like light metal needles or if you have hot hands, aluminum is a good choice. Brass and steel needles are heavy and smooth, but are sometimes nickel-plated. If you are allergic to

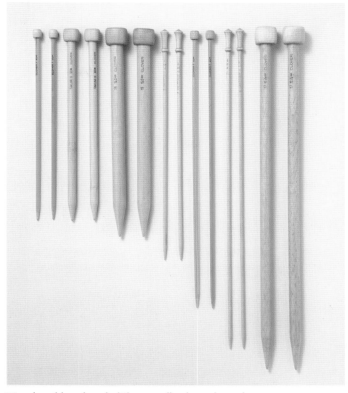

Wood and bamboo knitting needles in various sizes.

nickel, choose chrome- or Teflon-plated or aluminum needles, or choose something other than metal.

WOOD needles come in both single and double point, and sometimes in circular. They range in size from 0 to 17. They are made from light-colored woods such as birch, and dark woods like ebony, rosewood, and walnut, and are good if you knit ribbon or slippery yarn or like a light, warm needle.

BAMBOO needles, though technically made from a large grass, are similar to wood needles in weight, warmth, and texture. They are available in single point, double point, and circular. The sizes range from 5–15, and the lengths from 6" double point to 14" single point. Circular needles come in lengths from 16"–40".

FROM LEFT TO RIGHT: Bamboo flex knitting needles, various circular knitting needles, various straight double pointed knitting needles.

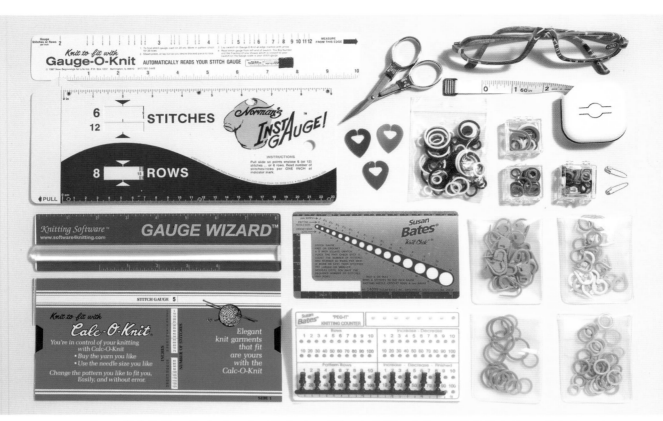

TOP ROW FROM LEFT: Gauge-O-Knit (New Beginnings for Life Inc.), Snip-its folding scissors, reading glasses, tape measure. 2ND ROW: Instaguage (Norman), markers, rings, safety pins. 3RD ROW: Gauge Wizard—Knitting Software, Knit Chek (Susan Bates), markers. BOTTOM ROW: Calc-O-Knit (New Beginnings for Life Inc.), Peg-it Knitting Counter (Susan Bates), markers.

Wood and bamboo are either finished with a coating of polish or have been resin-treated to keep them from wearing. Both wood and bamboo needles may warp or bend with use, and may be more comfortable than a metal needle because of this. If a needle feels too dry, wipe it with lemon oil or beeswax, and then buff dry with a chamois. If the points wear a little, smooth them with 600 grit sandpaper or garnet paper, or a nail-polishing chamois and talcum powder.

PLASTIC needles—circular, single and double point—are light, warm, and flexible. They are available in sizes 2 to 19, and in 5" double point to 16" single point. Single point plastic needles may be too flexible for a very heavy project such as an afghan, so consider using a circular needle. Some plastic needles are coated with aluminum, while other brands have steel cores covered with plastic. Plastic-only needles are kind to arthritic hands.

CASEIN needles, made from milk protein, are warm and flexible, and come in single and double point, sizes 1 to 15, in lengths from 7" double point to 14" single point. They have the same qualities as plastic needles except for the origin of the materials.

OTHER TOOLS

A NEEDLE GAUGE is the only thing that can tell you what size your needles are. Don't just go by the label or what is stamped on the needle—mistakes occur. Gauges come in paper, plastic, or metal. While you can stretch out a paper or thin plastic gauge, a metal gauge won't lie. Just be careful not to score the needle when you insert it into the gauge.

The stitch and row part of a gauge allows you to count the number of stitches per horizontal inch and the number of rows per vertical inch. While a simple tape measure can be used for this, a gauge allows you to read both measurements at once.

MARKERS identify anything you want to find easily: pattern repeats, increases or decreases, the beginnings of rounds in circular knitting. The most common markers are scrap yarn, coil-less safety pins, or rings. It is nice to have an assortment of markers in various colors for different jobs. If you use markers you won't have to count each stitch in a row to find the decrease.

Make a flag to mark a one-time event in your knitting. Use a tapestry needle to thread contrasting yarn through a stitch, then tie the yarn in a loose knot with 1" tails. Flags are easy to count, and when you are finished with the project, one snip removes them.

To mark the number of rows worked, use a long strand of contrasting yarn. Carry it along the edge and lay the strand of yarn between two stitches, moving it alternately from the front to the back of the work as you count off your progress. Having a bright strand show where you worked an invisible decrease is a lot easier than looking for an invisible stitch or counting rows.

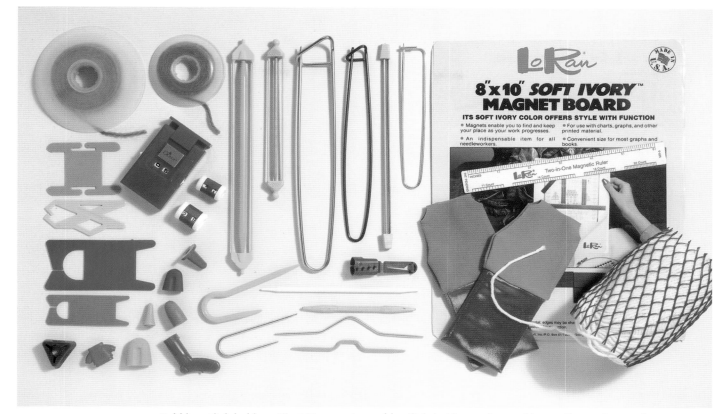

CLOCKWISE FROM TOP LEFT: Bobbins, stitch holders, 8" x 10" magnet board (Lo Ran), yarn bra, Thergonomic Hand-Aids (Connexxions Inc.), cable stitch holder, various cable needles, various point protectors, knitting bobbin, knitting counter, row markers.

COIL-LESS SAFETY PINS are good for marking increases and decreases in mid-row, or for repeated steps such as a decrease done every fourth row. Safety pins are especially useful when you need to mark a stitch as an afterthought.

RING MARKERS indicate repeated points of change, and are slipped back and forth on the needles between stitches. They mark shaping lines, such as the thumb gussets in mittens. They signal the end of a pattern repeat, so you can count the stitches, or let you know when you reach the center back of a garment. In circular knitting, rings mark the seams, shaping lines, and the beginning of the round.

Rings come in stiff plastic or stretchy rubber and silicone (called O-rings). Stiff plastic rings come in assorted colors and diameters, are very thin, and fit nicely between stitches. O-rings stretch to accommodate an inserted needle, come in a number of diameters and colors, and are readily available at hardware stores. You can also make rings of thread or yarn, but these tend to fray with repeated use.

Split rings are useful to slip into a stitch. They are also used between stitches like ring markers, but can scratch a wood or coated needle. Still, they come is a wonderful variety of colors and sizes, which makes them excellent for marking several different points in a row.

ROW COUNTERS will help you keep track of which row you are working in a multi-rowed pattern if you remember to use them.

CLICKERS are picked up and clicked each time you finish a row or a round. Many people "forget" to do this because it requires that you stop knitting for a moment.

ON-THE-NEEDLE COUNTERS actually sit on one needle (making the needles uneven in weight). Despite this, you still have to remember to dial up a new number each row.

MAGNETIC CLIPBOARDS allow you to have a chart conveniently before you and give you a magnetic ruler to show your progress. When working from a book or magazine, making a copy of a chart allows you to enlarge, mark up, and hang up the instructions. You can mark not only the rows worked,

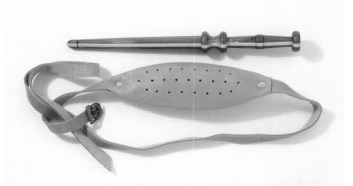

TOP: Wooden knitting pin, BOTTOM: Knitting belt or whisk from the private collection of Meg Swansen.

INTERNATIONAL YARN LABEL SYMBOLS

 4 x 4" 10 x 10cm / 30M or S 40 R — The manufacturer's suggested gauge/tension with the suggested needle size. This block of knitting stitches can be translated to read: In stockinette stitch, 30 stitches (S) [in French—Mailles (M)] and 40 rows (R) will equal 4" x 4" (10 x 10 cm).

F/4 mm — Manufacturer's suggested crochet hook size in metric and/or U.S. sizes.

 3½-4 mm (5-6) — Manufacturer's suggested knitting needle size in metric and/or U.S. sizes.

 Hand wash in lukewarm water only

 Hand wash in warm water at stated temperature

 DO NOT wash by hand or machine

 6 — Machine wash in warm water at stated temperature, cool rinse and short spin; more delicate handling

7 — Machine wash in warm water at stated temperature, short spin

40°C — Machine wash in warm water at stated temperature

CL — Bleaching permitted (with chlorine)

CL or — NO Bleach

— DO NOT dry clean

F — May be dry cleaned with fluorocarbon or petroleum-based solvents only

P — May be dry cleaned with perchlorethylene or flourocarbon or petroleum-based solvents

A — May be dry cleaned with all solutions

Press with cool iron   Press with warm iron

Press with hot iron   DO NOT press

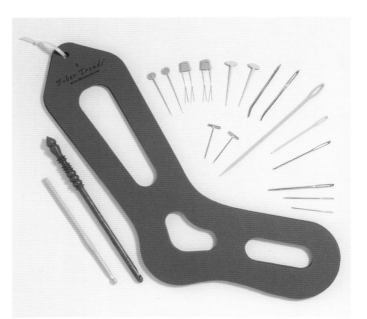

FINISHING TOOLS, CLOCKWISE FROM BOTTOM LEFT: Luxite crochet hook (Susan Bates), wooden crochet hook, sock form, marking pins, pins, seaming pins, jumbo tapestry needles, needles, darning set (Clover), T-pins.

but places that will need future attention for buttonholes, shaping, or whatever you tend to overlook.

NOTE PADS Some people swear by mechanical counters, other people keep a pad and pencil handy. Besides making a note of where you stopped in a pattern, you may sometimes want to change a pattern to suit yourself. Make a habit of immediately writing down a change you made during the course of a row. Otherwise you may not remember until after you have assembled the garment that you modified the front of a cardigan.

BOBBINS are small pieces of plastic or cardboard that allow you to wind on small lengths of yarn for intarsia work. They are essential for multi-color work, particularly intarsia work, when small lengths of five different colors can, while you are not looking, become one big knot. Butterfly-shaped bobbins catch the strand to keep the yarn from unwinding, but making a half-hitch around a piece of cardboard will do the same thing. You can also wind yarn around your fingers in a figure 8, finish it off with a wrap and a half-hitch.

A THREAD OR TENSION GAUGE is a small spring device worn at the tip of your yarn finger to carry the yarn. It

KEEP THE LABELS! If your project is a gift, send a label, and some extra yarn for mending, along with the gift. The recipient will need to know how to launder the gift. If you love the yarn, keep a label so that you can reorder. If you have a problem with the yarn after you have completed a project, the yarn labels will help the manufacturer solve the problem and make amends.

can be an improvement or a hindrance. It may keep ribbon from twisting as you knit. If you have arthritis, a tension gauge may require less lateral motion of your yarn finger, making knitting comfortable again. If you have just started knitting, a tension gauge controls the flow of yarn, giving you one less detail to deal with. In this case don't let it slow down the speed at which your hands learn to control the yarn.

STITCH HOLDERS allow you to slip stitches and set them aside to be worked later as necklines, pocket flaps, and other things. Holders come in different lengths, and have either a clip or a cap on the end, to keep stitches from escaping.

THE YARN LABEL

THE YARN LABEL is one of your most important tools. The label is the only place the manufacturer can tell you everything you need to know about the product. Every piece of information is designed to help you choose the yarn or thread that will give you a perfect finished product. Before you fall in love with a yarn, read the label.

FIBER CONTENT is basic, but it is amazing how many people choose yarn without ever looking beyond that. If you want to make felted slippers, don't buy resin-coated, no-shrink wool, even if it is in the wool section.

WEIGHT AND YARDAGE are not the same thing. If you are planning to substitute one brand for another, you need to be sure that one 50 gram ball has 100 yards, just like the other brand; a substitute 50 gram ball with only 75 yards will give you a very unpleasant surprise, even in a muffler. If the ball is labeled only with the weight, get a spare. Better yet, buy yarn that tells you the yardage.

CLEANING, BLEACHING, DRYING, AND IRONING (SMOOTHING) TEMPERATURES are shown in internationally recognized symbols (see chart, page 30). Ignore these at your peril. Even yarns with guarantees require proper handling.

PLY AND TWIST actually make a difference in your choice of yarn, or they should. If you choose a 4-ply woolen spun (which does not mean wool fiber) instead of a 4-ply worsted spun, the soft yarn will pill and wear badly. If worsted is what you need, even 1-ply worsted instead of 4-ply worsted is preferable to buying a woolen-spun.

YARN CLASS (SIZE) has replaced the confusing and esoteric ply and twist classification system. Yarn is now categorized by the working diameter of yarn, which is the way most people look for yarn. If you want a bulky sweater, you buy a fat yarn, right? (See Sizes of Yarn, page 32, for details.)

GAUGE AND NEEDLE SIZES appear on most labels. If the gauge and needle size recommended for the yarn surprise you, rethink your choice of yarn. A thin-looking mohair yarn may knit to only 2 stitches per inch because of the fuzzy halo around the yarn.

THE PRODUCT NUMBER AND THE DYE LOT are stamped somewhere on the label. Whatever you end up buying, purchase it all from the same dye lot. Tiny color differences not apparent under store light will be blatant in natural light. Even white is not always white. If you are match-ing yarn to a fabric, take the fabric with you and match under natural light.

There are some synthetic yarns with no dye lot. It is still a good idea to purchase all the yarn for a project at one time, because stores run out and companies discontinue colors and products.

YARNS AND FIBERS
SPINS, PLIES, AND SIZE

Yarn and thread are made up of strands that have been twisted together to form a larger diameter thread. The different ways fibers are spun, the number of strands, and the specific qualities that come from these differences, make a great difference in what you can do successfully with a particular product.

SPIN tells you the arrangement of the fibers while they were being spun, and also tells you about the tightness of the twist of each strand and the character of the yarn.

Yarn can be spun either clockwise or counterclockwise. If you look at a strand of yarn, the marks of the twist will either incline to the left (S-twist) or incline to the right (Z-twist). Depending on which hand you use to control the yarn, you will either untwist or twist the yarn as you use it. Normally this does not make a difference in the finished product, unless you have to pull out and reknit rows to correct a mistake. If you repeatedly work the same length of yarn you can twist it much tighter, or untwist it to the point that the strands separate. If you have to redo a section of a project and the twist of the yarn has changed noticeably, slip a rubber band on the ball of yarn and spin it in the correct direction to re-spin the strand. If the strand is worn looking, you may want to cut the yarn and start with a fresh strand. Save the cut piece for seams or mending.

In worsted yarns, fibers are parallel to each other and to the length of each strand (ply). The entire length of each fiber will be twisted, forming a very sturdy yarn that will not pill or fuzz easily. Worsted yarn is good for garments that take a lot of abrasion, such as mittens and socks.

In woolen-spun strands, fibers are spun crosswise to the length of the thread, so that the fibers form a vortex around a core of air. This gives the yarn very good insulation properties. The strands are loosely packed and softly spun so that the air-catching spaces are not squeezed shut. These warm yarns are good for garments that do not get a lot of abrasion, such as baby garments, scarves, and hats. "Germantown" also refers to a soft, woolen-spun yarn, 3 or 4 ply.

SPECIALTY YARNS have other qualities which define the yarn, such as bouclé, eyelash, slub, chenille, etc., and are chosen for appearance rather than wearing properties. Though they may wear very well, don't depend upon a specialty yarn to take hard wear unless you are very familiar with that type of yarn.

PLY refers to the number of spun strands twisted together to make up a yarn, usually two, three, or four. The number of plies does not tell you the diameter of the yarn because a ply can be large or small. Ply does not indicate either the type or size of yarn, though people frequently assume that it does. (See Sizes of Yarn, page 32.) Yarn is not just round, and ply has a great deal to do with how yarns wear.

SIZES OF YARN

Because of the confusion of the terms, categories based on the diameter of yarn have been devised. One classifies yarns into 5 categories by the approximate diameter of the yarn:

A = fingering or fine-weight yarns, good for thin socks and light baby clothes

B = sport or medium-weight yarns, good for indoor sweaters, baby things, dresses, and suits

C = worsted-weight or knitting yarns, good for outdoor sweaters, hats, mittens, afghans, and slippers

D = bulky-weight yarns, used for rugs, heavy jackets, and crafts

E = extra-bulky-weight yarns, used mostly for rugs

Some manufacturers also have a DK, or Double Knitting size, which falls between sport yarn and worsted weight.

The other system categorizes yarns into 6 classes, determined by the number of stitches per 4-inch swatch of stockinette stitch: the smaller the number, the smaller the yarn. There are 6 categories:

1 = fine = 29–32 sts
2 = light = 25–28 sts
3 = medium = 21–24 sts
4 = medium-heavy = 17–20 sts
5 = bulky = 13–16 sts
6 = extra-bulky =9–12 sts

Lace weight yarns are ultra-fine, generally knit up to 10 stitches to the inch or more, and fall outside of both systems.

SUBSTITUTIONS

Knowing the class of yarn is not enough information if you want to use a different kind of yarn. Substitutions are risky, and require that you take into account the length per ball, as well as the diameter of the yarn.

Substituting one diameter of yarn for another is generally not a good idea. Making the gauge work is difficult, and calculating how much yarn you need is even harder.

When substituting one brand of yarn for another, be careful to check the yardage. Fifty grams of yarn, 100 meters long will not give you the same amount of yarn as 50 grams, 80 meters long.

When substituting a different fiber of the same diameter, consider carefully whether the two fibers will act the same. Cotton, linen, and ramie are not stretchy, and will not act the same in a sweater ribbing as wool or acrylic. Mohair will not show off your stitches the way a reeled silk yarn will.

(1) 3 ply/ 1.75oz. 'Babi', Steinbach wolle; (2) 3 ply/ 5oz., 'Wool Ease, Sportweight', Lion Brand Yarn; (3) 4 ply/ 3oz., Caron Gold; (4) 4 ply/ 5oz., 'Wool Ease, Chunky', Lion Brand Yarn; (5) 2 ply/ 6 oz., 'Wool Ease, Thick & Quick', Lion Brand Yarn.

When uncertain, buy one ball of yarn and work several test swatches to see if what you want the yarn to do is, in fact, what the yarn does. Check for stitch definition, shrinkage, abrasion (pilling), or any other quality important in the finished product.

FIBERS

There are common properties in various groups of fibers, and these will help you understand some of the variables in yarns and threads. The diameter of fibers is of primary importance when wearing comfort, and the finer a fiber, the kinder it is to your skin. Staple (length) of a fiber affects its tensile strength as well as its price, with long fine fibers being the most costly. Your choice of fiber will help to determine the character of your finished project—the more you know, the fewer surprises there are.

The word "Virgin" on a yarn label means that the fiber used in your yarn is being used for the first time, rather than being reclaimed from previously used garments or products. Reclaimed animal fibers from a variety of sources are not consistent in their individual diameters or lengths, so that you will get both coarse and fine, and long and short fibers in the same yarn. These yarns are unpleasant to knit or wear.

Fibers made from recycled plastics, on the other hand, are indistinguishable from products made from virgin materials. The plastic from various sources is melted, reformulated to specific chemical standards, and extruded exactly the same way fibers from virgin plastics are.

Yarns combining both protein and cellulose fibers are difficult to maintain; the method used to clean one fiber harms the other.

PROTEIN FIBERS

Protein fibers come from animal hair and insect cocoon fibers, and have common properties. They are absorbent, weaker when wet, and tolerate acidic conditions, so they are best washed with mild detergents. They take dyes well, and can be dyed brilliant colors. Protein fibers tolerate very mild alkali conditions, including ammonia, so they can also be washed with soap, borax, and mild ammonia solutions. They are poor conductors of electricity, and build up static charges in dry climates. The fibers are elastic, but are damaged by stretching. Protein fibers resist creasing.

WOOL is the most commonly known animal fiber, usually shorn from the sheep; a few breeds shed their coats and are plucked. There are hundreds of breeds of sheep, each having a distinctive character. Merino and Rambouillet are the best known for fine, soft fleeces.

MOHAIR comes from the Angora (Ankara) goat, whose long, lustrous coat is shorn twice a year. Kid mohair is a fine, lustrous, and affordable luxury fiber, from goats up to 18 months old. Adult mohair can be as fine as cashmere or quite hairy, depending upon the individual goat. It is very durable.

CASHMERE comes from (Kashmir) goats, whose downy winter undercoat is plucked in the spring. A number of other "down" goats have plucked undercoats, and any goat hair 14.5–16.5 microns in diameter may be sold as cashmere.

CASHGORA comes from a hybrid of Cashmere and Angora goats, which makes it a longer-staple fiber than cashmere, but is lustrous and almost as fine.

ANGORA (Ankara) rabbits produce fibers for angora yarn. The rabbit fur is combed, plucked, or shorn, and is frequently spun with a strand of silk or wool for a yarn that sheds less, is less costly, but which has the silky texture of the soft fur. Angora felts easily.

THE LLAMA FAMILY is distantly related to the camel. There are two domesticated members of the group, the llama and the alpaca. The llama's rather coarse coat is used for utilitarian items, rather than clothing. The alpaca is bred for its fine, silky fleece, which is used for clothing.

VICUÑA AND GUANACO come from undomesticated and protected members of the Llama family, and the fibers are extremely rare and costly.

CAMEL HAIR is the winter undercoat collected from the Bactrian (two-humped) camel of the Gobi desert. It is very fine, soft, and lusterless, and is occasionally available in knitting yarns.

QIVIUT is the shed winter coat of the musk ox, which produces only about 6 lbs. per year. Finer than vicuña and extremely rare, this luxury fiber is collected in the wild and is good for light but extremely warm garments. It is available from Eskimo cooperatives.

SILK, extruded for the *bombyx mori* silk worm's cocoon, is unwound in a single strand. Other species of moths produce raw silk, called *Tussah*. After the moth has emerged from the cocoon, the short fibers (which cannot be reeled) are spun into

(1) Super Cashmere, Karabella; (2) Merino wool, 'Puffy', Karabella; (3) Angora Super, Anny Blatt; (4) Mohair/Wool blend, Stony Hill Fiberarts; (5) Wool, Klaus Koch Kollektion; (6) New Wool, Black Forest Yarn; (7) Lambswool/Mohair/Nylon blend, 'Kid Classic', Rowan; (8) Merino wool/Alpaca/Viscose blend, 'Felted Tweed', Rowan; (9) Mohair blend, 'Soft-Kid', GGH; (10) New Wool/Nylon blend, Travertino; (11) Acrylic/Wool blend, 'Wool-Ease, Sportweight', Lion Brand Yarn; (12) Acrylic/Wool blend, 'Wool-Ease, Chunky', Lion Brand Yarn.

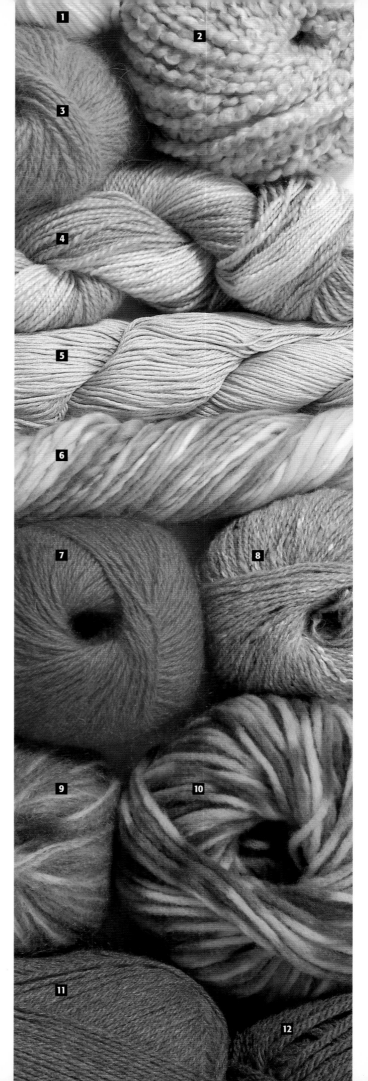

yarns. The waste silk from the combing process, called noil, is combined with wool, cashmere, or other fibers for textured yarns.

CELLULOSE FIBERS

Cellulose fibers can be both natural and man-made. The natural sources are from plant leaves, long stem (bast) fibers, and seed fibers. The most common natural cellulose fibers are cotton, flax (linen), hemp, and ramie. The fibers are hollow and absorb water readily, which makes them cool to the touch and pleasant to wear in hot climates. The spun fibers lie in one direction, giving cellulose threads a luster.

Cellulose fibers are stronger when wet than dry, and can take high temperatures, scrubbing, and abrasion. They also tolerate alkali conditions well, but are susceptible to acids, particularly hot acids. Clean with chlorine bleach (sodium hypochlorite), or by simmering in a soap solution (not detergent).

LINEN is a tall grass. If you have a yarn with stiff, crunchy linen fibers, try wetting it thoroughly, freezing it, and then ironing it while it is still frozen. This will soften it by driving steam into the core of the fiber. The process also works for garments.

COTTON fibers are less than 2" long; the soft fibers must be very tightly spun to hold together. Mercerized cotton has been boiled in sodium hydroxide (lye), which pre-shrinks, defuzzes, and increases luster. Most threads are mercerized: look for it on the label. Non-mercerized cotton will shrink, fuzz, and not behave the way you are used to cotton behaving.

RAMIE is the stem fiber of a nettle, called China grass. The lustrous, bleached fibers dry very quickly and are resistant to mildew. Somewhat stiff, the fibers are often found mixed with linen or cotton in yarns.

MAN-MADE CELLULOSE FIBERS

All man-made fibers are, strictly speaking, synthetic. But fibers made from regenerated natural fibers are no longer classed as synthetics; they are now called natural fibers. Man-made cellulose fibers fall into two categories: regenerated cellulose and cellulose acetate. Cellulose, frequently in the form of wood chips, is broken down and regenerated to produce viscose rayon, referred to both as viscose or as rayon. Rayon has properties similar to those of cotton, and blends well with other cellulose fibers, but is weaker when wet, and suffers abrasion

(1) Cotton, 'Cotton Tape', Rowan; (2) Cotton, 'Kitchen Cotton', Lion Brand Yarn; (3) Cotton, 'Chunky Chenille', Rowan; (4) Cotton/Silk blend, 'Cotton Silk Aran', Debbie Bliss; (5) Cotton/Rayon/Polyester, 'String of Pearls', Muench Yarns; (6) Acrylic/Wool blend, 'Kool Wool', Lion Brand Yarn; (7) Cotton/Acrylic blend, 'Cotton-Ease', Lion Brand Yarn; (8) Silk, Jaeger; (9) Silk/Polyamide, 'Baccara', Lang Yarns; (10) Silk/Wool blend, 'Silk Garden', Noro; (11) Super Kid Mohair/Silk, 'Kidsilk Haze', Rowan.

more easily. Rayon combined with wool tends to felt or mat together when machine-washed and dried.

A new regenerated cellulose fiber, Lyocell (Tencel®), is similar to rayon, and has a light, silky texture. In hand-knitting yarns it is currently found primarily in blends.

Cellulose acetate, commonly known as acetate, was developed after World War II. It is lustrous and drapes well. Its qualities are quite different from rayon and natural cellulose fibers, and more like those of synthetic fibers. It melts at 446° F, is not absorbent (so it will drip dry), and resists creasing.

SYNTHETIC FIBERS

Synthetic fibers are made from substances that are not fibers, but that are made into fibers by chemical means. Long chain polymer molecules of coal and oil by-products are combined into continuous molecules. These long strands are synthetic fibers, extruded much the same way silk fibers are. Synthetics have the shared properties of being very strong and elastic. They are light, do not absorb moisture (which makes them difficult to dye, but they drip dry), and are resistant to abrasion. Because they hold static charges, they soil more easily than natural fibers, and are harder to clean.

The first and most famous synthetic fiber is nylon (a polyamide), followed closely by polyamids, a subgroup of polyamides with less-rigid properties.

POLYESTER, which comes in a number of varieties under a number of names, such as Dacron, is a very fine fiber often used in commercially woven fabrics and high denier knits. In hand-knitting yarns these fibers are found in metallic and textural blends.

ACRYLIC fibers are a form of vinyl, and come under various trade names, such as Orlon. Knitting yarns with acrylic fibers have the hand properties of wool yarn. Acrylic is more flammable than nylon and polyester, though there are some types with good flame resistance. Acrylic is less elastic than nylon and polyester, so garments may distort if not cared for properly.

POLYPROPYLENE draws moisture away from the skin, does not develop static easily, and is a good insulator. It is spun into soft yarns and blends, and has very good insulating properties. 🧶

(1) Acrylic/Rayon/Nylon blend, 'Baby Soft', Lion Brand Yarn; (2) Acrylic/Polyester blend, 'Homespun', Lion Brand Yarn; (3) Rayon/Mohair/Nylon blend, 'Kid Slique', Prism; (4) Nylon, 'Dazzle', Prism; (5) Polyamide, 'Victoria', Anny Blatt; (6) Nylon, 'Quest', Berroco; (7) Rayon, 'Biwa', Prism; (8) Ganpi abaka/Rayon/Nylon blend, 'Ganpi abaka tape', Noro; (9) Polyamide, 'Segue', Trendsetter Yarns; (10) Acrylic/Wool/Polyamide blend, 'Lulu', Lang Yarn; (11) Polyamide, 'Muguet', Anny Blatt; (12) Polyamide, 'Fox', Lang Yarns; (13) Polyamide, 'Apart-Color', GGH; (14) Cotton/Viscose/Nylon/Poly/Linen, 'Light stuff skein', Prism; (15) Viscose/New Wool, 'Touch Me', Muench; (16) Acrylic, 'Lion Chenille Sensations', Lion Brand Yarn.

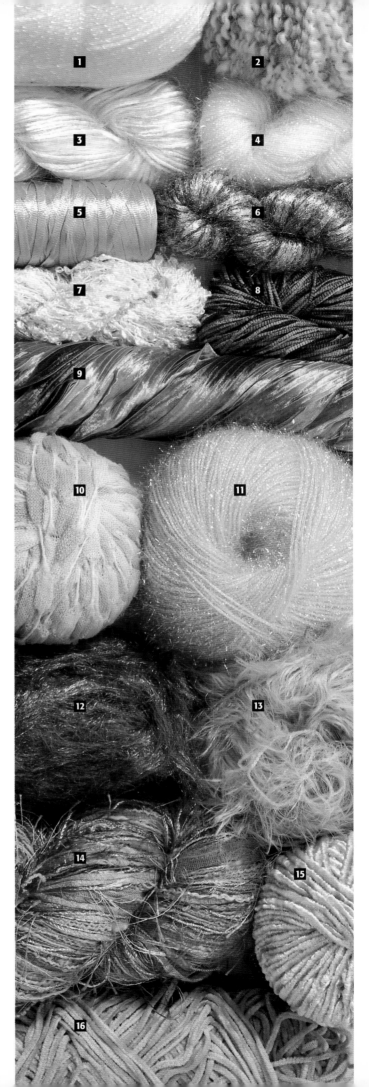

KNITTING RIGHT- OR LEFT-HANDED

Knitting itself is less right- or left-handed than the people who knit. Most knitting techniques work equally well for both left- or right-handed knitters. The issue is really initial awkwardness with knitting because it is a set of new skills for both hands. If you are a new knitter, learning and becoming comfortable with all techniques and knitting positions gives you a variety of skills for a variety of knitting situations. If you are already comfortable with one knitting style, expand your skills and enter new realms of fiber fluency.

Knitting with yarn controlled by the right hand seems the opposite of knitting with yarn controlled by the left hand; but, if you know both positions, you may switch from one position to another when your hands are tired. Likewise, double knitting (tubular knitting on two needles), two-end knitting, and multi-color knitting skills are all much simpler using different hands to control the different strands. Blending right- and left-hand skills takes the best of both styles and puts a new slant on them for greater speed and comfort.

Taken a step further, whether you are left- or right-handed, "backwards" knitting for you is simply the correct set of skills for reverse knitting, and reverse knitting is absolutely essential sometimes, and a blessed relief at other times. (Nevertheless, when you first begin to knit, your favored hand will want to feel in charge.) All in all, you will be much more comfortable and versatile by being familiar with several techniques, left and right, foreign and domestic.

Left-handers may wish to acquire new skills on their dominant side first. But we hope you won't stop there. If you start with the left-hand, branch out to right-hand techniques. If you are right-handed, learn the left-hand techniques equally well. I promise you, left or right-handed, someday you will be knitting a four-color Fair Isle sweater in the round, come to the armholes, and will be able to knit and shape from the front with reverse knitting. On that day you will thank yourself.

KNITTING FLAT OR IN-THE-ROUND

Knitting can be done "flat" on two single needles, with the work turned at the end of each row, to make flat shapes. Aside from scarves, shawls, and afghans, many knitted articles of clothing are made this way, with separate pieces sewn together. High-fashion knits are often made of flat knitted pieces, carefully shaped as they are knitted, then sewn together to produce a stylish garment.

Knitting is also done in the round, producing cylindrical pieces, such as socks, hats, and sweaters, or flat pieces such as tablecloths. Garments knitted in the round need little or no sewing, even the sweaters. Sometimes sweaters knitted in the round have armhole openings made by dividing the work into front and back, then rejoined at the shoulders. Armhole openings can be cut (yes, cut!) after the body is complete, and sleeves are knit or sewn on. Sweaters in the round are even cut down the front and made into cardigans.

The advantages to knitting in the round are both practical and self-indulgent. The practical advantages are 1) when you knit a sweater in the round there is very little additional assembly, 2) you can view the pattern work from the same side the entire time you are working, and 3) you don't have seams in your socks. The self-indulgent advantage is that you can just sit and knit, without having to stop to turn the work.

Whichever way you choose to knit, either flat or round, you can produce the same beautiful, textured, lace, or multi-colored fabrics, using the same knit and purl stitches with increases and decreases. Whether flat or round, whichever method you choose, knitting is a joy to make and a joy to use.

HOLDING THE NEEDLE

Holding the needles and yarn is a matter of culture and personal comfort. Knitting works in all sorts of different ways, and each has advantages and disadvantages. We offer the most familiar—at least in the United States—but there are more (see page 37). When you are familiar with one style, learn another so that you may select one that suits your need at any time.

There is much dispute as to which method is more correct, more "real," more traditional, and on and on. The methods are all traditional, they all produce real knitting, and they all are correct. Each style met the needs of the people who used it (for generations), and now you have the pick of all of them. Don't limit yourself to just one.

If you are interested in learning new styles, there are three steps common to all knitting: first, insert the needle; second, form the new stitch; and third, drop the old stitch. Identify each basic step in the new techniques and you will not get confused or leave one out. Pay attention to the direction the stitches face, so that you can properly adapt increase and decrease techniques. If you practice a couple rows of a new knitting style regularly, it will quickly become an old technique to you.

To avoid confusion with "right-hand," "left-hand" terms, whenever possible we will refer to the needle (or end of a circular needle) holding stitches to be worked on as the source needle. The working needle holds the new stitches, those being made in the current row.

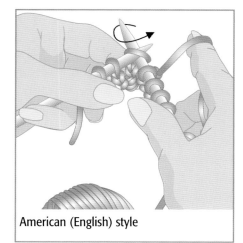

American (English) style

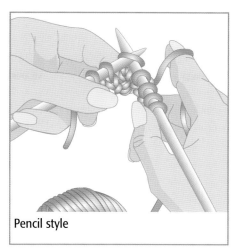

Pencil style

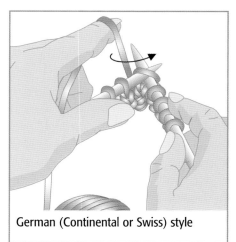

German (Continental or Swiss) style

HOLDING THE NEEDLE—STYLES

AMERICAN (English) knitting is the style used in this book. The needles are held under the palms. The yarn is wrapped counterclockwise for both the knit and purl stitches, and the right hand controls the yarn and the working needle. The left hand controls the (source) needle, which drops the stitch onto the working needle.

A variant of this style uses a knitting belt or whisk to support the working needle (see photo, page 29), which can be braced against the hip, or under the arm for stability, leaving the right hand free to work the yarn. This shares the work between left and right hands.

PENCIL knitting is a British variant and a French technique. The working needle is held as one would a pencil, and the yarn is wrapped counterclockwise for both the knit and the purl stitches. As the knitting progresses it is necessary to accommodate the increased bulk in your working hand and to balance the working needle on your arm. The tension on the yarn is loose, generally requiring smaller needles.

GERMAN (or Continental or Swiss) knitting is done with the yarn controlled by the left hand and the working needle by the right hand. Pick up the yarn for the new stitch with the working needle, which the index finger or the thumb can control, whichever is more comfortable.

There are two different ways to wrap the yarn in this style, and if you find someone who does it opposite to your way, prepare to defend yourself. One wrap is counterclockwise for both knit and purl stitches; the other is clockwise for both knit and purl stitches.

BLENDED STYLE is a hand-pampering and very sleek combination that carries the yarn in the left hand, in the German style, using clockwise-wrapped purl stitch and counterclockwise-wrapped knit stitch. The combination lets you pick up, rather than wrap on, both knit or purl stitches with the working needle. The unusual aspect of the combined style is that it places the knit stitch facing right and the purl stitch facing left.

The other knitting styles use either clockwise or counterclockwise wrap, but they don't combine the two. Using only one direction of wrapping the yarn means that both knit and purl stitches will face the same direction, but (depending on the style chosen) either the knit or the purl will require the more laborious wrapping of the yarn around the needle. Stitches facing different directions will not be any problem if you learn about the different positions of the stitch on the needle.

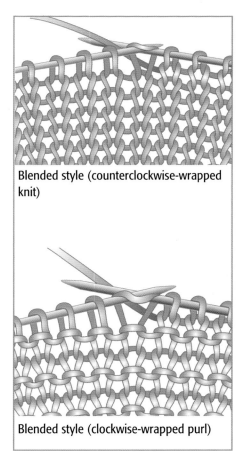

Blended style (counterclockwise-wrapped knit)

Blended style (clockwise-wrapped purl)

HOW MANY TO CAST ON?

A commercial pattern gives the correct number of stitches as well as the length of needle and the stitch gauge. Of course, you are going to knit a gauge swatch before you start a project! Then you will know how many stitches per inch you are knitting.

The yarn label should list the recommended gauge and needle size for the yarn. Check for recommended gauge of stitches per inch, then multiply the number of stitches per inch x the width you want. Using single-pointed needles, you can cast on as many or as few stitches as reasonably fit on the needle.

Using circular needles, a gap between the first and last stitches will make it impossible to knit in the round. There should be enough stitches on the needle to span from one point to the other without stretching. But you should not have so many stitches that they leap off the points. If the needle looks far too empty or full, it probably is.

Even if your needle is not the size recommended on the yarn label, you can use the following formula to approximate the right number of stitches: multiply the number of stitches per inch x the length of the circular needle. For example, for a stitch gauge of 5 stitches per inch on a 5 mm needle: 16" needle x 5 stitches per inch = 80 stitches. You can cast on a few more if it makes you feel secure.

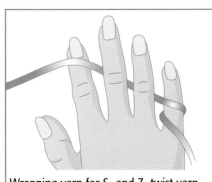
Wrapping yarn for S- and Z- twist yarn

WRAPPING THE YARN

As you knit, choose a comfortable way to carry the yarn across your hand; this may vary depending on the style of knitting you do. S- and Z- twist yarns (see Yarns and Fibers, page 31) wrap around your hand differently because they are spun in opposite directions, and the way you carry the yarn for American-style knitting may untwist the same yarn used in the German knitting position. If you make a mistake (it happens occasionally) and have to pull out a few rows, make sure that re-knitting with that part of the yarn will not untwist it even more. If needed, place a rubber band around the ball of yarn to keep it from unwinding, then dangle it in the air and spin it in the direction that tightens the yarn. Wind the re-spun yarn onto the ball and slip the rubber band over it as you progress, until all the yarn is smooth and nicely twisted again. If you have re-knit the same area a few times (it happens occasionally), and the yarn looks positively frowsy, you may prefer to cut the worn yarn and attach a new strand. Save the cut yarn for mending the sweater later.

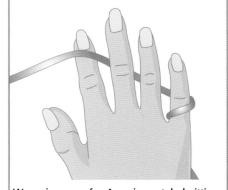
Wrapping yarn for American-style knitting

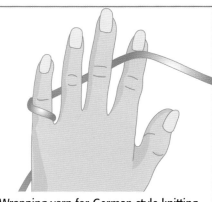
Wrapping yarn for German-style knitting

CAST-ON

Casting-on begins every knitting project. One way or another you have to get loops on the needle, and to "cast on" begins the process.

CHOOSING CAST-ON METHODS

As with any traditional craft, there are people who believe there is only one right way to do something. However, there are regional traditions for doing practically everything. Anything that works, *works*, and it is pointless to argue with success. Some knitters have a favorite beginning and ending pair, while others are eclectic and use lots of different combinations. Choose your own tradition or borrow someone else's.

The casting-on methods here are a good basic repertoire: finger, needle, or crochet; firm or stretchy, decorative, and even vanishing. Specialized methods are included where they pertain, and notes are tucked in that may solve problems you haven't yet encountered. If you invent, devise, or discover a technique that meets a need, use it and share it! So long as there are knitters, the last word on knitting has not been written.

STAY LOOSE

Casting-on tightly makes the first row difficult and uncomfortable to work, and may interfere with a stretchy stitch pattern. It also makes an edge that is more likely to break under strain. An easy way to avoid this is to cast on over two needles held together, removing one needle before you start knitting. If this becomes a perpetual problem, try one of the special, stretchy cast-on techniques. Make sure the loops slide easily along the needle, and that the other needle point can be inserted into the loops without having to use force.

CASTING-ON TECHNIQUES
BASIC CAST-ON

Form a slip knot. The slip knot is counted as a cast-on stitch, since you will knit into it on the next row. Pull a 10" length of yarn from the skein. Make a circle and place the working yarn (the yarn coming from the skein) under the circle. Insert the needle and pull on both ends of the yarn to complete the slip knot. The slip knot counts as your first cast-on stitch.

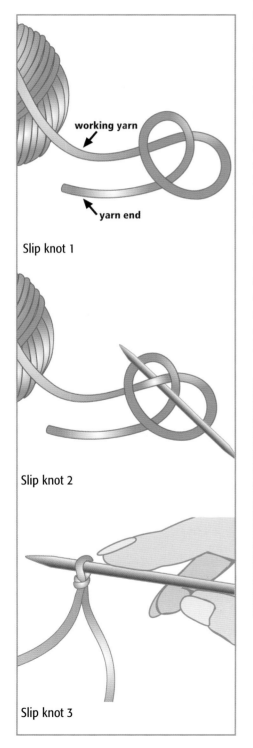

working yarn

yarn end

Slip knot 1

Slip knot 2

Slip knot 3

FINGER CAST-ON

Works either right or left handed. This cast-on produces a firm edge by "knitting-on" the first row, which will be facing you as you cast on. When you turn the needle you will see the back of a knit row, with a line of small bumps above the casting on. If you are doing circular knitting, you will begin knitting on the right side of the fabric.

Make a tail by measuring out about the width of knitting you wish to work x 4, or measure about one inch of yarn per stitch you intend to cast on.

Make a slip knot, put it on the needle with the tail to the inside. Catch both the tail and the working yarn in your palm, under the last two fingers, and slip the index finger, between the strands.

Slip your thumb under the inside strand to make an open loop. With the tip of the needle coming up under the inner strand of the thumb loop (tail), pick up the loop, catch the working strand over the index finger, and draw it through the thumb loop.

Tighten the thumb loop beneath the needle. Repeat for the desired number of stitches, counting the slip knot as a stitch. (As you move your thumb to pick up the yarn tail, move it consistently either clockwise, or counterclockwise, to keep the stitches consistent.)

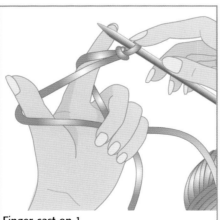

Finger cast-on 1

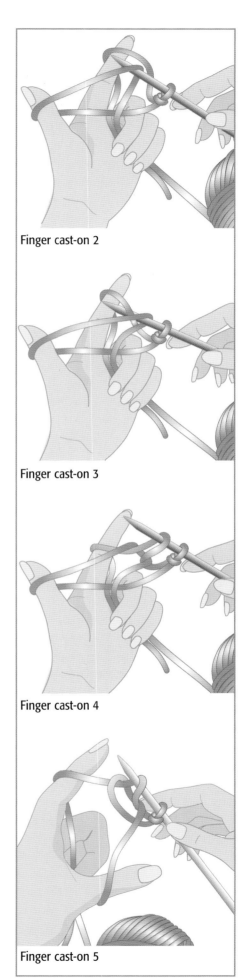

Finger cast-on 2

Finger cast-on 3

Finger cast-on 4

Finger cast-on 5

TWO-NEEDLE CAST-ONS

Start with a single slip knot, into which you knit or purl stitches that are then slipped back on the needle. The motions are the same as knitting and purling. To keep the edges as stretchy as the knitted fabric, cast on with needles a few sizes larger than you plan to use for the rest of the piece.

KNITTED CAST-ON

Leaving a short tail, make a slip knot and put it on the needle.

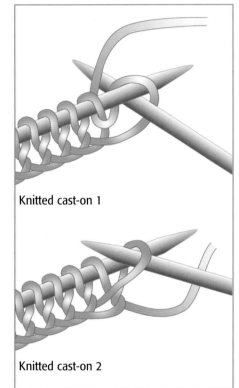

Knitted cast-on 1

Knitted cast-on 2

Insert the working needle from front to back through the loop, under the source needle. At the back side of the work, wrap the yarn clockwise around the working needle, catch the strand and draw it through the slip knot. Holding the needles point to point, transfer the loop just formed onto the source needle.

OPEN KNITTED CAST-ON

Work as you do the knitted cast-on, up to the point where the new stitch is transferred to the source needle. At this time, turn the working needle so that it points in the same direction as the source needle. Slip the point of the source needle into the new stitch and back the working needle out of the loop. This will twist the new stitch and open the base.

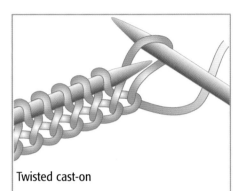

Twisted cast-on

This variation of the knitted cast-on produces a deeper, twisted edge with smaller openings (useful if you wish to add fringe). It is also attractive if you are working a lacy pattern.

CABLED CAST-ON

Follow the directions for making a knitted cast-on to make the first two loops. For the third and successive stitches, insert the working needle from front to back between the two stitches on the needle. Wrap the yarn counter-clockwise around the working needle, draw loop through, and slip it onto the source needle.

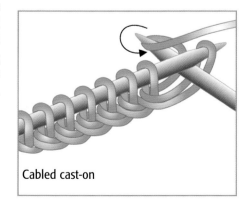

Cabled cast-on

This is very similar to the knitted cast-on, but the edge is a double strand of yarn. It is pretty and rather stretchy.

PURLED CAST-ON

Leaving a short tail, make a slip knot and put it on the needle. Insert the working needle from back to front through the loop. With the yarn in front, wrap the yarn counterclockwise around the working needle, and draw a loop through to the back, then put the needles point to point and slip the loop onto the source needle.

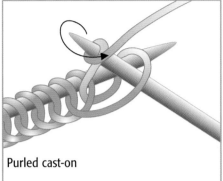

Purled cast-on

This cast-on is easier to do than the knitted cast-on simply because slipping the stitches onto the source needle requires less twisting of the working needle—it is a more natural motion. The purled side is the front.

RIBBED CAST-ONS

Alternating knitted and purled cast-on stitches form the pattern. If you prefer the cabled cast-on edge, alternate knitted and purled cast-on stitches to produce cabled cast-on ribbing.

TEMPORARY OR TUBULAR CAST-ON

Tie together the ends of the waste yarn and working yarn. Hold the knot and waste yarn under the needle with your thumb. Catch the strands in the other hand, holding the short end over the thumb, and the working strand over the index finger, catching the ends in your palm.

Wrap the working yarn, back to front, over the top of the needle, then give one clockwise twist to the working and waste yarns, putting the waste strand on top; the working yarn will now be to the front of the needle, twisted with the waste yarn under the needle.

Bring the needle up under the working yarn, wrapping the working yarn over the needle. Twist both strands counterclockwise, catching the working yarn in a twist under the needle. Each time you wrap the working strand and twist the two strands under the needle it casts on a stitch. Be careful to keep the waste yarn taut under the needle, and to carry the working yarn less tightly around the needle, so that the stitches will be the right size.

As you cast on, hold the stitches in place with your thumb to keep them from shifting around on the needle.

Knit the rest of the piece until you are ready to pick up the cast-on stitches to work in the other direction. Then clip the waste yarn and pull it out as you pick up the stitches on a needle.

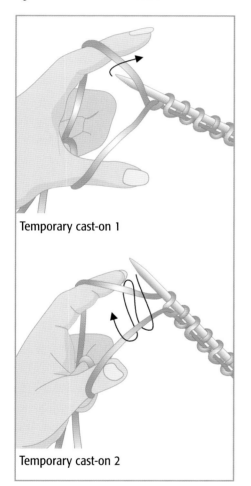

Temporary cast-on 1

Temporary cast-on 2

This method makes stitches without the beginning yarn ridge from the usual casting-on processes. Use when you want to knit in the other direction later on in the project, such as when you want to work a ribbing last. The temporary cast-on leaves stitches like those on the needle during the knitting process. It is simple to perform and just as simple to remove.

HALF-HITCH CAST-ON

Use for emergency only, since it is really more of an increase than a cast on. Use when you need to cast on a few unobtrusive stitches in the middle of a row, perhaps for a buttonhole, or at the end of a row for a vent or kick pleat. When working with really strange novelty yarns and ribbon, this is sometimes the only cast-on method that works well.

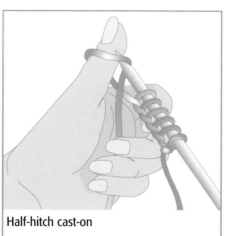

Half-hitch cast-on

CROCHET IN KNITTING

If you have never crocheted it is well worth learning. Aside from its intrinsic beauty, crochet is invaluable in expanding and simplifying aspects of knitting. Take the time to learn at least as much crocheting as we cover in this book. You may find that you have acquired another hobby.

Crocheted cast-ons are numerous and versatile because the crochet chain has many useful loops. While the diameter of the knitting needle determines the size of the knit stitches on the first row, the diameter of the crochet hook determines the amount of stretch in the edge. (This is very useful when you may need a lot of stretch on a border, such as in socks or sweaters.)

SIMPLE CROCHET CHAIN CAST-ON

Chain with one stitch for each knitted stitch you need. Count the slip loop as well as the chain on the hook. Insert the knitting needle into the loop on the hook, then draw up a loop through each spine bump on the back of each chain stitch. You can use the crochet hook to draw up the loop if this is easier, then just slip the loop onto the needle. If you draw up the loop from back to front, the

stitch will be knitted. If you draw up the loop from front to back, the stitch will be purled.

This technique is appropriate for casting on ribbing or pattern stitches. Bind off to match with lift-over bind-off (see page 50).

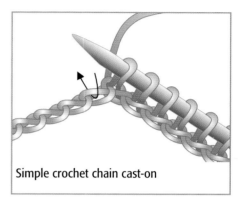

Simple crochet chain cast-on

VANISHING CROCHET CAST-ON (PROVISIONAL CAST-ON)

Using waste yarn, make a chain a few stitches longer than you need. Finish the chain loosely, so that you can easily pick out the last chain later. With your project yarn, pick up the desired number of stitches through chain spine bumps. You can do this by knitting into the spine bump directly, or by using the crochet hook to draw up a loop through the spine bump, then slipping the loop onto the needle. Knit the rest of the piece as needed, up to the point where you are ready to use the first row stitches. Simply take out the last crochet loop and pull out the chain. Your knitted loops will be ready to pick up and knit in the other direction. This doesn't work for ribbing.

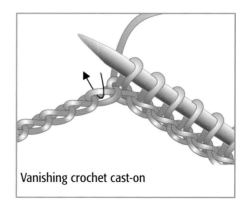

Vanishing crochet cast-on

KNITTING A STITCH

Once you have loops on a needle you can start knitting—finally. If you have never knitted before, for the sake of simplicity hold the source needle (with the cast-on loops) under your left hand and the working needle under your right hand, and use your right hand to work the yarn. We can debate about it after you have worked a couple of rows.

If you are knitting on 2 needles, turn the needles point to point, and work into the last loop you cast-on.

If you are trying circular knitting, you will be working into the slip knot, which was the first loop on your needle.

Whichever it is, it will be the first loop you knit into so we will call it the first stitch.

Make sure the yarn is on the far (back) side of the needle. Insert the working needle, front to back, into the first loop. The point should be sticking out on the far side, pointing somewhat away from you. Wrap the yarn in back counterclockwise around the projecting point. Catch the wrap of yarn on the working needle, draw a loop through to the near side, facing you. Then drop the first loop off of the source needle (nudge it off with your finger, if you need to). You will now have one loop (a knit stitch) on the working needle, and one less loop of your original cast-on row on the source needle.

The working strand of yarn will now be behind the working needle, instead of behind the source needle. If you ever have to put your knitting down in the middle of a knit row, when you pick it up make sure the working yarn is on your "working" side.

That is all there is to it—drawing a loop through another loop. Do this across the row of cast-on loops, making sure that once the new stitch is on the working needle you discard each cast-on loop.

The first stitch of the row requires a little attention. At the end of a row, pull

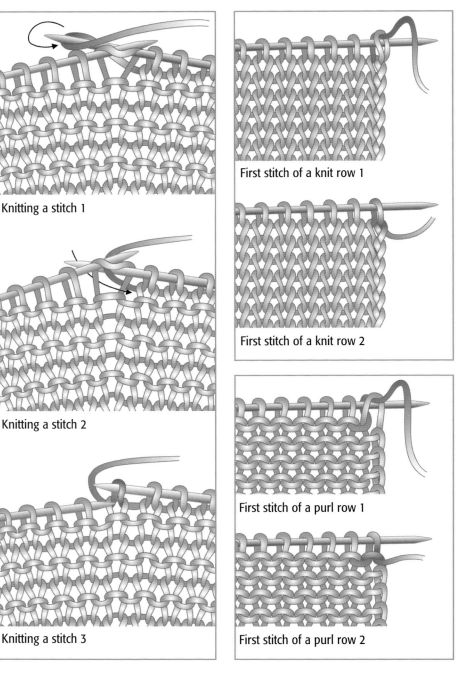

Knitting a stitch 1

Knitting a stitch 2

Knitting a stitch 3

First stitch of a knit row 1

First stitch of a knit row 2

First stitch of a purl row 1

First stitch of a purl row 2

the strand of working yarn down toward the back of the needle, whether you have worked a knit or a purl stitch. Turn the needle for the next row, and before you begin to knit the next row, check to make sure that the yarn lies on the front side of the needle. This will keep you from looking at the first stitch and seeing two stitches where there is only one. If the yarn is pulled over the needle toward the back at the beginning of a row, both legs of the stitch below will lie across the top of the needle and will look like two separate stitches. If you knit into both of them you will increase one stitch each row; your knitting will get wider and wider.

If you are new to knitting, knit several rows (or even several feet) until the movements are comfortable and you don't even have to think about them.

PURLING A STITCH

The purl stitch is the other half of basic knitting. The bumps formed on the front of the fabric look like pearls, which is why the stitch is called purl. Make sure the yarn is on the front side of the needle. Insert the working needle from back to front in the loop on the needle. Wrap the yarn counterclockwise, and draw the new loop in through to the back; drop off the old loop. The strand of working yarn will now be in front of the working needle, instead of in front of the source needle.

The purl stitch is exactly as easy as the knit stitch, because purling is simply knitting from the back of the fabric to the front. The proof of this is that after you have made a swatch of 8 rows of purl stitch only, then compare it to a swatch of 8 of knit stitch only. You will see that there is no difference.

When you feel comfortable enough with purling to experiment, wrap the yarn both ways, to see how you can control the direction of a stitch as you make it.

If you need to reverse the way a stitch faces, lift the stitch off with the tip of the working needle, reverse the legs over the needle, and set it back facing the other direction.

Or simply insert the needle on the face you usually use, and purl it as it sits.

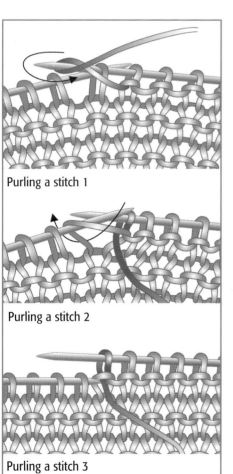

Purling a stitch 1

Purling a stitch 2

Purling a stitch 3

POSITION OF A STITCH ON A NEEDLE

Now that you can put a stitch on a needle, it's time to do a little restful observation of your knitting. If you followed the knit stitch instructions exactly, each time, your stitches will face left. If you didn't, stitches may face left or right, or perhaps some of each. Since you will need to use stitches in both these positions, this is a good time to learn the whys and hows.

The shape of a stitch as it sits on the needle is like a croquet wicket: There is the arch on top and a leg on either side. Each leg is anchored in place by the stitch below, but the arch straddles the needle and the stitch faces either the right or left side.

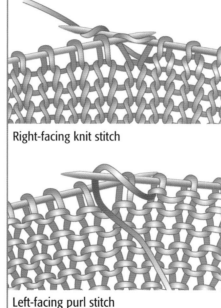

Right-facing knit stitch

Left-facing purl stitch

A stitch points in the direction of the back leg, i.e., if the left leg is in back the stitch faces left. But the stitch can pivot once it is removed from the needle. (We refer to stitches assuming that they start out facing left, and the illustrations are drawn from this point of view.)

The leg in back is determined by the direction the yarn is wrapped as you make a stitch. If you wrap the yarn counterclockwise around the working needle, as shown here, the new stitch will face left.

CLOCKWISE WRAP

If you wrap the yarn clockwise, the stitch formed will face right. Some knitting traditions have the stitch facing the knitter's right side because of the way the needles are held and the yarn is wrapped. The knitting movements look different, the stitch faces the other direction, but the outcome is knitting.

Knitters tend to use either a clockwise wrap for both knit and purl, or a counterclockwise wrap for both knit and purl. But you don't have to (see Blended Style, page 37). If you know how to produce both of these you can mix and match. When you feel comfortable enough with knitting to experiment, wrap the yarn in different directions, just to see what happens. Purling works the same way.

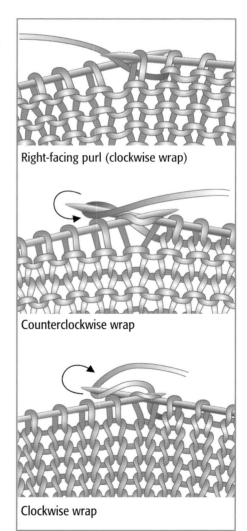

Right-facing purl (clockwise wrap)

Counterclockwise wrap

Clockwise wrap

UNDERSTANDING THE KNITTING STITCH

If you understand a little about how a stitch works you will better understand all knitted fabrics. The knit stitch is wider at the top because the two strands at the base of each stitch squeeze into the arch of the stitch below. The arch at the top contains the legs of the stitch above. A purl stitch has exactly the same qualities, but they are visible on the back of the fabric.

Combine knit and purl stitches to make pattern stitches. Individual purl stitches rise above the surface of stockinette fabric, catching the light and making a visible pattern. On the other side of the fabric—reverse stockinette—individual knit stitches recede to the point of invisibility. Groups of knit stitches are smooth and reflective, while the pebbly texture of purl stitch groups breaks up the light and gives depth. Combinations of these stitches can be intricate or simple, and are easy to adapt to all sorts of projects.

CHANGING YARN FROM BACK TO FRONT

When working with both knit and purl stitches in a single row, you will be changing the side (back or front) on which you insert the needle and wrap the yarn. When you switch from purl to knit or from knit to purl, the strand of working yarn must also switch to the other side before you work the new stitch. To do this without inadvertently adding another stitch, simply pass the strand of yarn to the other side **between** the points of the needles. Do not lay the strand of yarn across the top of either needle or you will mistake it for a stitch in the next row and knit it. This would add a stitch and throw off the pattern in every repeat to the end of the row.

GARTER STITCH

Rows of the knit stitch, turned at the end of each row, produce garter stitch fabric. Since the purl stitch is simply the knit stitch done from back to front, rows of purl stitch produce garter stitch fabric, too.

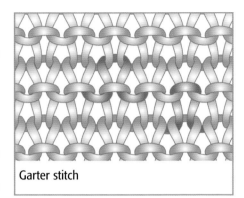
Garter stitch

A garter stitch is identical on both sides, with a ridge where two rows of knitting interlock; each ridge equals two rows of knitting. This makes it thick and warm because of the air pockets on both sides of the fabric.

Because knitting done in the round is not turned at the ends of the rounds, the stitches can interlock only on one side to produce stockinette fabric. Rows and rounds of stockinette are often counted on the smooth side. Garter stitch in the round is done by alternating a row of knitting with a row of purling. Sometimes a technique is easier in one method than the other, so it is sensible to learn both round and flat knitting techniques.

A nice feature of garter stitch is that it works square, i.e., 15 stitches in width is 15 ridges (30 rows) in height. Because of this it is often used for lace knitting, to keep the proportions of the designs. It also allows you to miter corners with exact 45° angles, which is useful in making corners for button bands, collars, and shaped garments.

STOCKINETTE STITCH

To produce stockinette fabric, knit one row of knit stitch, turn the work, and then work one row of purl stitch. The smooth knitted fabric of T-shirts is the most familiar kind of knitted fabric, with a smooth side with an allover pattern of small Vs on the front and an allover pattern of bumps on the back.

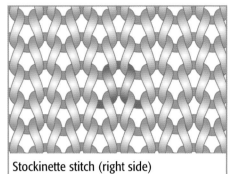
Stockinette stitch (right side)

REVERSE STOCKINETTE

Because reverse stockinette is very hard to count, it has been called "beggar's wealth." The bumps of the knit and purl stitches, formed by the arch of each stitch, are all interlocked on the back side of the fabric, and the Vs (the legs) of the knit and purl stitches are pushed to the front side of the fabric. Stockinette stitches are wider than they are tall, so the fabric does not work square, that is, 15 stitches in width do not equal 15 rows in height. The proportions are more like 2:3, where two stitches are as wide as three rows are tall. This is useful to know when you are picking up stitches along the edge of a sweater to make a button band. If changing a pattern from garter stitch to stockinette, or vice versa, you may have to recalculate the shaping of armholes and necklines, etc.

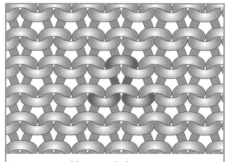
Reverse stockinette stitch

PATTERN STITCHES WITH KNIT AND PURL

Ribbing is the easiest pattern knitting. It makes the stretchy bottom edges of most sweaters and sleeves by alternating stacks of knit and purl stitches. This is done by repeating a pattern of knit and purl (such as Knit 1, Purl 1) for several rows. The alternating stacks appear in reverse on the other side of the fabric, i.e., knit on the front is purl on the back. A stack of knit stitches protrudes on the right side of fabric, while a stack of purled stitches recedes on the right side of the fabric, creating the ridges of ribbing. The small amount of extra yarn used to alternate from knit to purl stitch allows ribbing to stretch more, and makes the stretchiness characteristic of ribbings.

The stretchy quality of groups of stacked stitches gives us the family of ribbed patterns. You can alternate even numbers of knit and purl stitches for Knit 2, Purl 2, Knit 3, Purl 3, Knit 4, Purl 4 ribbings and even higher, though the wider the knit or purl segments, the less ribbing will act like a ribbing, and the more it will act like stockinette fabric.

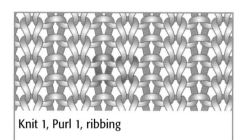

Knit 1, Purl 1, ribbing

You can also alternate odd and even numbers of stitches for uneven ribbing. Knit 1, Purl 2 gives a thin rib that stands out against reverse stockinette, while Knit 3, Purl 2 has broad, flat ribs. If you are using broad cables across a sweater the broad ribs may be more aesthetically pleasing than narrow ribs, while a single rib may blend beautifully with a Knit 1, Purl 1, broken ribbing pattern.

Knit 2, Purl 2, ribbing

TWISTED RIBBING

Twist the knit stitches of ribbing to create a braided stitch. This decorative variation droops less than an untwisted ribbing, but is a little less stretchy. If you are knitting with wool, the thing you will notice is how pretty it is, since wool is a stretchy fiber. The twisted rib is useful when you are working with cellulose yarns such as cotton or linen, which are not in themselves stretchy fibers. A twisted rib will diminish sagging ribbing, which is a torment often seen in cotton socks and sweaters.

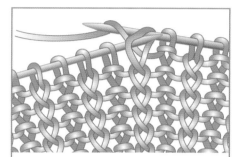

Twisted ribbing 1

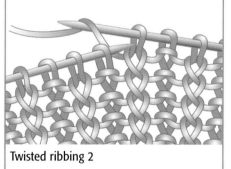

Twisted ribbing 2

BROKEN RIBBING

Work the orderly ribbing patterns for a few rows, then reverse the knit and purl stitches for a few rows to create broken ribbing patterns. This creates all-over patterns, which are as easy to remember as Knit 1, Purl 1, but have different and interesting textures. And when orderly vertical stacks of knit and purl stitches are interrupted the stitches flatten out instead of drawing in like ribbing.

Perhaps the most famous of these is the Seed Stitch, which is one row of Knit 1, Purl 1. Then the knit and purl stitches are reversed for a row. The pattern of alternating purl bumps and knit stitch Vs, both across and vertically, creates a lovely pebbled effect.

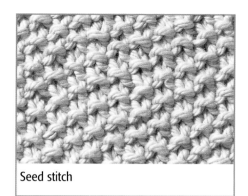

Seed stitch

If you alternate 4 rows of Knit 4, Purl 4, with its reverse, you see a checked pattern emerge, while alternating 4 rows of Knit 3, Purl 5 creates a basketweave pattern.

Knit 5, Purl 5, basketweave pattern

WHICH STITCH? If you are knitting stockinette stitch and don't recall whether you were knitting or purling when you finished the last row, take the needle as if you are about to start the new row. If you see smooth columns of Vs in front of you, knit the new row. If you see nothing but purl bumps, purl the new row.

If you ever have to put your knitting down in the middle of a row, when you pick it up make sure the working yarn is on your "working" side. If you knit rows from right to left, the working yarn in the middle of a row will be on the right needle. If you knit rows from left to right, the working yarn in the middle of a row will be on the left needle.

BASIC ERRORS

TWISTED STITCHES AND REVERSING (FLIPPING) A STITCH

To reverse (flip) a stitch, switch the leg in back since a stitch points in the direction of the back leg.

Remove the stitch from its perch with the tip of the working needle. Pivot the stitch so that you can see it straight on, then set the other leg at the back of the source needle; the stitch will still be facing front but the angle will change. The front of the stitch is still in front as long as the legs are not twisted.

Once you become familiar with this you can simply insert the needle on the correct face (knit from the front, purl from the back); work the stitch as it sits.

TWISTED STITCHES

When you reverse the direction of a stitch, the legs should not twist around each other, but should rise straight to the arch of the stitch. If the legs twist around each other the stitch will be twisted when it drops off as you knit the next row. Doing this deliberately makes both left- and right-twist stitch patterns.

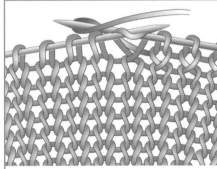

Counterclockwise twist

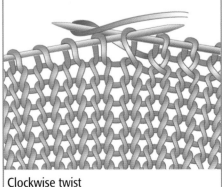

Clockwise twist

SLIP STITCH

The slip stitch is used in decreases and decorative patterns. It is the easiest stitch of all, because you do nothing but pick up a stitch from the source needle, and slip it onto the working needle. No yarn is wrapped or pulled through because the stitch from the row below is simply carried unchanged into the new row. You can slip the stitch either from the back of the stitch (purlwise) or from the front (knitwise). *Important:* When using a slip stitch to decrease in a knit row, make sure to slip the stitch knitwise (through the front) or it will be twisted in the finished decrease.

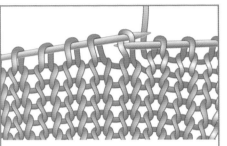

Knitwise slip stitch

Purlwise slip stitch

WYIB (WITH YARN IN BACK) OR WYIF (WITH YARN IN FRONT)

When you slip stitches the working strand of yarn is not used until the next time a stitch is knit or purled. In some decorative stitches the yarn is carried across the front of the work as stitches are slipped, leaving the strand to show on the right side of the pattern. The right side of the pattern may be in front or in back of the work, depending on which row you are working. Move the yarn to the side of the work specified for that row, slip the required number of stitches, and return the yarn to the side needed to work the next stitch.

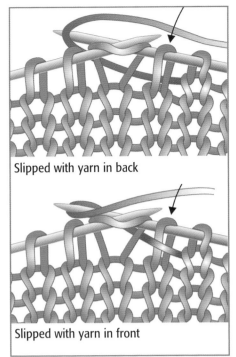

Slipped with yarn in back

Slipped with yarn in front

DROPPED STITCHES

Dropped stitches happen when a stitch falls off the needle without being knitted. Speed is usually the culprit; sometimes you drop a stitch despite all precautions. Fix a stitch with a knitting needle, or a crochet hook (keep one handy, just in case). Consider making a disaster swatch now to practice fixing a stitch, instead of waiting until you are working on a Very Important Project.

If you practice in a panic-free atmosphere you will notice that: a run (ladder) will only go in one direction—down. There is a horizontal yarn "rung" for each row the stitch has dropped. You can pick up a stitch from either side of the work. If the stitch has just slipped from one of the needles and hasn't started to run, simply insert the point of either needle back into the loop and return it to the proper needle, facing the correct direction (see Position of a Stitch on a Needle, page 43).

If a dropped stitch has run, leaving a long ladder, look just below the bottom rung to find the stitch loop. Insert the crochet hook through the loop—from the front to make a knit stitch, from the back to make a purl stitch. Catch the lowest rung of the ladder and pull it through the stitch loop—from the back to make a knit stitch, from the front to make a purl stitch. If you have several stitches to repair, remove the hook from the new loop so that you can re-insert it from the correct direction to pick up the next rung of the ladder. Repeat the process as many times as it takes to catch every rung, then check the back of the piece to make sure you haven't missed any. When you have finished you will have no rungs left and one loop to slip onto the needle.

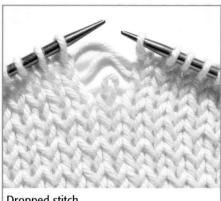
Dropped stitch

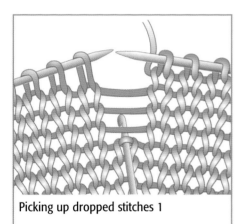
Picking up dropped stitches 1

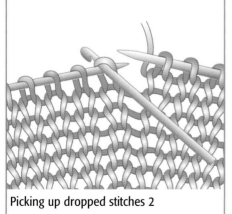
Picking up dropped stitches 2

LURKING ERRORS

Sometimes you don't notice a dropped stitch until several rows later. This is most likely to happen in stockinette knitting, which doesn't have pattern repeats to alert you to a problem. It is very easy to fix. Notice that there are strands between stitches, which are just like the rungs of a stitch that have run. Insert a crochet hook into the loose stitch loop and catch the strands above it just as if they were part of a ladder down to the stitch. The tension here will be a little tighter than in the other stitches, but this will even up when you block and wear the sweater.

USING DROPPED STITCHES

Not all dropped stitches are errors. You may find one purl stitch on stockinette, visible for miles. Follow the line of stitches above the wrong stitch all the way up to the stitch on the needle. Deliberately drop the stitch and make it run all the way down to the mistake. Then fix the mistake and repair the ladder, taking care not to make any new mistakes on the way up.

You may find a large error, such as a cable twisted in the wrong direction for the entire length of the piece. In this case you can drop several stitches—the width of the cable—and re-knit it using double-pointed needles. This is a lot less aggravating than pulling out the whole piece. People with very robust egos ignore such trifles and use them as proof the garment is a rare and costly hand-knit.

A ladder can be made for the full length of a piece and yarn or ribbons can be woven in various decorative patterns through the strands of yarn.

Incomplete stitches occur when you don't lift an existing stitch off the needle before moving on to work the next stitch. When you turn and work back across the row you will notice a strand lying diagonally across the needle. It looks like yarn over, except that it crosses another stitch. This is a warning that something is amiss. If you knit it you will increase one stitch. Instead, see which stitch it crosses—that is the stitch which didn't get completed. Pick up that

stitch with the tip of the needle, lift it over the diagonal strand, and drop it from the source needle. Then work the newly completed stitch.

✿
INCORRECT STITCHES

When the numbers are wrong and a pattern repeat or row count ends up with the incorrect number of stitches, immediately find out why. Go back to the beginning of the row and check each stitch. Do not just add a new stitch, or you will have a very rude surprise later. If you are working a complex pattern with several repeats, put markers between each repeat to alert you to a problem before you finish the whole row incorrectly.

✿
AVOIDING DROPPED STITCHES

A dropped stitch can start a run that continues all the way down to the casting on stitch—the ladder of thread is an entire column of stitches coming undone. The results of a dropped stitch range from mildly annoying to complete disaster. The best thing, of course, is to prevent dropping a stitch.

Do not put your knitting down when you are in the middle of a row. Stitches leap off the needles as soon as your back is turned. If you are knitting on a circular needle and you must stop in the middle of something, put point protectors on your needle when you put the knitting down. This one habit will save a lot of time spent fishing for stitches.

If you are knitting with slippery yarn, use wooden or bamboo needles. This is especially true if you are knitting on double-pointed needles; slick chrome needles practically launch themselves out of the knitting.

PICKING UP STITCHES AND KNITTING ON is often, (but not always) coupled with a catastrophe. When you have to pull out a row and re-stitch, do so with the simplest method to make things easier. On the other hand, you'll find picking up stitches to put the finishing touch on your creation can't go fast enough.

There are live stitches and dead stitches. Live stitches can escape and run. Dead stitches can't run anywhere; they are found at the sides and at the bottom of knitting. These stitches are picked up to add borders, sleeves, and necklines.

RIPPING BACK SEVERAL ROWS offers the option of picking up the stitches before you rip. Pull back to a row below the mistake you are fixing. This is easiest in a row without decreases or increases, if you have any options. Take a smaller diameter needle and go back to the row where you want to stop. If possible, leave the "real" needle in the top of the knitting for the time being.

Slip the needle into the center of each stitch across the stopping row, preferably so each stitch faces the same way. Miss no stitch or you will be doing this again very soon. When you are confident that you have every stitch, pull the "real" needle out of the top of the knitting, take the strand of yarn and start to pull.

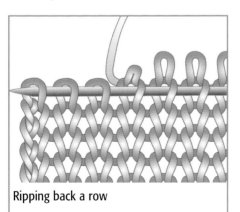

Ripping back a row

Don't jerk the yarn if it gets stuck. Stop, carefully disconnect the yarn, then resume ripping. Wind the yarn frequently as you go to avoid creating (and emitting) large snarls.

The stitches may be on the needle from the wrong direction, with the first stitch of the row by the button end of

the needle. If that happens, just slip the stitches one by one to the original needle and start working again. If you discover that some stitches are facing the wrong direction as you begin to re-knit, flip them so that they don't twist as you knit. (See Position of a Stitch on a Needle, page 43.)

RIPPING BACK

Ripping back stitch by stitch, one row after a mistake, shows you are alert. You may miss the lyric highs of ripping out several inches of knitting, but you also miss the aggravation of watching an evening's work disappear. Of course you can use this technique if you need to rip back several inches, and then rip back the last row stitch by stitch.

Hold the work as it was when you were working the row, with the empty source needle waiting to take the stitches back. Carefully pull the yarn out of one stitch and slip in the source needle. Slip the needle in before you pull out the yarn for an added bit of security, especially if you are using a slippery yarn. Repeat this for every stitch back to the mistake. Then begin knitting again to finish the row.

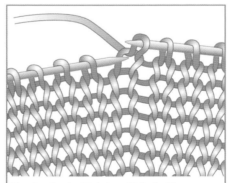

Ripping back stitch-by-stitch (knit)

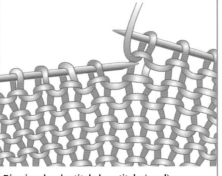

Ripping back stitch-by-stitch (purl)

PICKING UP STITCHES (KNITTING UP)

Use when you are knitting sleeves onto an armhole, knitting a border onto a scarf, adding ribbing to a neckline, and similar situations. The chief advantage to picking up to knit is that you don't have to sew pieces together. You can adjust sleeve length and repair cuffs without having to remove the sleeves.

Pick up the new stitches, on a needle with a smaller diameter than you intend to use to knit, keeping the new stitches from being loose or sloppy. You may be able to use a single-pointed needle for short work.

PICKING UP STITCHES CROSSWISE

Space the new stitches evenly along the other knitting, and to lie smoothly. Stockinette fabric, and any knitted fabric with obvious knit and purl sides, has stitches wider than they are tall (see Garter Stitch and Stockinette Stitch, page 44). When picking up stitches to knit in a different direction, such as sleeves, the rule of thumb about proportion is 3:2, that is, 3 rows of height = 2 stitches width.

For example, on a stockinette sweater, worked as usual from hip to shoulder, if you are picking up sleeve stitches around the armhole, pick up 2 sleeve stitches for every 3 rows in the armhole opening. Pick up buttonhole bands knitted perpendicular to the body in the same way—2 new stitches for every 3 rows of body stitches. To make sure it will work on your knitting, test the pick-up proportions on your test swatch.

Instead of picking up stitches through the uneven turning stitches at the ends of the rows, if you didn't make selvages, pick up a new stitch between the turning stitch and the second stitch. Just threading a knitting needle through the edge stitches and knitting them sideways will distort the new knitting. Use a separate strand of yarn to create new stitches.

To get the new stitches onto the needle, you can insert the needle into the stitches, wrap the yarn around the needle, and draw it up as if you are knitting. Or you can take your handy

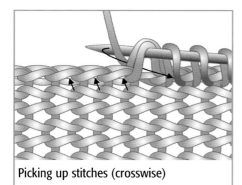

Picking up stitches (crosswise)

crochet hook and snag the yarn loops up without further ado. Set the new stitches on the needle facing the correct direction, so that when you knit the first row you don't inadvertently twist any. (See Position of a Stitch on a Needle, page 43.)

PICK UP STITCHES LENGTHWISE

This is frequently used on shaped necklines, where some of the stitches are bound off for the shaping but are needed later to hold ribbing. Draw up the new stitch from the center of each existing stitch with a smaller diameter needle or crochet hook.

Picking up stitches on a garment requires picking up stitches both cross-

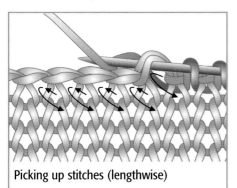

Picking up stitches (lengthwise)

wise and lengthwise, such as working a buttonhole-neck band around a cardigan, or knitting sleeves onto a sweater from armhole to cuff. Use double-pointed needles or circular needles for picking up sleeve stitches. For long buttonhole bands and borders, use a circular needle if convenient, or pick up the stitches in sections on several circular needles. You may work buttonhole bands as a continuous band, or work sections separately and graft them together at the center back or at the shoulder seams.

JOINING METHODS
ATTACHING A NEW STRAND

Delightful knitting comes to an abrupt end when the yarn runs out. There are a couple of different ways to attach a new strand of yarn, depending on what yarn and technique you are using in your project.

Join at the beginning of a row whenever possible, to eliminate lumps, knots, and bulk in the middle of a piece. When knitting with novelty yarns such as chenille, this is often the only way to join neatly a new strand of yarn.

Take up the new strand, insert the needle into the first stitch, wrap the new strand around the needle and complete the stitch. After you have knitted a few stitches, go back and make a single knot or a bow to keep the ends joined. This is not a permanent join, and will be taken out and the ends worked into the seam later. When knitting in the round, attach a new strand at the beginning of a new round to eliminate random ends throughout the sweater.

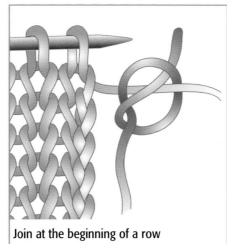

Join at the beginning of a row

SURPRISE ENDING!

One way to keep from having the end of the yarn come as a rude surprise is to pull out a row's worth of yarn at the beginning of each row. Four x the width of the row will usually be the correct amount.

MID-ROW SPLICE

Use to join two identical strands of yarn. This is a helpful technique if you are knitting a large piece and either edge is yards and yards away. Untwist 3" at the ends of both yarn pieces so that you can see the separate plies. Cut half the plies from each end and abut the short ends of one strand to the long ends of the other. Put the splice between your palms and roll the splice in the correct direction to re-twist the strand (see Yarns and Fibers, page 31).

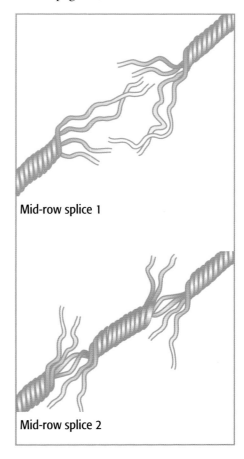

Mid-row splice 1

Mid-row splice 2

OVERLAP JOIN

Use in traditional knitting with fine yarns. If you are tempted to use this join, evaluate it when you work the gauge swatch to make sure it is invisible. Overlap the old and new strands for about 6", and knit with a double strand until the old strand runs out.

WOVEN JOIN

Work the ends in as you continue the row, the way you would work with two-color weaving (see Color-Weave Knitting, page 80). Knit with the old strand in the left hand for a few stitches, lifting the old strand over the working needle on alternate stitches, using the new strand to make the stitch and catching the old strand behind it.

Variation: Knit alternate stitches with the new and old strands.

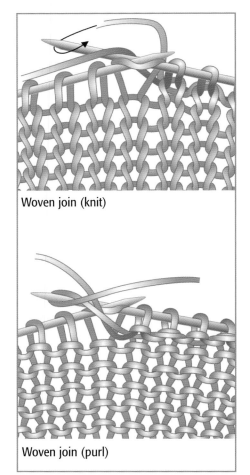

Woven join (knit)

Woven join (purl)

BINDING OFF (CASTING OFF)

Binding off is the opposite of casting on; stitches are removed one by one and locked so that they will not ravel. The number of stitches in the row does not change. Binding off is either done across the whole row at once for a straight edge, or a few stitches at a time to create necklines, sleeve caps, or slanting shoulders.

Within a piece, binding off occurs to create buttonholes, pockets, and sometimes neck and armhole openings. The terms "binding off" and "casting off" are interchangeable, although British publications use "casting off" more than American publications.

The bound-off edge should be stretchy but firm enough to hold its shape (unless you have a reason to pull in the edge, such as for a puffed sleeve). Binding off may tighten up the last row of stitches, but using a larger needle to bind off will diminish or eliminate this problem. Binding off with a sewn technique will also leave the end very stretchy, and is virtually invisible.

"BINDING OFF IN PATTERN"

When working in a pattern stitch and you come to binding off, simply work across the row knitting or purling each stitch just as you would if you were not binding off. Bind off after each stitch is worked. This continues the decorative pattern to the end of the piece.

When working a lace pattern that has the yarn-overs (increases) in one row and the balancing decreases in the next row, bind off in pattern on the decrease row so that the piece will not flare at the edge from excess stitches.

LIFT-OVER BIND-OFF

This basic technique is adaptable to many needs. Knit 2 stitches, pick up the first stitch with the point of the source needle, lift it over the second stitch knitted, and drop it off the working needle. The process is the same whether you are knitting or purling the stitches, so this is useful for binding off in pattern. This bind-off exactly matches the simple crochet cast-on (see page 41).

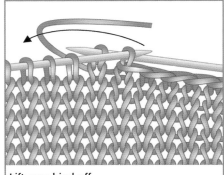

Lift over bind-off

DECREASE BIND-OFF

Use to create a very even but somewhat un-stretchy edge. If you wish to control a spreading pattern, such as allover cables, this works well. When worked with a needle a few sizes larger than the source needle, the edge will be both stretchy and beautifully even. It can be done in knit or purl, and can be combined with other binding-off methods (see Ribbing Bind-off, below).

On a knit row: Knit one stitch, *slip the next knitwise, knit 2 stitches together. Repeat from * across the row.

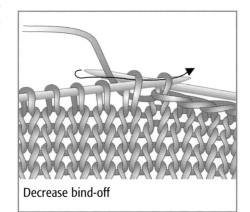

Decrease bind-off

On a purl row: Purl one stitch, *slip it back to the source needle, purl 2 stitches together. Repeat from * across the row.

RIBBING BIND-OFF

Keep the stretchy qualities of ribbing while making an attractive flat edge.

This is a lovely bind-off, and can be adapted to any ribbing: even (3 x 3, 4 x 4, etc.) or uneven (2 x 3, 3 x 4, etc.). What happens here is that the transitions between knitting and purling are treated differently. The transition from the knit rib to the purl rib (K+P stitch) is always returned to the source needle and used to purl again. The transition from the purl rib to the knit rib (P+K stitch) is always used in a simple lift-over bind-off (see above). Any side-by-side K, K or P, P portions of the rib are bound-off with a simple lift-over bind off.

FOR 1 X 1 RIBBING: Beginning with a knit stitch: * P2 tog, move the yarn to the back; k1, lift over the first stitch over and bind off. Yarn forward, slip the stitch from the working needle back to the source needle. Repeat from * across the row.

FOR 2 X 2 RIBBING, beginning with knit 2: Knit 2, lift the first stitch over the second and bind it off; yarn forward, slip the knit stitch on the working needle back to the source needle, p2 together, slip it back to the source needle, p2 together. Yarn back, knit 1 (2 stitches on working needle), lift first stitch over knit stitch and bind it off.

STEPPED BINDING-OFF

Use to create an angle, such as for a shoulder. It can be bound-off as you go, or the angle can be worked in short rows, which are rejoined and completed in the last row or two. In both methods, making the final row as straight as possible gives a smoother seam or a more attractive edge.

BIND-OFF AS YOU GO

The usual way to create an angled edge, binding off a few stitches each knit row. Avoid a 2-row jog at the beginning of each segment by working a transitional stitch between bound-off segments. On the row before the bind-off, work the last two stitches together in a decrease. This creates a stitch one row taller than the preceding bound-off segment and one row shorter than the new segment, allowing a smooth line in the finished edge.

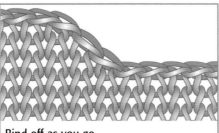

Bind off as you go

To eliminate a long and loopy last stitch on the bind off row, slip the first stitch of the row before the bind-off row, working the rest of the row as usual. Turn and bind off the row, working and binding off the slipped stitch as usual.

SEWN BIND-OFFS

Use a tapestry needle and a single strand of yarn to pick up the loops and keep them from raveling. Because the stitches are not looped over each other to lock them in place, a sewn bind-off is less visible and can be more elastic than knitted bind-offs.

TWO STITCHES FORWARD AND ONE STITCH BACK is simplicity itself. This is a perfect end to garter stitch, but is also an elegant final flourish to stockinette or reverse stockinette. If you knit your cast-on, this is an almost perfect match to the smooth cable edge.

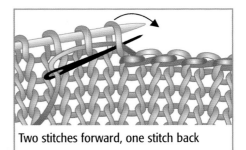

Two stitches forward, one stitch back

Thread a tapestry needle with a yarn tail about 3 times the length of the edge you are finishing. *Thread the tapestry needle purlwise through the first 2 stitches on the needle and bring it out on the front of the work. Insert the needle back into the first stitch on the needle knitwise, then drop that stitch off the needle. Repeat from * across the row.

INVISIBLE BIND-OFF is smooth, stretchy, and worth learning for a perfect tubular end to tubular ribbing but can be used for any 1 x 1 or 2 x 2 ribbing. Think of each rib as being paired with its twin on the opposite side of the work. When you link these together you are using grafting techniques to bind off. It can be done on or off the needles.

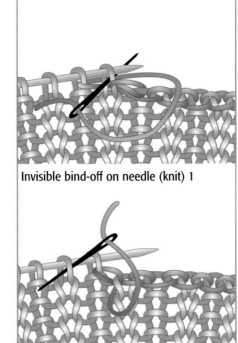

Invisible bind-off on needle (knit) 1

Invisible bind-off on needle (knit) 2

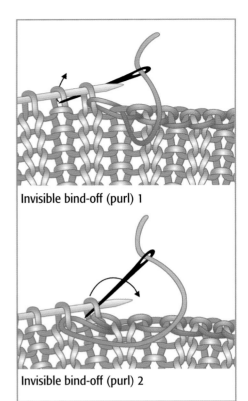

Invisible bind-off (purl) 1

Invisible bind-off (purl) 2

Invisible bind-off done off needles 1

Invisible bind-off done off needles 2

You can sometimes enlarge or reduce areas of a garment by changing the size of the needles used, such as using a larger needle at the chest than at the waist. This method of shaping is limited, though it is useful in circular knitting, and to avoid interrupting a multicolor pattern or texture pattern such as ribbing.

SHAPING
INCREASES AND DECREASES FOR SHAPING AND DESIGN

Garments are shaped by adding or subtracting a few stitches here and there with increases and decreases. There are techniques that allow you to hide an increase or decrease in the surrounding stitches, and techniques that let you make a decoration of a necessity, adding visual interest to the piece. Decreases and increases are limited to a change of 1 or 2 stitches in a single stitch. You can group decreases if you need several in one area, such as for shaping a raglan sleeve. But if you need to add or subtract 3 or more stitches in one spot, perhaps for a collar or a kick pleat, casting off or casting on is necessary.

To conceal the shaping in the seams, you can work increases and decreases at the very edges of flat-knitted garments.

This is frequently done in high fashion knits that emphasize the line of the garment rather than the construction. Shaping worked at the edges should not interfere with a decorative edging or a smooth, flat seam.

Full-fashioning in a garment (see Quiet Reflections project on page 138) uses increase and decrease lines as design elements. Shaping stitches are visible—even obvious—in the body of the garment, instead of being concealed in seams of the garment pieces. Barred shapings leave a horizontal thread on the right side of the fabric. Smooth shapings show as a smooth chain of Vs raised above the surface of the knitting, or show as a differently-slanted area of fabric. There are also openwork increases and decreases that create holes as you work them.

CALCULATING INCREASES OR DECREASES

Calculate placement of increases and decreases to distribute changes evenly throughout a piece. Sometimes all the changes are in one row, or they may occur at regular intervals of rows as you work the piece. To stack several increases in a straight vertical line, use a marker on the inside edge of the line of increase.

Increase evenly across the row by adding (for calculation purposes only) one increase to the number you really need. Divide this number into the number of stitches in the row. The answer is the number of stitches between increases.

Example: 54 stitches to be increased to 60 = 6 increases

6 increases + 1 = 7 (remember, the additional 1 is for calculation purposes only—you won't work a 7th increase)

54 stitches in row divided by 7 increases = 7.7. Round this down to 7 stitches between increases. Add it all up to make sure you end up with the exact number of stitches you need—60.

7 x 7 = 49 space stitches

6 x 2 = 12 stitches (remember, you work 2 times in a stitch for an increase)

61 total stitches, 1 stitch too many

If the total number is higher than the total number you want in the row, work one stitch fewer between the increases in as many segments as you must. Here there is only one stitch too many, so in one space between increases, work 6 instead of 7 stitches.

7 V 7 V 7 V 6 V 7 V 7 V 7

V= increase of 1 stitch worked in 1 original stitch

Ideally this will be done in the center space for perfect symmetry. If you end up with more than one extra stitch you may want to calculate exactly where to put the extras, or you may have had enough math for one day.

Decrease evenly across the row uses a similar process, but you subtract half the number of stitches involved in each decrease.

Example: 28 stitches to be decreased to 24 = 4 decreases

4 decreases x 2 stitches = 8 stitches (remember, there are 2 stitches at the beginning of each decrease)

28 stitches – 8 decrease stitches = 20 stitches

Next: Increase the number of decreases planned by 1, to avoid having a decrease occur on an edge. As above, this is simply a number used for calculation and you will not be working the extra decrease in your knitting.*

20 stitches divided by 5 decreases = 4 space stitches between decreases

Check your calculations to see what the final number of stitches will be:

20 space stitches + 4 decrease stitches (8 beginning decrease stitches divided by 2 stitches involved in each decrease) = 24 stitches total

4 ^ 4 ^ 4 ^ 4^ 4

^= decrease of 1 stitch begun with 2 original stitches

* The technical name for this is "Finagle's Constant," which is the number you add to an equation to make it work out.

ROW-BY-ROW CHANGES are used to increase evenly over the length (height) of a piece. In garments this is generally done with matching increases or decreases at both ends of a row. The interval of increase depends on your row gauge.

Increase 20 stitches over the length of 10 inches, and your row gauge is 4 rows per inch:

4 rows x 10 inches = 40 rows

Example: 20 stitches divided by 2 ends of each row = 10 decrease rows

Here it is expected that the last increase will occur at the end of the 10 inches. (We don't have to use Finagle's Constant, however much fun it is.)

40 total rows divided by 10 decrease rows = A decrease row occurs every 4th row.

Full-fashioning is an indication of careful design and construction, unlike knit yardage that is simply cut to shape and seamed. Hand-loomed knits (those made on knitting frames) may be full-fashioned. Garments knit in the round must be full-fashioned, since there are no seams where you can hide increases and decreases.

Slant occurs to the right or to the left in most increases and decreases. Though this may not be obvious in a single shaping stitch, in a series the direction becomes more obvious. Balanced, mirror-image shaping is visually pleasing in a garment. Unless a designer specifies a shaping technique, the choice of which type of increase or decrease is left up to you. Be alert to the slant of the stitch, whether it is smooth or barred, invisible or open.

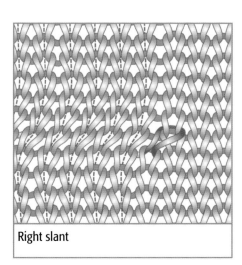

Left slant

Right slant

Usually, just because it is easier to keep track of what you are doing, a matched pair (or set) of shapings is done on the same side of the fabric. Sometimes one of a pair must be worked in a knit or right-side row and its mate in a purl or wrong-side row. The difference of a single row is seldom visually annoying, or even noticeable. (If anyone is looking so closely as to notice, smack him.) Just remember that when you use paired decreases worked on different rows, the left leaning ones on the back will be right leaning on the front, and vice versa. Use your eye to help you out as you go along—if it points in the correct direction on the side you are working it, it will point in the correct direction on the other side, too.

Circular knitting requires shapings that can be worked on one side of the work, generally the knit side. If you are working reverse stockinette, choose shapings that look good on the purl side.

Markers at shaping points are especially helpful to keep the increase or decrease from straying out of line or from being omitted. Place the markers between stitches on the side of the shaping where the stitch count will not change. If you are working several changes in a single row, or on both knit and purl rows, use very differently colored markers to keep the different actions obvious. This is also true of work in the round, where you may need one marker to let you know the beginning of the round, and 2 other pairs to distinguish the fronts and backs of raglan sleeves.

Names are attached to the techniques to locate something in the index. They are not standardized because different writers use different language to describe what happens. Knitting will be easier if you understand what an increase or decrease does to the fabric when you knit it. Then, even though the name of a technique may be unfamiliar, you will be able to choose an appropriate increase or decrease because of its function. Being an intelligent knitter saves time and heartburn.

DECREASES

Types of decreases fall into 2 basic categories: working stitches together, or passing one stitch over another. Both of these can be worked on knit and purl stitches.

Knitting (or purling) stitches together is a quick way to eliminate an extra stitch. The working needle is inserted in 2 (or more) stitches at once, the yarn is wrapped around the needle, and one stitch emerges in the new row. For shaping you will not commonly work more than 3 stitches together. Decorative pattern stitches sometimes have several stitches worked together. This technique can be used with 2 or more stitches.

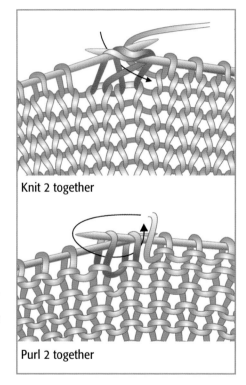

Knit 2 together

Purl 2 together

Slip two stitches, separately, knitwise, then return them to the source needle, and knit together through back loop.

Passing one stitch over another is

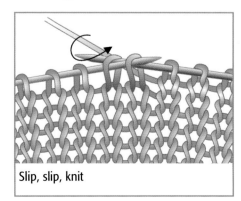

Slip, slip, knit

done by picking up a stitch and dropping it off the end of the needle, over any stitch between it and the point. The "passed" stitch loops around the stitch still on the needle. You can pass a stitch over another on either needle, creating left and right slants.

Psso—pass slipped stitch over—produces a left slant. At some point you are told to slip a stitch (see Slip Stitch, page 46) from the source needle to the working needle. When you see psso, lift that same slipped stitch over whatever is between it and the point of the working needle and drop the slipped stitch off the needle.

When using a slip stitch to decrease in a knit row, slip the stitch knitwise (through the front of the stitch) or it will be twisted after you complete the decrease.

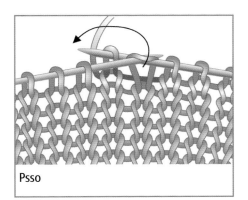

Psso

Pnso—pass next stitch over—is the psso process worked in the other direction, producing a right slant. On the source needle, one unworked stitch is lifted and passed over another unworked stitch, which is then worked. The variation of this is to slip a new stitch back to the source needle, pass the unworked stitch over the new stitch, then return the new stitch to the working needle.

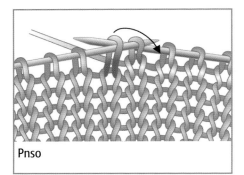

Pnso

KNIT ROW DECREASES

The standard pair of smooth decreases is ssk and k2tog, worked on a knit row as a mirror image pair. They will get you through most narrowing situations. The alternate written form of ssk, found in most publications prior to 1975, is s1, k1, psso.

LEFT-SLANTING SINGLE DECREASE

SLIP, SLIP, KNIT 2 TOGETHER (**ssk**): Slip 2 stitches, separately, knitwise, then return them to the source needle, and knit together through back loop. Two left-slanting stitches will be suspended from the new stitch. Pair ssk on right-hand edge and k2tog on left-hand edge.

SLIP 1 KNITWISE, KNIT 1, PASS SLIPPED STITCH OVER (**s1, k1, psso**): is identical to ssk in the outcome, but the steps are worked in a different order. Slip the first stitch knitwise, knit the second stitch, then pass the slipped stitch back over the knit stitch. You end up with 2 left-slanting stitches suspended from 1 new stitch.

OUTER EDGE DECREASE, LEFT-SLANTING: Flip edge stitch to face right, then knit 2 tog through back loop. Pairs with right-leaning k2tog.

RIGHT-SLANTING SINGLE DECREASE

KNIT 2 TOGETHER (**k2tog**): Insert working needle through 2 stitches at once, then knit them as if they are one stitch. Use this decrease at the left-hand edge, paired with ssk at the right-hand edge.

KNIT 1, PASS NEXT STITCH OVER (**k1, pnso**): This is the right-leaning equivalent of s1, k1, psso. Knit 1 stitch, slip it back onto the source needle; pass the next stitch over it; then slip the knitted stitch back onto the working needle.

FAGOTTED DECREASES are useful for shaping lacy garments. This uses a yarn over (see Yarn Over, page 57) for openwork, while working a double decrease to subtract both the stitch to be decreased for shaping PLUS the stitch added with the decorative openwork. These can be paired with left- and right-slanting fagotted increases.

ON THE RIGHT-HAND SIDE OF THE SEAMLINE OR BAND OF STITCHES (**k3tog, yo**): Knit 3 together, then yarn over.

ON THE LEFT-HAND SIDE OF THE SEAMLINE OR BAND OF STITCHES (**yo, sssk3tog**): Yarn over, Slip 3 stitches separately knitwise, then Knit 3 together.

CENTERED DOUBLE DECREASE (**sl 2tog, k1, p2sso**): Slip 2 at once knitwise, knit 1, pass the 2 slipped stitches over the knit stitch. This elegant, perfectly centered double decrease is a lifesaver in multicolored patterns, especially for hats and yokes.

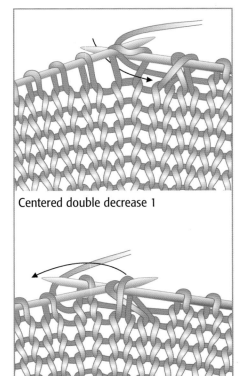

Centered double decrease 1

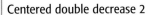

Centered double decrease 2

PURL ROW DECREASES are a blessing in disguise because purled decreases also make even, attractive chain decreases on the knit side of the fabric. If it suits your purposes to work the shaping on purl rows it will be just as attractive as shaping on the knit rows.

The standard purl-side pair of decreases is the LEFT-SLANTING PURL 2 TOGETHER (p2tog), and the RIGHT-SLANTING SLIP, SLIP, PURL (ssp): Slip 2 stitches knitwise, return them to source needle, and purl 2 together through the back loop.

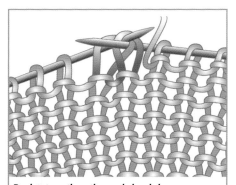

Purl 2 together through back loop

LEFT-SLANTING PURL DECREASE (p2tog): Purl 2 together.

RIGHT-SLANTING PURL DECREASE (s1k, s1k, p2tog tbl): Slip 1st st kwise, slip 2nd st kwise, return both stitches to source needle; purl 2 together through the back loop. This is fine on the knit

There are dozens of increases and decreases which are found occasionally in decorative pattern stitches or are specified by a designer for a particular effect in a design. In order to keep the number of different chart symbols reasonable, and to keep them visually uncluttered, only the slant direction or basic type of increase or decrease is marked on a chart. Any further details regarding specific techniques used in a particular chart will be noted in a chart key.

side of the fabric, but if you are working Reverse Stockinette fabric use the following decrease. It looks better on the purl side of the fabric.

REVERSE STOCKINETTE LEFT-SLANTING DECREASE (s1, p1, psso): Slip the first stitch of the decrease pair, purl the second stitch. Pick up the back loop of the slipped stitch and pass the slipped stitch over.

LEFT-SLANTING PURL DECREASE (s1p, s1k, p2tog): 2 stitches separately, knitwise; return to source needle and purl together. This is like the distinction between ssk and s1, k1, psso—the psso occurs later in the process, but the stitches are identical in what results.

RIGHT-SLANTING PURL ROW DECREASES

RIGHT-SLANTING PURL DECREASE (p1, s1k, pnso): Purl 1 st, slip next st knitwise; return both sts to source needle; psso purled st, slip purled st back to working needle.

RIGHT-SLANTING PURL DECREASE (s1p, s1k, p2tog tbl): Slip 1 purlwise, slip next purl stitch knitwise; place slipped stitches back on source needle, then purl 2 together through back loops. This looks nice on the knit side, even though the stitch that ends up on the bottom is twisted. Don't let it make you crazy.

BARRED SINGLE DECREASE PAIR: This pair of decreases is worked on the purl side of the fabric and leaves bars on the knit side of the fabric. I cannot imagine why anyone would want to leave decrease tracks, but these will do it.

RIGHT-SLANTING (s1p, s1k, pnso): Slip 1 stitch purlwise, slip next purl stitch knitwise, place slipped stitches back on source needle; pass next stitch over.

LEFT-SLANTING (s1k, p1 tbl, psso): Slip 1 stitch knitwise, purl 1 stitch through back loop, pass slipped stitch over.

CENTERED PURLED DOUBLE DECREASE (s2k, p3tog) is as smooth and elegant as its knitted version, but is a little more complex to work. Some things are worth it.

On the purl side of the fabric, slip the first two stitches of the decrease knitwise, then insert the source needle back into them on the near side, from the right. This twists them back on the source needle. Then slip the working needle purlwise through the twisted pair and the third stitch, and purl the 3 together normally. When you look at the knit side of the fabric you will see one smooth, centered stitch.

Smooth "mixed pair" decreases on separate rows (remember, if it points in the correct direction on the side you are working it, it will point in the correct direction on the other side, too.) Do not brood over these; we tested them.

FIRST PAIR:

Right-slanting purled side (s1p, s1k, p2tog tbl): Slip 1 purlwise, slip next purl stitch knitwise, place slipped stitches back on source needle; then purl 2 together through back loop.

Left-slanting on purled side (K2tog): Knit 2 together.

SECOND PAIR:

Left-slanting on knit side (ssk): Slip 2 stitches separately, knitwise; return them to source needle, and knit them together.

Right-slanting on knit side (p2tog): On the purl side, purl 2 stitches together.

THIRD PAIR:

Right-slanting on knit side (s1p, p1, psso): On purl row, slip purlwise the first stitch of the decrease pair, purl the second stitch. Pass the slipped stitch over.

Pair with left-slanting ssk on knit side.

INCREASES

Added stitches, knitted or purled, with or without holes. When you are doing a decorative pattern or a lace, holes are fine. When you are knitting a ski sweater the thought of increases with holes may leave you cold. Choose your technique accordingly.

There are 2 basic ways to increase the number of stitches in a row: cast on a new stitch or knit more than once into a stitch, and there are variations of each of these.

Cast on a new stitch by wrapping the yarn over or around the needle as you knit the row, or pick up a thread between stitches of a preceding row.

Knit more than once in a stitch as you knit the stitch of a preceding row.

There are so many of ways to do this that we will present only a few here, to acquaint you with the basic technique. You will find more variations in the Pattern Gallery, and others in designer patterns in this book. You may even invent a few yourself.

INCREASES WITH HOLES cast-on a new stitch between already existing stitches, leaving a noticeable gap between the stitches on either side. You can use the yarn in your hand to cast on a new stitch, which is worked in the next row, or pick up the strand of yarn between the stitches already on the needle, borrowing from the stretchiness of the neighboring stitches. The new stitch can be twisted to make the hole beneath the new stitch smaller, or it can be left untwisted over a larger hole.

A YARN OVER (yo) adds a length of thread that will be a stitch in the next row. This creates a hole under the new stitch. You can make a yarn over in either a knit or purl row simply by working the stitch before the increase, wrapping the yarn around the needle—front to back for a knit increase, back to front for a purl increase; then work the next stitch as usual. In the next row, knit or purl the yarn over. This is a very stretchy increase. It is wonderfully easy to recognize because it forms a diagonal wrap around the needle, quite distinct from the straight loops of regular knit and purl stitches.

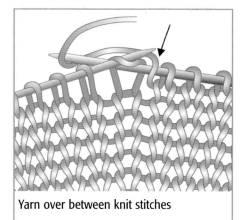

Yarn over between knit stitches

In lacy patterns a multiple yarn over makes a very large hole into which two or more stitches are worked in the next row. To make a double yarn over (yo2), simply wrap the yarn around the needle twice before working the next stitch, and work two stitches into the yarn over loops in the next row—one will be knitted, the other purled. A triple yarn over (yo3) wraps the yarn around the needle 3 times between stitches, alternating knit and purl stitches (or vice versa) as you knit the wraps on the next row. In lace patterns the increases are balanced by decreases, so that the hole remains but the fabric does not get wider.

YARN OVER BETWEEN KNIT AND PURL STITCHES may be necessary when working decorative patterns. Remember that the knit stitch is formed with the yarn strand at the back of the work, while the purl stitch is formed with the yarn strand in front of the work. To increase between different types of stitches the yarn will have to change position. If the first stitch is a purl, simply laying the yarn across the needle to the back will make the yarn over while it puts the strand of yarn in position for working a knit stitch.

After completing a knit stitch, bring the yarn forward to the front of the work, then wrap the yarn around the working needle before purling the next

stitch. This will form the yarn over while putting the yarn in the correct position for the purl stitch. If you simply lay the working strand from back to front over the needle it will distort the preceding knit stitch and make working the following purl stitch very awkward.

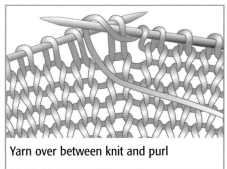

Yarn over between knit and purl

A PICK-UP INCREASE uses the connecting strand between stitches as a base for the new stitch. It is just as if you made a yarn over in the preceding row, but the hole left by a pick-up increase will be smaller. Slip the working needle under the connecting strand between two stitches. Lift the strand onto the source needle—from the back to knit, from the front to purl—then knit or purl into it. This adds one stitch to the row count.

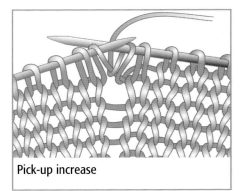

Pick-up increase

HALF-HITCH INCREASE is a hybrid of the yarn over and pick-up increases. You twist a loop and put it on the needle, which gives you the open and stretchy increase characteristic of a yarn over with the completed new stitch characteristic of the pick-up increase. These can be made at either end of a row or in the middle.

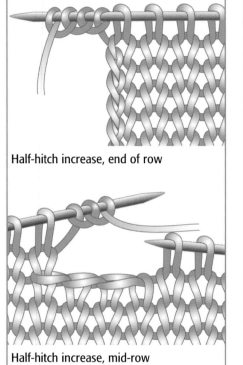

Half-hitch increase, end of row

Half-hitch increase, mid-row

TWISTED PICK-UP INCREASE is virtually invisible, though in the hole-making increase category, because the connecting strand is twisted into a loop before the new stitch is worked in it. It is the equivalent of making a half-hitch increase in the row below. Slip the point of the working needle under the connecting strand, twist it into a loop, then slip the loop onto the source needle. Work the stitch as needed.

FAGOTTED INCREASES are useful in lacy garment shaping. Work 1 yarn over increase on either side of a seam or band of stitches. This can be used with the fagotted decreases above.

KNIT TWICE IN 1 STITCH INCREASES are made by working twice into one stitch, either knit or purl. This makes a new stitch without a hole, but the stitches will be less stretchy than a single stitch.

Knit twice in 1 stitch produces 2 knit stitches, the second with a small bump at the base of the stitch. Slip the stitch from the source needle knitwise (faces right), and return it to the source needle. Knit into the back of the stitch; keep the old stitch on the needle, then (holding the working yarn under the needle) knit into the front of the stitch.

Knit twice in 1 stitch 1

Knit twice in 1 stitch 2

A bump will always occur at the base of the second stitch of this increase, so if you are balancing a pair of increases, place them so the bumps are evenly spaced. For example, to increase one stitch on either side of a marker, for the first increase of the pair you will work the increase on the second stitch before the marker, and the second increase of the pair will be worked in the stitch immediately following the marker. The bump from each increase will be between the first and second stitches on either side of the marker.

INCREASE IN A LOWER ROW by working a second time into a stitch a row below, either on the right or the left side. (Note that this is counted below the source needle, because once you have worked into a stitch you have added another row to that stitch.) These wonderful increases permit paired, mirror-image increases (a technique used in Viking cables), or you can do an increase as an afterthought.

Increases in a lower row are virtually invisible when done randomly throughout a piece. They can be worked equally well on knit or purl rows. When increases on one side of a stitch are stacked in a straight vertical line, the knitting slants off in that direction.

INCREASE LEFT, ONE ROW BELOW: Insert the needle into the left side of the stitch one row below the stitch on the source needle; draw up a new stitch.

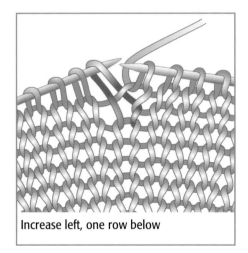

Increase left, one row below

INCREASE RIGHT, ONE ROW BELOW: To make the increase, work into the right of the stitch one row below the stitch on the source needle; draw up a new stitch.

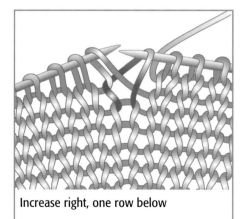

Increase right, one row below

INCREASES BELOW NEIGH-BORING STITCHES are worked exactly like the other increases in a lower row. Stacked increases slant to the side on which they are worked, either left or right. Paired increases allow you to create mirror-image shaping and decorations (such as cables).

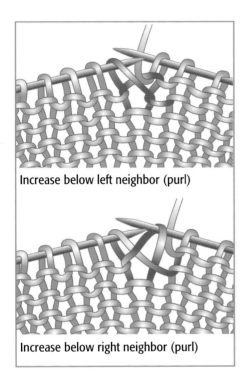

Increase below left neighbor (purl)

Increase below right neighbor (purl)

PURLED INCREASES

RIGHT-SLANTING: Purl 1, pick up thread between stitches to face right, then purl into it. Worked on the purl side, this increase is without holes, left leaning on knit side, and pairs with a twisted lifted increase on knit side.

LEFT-SLANTING: K1, pick up thread between sts, knit into back of loop.

SHORT ROWS ARE A FORM OF DECREASING done by NOT working some stitches at the end of a row. It is very surprising the first time you are asked to turn the work without finishing the row. It is even more surprising to make short rows by mistake when you set your knitting down in the middle of a row, then pick it up later and knit in the wrong direction.

The basic short row can be worked at one or both edges of a piece on flat knit-ting, or in the round (often used to turn heels on socks). To work a short row, knit the specified number of stitches, leaving the rest on the source needle. Turn the work, and without doing anything to the resting stitches, work the stitches on what is now the source needle.

When the shaping is completed and you wish to reactivate resting stitches, pick up the resting stitches as required and knit them again as you continue the overall piece.

Because a knit stitch met on the other side of the fabric is a purl stitch, working short row shapings in complex pattern stitches will mean that when you pick up a pattern repeat in the middle, suddenly the stitches of the front side may have to be worked as their opposites.

When I encountered this problem in a simple seed stitch garment it caused such a mental grinding of gears that I switched to garter stitch for the duration of the shaping. If you are not up for such excitement, confine short row shaping to garter stitch and stockinette fabrics. If you think you can handle it, work a good-sized shaping swatch and chart what the pick-up pattern will be.

WRAPPED SHORT ROW SHAP-ING is used to eliminate the small hole that occurs when you pick up resting stitches. To work a short row with a wrapped stitch, work up to the point where you intend to turn the row. Leave the yarn where it was as you worked the row: on the back, if you were knitting, on the front if you were purling. Slip the first stitch of the resting stitches, move the yarn to the other side of the work (this creates a wrap around that stitch), then replace the slipped stitch on the source needle.

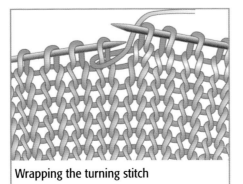

Wrapping the turning stitch

Turn the row, move the yarn to the side where you need it, and work the active stitches. Some people like to slip the first stitch after the turn, to eliminate any small hole. You can work the stitch or slip it, as you like.

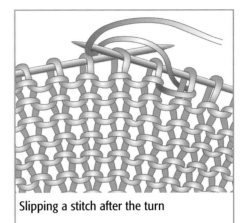

Slipping a stitch after the turn

When you are ready to work a resting stitch again, pick up both the stitch and the wrap and knit them together. This works best when you are doing gradual shaping, one stitch per row, such as turning a sock heel. If you are picking up on garter stitch or reverse stockinette, you may just leave the wrap as you knit. The bump of the wrap will blend in with the other stitches.

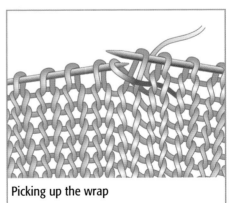

Picking up the wrap

For more significant shaping, such as in a beret, you can leave several stitches resting for a few rows, but there will be a hole when you pick up the resting stitches. Wrapping will diminish this, but will not eliminate it. 🪡

sweet baby of mine

Beginners can easily master the simple stitches used to create this soft snugly blanket. This project is a pleasure to knit and, just like peanuts, you won't be able to stop with only one.

DESIGN BY MARSHA HINKSON
Skill level: Beginner
Finished project size: 32" (81.5 cm) square

MATERIALS
Lily Sugar 'n Cream, Article 930H, 4-ply 100% Cotton Yarn
(2½ ounces/70.9 grams, 125 yards/114.5 meters per skein): 6 skeins of Cream (#3)
Size 5 (3.75 mm) circular needle or size needed to obtain gauge

GAUGE
18 sts and 36 rows = 4" (10 cm)
Take time to check your gauge.

STITCH PATTERN
This baby blanket is worked on a diagonal alternating knit and purl rows creating a textured stripe. These stripes are also referred to as welts. The yarn over at the end of each row creates a border as you knit.

INSTRUCTIONS
FIRST HALF (INCREASE)
Cast on 3 sts.
Row 1: Knit across.
Rows 2–4: K2, yo, knit across.
Row 5: K2, yo, knit across.
Row 6: K2, yo, purl across to last 2 sts, k2.
Rows 7–12: K2, yo, knit across.
Repeat rows 5–12 until piece measures approximately 36" (91.5 cm) long, ending by working Row 12.

SECOND HALF (DECREASE)
Row 1: K1, k2 tog, yo, k2 tog, knit across.
Row 2: K1, k2 tog, yo, k2 tog, purl across to last 2 sts, k2.
Rows 3–8: K1, k2 tog, yo, k2 tog, knit across.
Continue pattern and decrease each row until you have 3 sts remaining. Bind off last 3 sts. ✤

Marsha Hinkson has been a member of the Kooler Design Studio for the past twelve years as an expert on counted-thread work and embroidery. Her needlework interests and talents include designing knit and crochet afghans.

beyond the basics

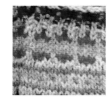

CONGRATULATIONS! You made it through the basics and are now ready, willing, and anxious to practice your new skills. Here you will learn to twist cables as cannily as any sailor, while making stitches play leapfrog on the needle.

Should you prefer glorious, wonderful color, we will show you how to use as many colors as Renoir, and sprinkle your knitting with beads and sequins like the night sky. While beneath it all are the basics that you came to love. Now we can begin to play with them a bit. Tall stitches, wrapped stitches, dots and spots, all the fun things that you can do with knitting when you want something just a bit different, trendy, or even wildly extravagant.

On the following pages, the world's top designers let you in on their secrets. Their projects will expand your new skills into glorious hats and whisper-smooth sweaters, so chic you could swoon just to wear them, and afghans so cozy that you might snooze under one all afternoon. We even have some fleecy felted lambs that would love to find a good home.

Remember those beads and colors we mentioned? The beads are on a scrumptious scarf and three tiny purses, which you will surely want to show off when stepping out on the town. Should you prefer to stay home, you can feast your eyes on an alabaster appliquéd floral pillow or small Baltic cushions. Colors also pop up on man's best-dressed friends, a bright coat for Fido the dog and matching socks for you.

Lest someone special be jealous of Fido's good fortune, there is a glorious vest for the man in your life. There is no reason for anyone to be left out in the cold when you know how to knit. From the first cast-on loop to the last swirl of the cable, you will love your new skills, and so will everyone around you.

BASIC LACE PATTERNS

Lace looks much harder than it is. Even a novice knitter can make a beautiful piece with only the knit stitch, yarn over, and k2tog. In fact garter stitch (knit every row) was ordinarily used for the famous traditional laces—Shetland, Orenburg, and Unst among them. The simplest lace is a row of eyelet openings—elegant and practical. (See Ribbon Eyelet in gallery, page 200.)

Lace can be worked lengthwise, crosswise, or in the round, as an allover pattern whose width does not change, or as a shaped lace whose outline is the focal point. There is a lace knitting technique to dress up any project you have in mind.

ALLOVER LACE PATTERNS balance increases with decreases to keep the width of the piece even, so that the fabric can be used for clothing. The simple and delicate lace grounds used as background stitches in figured-lace masterpieces are lovely in their own right, and are perfect for scarves and afghans. Sometimes the openwork of lace is combined with knit and purl patterns for richly textured lacy fabrics, excellent for socks, layettes, wraps, and sweaters. (See Snowdrops in gallery, page 201.)

Illumination Lace project, page 108.

SHAPED LACE uses increases and decreases both to form the lace design and to shape the outline of the work. In some laces the pattern repeats are horizontal, used to widen the piece. They can be used as overall lace patterns, but the unusual shape of the beginning or ending edges is often used as a decorative hemline or cuff on a simple stockinette garment.

There are edgings that lengthen with each repeat. This kind of lace has long been used in thread edgings for linens, but worked in yarn is beautiful for shawls, hats, and other dressy garments. Yarn that does not obscure the lace pattern is a good choice, though angora and mohair yarns can give lace a romantic mistiness. In an edging the number of stitches may vary widely from row to row, so counting the stitches each row is very helpful. (See Horseshoes in gallery, page 203.)

Knitted lace or lace knitting? Some designers and writers distinguish between the two. In lace knitting the design elements are made in one row, and each alternate row is knit without yarn overs or decreases. In knitted lace the openwork design is made by using yarn overs and decreases in any row, odd or even. You may never need to know this fine distinction, but when a lace pattern says to "knit across" or "purl across" every other row, it is lace knitting, and you only have to memorize half the rows.

TECHNIQUES

MULTIPLE INCREASES: The standard lace increase is a yarn over (see page 57). A single yarn over usually has one stitch worked into it in the next row. A double yarn over (yo2) will have two stitches worked into it in the next row, one knit and one purl; there is no way to work two identical stitches into one yarn over. A triple yarn over (yo3) will have either a knit-purl-knit sequence or a purl-knit-purl sequence worked into it. (See Mermaid's Mesh in gallery, page 198.)

MULTIPLE DECREASES: There are many lovely, traditional designs that have only the k2tog decrease, but knowledge of left- and right-slanting decreases will make the lines of complex laces clearer. Because holes are part of the design, here you will find slanting knit-together decreases of 3 and more stitches. If you have trouble drawing a new stitch through all the stitches to be decreased, lift the decrease stitches off the needle, over the new stitch, one by one.

RIGHT-SLANTING MULTIPLE DECREASE: Knit 3 together is no more complex than k2tog. For a multiple right-slanting decrease, insert the working needle under the necessary number of stitches; knit (or purl) them together in one step. (See Eyelet Diamonds in gallery, page 201.)

LEFT-SLANTING MULTIPLE DECREASE can be worked in two ways, either as ssk or as psso (see page 55). The result is identical. Simply increase the number of stitches worked in the decrease. You may need to tighten the yarn tension for one stitch as you knit several stitches together, but relax it again as soon as the decrease is finished.

MULTIPLE SSK: Slip each stitch, one by one, knitwise; re-insert the source needle in the front loops, and knit all the slipped stitches together. (See Eyelet Diamond's in gallery, page 201.)

MULTIPLE PSSO: Slip the first stitch knitwise, knit the rest of the decrease stitches together, then pass the slipped stitch over the knit-together group. (See Horseshoes in gallery, page 203.)

CENTERED DOUBLE DECREASE: Slip 2 stitches together, knitwise; knit 1 stitch, then pass the slipped stitches over it. (See Mermaid's Mesh in gallery, page 198.)

SELVAGES

The purpose of adding selvage stitches is to create a smooth, even edge to a knitted piece. Selvages added to the sides of each piece make flat, even seams in a garment. There are various ways to work the selvage, but the basic choice is whether you will have one or two selvage stitches at each edge. Anything wider than 2 stitches is really a border.

Selvage stitches are calculated into the overall dimensions of the garment because they give the width for seams. Do not include selvage stitches in pattern repeat calculations. To keep from accidentally working the selvage stitches in pattern stitches or shaping, put markers between the selvage stitches and the main pattern stitches.

1-STITCH CHAIN SELVAGE makes nice narrow seams. Slip the beginning stitch of every row knitwise (see Slip Stitch, page 46). Knit the last stitch of every row. If you are planning to weave the garment seams, this gives you half the number of edge stitches as rows, with no loopy edges. This selvage is excellent for garter stitch.

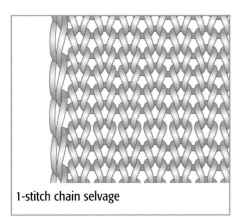

1-stitch chain selvage

A variation of this is to slip the first stitch knitwise and knit the last stitch on each right-side row. On each wrong-side row slip the first stitch knitwise and purl the last stitch.

2-STITCH GARTER STITCH SELVAGES are good for exposed edges, since they are wide enough to hold the edge flat. A garter stitch selvage will not curl, and is easy to count (2 rows per ridge) and seam. It works well with backstitched or chain-stitched seams. Add 2 stitches at each side, knit OR purl both stitches at the beginning and end of every row.

If you want the chain look on a 2-stitch selvage, slip the first selvage stitch of each row knitwise, and knit the last selvage stitch each row.

BORDERS

BORDERS are stitches anywhere around the perimeter of a knitted piece. They are used to make the edges match each other, behave in a certain way, or as a finishing touch. They can also be worked with the piece as a whole or added around the outside as the last step. Borders can be plain or fancy, a sigh of relief as you escape the coils of intricate cables, or a final yahoo of triumph.

GARTER STITCH BORDER flattens out the curling edges of stockinette stitch. It can be worked as you work the piece by starting out with several rows of garter stitch before you begin the pattern stitch. Remember that garter stitch works square (see Garter Stitch and Stockinette Stitch, page 44), 1 stitch width = 2 rows height, so you can calculate side borders to exactly match the beginning and ending borders.

OPENINGS

Garments need openings. Some openings are made as you go. Some openings can be worked as you go or added as afterthoughts. Openings may be loosely categorized as horizontal or vertical, though openings like necklines are often a combination of the two. Horizontal openings are the easiest to make because you can bind off a section of the row and cast on stitches above it in the next row. (See pages 39 and 50 for casting-on and binding-off techniques.) Vertical openings usually involve working parallel knitting on either side of the opening, then rejoining the two sides at the top of the opening.

BUTTONHOLES can be eyelet, horizontal, or vertical. They can be made in the body of a garment, placed on separate buttonhole bands, or placed between the garment body and a decorative edging. Buttonhole bands can be knitted as you work the body of the garment, or they can be knitted on or sewn on when the garment is assembled.

BUTTONHOLE BANDS can be worked lengthwise, parallel to the front opening of a garment, and on them horizontal buttonholes will look horizontal. The direction of knitting in buttonhole bands can also be perpendicular to the garment opening, which would make horizontal buttonholes appear vertical. Bands can also be single thickness or double, which requires two sets of identical buttonholes so that they match when the band is doubled over.

As with much of knitting, there are different opinions about when to make the buttonholes. Some sources recommend making the button side of a gar-

Buttonhole band from Sunshine Duo project, page 151.

ment first. This works when you want to see how the buttons look on the garment, then make the holes to match the final arrangement. On the other hand, if you need to space buttonholes to accommodate pattern stitches—either vertical or horizontal—it may be much easier to make the holes where they must go and to sew on the buttons to match.

Usually the buttonhole is worked from the right side (outside) of the garment. This works well, but sometimes a buttonhole worked on the wrong side of the garment looks better. Testing the buttonhole in a swatch will let you choose which buttonhole works best with your yarn and pattern stitch. It also allows you to practice refinements so that you can breeze through the buttonholes with confidence.

THE SIZE OF THE OPENING influences how the buttonhole will function—the smaller the buttonhole, the more solid it will be. Buttonholes bigger than 4 rows or 4 stitches will be more likely to let the button slip out, even if the button is a large one.

Openings that fit the button are essential. Buying the buttons first allows you to fine-tune buttonholes as you make them. Knitted fabric is stretchy, so you can get away with having snug buttonholes, but stretchiness can let a button slip out of a slightly-too-large buttonhole. Flat buttons require smaller buttonholes than domed buttons of the same diameter. All these things can cause problems if you make the buttonholes before you buy the buttons.

Measure the diameter of the button to see how many stitches it equals in the gauge you are knitting. If it is off by a fraction of a stitch, err on the side of making the buttonhole smaller. After you have completed ONE buttonhole this size, slip the button through the hole. If the button is still attached to the card you can tug on the card to see if the button pulls out of the buttonhole too easily. You can also tell if the knitted fabric is the right thickness for the button shank.

EYELET BUTTONHOLES are the simplest kind, frequently used on baby clothes and dressy sweaters with small buttons. The eyelet is completed in one row. A row of eyelets is also useful as a path to run a drawstring or decorative ribbon.

1. Knit to the location of the buttonhole.

2. Yarn over, knit two together. Complete the row.

Eyelet buttonhole

Variation:

1. Knit to the location of the buttonhole.

2. Slip 2 stitches knitwise. Return them to the source needle and knit the 2 together. Yarn over. Complete the row.

HORIZONTAL BUTTONHOLES are made by binding off a button-sized length on one row and making another button-sized length above it. Between the two is a slit for the button.

1-ROW BUTTONHOLE: This is the neatest, best constructed horizontal buttonhole, and looks even better when worked from the back (wrong) side of

the fabric. Both the back and front version instructions are included so that you can work a swatch to see which side you like best.

Made from the back:

1. Purl to the starting point of the opening.

2. Bring the working strand to the back of the work, slip one stitch purlwise, and return the working strand to the front. This wraps the stitch as if you were working a short row. (See Short Row Method, page 59.) Only the first slipped stitch will be wrapped.

3. Slip a second stitch purlwise, then lift the wrapped stitch over it to bind-off one stitch. (See Binding off, page 50.)

4. Do this for as many stitches as you wish the opening to measure. Return the loop of the last slipped stitch to the source needle.

5. Turn the work immediately and knit cable cast-on (see page 40) the number of stitches bound-off + 1 stitch.

6. Turn the work and knit across the new stitches, purling the last new stitch together with the first stitch of the source needle, then complete the rest of the row.

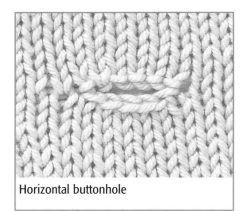

Horizontal buttonhole

Variation: 1-row buttonhole made from the front

1. Knit to the starting point of the buttonhole opening.

2. Bring the strand of wool to the front of the work, slip 1 stitch purlwise, and return the working strand to the back. This wraps the stitch as if you were working a short row. (See Short Row Method, page 59.) Only the first slipped stitch will be wrapped.

3. Slip a second stitch purlwise, then lift the wrapped stitch over it to bind off one stitch. (See Binding-off, page 50.)

4. Do this for as many stitches as you wish the opening to measure. Return the loop of the last slipped stitch to the source needle.

5. Turn the work immediately and purl cable cast on (see page 39) the number of stitches bound off + 1 stitch.

6. Turn the work and knit across the new stitches, knitting the last new stitch together with the first stitch of the source needle, then complete the rest of the row.

3 - R O W   B U T T O N H O L E is one of the places where the half-hitch cast-on is just what you need.

Row 1:

1. Knit to the point where the opening begins.

2. Knit 2, bind off 1.

3. Continue to knit 1, bind off 1 for the required number of stitches.

4. Knit across the rest of the row.

Row 2: Purl to the first bound-off stitch of the row. Pick up the first bound-off stitch and cast on an equal number of stitches as were bound off. Purl across the rest of the row.

Row 3: Knit to 1 stitch before the buttonhole begins, knit that stitch, the buttonhole stitches, and the stitch following it through the back loop (that is, twisted). This will tighten them up a bit.

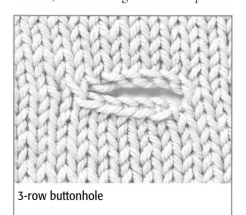

3-row buttonhole

V E R T I C A L   B U T T O N H O L E S are tall and graceful, and need reinforcing when buttons pull on the sides. The edges can be sewn with a strand of thread, or the buttonhole can be faced by being sewn on a ribbon, or on a knitted facing with identical buttonholes. This type of double band is folded over and the openings are sewn to each other. Because of the thickness of the fabric, this is best done with stockinette fabric for one or both layers of the band.

2 - S T R A N D   B U T T O N H O L E S are made with one strand on one side of the opening and a different strand on the other side. When the opening is the correct height, unite the two sides by using one or the other of the strands to knit across the two sides. In fact, what you are doing is knitting parallel sets of short rows. (See Short Row Method, page 59.) You can arrange it so that there are loose yarn ends only at the outside edges of the piece, rather than at the edge of the button slit.

Whichever type of vertical buttonhole you use, do not make more ends of yarn than you need. Instead of breaking the working yarn to wind some off for a buttonhole, just use another ball of yarn. If you have only one ball, find the other end, even if it requires fishing about on the inside of the skein. Then knit as much as you need from both ends of the ball. At the end of the buttonhole section, cut the yarn. You will have created no extra ends to darn in.

A 2-strand buttonhole can be made any height. If you want to reinforce the finished buttonhole by sewing, leave a long tail when you attach the second strand, or work with an additional strand of thread. You can also work twisted edge stitches on both sides of the opening. (See Twisted Stitches, page 46.)

1. Knit to the buttonhole location.

2. Attach the second strand and knit to the end of the row. Turn.

3. Work to the buttonhole. Switch working strands and continue to the end of the row. Turn.

4. Continue working the two sides of the buttonhole with the different strands for the desired height.

5. Use whichever strand is most convenient to reconnect the two sides of the row. Work in the loose yarn ends.

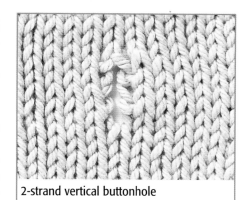

2-strand vertical buttonhole

Y A R N   O V E R   V E R T I C A L   B U T-T O N H O L E is a versatile technique that can be worked in any pattern stitch. We describe it in stockinette stitch.

1. Knit to the location of the buttonhole. Knit 2 stitches together, yarn over twice. Knit across the row.

2. Purl to the yarn over. Purl the first yarn over, drop the second. Complete the row.

3. Knit to the opening. Knit into the hole left by the yarn over, drop the purl stitch made in the yarn over in the previous row. Complete the row.

Variation: Worked this way the buttonhole is still 2 rows tall, but by working the k2tog decrease one row below the yarn over, the buttonhole will be slightly shorter.

1. One row below the location of the buttonhole, purl 2 stitches together.

2. Knit to the p2tog decrease. Yarn over twice, knit the decrease, then complete the row.

3. Purl to the yarn over. Purl the first yarn over, drop the second. Complete the row.

4. Knit to the yarn over opening. Knit into the hole left by the yarn over, drop the purl stitch made in the yarn over in the previous row. Complete the row.

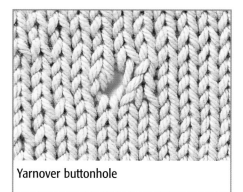

Yarnover buttonhole

BUTTONLOOPS are worked on the edge of a piece and are frequently used for baby clothes and dressy sweaters, but are also suitable for coats. Combine them with frogs and knots for highly decorative closures. (See I-cord, page 69.)

Sewn buttonloops are made with a tapestry needle and yarn or thread, with a reinforcing thread if desired. Use a gauge the size of the button to assure that the loops are all the same size. Mark the placement of the loops along the edge of the piece, bring the needle up from the back side of the knitting, and insert it down through the front side. Do this until there are 2 or 3 strands of yarn, depending on the size of the button, using the gauge to keep all the loops even. Then work the buttonhole stitch around the loops, making only enough stitches to make a smooth loop without stretching it. Slip the needle back under the buttonhole stitches to hide the tail of the yarn. Cut the yarn.

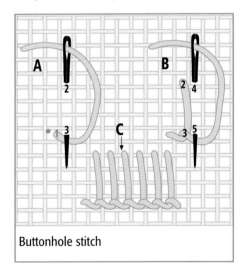
Buttonhole stitch

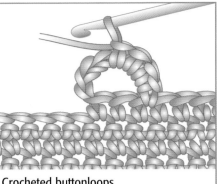
Crocheted buttonloops

CROCHETED BUTTONLOOPS are made by marking the placement of the loop, then drawing up a thread or yarn loop with a crochet hook and making a chain the desired length. Work a slip stitch to secure the other end of the chain. Work single crochet stitches around the chain, not packing the single crochet stitches so tightly as to stretch the loop. Work in the tails. Use a gauge to make sure all the chain loops are the same length—do not depend on the number of chain stitches in each loop to be exactly equal in length.

AFTER THE FACT HORIZONTAL BUTTONHOLES can be a complete afterthought or planned and set up when the garment is being knitted, then worked at the end. These same techniques can be used for inserting pockets and mitten thumbs.

Contrasting stitches help identify the exact spot for an opening to be made after the fact. Use a different color yarn to knit the stitches that will form the buttonhole, then slip the contrasting stitches back onto the source needle. Take the working strand of yarn and knit across the contrasting stitches and continue the row as usual. Do this at every place you want a buttonhole. These can be finished in a number of ways.

STEEKS are straight vertical openings made by cutting the strands between two columns of stitches. They are used in knitting in the round to make armholes and front openings after the sweater body is finished. It is easier to cut knitting in a straight line between columns of stitches than to match pattern stitches or color intervals in space-dyed yarn. The most important aspect of

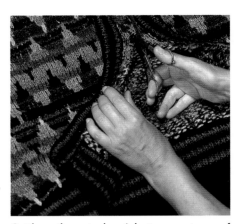
Cutting the steeks (photo courtesy of Martingale & Company from the book *Fair Isle Sweaters Simplified*). See "Sunshine Duo" project on page 151.

making a steek is securing the stitches on either side of the cut. After this is done you can pick up stitches and knit sleeves or buttonhole bands without fear of your hard work disintegrating completely.

If the cut is to be from top to bottom of the knitting, such as for a cardigan sweater, you need only secure the stitches on either side of the cut line. Place markers to show the steek lines and cast on a few extra stitches between what will be the finished edges. These added steek stitches are knitted each round with the rest of the sweater, cut down the center, and stitched down like facings on the wrong side.

SECURING THE STEEK: Machine sew through the center of the column of stitches on either side of the steek. (Pivot the machine stitching across bound-off stitches at the bottom of sleeve steeks.) The machine stitch length should be small enough to catch all the horizontal strands of the knit stitches.

Twist and crochet the side stitches if you don't want to mess with a sewing machine, then twist each steek line stitch as you knit. To secure the steek before cutting, use a crochet hook to slip stitch through each of the twisted stitches.

SHAPING AROUND STEEKS, such as necklines and armholes, must be done outside the edges of the steek stitching line. A V-neck, for example, would have straight lines of decreases on either side of the steek. When the steek is finished and cut, the neckline opens out to the full width of the V. Crew necks can be worked by binding off half the opening stitches at the base of the steek, working the remaining shaping decreases outside the steek line.

ARMHOLE STEEKS have a bottom edge, so there are a few different ways to set up an armhole. Any sleeve type can be used if it has a straight edge for the steek line. These include dropped, set-in, and raglan sleeves.

At the lower edge of the opening, bind off the required number of stitches. In the next round, above the bound-off stitches, cast on enough steek stitches to provide fabric for cutting and turning under. A dropped sleeve has no shaping or bind-off under the opening, but cast on a few steek stitches so that there is enough fabric to cut and turn under. Any shaping beyond the initial bound-off stitches will be full-fashioned, worked outside the steek line.

Pick up stitches to knit-on a sleeve as you would to knit-on a buttonhole binding. The normal proportion for patterns with a knit and a purl side is 3 rows: 2 stitches. For garter stitch pick up 1 stitch per ridge.

FINISHING THE STEEK EDGES. If you are using a wool yarn that is not machine washable, steam it to create a felted edge. Otherwise, hem it with stretchy herringbone stitch. I-cord (formerly called "idiot cord") is a dandy little cord useful in a multitude of tasks. By itself, it can be a drawstring, but it can be used as an edging for buttonholes, trim for garments, and braid that can take any shape you like. Use 2 double-pointed needles, and cast on 3 stitches. Knit across the row, then slide the row to the other end of the needle and begin again, knitting the first stitch without turning the work. Pull the yarn up tightly after each row. After a few rows you will see a cord forming, and you can keep going as long as you like.

APPLIQUÉD I-CORD will take any shape you choose. It can be used to form mock cables, Celtic knots, and other improbable shapes. With a tapestry needle, catch the underside of the cord with a stitch through the background fabric and draw it down securely without distorting the fabric. Continue shaping the cord and securing it to the background fabric. Use this to form frogs, ornate closings, and buttonloops.

KNITTED-ON I-CORD is a lovely way to edge a piece of knitting, either in the same or a contrasting color. Pick up stitches along the edge you wish to cord on a double-pointed needle. Cast on 3 stitches on a double-pointed needle and knit a round of I-cord to start. The next round, knit 2, slip the last stitch, knit the first stitch from the edge of the knitting, and pass the slipped stitch over it. *Slip all 3 stitches onto the garment needle with the stitches to be picked up. Knit 2, slip one, knit the next reserved stitch, pass the slipped stitch over. Repeat from *, making one round of I-cord for each stitch to be picked up along the edge of the garment.

If you wish to conceal a buttonhole between the edging and the garment, knit rounds of plain I-cord the length of the buttonhole without catching up any edge stitches from the garment. When the buttonhole is long enough, begin to pick up edge stitches into the I-cord again.

I-cord has been little explored but merits some further consideration. An I-cord of several stitches will be large enough to be adapted as glove fingers, once the loose stitches at the back of the cord have been hooked up into a column of stitches, like a ladder repaired.

I-cord can also be used as a method of casting on and hemming at the same time. Make a cord with as many rounds as you need to cast on stitches, then pick up stitches the length of the cord and knit them as a row. The end stitches of the cord can be grafted to other similar hem pieces, or the I-cord stitches can be picked up and continued as edging around the piece, or can be sewn into seams.

DECORATIVE STITCHES

Once you can knit, purl, and manipulate the needles comfortably you can expand your knitting skills to highly decorative techniques—highly decorative but not highly complicated. Many of these techniques come from regional knitting styles with a long and venerable history, but the techniques are not difficult and they will enrich your understanding and enjoyment of 21st century knitting.

TALL AND DROPPED STITCHES

Taller stitches can be used in lacy fabrics, or to work decorative stitches that require more yarn than you get in a plain knit or purl stitch.

Use yarn overs between stitches to create areas of lacy openwork. In tall stitches the yarn overs are dropped before they are ever knitted, and the extra lengths of yarn are taken up as extra height in the existing stitches. Vertical threads form lacy horizontal sections across the row. Though dropped yarn overs are used in other lace stitches, the purpose in tall stitches is to allow the stitches to become long, rather than to form discrete holes in the fabric.

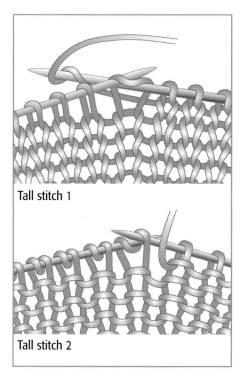

Tall stitch 1

Tall stitch 2

For a simple and consistent tall stitch across the row, yarn over between each stitch—as many times as you need, but the same number of yarn overs between each stitch. In the next row, knit or purl the real stitches and drop the yarn overs.

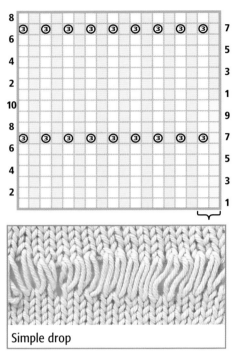

Simple drop

You can vary the number of yarn overs between stitches to form differently shaped open spaces. Tall waves are made by working different numbers of yarn overs between stitches in a repeat, then dropping the yarn overs as you work the stitches in the following row.

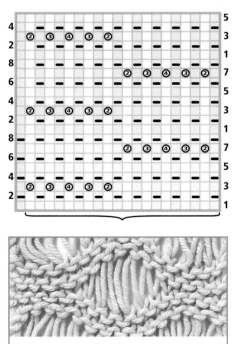

Seafoam

A variation of these tall stitches creates a twist in the vertical strands. Insert the working needle in the stitch to be worked, wrap the yarn around both needles once, then yarn over in the usual way, knitting only the original working stitch and dropping the extra wrap. This produces a horizontal fagotting effect across the row.

You can wrap the yarn around both needles more than once if you wish, and each additional wrap will produce a longer, more-twisted stitch. The stretchy fabric has utilitarian possibilities, but it looks messy.

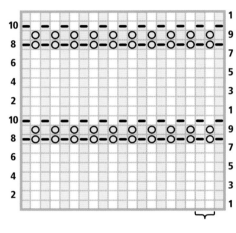

Double twist drop stitch

DROPPED STITCH PATTERNS

Knit the added yarn overs as extra stitches for a few rows, then drop the stitches and deliberately create short runs that stop at the point where the yarn overs were added. (See Drop Stitches, page 197.) The liberated horizontal threads (the "ladder rungs" that are the bane of nylon stockings) create vertical lace sections. You can open vertical spaces through the entire length of the knitting, or make short openings for regular patterns.

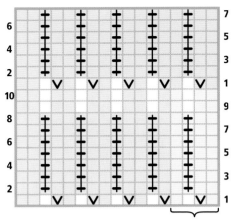

Ladder stitch

TRAVELING AND CROSSED STITCHES

The basic crossing technique is the same whether the crossings are confined to one row or keep going from one row to the next, leaving delicate, 1-stitch trails across the fabric. Crossings show only on the knit side, though they can be worked on both the knit and purl sides of the fabric to give the trails different angles. A stitch is taken out of order, moved either behind or ahead of another stitch, and the two stitches switch the order in which they are worked. Pay attention if you are working crossings from the purl side of the fabric because you can't see what is going on; make sure you get the correct stitch in front. (See Double Lattice in gallery, page 173.)

ON THE NEEDLE TECHNIQUES

Cross stitches while they sit securely on the needle. This is done by making a decrease and an increase in the same stitches instead of actually crossing two stitches. This keeps the fabric very flexible, while making even stitches.

The stitches are described by the direction they are traveling on the knit side of the fabric, where the trails will show. You are not going to see anything great on the purl side. "1st stitch" and "2nd stitch" refer to the order in which you encounter the stitches in the crossing maneuver. "Traveling stitch" is the traveling stitch, no matter which side of the fabric is facing you.

RIGHT-TRAVELING STITCHES

KNIT SIDE: Knit 2 together, keep them both on the source needle; knit a second time into the 1st stitch. Discard the 1st and 2nd stitches from the source needle.

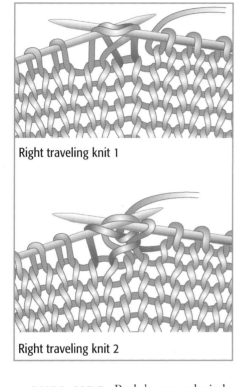

Right traveling knit 1

Right traveling knit 2

PURL SIDE: Purl the second stitch, leaving it on the needle; purl the 1st and 2nd stitches together. Discard the 1st and 2nd stitches from the source needle.

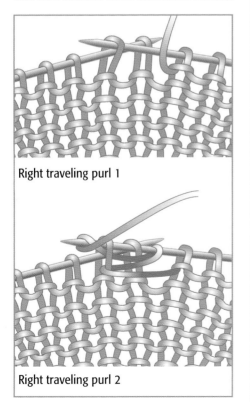

Right traveling purl 1

Right traveling purl 2

LEFT-TRAVELING STITCHES

KNIT SIDE: Slip 2 stitches knitwise, separately, and return them to the source needle. Knit into the back leg of the 2nd stitch, then knit again into both through the back legs. Discard the 1st and 2nd stitches from the source needle.

PURL SIDE: Slip 2 stitches knitwise, separately, and return them to the source needle. Purl both together through the back leg, then purl the 1st stitch again through the back leg. Discard the old stitches from the source needle.

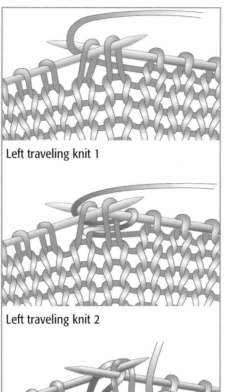

Left traveling knit 1

Left traveling knit 2

Left traveling purl 1

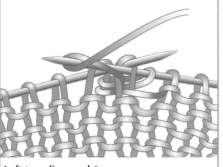

Left traveling purl 2

FREE LOOP TRAVELING STITCHES

These stitches come off the needle to cross others. The stitch that will be worked second is slipped off the working needle and out of the way, onto a cable needle if you are using one, and the second stitch is moved into its place. They are worked in their new order. You may prefer a cable needle to hold the loose stitch, but once you have worked a few, set the extra needle aside and leave that free loop flapping in the breeze. Make a practice swatch and get used to your stomach dropping away as you step out without a cable needle. Soon you will find it efficient rather than thrilling to leave a live stitch unattended. It is best to experiment with a non-slippery yarn like knitting worsted.

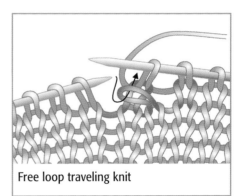

Free loop traveling knit

Insert the working needle into the 2nd stitch of the crossing pair, from the back side of the work if the stitch will cross behind, from the front of the work if the stitch will cross in front. Let the 1st stitch of the pair slip off the source needle; it will move to the side where it will cross. Slip the source needle back into the 1st stitch, then slip the 2nd stitch back onto the source needle. Work the two stitches in their new order.

71

THREADED STITCHES are crossed through the centers of other stitches, rather than to the front or the back of those stitches. You can thread one stitch or several, to the right or to the left, with a passing technique similar to the decrease techniques of **psso**—pass slipped stitch over, and **pnso**—pass next stitch over (see Multiple Threaded Stitch, page 185). They are usually worked on the knit side of the fabric, but this is not a rule, just an observation.

THREADED RIGHT-SLANTING: Ignore the 1st stitch of the pair initially. Insert the working needle knitwise in the 2nd stitch and lift it over the first stitch without discarding it from the point of the working needle. Yarn over the point of the working needle and draw the new knit stitch through the 2nd stitch; then discard the old stitch. Next, insert the working needle into the 1st stitch of the pair and knit it normally.

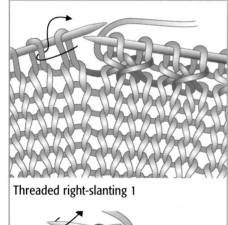

Threaded right-slanting 1

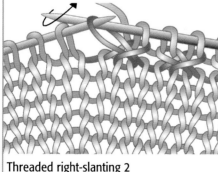

Threaded right-slanting 2

THREADED LEFT-SLANTING: Slip both the 1st and 2nd stitches purl-wise onto the working needle; lift the 1st stitch over the second and back onto the source needle. Then return the 2nd stitch to the source needle, and knit it. Knit the remaining stitch through the back leg to keep the crossing threads at the same angle on both left- and right-threaded stitches.

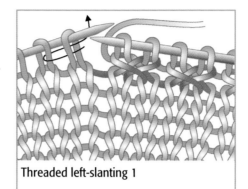

Threaded left-slanting 1

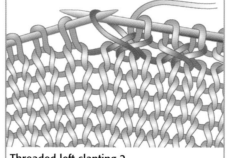

Threaded left-slanting 2

WRAPPED STITCHES use the working strand of yarn to bind groups of stitches across the row, bundling them into clusters. It is quite easy to do. Slip stitches without working them, bring the working yarn to the other side of the work around the slipped stitches, then slip them back to the source needle, and return the yarn to the working position.

In order to have the working yarn come out at the end of the wrap positioned to continue knitting, on a knit row, wrap the stitches counterclockwise; on a purl row, wrap clockwise. Draw the working strand up as tightly as desired and knit the wrapped stitches. Very tightly wrapped stitches will be more awkward to work; this is the price of "art."

The other method of making wrapped stitches uses a psso or a pnso (see Wrapped Eyelet, page 195) over the stitch bundles. This kind of wrapping produces a lacy fabric because each passed-over wrap is a decrease, and a replacement increase must be worked for each wrap, either in this row or the next.

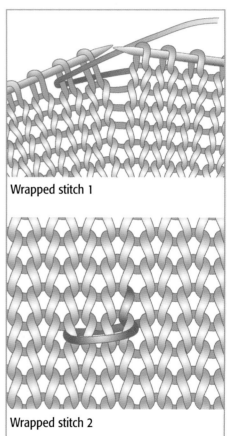

Wrapped stitch 1

Wrapped stitch 2

CABLES

CABLES are arguably the most popular decorative techniques because they are easy to do and endlessly variable. The only constant is that a group of stitches regularly changes places with other groups of stitches. Cables can be simple 2-section twists or complex braids with 3 or more strands. Variations are created by the twists and turns of the cable itself, as well as by the number of rows knitted between twists. Intertwining sections of a cable do not need to be the same width (though braids are usually regular), and the section widths can change, especially when the cable is used like a dart to shape a garment. In fact there are very few hard and fast rules about cables, which only adds to their charm. Here beauty and innovation are in their element.

SIMPLE CABLES can be named by the number of stitches and sections: 2/2 means that there are two, 2-stitch sections to the cable. 3/2 means that there is one 3-stitch section and one 2-stitch section. Sometimes a cable is called by one number, such as a 4-stitch cable. Is it 4 stitches total, or is each half of 4 stitches? Either is possible. When in doubt, read the instructions or look at the chart.

There tends to be a gap at the last edge of a cable because of the pull of the knitting. Counter this by pulling the working strand of yarn tighter to work the last stitches of the cable and the adjacent stitches. On turned work, as you work back across the row, insert the point of the needle into the stitches at the edge of the cable and draw yarn back to the center stitches of the cable to tighten up the edge. In the round, tug yarn back from loose stitches farther along in the row to even things out.

CABLE MANEUVERS in this book refer to cable needles. The double-pointed cable needle allows you to shift blocks of stitches easily to create the sections of a cable. You can purchase specially shaped cable needles or just use a double-pointed needle (wood and bamboo are less slippery than metal). (See Materials, pages 26–27.) The cable needle should be smaller than the needles you are using for the body of the project, to keep from distorting the cable stitches. You can also practice the free loop techniques of traveling stitches (see page 71) and adapt them to cables. Slipping 4 stitches from a needle into thin air, even for a moment, is a heady experience. Do whatever makes your knitting experience more enjoyable.

Cables are frequently worked in stockinette stitch on a reverse stockinette background, to better display the smooth twists and turns. This is far from a rule, but it is a good place to start. Usually cable crossings are worked from the front of the fabric because it is easier to see which stitches you are moving. Working cables from the back merely requires a little more attention.

While I tell you officially to slip stitches from the cable needle back to the source needle before knitting them, I tell you unofficially that I don't really know anyone who does this. Most people just knit straight from the cable needle and the cables look just fine.

ROTATED CABLES make a 180° twist in a single group of stitches to create the cable. These interesting cables are very easy to work because you are simply twisting a single group of stitches. They look nice worked in stockinette, garter, or seed stitch, and are attractive in widths of 6 stitches or less, though this is a suggestion rather than a rule. Experiment to see what works best with your yarn.

Slip all the stitches for the cable onto the cable needle. For a left twist, rotate the cable needle clockwise. For a right-twist, rotate the needle counterclockwise. Then knit the cable stitches onto the working needle. If you are working in stockinette stitch, it is customary to knit the top face of the cable despite the fact that you have just turned the purl side up. Between rotations work at least as many rows as the number of stitches the cable is wide. This will allow the cable to rotate without being bunchy or distorting the fabric beside it.

Right cables

Left cables

ROPE CABLES are two sets of stitches wrapping around each other. You will need to knit as many rows of uncrossed cable between turnings as you have stitches in the cable to make the cable sections long enough to twist. You can also vary the lengths of different sections of a cable to create a visual rhythm.

RIGHT-CROSSING (COUNTERCLOCKWISE) CABLES move the first cable section to the back; they are sometimes called back cables. Purl to the beginning of the cable stitches, slip them purlwise onto a cable needle, and park the cable needle behind the work. Knit the left section of the cable onto the working needle, then knit the stitches from the cable needle. Purl the framing stitches after the cable. On the wrong side of the fabric, knit the knit stitches and purl the purl stitches. (Refer to Classic Right Cable in gallery, page 179.)

LEFT-CROSSING (CLOCKWISE) CABLES cross the first section to the front, and are sometimes called front cables. Purl to the beginning of the cable stitches, slip them purlwise onto a cable needle, and park the cable needle in front of the work. Knit the stitches from the source needle, then the stitches from the cable needle. Purl the framing stitches after the cable. On the wrong side of the fabric knit the knit stitches and purl the purl stitches. (Refer to gallery, page 179.)

BICOLOR CABLES are made when two different colors are used to knit the cable sections. The cable can be separate sections of a garment united by colorful twists of cable, or can simply be vertical stripes made with bobbins of different colors, like intarsia knitting (see page 83). The method of construction is the same as a simple rope cable twist.

AXIS CABLES have a center cable (2 stitches wide at most) which stays in the center as the side sections cross behind or before it. This produces a chain link effect in the cable.

Axis cables

Back crossing: Slip the first cable stitches plus the center stitch to the cable needle and hold behind or before the fabric, depending on whether it is right or left twisting. Knit the second cable section, slip the center stitches from the cable needle onto the source needle, and knit them. Then knit the reserved section from the cable needle.

Front crossing: Slip the first cable section plus the center stitch to the cable needle and move behind the fabric. Knit the second cable section. Slip the center stitch to the source needle, then move the cable needle to the front of the fabric. Knit the center stitch from the source needle, then knit the reserved section from the cable needle.

TRAVELING CABLES combine traveling stitches and cables, allowing cables to cross groups of stitches without twisting around them. The cables wander across the fabric to create vignettes, produce tree of life designs, braids, Viking interlace, ad infinitum.

The method of crossing is the same as for rope cables. The first section of stitches to be moved is slipped onto a cable needle and parked in front or in back of the fabric, as needed. The amount of sideways movement you get from a cable depends on the yarn, the tension, and the stitch pattern. Generally speaking, the sideways movement is limited to the width of the cable, just as in rope cables. It is a good theme for an investigative swatch on a rainy afternoon. (Refer to Saxon Braid in gallery, page 181.)

CASTING ON CABLES between sections of ribbing allows you to have a continuous cable design from the edges of the piece without sacrificing the convenience of ribbing. It is no more difficult than casting on a ribbing, and produces an extremely fashionable garment.

Using smaller needles as you would to cast on an ordinary ribbing, cable cast on (see page 40) the stitches that will make up the sections of the cable, but replace the background stitches in the rest of the pattern with ribbing. Choose a ribbing pattern that is visually harmonious with the size of the cables. If you have several different sized cables in the piece, cast on all the cables with ribbing between them. You may have to decrease the number of stitches in the ribbing if the width of the cables makes the ribbed edge too wide. If this is the case, use pick-up increases or increases in the stitch below (see pages 57 and 58) in the last row of ribbing to bring the stitch count up to the number needed for the body of the piece.

If you decide to allow a cable to rise from the ribbings, it is best not to work a crossing in the first row of the ribbing because it will make a loose, loopy edge.

SHAPING WITH CABLES allows cables on a straight vertical axis to swoop around curves. You can shape either the cables themselves or the backgrounds to create a garment that actually fits you, rather than just serving as a display area

---

CABLE EASE

Because the crossings of cables pull the knit fabric in more than stockinette knitting, it is necessary to add stitches if you are adding cables to a plain sweater pattern, or to your gauge in stockinette stitch. A good rule of thumb is to calculate ¼ of a stitch of ease for each stitch used in a cable. If you have one 3/3 cable in the sweater,

6 cable stitches x ¼ stitch per cable stitch = 6 x ¼ stitches, or 1½ ease stitches.

If you have 4 of the 3/3 cables,

4 cables x 1½ ease stitches per cable = 6 stitches ease.

for cables. The back crossing of a cable is an excellent place to make invisible changes. Behind the front section of cable you can insert a stitch invisibly and convert the edge of the cable to a framing stitch, or take a framing stitch surreptitiously and use it to enlarge a cable. To increase in a cable strand, inserting a stitch in the back crossing or at an edge of the front crossing works well.

Shape between cables by working increases or decreases in the stitches that frame the cable. There are so many types of cables and so many increases and decreases that it is not possible to cover every situation. Careful consideration of where you need to make a change will guide you to choose an appropriate shaping stitch.

INCREASES AT THE EDGE OF A CABLE can have gaps. Firm tension in the working yarn may control this problem, but you are better off working the increase either in the cable or in the background rather than straddling the gap. A purl increase in a purl stitch one row below is a very effective increase for reverse stockinette. Remember that an increase done in a stitch one row below creates a smaller gap because it is tucked in between two already existing stitches. But if you must increase between stockinette and reverse stockinette, an increase made by working twice in one stitch, either knit-purl or purl-knit with the bump on the appropriate side, will blend in. An increase here is best worked in any row other than the crossing row, where it may gap from the extra pull.

DECREASES AT THE EDGE OF A CABLE are very successful, especially when a cable stitch lies across the framing stitch, because the edge of the cable is emphasized.

CABLE DARTS borrow stitches and use the crossings and twists of cables to disguise darts that would otherwise require increases and decreases. Subtle

and elegant effects are possible by borrowing neighboring stitches to enlarge cable strands, decreasing the stitches available for ease in the adjacent areas. This is useful at the waist, temporarily relocating bulky stitches in cable crossings, releasing the stitches as they are needed again for the bust with nothing but a sinuous curve of cable to tell the tale.

Use the convenient Cable Ease formula, page 74, to calculate how many stitches you will need to lend to cables to temporarily narrow an area of knitting. Borrow background stitches at a rate of one stitch per cable strand per twist at most—more than this will cause the cable strand to buckle and fold rather than lay flat. Add a row between twists to accommodate the additional width of the strand. This may not be possible if you have a number of cables and wish to use only a few of them as darts, since it would throw off the symmetry of the cables. In this case you could more easily sneak one stitch into only the back strand of twice as many cables, without varying the vertical row count between twists.

CABLE DECREASES remove blocks of stitches gracefully on full-fashioned knits. They are especially helpful on a raglan sweater with a cable design that should not simply be chopped off as the raglan decreases are worked. One section of a cable is moved directly over its mate, rather than across it, and the stitches on the separate needles are paired and knitted together in the same way that a joinery bind-off seam is worked (see Joinery Bind-off, page 95). This leaves a pretty curve instead of a straight line where the stitches overlap. It can be done without a cable needle handy, and is helpful on very fine-gauge knits where an inch decrease can involve 8 or 10 stitches in an otherwise unattractive series of decreases.

DOTS, KNOTS, AND BOBBLES

Dots, knots, and bobbles punctuate your knitting with texture by adding stitches and rows to a single stitch. These stitches comprise some of the classic texture patterns of Aran knitting, such as the famous Trinity stitch. They can be added as a dash of whimsy here and there, or even as a dash of color. When working any of these stitches, pull the working yarn very tightly when beginning and ending the stitch, and above it in the next row, to settle the stitch firmly into the surrounding knit fabric. Though you do not have to know reverse knitting, it is a wonderful timesaver here. And if you are so inclined, this is another area to expand crochet skills.

DOTS, also called peppercorns or nubs, increase a knit or purl stitch vertically and the extra height bulges forward. Work a stitch as usual; yarn over a second time around the point of the working needle and lift the stitch over, the way you would pass a slipped stitch over. Each time you do this, it knits one stitch in height and increases the texture. Two to three of these vertical increases make a dot, while a dozen can make a long dangle. Feel free to experiment.

For bigger dots (1 row tall):

1. Work a knit-purl-knit increase into one stitch.

2. Yarn over on the point of the working needle, and lift each loop of the increase over the yarn over, to decrease back to one stitch.

3. Push the dot through to the front before moving on to the next stitch.

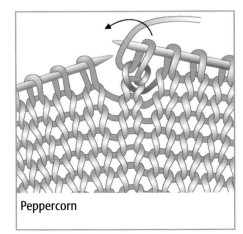

Peppercorn

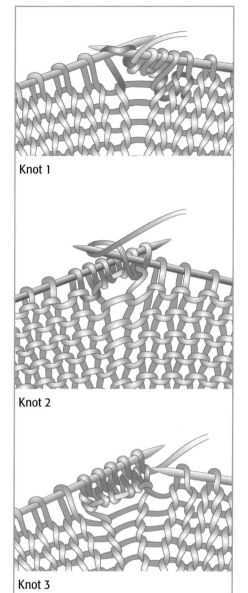

Knot 1

Knot 2

Knot 3

KNOTS (3 rows tall) have a row of increases, the increases are purled, then decreased back to one stitch. You will need to turn the knitting to work the purl row of each knot unless you use reverse knitting across those rows. It is worth the minimal effort of learning.

Knit-purl increase 5 times in one stitch. Turn the work and purl across the increases. Turn the work. Slip all 5 stitches to the working needle. Yarn over, and lift all 5 stitches over it, one at a time. When you knit the next stitch draw the yarn very tightly to anchor the knot in place.

Knit-purl increase 5 times in one stitch. Purl the increases. Knit the first 3 increases together. Ssk the last 2 increase stitches together. Pass the loop of the 3-stitch decrease over the ssk loop. Pull the yarn tightly when you work the next stitch to anchor the knot.

BOBBLES (5 rows tall, also called popcorns) are very large knots. They tend to be limp and loosely attached, and anything that tidies them up is a good thing. The best-looking bobbles I have seen are crocheted, solid, and without gaps around them. For knitted bobbles, see page 169 in gallery.)

CROCHETED SINGLE BOBBLES are individual bobbles that can be made in any color you like and used whenever and wherever you want a bobble. A baggie of bobbles in your knitting equipment is a cheerful sight. (If you already know how to crochet, these bobbles are popcorns made of 3–5 double crochets.)

1. Make a slip knot, leaving a 4" tail. Chain 3.

2. * Yarn over and draw up a loop through the first chain. Yarn over and draw through 2 loops. *

3. Repeat from * to * 3 or 4 times, depending on how large you want the bobble to be. (There will be on the hook one loop for each repeat, + 1 starting loop.)

4. Yarn over once and draw through all remaining loops on the hook.

5. Insert the hook into the first chain, yarn over, and draw the loop through the last loop of the bobble, pulling the base and top together.

6. Cut the yarn leaving a 4" tail, and draw the cut end through the last loop on the hook.

When you use the bobble, draw one tail through the knit fabric, and draw the other tail through the fabric one strand below the first. Tie the 2 tails around the strand, then work them into the back of the fabric with a crochet hook or tapestry needle. If the bobble color is different from the background be sure that the tails do not show on the front of the work.

EMBOSSED KNITTING forms texture by working extra rows and stitches within the vertical and horizontal pattern repeats, unlike bobbles, which do it in the space of one stitch. The extra bulk raises the front of the stitch and creates heavily textured patterns. The basis for the additional stitches for each motif is the Cabled Cast-on which will create a smooth, neat edge. However, in some cases, the Half-hitch Cast-on can be used (see page 41). The new stitches, combined with various decorative decreases slant the work to the left and right for shaping and highlights as you whittle your way back down to the original stitch count at the end of the vertical repeat. (See motif pattern and explanation for Bell Insertion, page 170.)

WORKING WITH COLOR

MULTI-STRAND AND COLOR TECHNIQUES (2 colors in a row) add another layer of warmth as beautiful designs dance across your fingers and into your knitting. The techniques are varied, and you will surely find at least one to lure you into the polychrome world. Knit a gauge swatch before you start a project. Knitting with two colors always affects gauge.

STRIPES are a classic way to break the color barrier. They are simple, lovely, and can make a plain sweater as exciting as a candy cane. As basic as the stripe is, here are hints to make it even easier.

STRAIGHT STRIPES change color strands at the beginning of a row. Stripes with an even number of rows (2, 4, 6, etc.) get you back to the needle point to pick up the other color. If you are making broad stripes, carry unused colors along the edges, knitting an edge stitch of the waiting color or twisting the strands.

THE REVERSE SIDE OF STRIPES is very exciting. Instead of a smooth band of color you get a line of colored purls, as reticulated as a reptile. Here you may indulge your desire for a single stripe of color, though it will be a syncopated stripe instead of a sedate drawing room stripe. Reverse garter stitch stripes are almost evenly divided colors, though the depth of the fabric tends to obscure this and to resemble a 2-row stripe.

Reverse stockinette fabric produces a bordered stripe with each 2-row stripe of color. A 2-row stripe between broader contrast stripes will remain a simple bordered stripe, but two 2-row stripes will interlock, every 4 rows making a jazzy pattern of single stripes of 2 colors and a double stripe of one color. (See Brick Pattern in gallery, page 223.)

STRIPES IN RIBBING have a reverse stockinette double stripe in the purl ribs at each color change. To avoid this, knit the new color across purl stitches instead of purling. The interruption to ribbing is not noticeable in a single row, but changing colors every 2 rows turns purl ribs into garter stitch, completely changing the character of the ribbing. Decide if you prefer texture changes to color changes in ribbing, and

work a swatch to make sure. A space-dyed yarn may be the answer.

SLANTED STRIPES are possible in flat knitting by using short rows to create uphill and downhill slopes. Making slanted stripes is the best way to become really familiar with the way short rows work. The different colors are like arrows pointing to the turning stitches. The process is described in stockinette stitch because anything else will make you crazy.

LEFT EDGE ROWS (on the front side) begin on the purl side of the fabric. Purl across to the turning point. Turn the work. Bring the working yarn forward, to your side of the fabric. Behind the working strand of yarn, insert the working needle into the turning stitch purlwise, then lay the yarn across the top of the working needle from front to back, making a counterclockwise yarn over at the beginning of the short row. Complete slipping the turning stitch to the working needle and knit the new row. The next time you encounter this stitch will be on a purl row. Purl together both the slipped stitch and the yarn over following it.

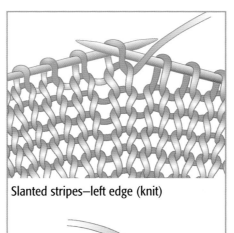
Slanted stripes—left edge (knit)

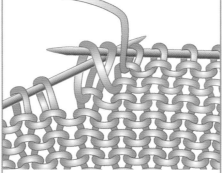
Slanted stripes—left edge (purl)

RIGHT EDGE ROWS (on the front side) begin on the knit side of the fabric. Knit across to the turning point. Turn the work. Bring the working yarn forward, to your side of the fabric. Slip purlwise the first stitch on the purl row and make a counterclockwise yarn over on the point of the working needle, then purl back across the row. The next time you encounter this stitch will be on a knit row. Knit together the yarn over and the slipped stitch following it.

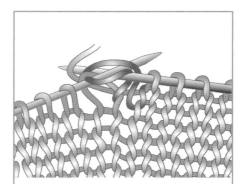
Slanted stripes—right edge (knit)

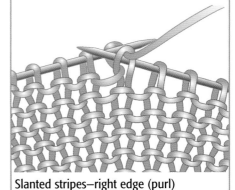
Slanted stripes—right edge (purl)

SLIP STITCH COLOR is an ingenious way to get to 2 colors in a row knitted in only one color. This works on striped fabric by using slipped stitches to borrow the color of the lower row. Two colors are knitted in alternating rows, and where you need the 2nd color to appear, stitches of the row below are slipped into the current row. This can be done with a knit or purl stitch, on turned work or in the round. The possibilities are virtually limitless, from simple vertical stripes to intricate patterns. It also allows you to knit comfortably with 2 strands and still have 3 colors in a row.

To make sure the yarns all start at the beginning of the row, work a selvage stitch of that row's color at each end. This will also give you a hint, should you become muddled, as to which color comes next. (See Plaid Ladders in gallery, page 222.)

SLIP STITCH PATTERNS are a bit less stretchy than plain stockinette. This is useful if you are knitting with a yarn that tends to stretch lengthwise. Carry the unused strand loosely behind the slipped stitches to avoid puckering the knitting. A balanced pattern with regular use of both colors and without long expanses of one color will give the best result.

SINGLE-POINT NEEDLES require 2 rows with each color in order to get back to the beginning of the row to change colors. The second color also makes two rows, slipping stitches from the first color row to create a pattern, carrying the unused yarn on the wrong side. On the return row, slip the slipped stitches and knit the knit stitches for a solid block of color (to follow a charted pattern on graph paper).

ONE STRAND IN EACH HAND

Some knitting traditions are synonymous with multicolor. Can you even imagine a monochrome Norwegian ski sweater? Though it is possible (and sometimes necessary) to knit with two strands in one hand, knowing how to manipulate the yarn with both left and right hands speeds up color knitting, and is essential in some of the 2-color techniques. If you have never learned how to knit with "the other hand," learning with a separate color in each hand is an easy and natural process. The dominant color is held English-style, and the second color is held German-style. (See page 37.) With a strand in each hand, each hand is occupied with its own business and not fighting for control. This quickly becomes second nature, and you will have no trouble knitting in either style without thinking about it.

If you will be adding a border, avoid having to pick up new stitches by knitting the border color at the end of each row.

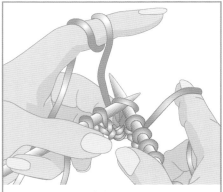
One strand in each hand

JACQUARD AND FAIR ISLE share techniques. Fair Isle (one of the Shetland Islands) and Jacquard (the designer of a loom that worked multicolored, figured designs) both refer to stockinette fabric worked with 2 or more colors in a row. Fair Isle knitting, strictly speaking, has traditional OXO and "peerie" patterns, but the name is often used simply to refer to multicolored, stranded knitting. (See Houndstooth Check (Jacquard), page 225, and Fair Isle Diamond, page 227, in gallery.)

MULTICOLORED KNITTING often limits itself to 2 colors in a row for ease of knitting. Even Swedish Bohus knitting, known for its intricate color designs, used only 2 colors in a row. If needed, a third color was a slipped stitch from a lower row. But there are traditions (such as Finnish) that routinely use 3 colors in a row. To do this, hold the main color English-style and hold both alternate colors German-style, ready to pick up as you need them.

CHARTED DESIGNS allow you to adapt any number of color designs to knitting. The only real problem you may encounter is that stockinette stitch does not knit up square. Special knitters' graph paper is available to adapt designs to stockinette knitting. To avoid the problem use color-weave knitting (see below), which produces square stitches.

STRANDING carries strands of unused color on the back of knitting. These strands (called floats) catch on fingers and jewelry. One way to control this is to catch the unused color on the back of a stitch every few stitches (no more than 4 or 5) or once every inch. This

does not show on the front of the fabric. An alternative is to knit a stitch in the unused color.

There are four different situations where you will need to know a stranding technique: the right-hand yarn knit and right-hand yarn purl stitches, to catch in the unused strand from your left hand; and the left-hand yarn knit and left-hand yarn purl stitches, to catch in the unused strand from your right hand.

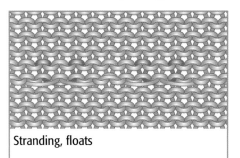
Stranding, floats

Right-hand knit: Insert the working needle into the stitch and lay the left-hand color across the working needle; yarn over clockwise from beneath the working needle with the working color; and draw through the stitch without catching the unused color.

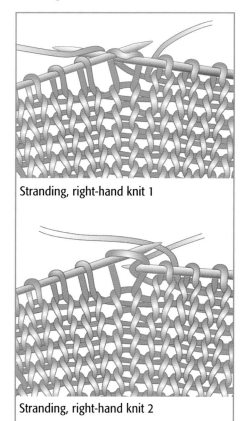
Stranding, right-hand knit 1

Stranding, right-hand knit 2

Left-hand knit: Insert the working needle into the stitch and bring the right-hand yarn (the unused color) clockwise up from below the working needle and lay it across the top. Bring the left-hand yarn (the color you are using to knit the stitch) up clockwise the same way. Take the unused right-hand color back down to its starting position, then finish knitting the stitch with the left-hand color. Give the right-hand yarn a tug to make sure it has not been caught into the finished stitch.

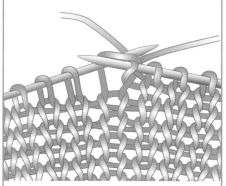
Stranding, left-hand knit 4

Right-hand purl: Insert the working needle and lay the left-hand (unused color) yarn across it. Purl across the unused yarn without drawing it through the stitch. This will catch the unused strand between the purl side of the fabric and the new purled stitch.

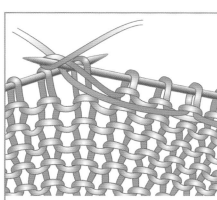
Stranding, right-hand purl

Left-hand purl: Insert the working needle and wrap the right-hand (unused) color clockwise from beneath the needle; then lay the left-hand (working) color counterclockwise across the working needle. (The two strands of yarn will cross above the needle.) Then unwrap the unused color and draw through the stitch of working yarn. Tug the unused color slightly to make sure it has not been caught up in the new stitch.

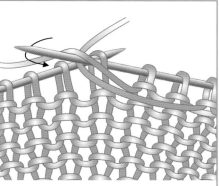
Stranding, left-hand purl

79

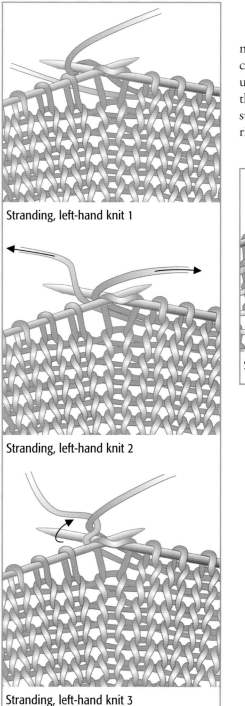
Stranding, left-hand knit 1

Stranding, left-hand knit 2

Stranding, left-hand knit 3

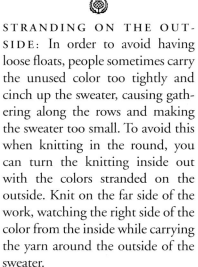
STRANDING ON THE OUT-SIDE: In order to avoid having loose floats, people sometimes carry the unused color too tightly and cinch up the sweater, causing gathering along the rows and making the sweater too small. To avoid this when knitting in the round, you can turn the knitting inside out with the colors stranded on the outside. Knit on the far side of the work, watching the right side of the color from the inside while carrying the yarn around the outside of the sweater.

COLOR-WEAVE KNITTING is a specialized form of stockinette stranding preferred by those of us neat-freaks who cannot bear to have floats even as long as 4 stitches. But in addition to producing the tidiest insides of sweaters, it is loved in its own right for producing beautiful, firm, tapestry-like patterns. It produces a square stockinette stitch that can be used to knit from ordinary square-block charted designs, because it catches the unused color alternately above and below the stitches of the color in use, and locks the unused color in behind every second stitch.

The movements for color weave knitting are the same as those used to catch up floats in regular stranded knitting, but they are used in a methodic system of 4 movements, 2 for each hand. To use color-weave knitting for general knitting, imagine every stitch is either an odd or an even numbered stitch in that color: the first, third, fifth stitches, etc., are Odd stitches. The second, fourth, sixth stitches, etc., are Even stitches. Each stitch you knit of either color is either an Odd or an Even stitch. When knitting an Odd stitch, use the Odd technique for the appropriate hand. When knitting an Even stitch, use the Even technique for the appropriate hand.

To work a sample swatch, make 2 stitch-wide vertical stripes until you are comfortable with the Odd and Even movements. Then be daring and try 3 or 5 stitch-wide vertical stripes until it becomes second nature.

KNIT ROWS
Right-hand color:

Odds: Insert the working needle in the stitch; carry the left-hand color below the working needle and knit as usual.

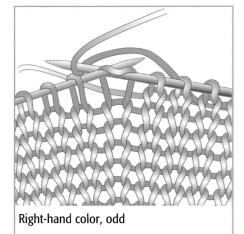

Right-hand color, odd

Evens: Insert the working needle in the stitch. Lay the left-hand color across the top of the working needle. With only the working color, knit the stitch. If the next stitch is with the right-hand color, the left-hand strand will be caught under it.

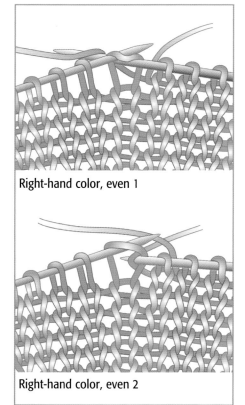

Right-hand color, even 1

Right-hand color, even 2

Left-hand color:

Odds: Insert the working needle into the stitch and knit as usual with the left-hand strand. The right-hand color is behind the stitch you are knitting; don't worry about it.

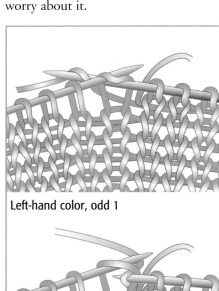

Left-hand color, odd 1

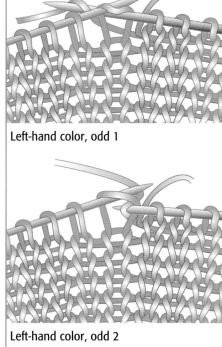

Left-hand color, odd 2

Evens: Insert the working needle into the stitch; bring the right-hand color up from below the needle and wrap it clockwise around the working needle. Bring the left-hand color up the same way and wrap it clockwise around the needle, then lower the right-hand yarn and knit the stitch with ONLY the left-hand yarn.

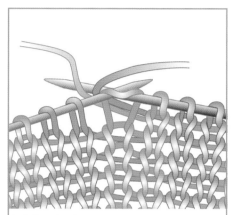

Left-hand color, evens 1

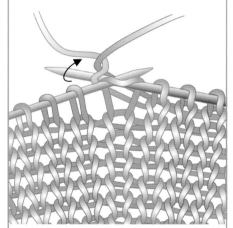

Left-hand color, evens 2

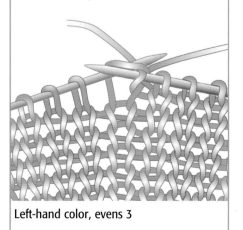

Left-hand color, evens 3

PURL ROWS
Right-hand color:
Odds: Insert the working needle to purl, holding the left-hand strand below the stitch and out of the way. With the right-hand yarn purl the stitch as usual.

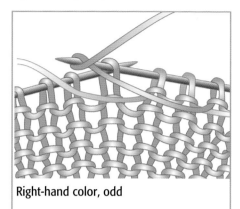

Right-hand color, odd

Evens: Insert the working needle to purl and lay the left-hand strand across the top of the working needle; purl with the right-hand yarn.

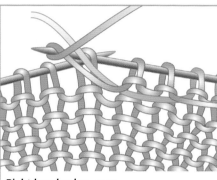

Right-hand color, even

Left-hand color:
Odds: Insert the working needle to purl, and with the left-hand strand purl as usual. The right-hand color is behind the stitch you are working; don't worry about it.

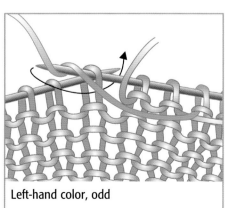

Left-hand color, odd

Evens: Insert the working needle to purl. Bring the right-hand yarn clockwise, from below the working needle. Bring the left-hand yarn counterclockwise across the top of the working needle; lower the right-hand yarn. Purl the stitch with the left-hand yarn, being careful not to catch in the right-hand strand.

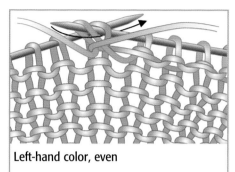

Left-hand color, even

CASTING ON IN COLOR starts the excitement of varied colors at the very beginning of the knitting. Aside from the fun of color, learning how these cast-ons work is easier when you can see the separate colors. Done in a single color, the beautiful structure is an elegant edge to any number of projects. There is a right side and a wrong side to 2-color ribbings, and you must always carry the unused color on the wrong side between stitches. If you hold 2 strands in 2 hands, you will discover one of the great inequities of life: the same strand has to do all the shifting to achieve this.

- -

Knot the two colors together in a slip knot and put it on the needle. This is the first stitch, and is worked as one stitch when you being to knit. You can also pick out the knot before knitting, and start with only the cast-on stitches. The outer edge color of the knot is held in the right hand. The second color is held in the left hand.

Make a half hitch with the left-hand color and slip it on the needle.

Lay the right-hand color across the needle.

Slip the left-hand loop off the needle and tighten it around the base of the stitch.

Twist the yarns clockwise so that the colors reverse hands.

Repeat the steps.

When you begin the first row of knitting, if doing turned work, begin with a purl row. If knitting in the round, begin with a knit row.

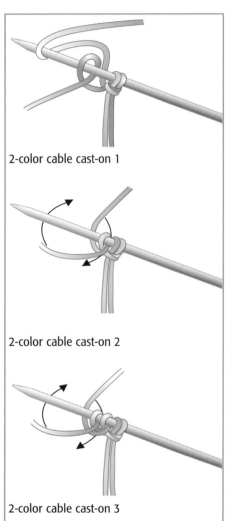

2-color cable cast-on 1

2-color cable cast-on 2

2-color cable cast-on 3

VARIATION: 2-COLOR CORD CAST-ON

Twist the yarns counterclockwise so that the colors reverse hands.

CORRUGATED RIBBING sets the tone for a vibrant sweater or hat, and is part of many knitting traditions. It is a

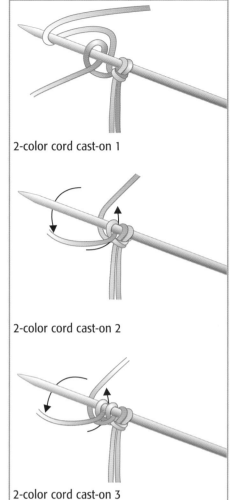

2-color cord cast-on 1

2-color cord cast-on 2

2-color cord cast-on 3

2 x 2 ribbing (knit 2, purl 2), with the knit stitches done in one color and the purls done in another, sometimes changing colors in the ribbed section for even more excitement (rather like watching a sunrise through a mullioned window). It is, interestingly, cast on in a single color, with the second color added in the next round or row. A cabled cast-on, ribbed or plain, or a tubular cast-on adapted to 2 x 2 ribbing give a nicely finished edge, but you may use your favorite method to cast on.

Cast on a multiple of 4 with one color. Begin the second color when working the first row, knitting 2 stitches with the main color, purling 2 stitches with the second color. Carry the unused color behind the work. Corrugated ribbing is less stretchy than single color ribbing, but it is consistent with the stretchiness of multicolor stranded knitting.

Close-up of entrelac. See Kaleidoscope project, page 128.

ENTRELAC

Entrelac or Basketweave knitting is an intriguing technique that knits rectangles into a basketweave pattern, worked either flat or in the round. Knitting the separate levels of rectangles in alternating colors emphasizes the illusion that the fabric is woven of knitted strips. As if basic basketweave were not exciting enough, you can knit patterns or colored designs into the individual rectangles. Cables, flowers, a picture in every segment—whatever makes your knitting more exciting and enjoyable.

A base row of triangles begins the work; after that each level is made of rectangles. Each additional level is built off the preceding segment. When worked flat, a triangle begins and ends each level of rectangles to make a straight edge. Each rectangle has two sides connected to the neighboring segments and two free edges: one side of "live" loops, and one edge that serves as a base for the next level of rectangles. The workings of entrelac are explained in the project, (Kaleidoscope) on page 128. Once you understand them you can invent and adapt to your heart's content.

INTARSIA

Intarsia (inlaid) colors create discrete islands of color by using individual bobbins or skeins. The classic example is argyle knitting, whose distinctive diamonds decorate socks and sweaters. The color change occurs at the edges of the island as you work across each row.

A short length of yarn on a bobbin works for a small area of color. For large color areas that require skeins of yarn, keep each skein in a separate container, lined up in order of use. These will twist as you work across each row and change colors. *If* you turn the work consistently between rows, all these strands uncross on the return row. Working a purl row before you stop knitting leaves a lovely, untwisted row when you begin again.

After a knit row, turn the full needle counterclockwise.

After a purl row, turn the full needle clockwise.

The crossing rules are delightfully simple:

The new strand crosses over the top of the old strand.

Vertical line of color changes = cross the yarns every row

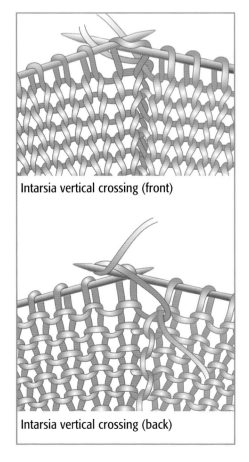

Intarsia vertical crossing (front)

Intarsia vertical crossing (back)

INTARSIA DIAGONAL CROSSINGS

Diagonal lines of color changes cross every other row. Right diagonal color changes cross on the knit side, and left diagonal color changes cross on the purl side.

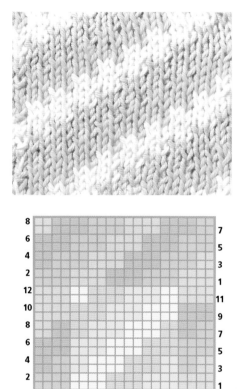

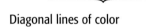

Diagonal lines of color

INTARSIA ARGYLE CROSSINGS

ARGYLE CHARTS are printed flat, but don't let this persuade you that they must be knitted that way. Though done in rows rather than rounds, intarsia knitting can be used for round garments by creating a seam of one shared edge stitch that is knitted and slipped to the other needle at the end of the row. The direction of work is reversed (you will be purling every other row, just as in flat knitting) and the stitch is worked at the end of the next row. This makes possible argyle socks and sweaters without sewn seams.

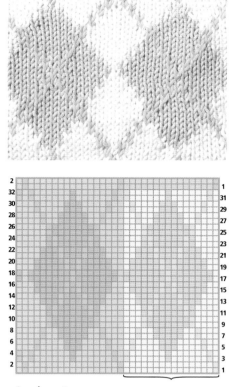

Argyle pattern

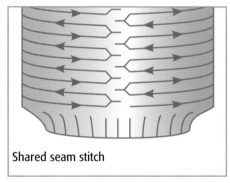

Shared seam stitch

An even more brilliant solution to the intarsia problem can sometimes be solved by knitting the motifs individually, then knitting them into place as you knit the background with short rows. While knitters slaved over intarsia in the round, industry used individual diamonds, caught into the background of the sock as it was knitted.

THE SLIDING LOOP JOIN at edges makes possible flat, beautiful joins that are new to most knitters. The technique is simple to understand, and can be taken to who knows what heights? Time alone will tell. But you can add to the research.

Each time you turn a row while knitting, the strand of yarn loops up to begin the new row. (Of course, if you slip the first stitch of a row for a chain edge this loop does not exist.) This loop can be picked up and used to join a row being knitted on a completely different piece as invisibly as if the yarns were twisted. This technique will work on either the left or the right edge of knitting, and works equally well on both knit and purl stitches.

To identify where this occurs, knit a small rectangle in stockinette stitch. Cast on, then turn to work the first row. Lay a strand of yarn across the working yarn as you bring it up to wrap for the first stitch. Do not catch it into the stitch itself, but only into the turn of the row. The marking strand will lie across the working yarn and be caught into the very outermost edge of the row.

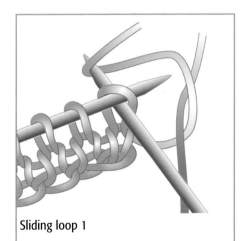

Sliding loop 1

Work across the row as usual, turn and work the second row. Each time you meet the marking thread, mark the turn of the row. After several rows you will begin to recognize that the marking yarn

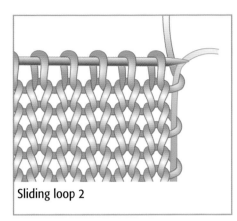

Sliding loop 2

is in the bulge at each turning stitch.

To use the sliding loop, begin another rectangle by casting on. Choose the side of the marked rectangle to abut the new knitting. Where the marking yarn threads through the edge, draw up a long loop of the working yarn of the new rectangle. This long loop is the sliding loop that will join the new rectangle to the old. Pull it to find the end that is attached to the new cast-on and the end that slides. Use the attached, non-sliding yarn to knit the next row.

Turn the work to purl back (or work in reverse knitting) across the new rectangle. At the end of this row—the free edge of the new rectangle—turn and pull on the sliding loop to draw up more yarn; knit back across the row to the joining edge. When you reach the joining side, tighten the last stitch of sliding yarn on the knit row. Pull the sliding loop out of the finished row. Draw up a new sliding loop for the new row through the marked edge stitch of the old rectangle.

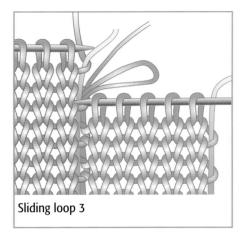

Sliding loop 3

The sliding loop join works beautifully on straight edges of knitting, but you can also use it on slanted shaped edges, such as argyle diamonds. Knitting between two diamonds would have to be shaped by increases, decreases, or even short rows, to fit the open space, but once shaping was accomplished any suitable edge stitch could be used to join two edges with a sliding loop. With the sliding loop method, diamonds knitted while watching a soccer game can be joined into a sweater later, like other motif knitting.

Binding off will have jags of color out of line unless the last stitch of one color is knit with the following color. When bound off, the stitch lifted over the following stitch will not overlap the boundaries of the preceding color.

SPECIAL MEDIA AND TECHNIQUES

REVERSE KNITTING allows you to work back across a row without turning the work. Whichever way you normally knit, reverse knitting works in the other direction. This is a brief trip back to being a complete novice at knitting.

Work with the right side of the fabric facing you no matter which row you are working, and work mirror image to the normal direction of knitting. If you normally knit American (English-) style, leave the yarn in your right hand. This will automatically carry the yarn ahead of the reverse knitting, German-style (see page 37), though in the other hand. Working backwards is easier to learn if you do not have to throw the yarn, too.

Knit the first row in the usual way. At the end of the row, DO NOT TURN THE WORK. Instead, the full needle stays where it is, pointed in the same direction. The working strand of yarn is behind the work. Insert the empty needle from front to back, left to right, through the stitch. Bring the yarn up under the (new) working needle, between the two needles. The wrap is clockwise, though you may not realize it since you are busy thinking backwards. Draw the loop through the old stitch. Drop the old stitch. Work across the row and heave a sigh of relief.

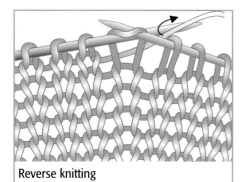
Reverse knitting

When you insert the working needle to knit the next row in the usual direction, the stitches are right-facing instead of left-facing (see page 43). This is because it is easier to wrap the yarn clockwise to form the reverse knit stitches. After a few inches of alternating forward and reverse knitting, it will feel natural enough to experiment with counterclockwise wrapping.

REVERSE PURLING produces purl bumps on the side of fabric facing you, like regular purling does. Carry the yarn ahead of the work on the front side, German-style. For garter stitch without turning, work a row in forward knitting and a row in reverse purl. Make sure the working strand is at the front to start. Insert the (new) working needle from back to front, under the back leg of the stitch, left to right through the stitch. Bring the yarn up under the working needle, (this wraps counterclockwise) and draw the new loop through to the back. Drop the old stitch.

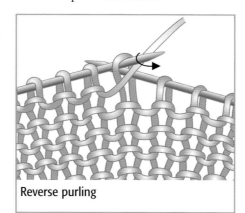
Reverse purling

For additional practice or fun, skip the forward rows and turn the work between rows to work ONLY reverse knit and reverse purl rows. It is just like turning forward knitting and purling, only backwards. So knitting puts the smooth side of the stitch on the front, whether you are working forward or reverse, and purling puts the purl bump on the front, whether you are working forward or reverse. Tempted to bang your head on the wall at this point? Each new technique you master actually creates new brain connections to keep you mentally agile.

BEADS AND SEQUINS

BEADS AND SEQUINS add sparkle to knitting. Whether you want to fling a handful of stars across an evening wrap or encrust a tiny purse with jewels, the techniques are simple. Test swatches are essential. The weight of added decoration affects the drape of knitted fabric. Because of the materials used for sequins, beads, and paillettes, cold blocking is the only completely safe way to finish a garment. You can experiment with steam blocking on a swatch. How do decorations stand up to laundering? Delicate pearl and iridescent finishes can flake off or dull unless treated gently. Test swatches allow you to choose the correct knitting, blocking, and laundering methods. Any cleaning method, including dry cleaning, must work for both yarn and decorations.

SPARKLY DOODADS come in a multitude of shapes, colors, facets, and sizes, but the part that you work with first is the hole. An ornament must slide along the strand without fraying it. If you have to force a bead onto the yarn, reconsider your choice of materials or methods. Beads come in different sizes, and if you love a color or finish, look for it in a larger size. If you love sequins and don't mind the effort, a large tapestry needle or paper punch can enlarge a hole significantly. Sometimes sewing on a few beads or sequins is the best choice.

THREADING can be done a few different ways. If you are able to find sequins or beads in hanks, simply make a loop of the hank strand, slip the yarn end through it, and begin sliding the ornaments onto the yarn.

To thread items one at a time, a sequin hole accommodates a medium tapestry needle (NOT a large yarn needle) and a strand of sport weight yarn, or use a loop of dental floss in a needle to hold the yarn end. Tie the floss around the yarn if you need to.

If you have multitudes of dazzlers and doodads to thread onto the yarn, do it in small batches as you need them rather than putting them all on at the beginning. Cut the yarn just before you need the first batch, thread a few rows' worth, then knit them up and repeat the process as needed.

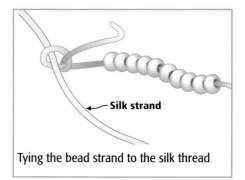
← Silk strand

Tying the bead strand to the silk thread

SEQUINS are reflective disks, flat or cupped. Some sequins are actually metal or shell, but lightweight plastics add shimmer without adding a great deal of weight. They are beautifully effective when used in a seed stitch pattern of alternating stitches on alternating rows. Sequins look best with space to lie flat; do not crowd them. Leave a selvage stitch at each edge to keep the sequins from sliding around to the back. Thread cupped sequins with the cupped sides all facing the same direction, up or down according to taste. Both directions reflect light equally well.

The basic sequin pattern is a 4-row seed stitch. Purl bumps on the sequin side of the fabric keep the sequins from twisting. Even if just placing sequins randomly across the fabric, work flanking purl stitches one row above each sequin to keep it flat and centered.

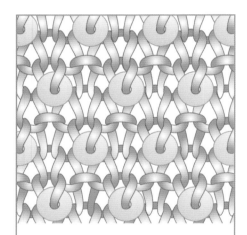
Sequins on seed stitch fabric

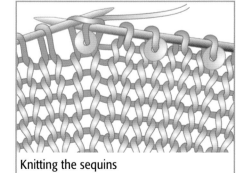
Knitting the sequins

Get the sequin through the stitch by poking it through with your finger or coaxing it through with the point of the knitting needle.

ON FLAT KNITTING

Row 1 (right side): Knit 1 stitch without a sequin; knit the second stitch with a sequin. Repeat across the row.

Row 2 (wrong side): Purl the stitches that have sequins. Knit the stitches that do not have sequins.

Row 3: Knit 1 stitch with a sequin. Knit the second stitch without a sequin. Repeat across the row.

Row 4: Purl the stitches that have sequins. Knit the stitches that do not have sequins.

ON CIRCULAR KNITTING (RIGHT SIDE)

Round 1: Knit 1 stitch without a sequin; knit the second stitch with a sequin. Repeat this across the row.

Round 2: Purl the stitches that do not have sequins. Knit the stitches that do have sequins.

Round 3: Knit 1 stitch with a sequin; knit the second stitch without a sequin. Repeat this across the row.

Round 4: Purl the stitches that do not have sequins. Knit the stitches that do have sequins.

While it is certainly technically possible to place sequins on a purl stitch, the supporting thread runs horizontally and tends to project the sequin sideways, making it more liable to catch and bend. If this will not be a problem, you can use the technique on both stockinette and reverse stockinette fabrics.

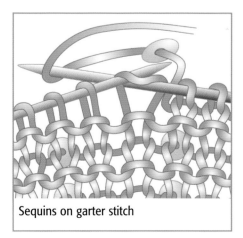
Sequins purled on stockinette

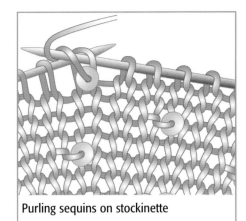
Purling sequins on stockinette

ON REVERSE STOCKINETTE fabric, hold the sequins on the leg of the stitch with a knit stitch, as on the knit side of stockinette, or purl stitch. A purl stitch will place the sequin between stitches on the purl bump.

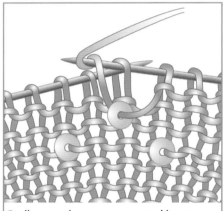
Purling sequins on reverse stockinette

ON GARTER STITCH place the sequin while working the wrong side row, so that it lies between stitches, as it does on reverse stockinette. Knit the stitch before the sequin and slip the sequin against the back of it; then knit the next stitch.

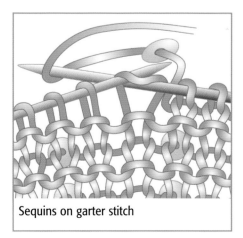
Sequins on garter stitch

BEADS

One glass bead doesn't weigh much, but a hank of beads adds quite a bit of weight. Wool yarns or a very open pattern may be pulled out of shape by extensive beading. Cellulose fibers (see Materials, page 34) stretch less under an equal burden of beads, and frequently come in thin strands that can accommodate seed beads. Work a long swatch and let it hang for a few days to see if stretching is going to cause a problem. If it is, a different fiber, fewer beads, or a different method of attaching the beads may provide a more stable fabric.

WHEN WORKING WITH YARN, beads are usually placed intermittently. Instead of stuffing a plump yarn into tiny bead, consider carrying a separate thread of beads along with the yarn when working the beaded rows, or sew the beads on separately. For bead-encrusted pieces, use a yarn or thread that allows beads to slide very freely. Where beads are the focal point, consider using crochet thread in a matching or complementary color.

BEADS CAN BE PLACED HORIZONTALLY OR DIAGONALLY on stitches. This allows some interesting directionality if you are using long beads. Placed on the leg of a stitch a bead will slant diagonally.

There are 3 ways to hold a bead horizontally: on a purl thread at the arch of a stitch, carried in front of a slipped stitch, or on the strand between stitches.

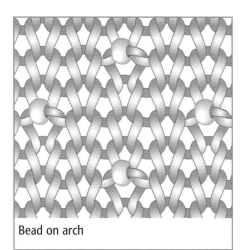

Bead on arch

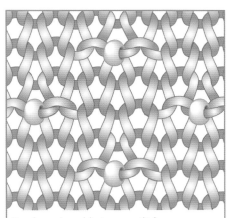

Bead on strand between stitches

Beads between stitches or in front of stitches are rather independent; the strands that hold them are not immediately involved in a stitch. Beads incorporated in a stitch must be locked into position by twisting the legs of the stitch or putting the bead on a purl bump (the arch). The final positions of the beads are different with these two methods, but both hold the beads securely in place. It is always nice to have a choice.

Slip stitch beading provides a firm fabric background, but the beads themselves sit rather loosely. This can be worked on either side of stockinette, or on any pattern that will tolerate a slipped stitch. These include stockinette and reverse stockinette, as well as patterns with stitches worked with the yarn carried in front (see WYIF, page 46). If necessary, slip several stitches to accommodate the length of a bead. The slipped stitches of this method will diminish some vertical stretching in the garment, but will also affect the horizontal stretch. Make test swatches to check the way this affects the garment ease.

Row 1: Work the stitch before the bead position. With the yarn on the right side of the fabric, slide the bead into place, then slip the stitch without slack in the working strand. Continue working across the row as required.

Row 2: Work across the row, working the slipped stitch as needed.

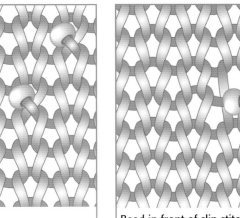

Bead on leg of stitch

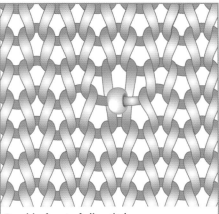

Bead in front of slip stitch

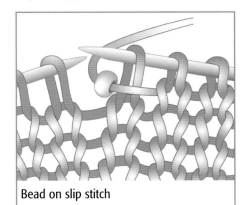

Bead on slip stitch

For allover beading alternate knit stitches with bead slip stitches. In the following row, carry the bead on the right side of the fabric, slip the bead stitches of the preceding row and place beads above the blank stitches. Make sure all the beads are on the right side of the fabric. The effect will be that of seed stitch, with beads replacing purl stitches on the right side of the fabric. The overall slipped pattern takes both horizontal and vertical stretch out of this fabric, so test swatches to make sure there is enough ease for any garment you are planning.

PURLED BEAD STITCH is extraordinarily versatile. The bead is placed in a stitch one row before it is required. On whichever side of the fabric you are working, insert the bead into the stitch. On the next row work the bead stitch so that it is a purl stitch on the right side of the work, locking the bead into the arch of the stitch. The purl stitch will not be noticed, but the bead prominent on it will be. When sliding the bead into place initially, push the bead through the stitch with your fingertip or the needle.

Knit row placement:

Row 1: On the knit row, insert needle, wrap the yarn, pop the bead through the stitch, and finish the stitch.

Row 2: On the purl row, purl the stitches without beads. On stitches with beads, insert the needle to knit, slide the bead over the source needle to face you; wrap the working yarn and draw the stitch through. (The bead will still be facing you.) Before sliding the bead stitch off the needle, bring the working yarn under the bead and to the front of the work, preparing to purl the next stitch.

Purl row placement:

Row 1: On the purl row, insert the needle, wrap the yarn with the bead on it, and finish the stitch.

Row 2: On the knit row bead stitches, push the bead to face you. Insert the needle beneath the bead and knit the stitch. Carry the working strand below the bead to the next stitch.

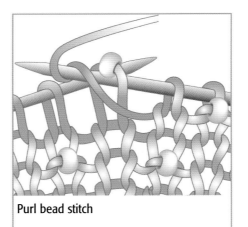

Purl bead stitch

Variation:

Worked on a purl row, this variation places the bead between stitches on the fabric knit side and twists the stitch.

Row 1: Knit the stitch before the bead. While the yarn is still in the knit position, slip the bead to the far side (the right side) of the knitting. Bring the yarn back to the purl position and purl the stitch following the bead.

Row 2: Knit across the row, knitting the bead stitch through the back loop to twist the stitch. This makes the fabric firmer and keeps the bead from slipping through to the back.

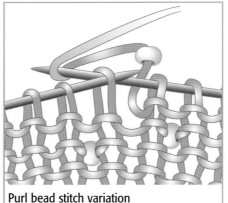

Purl bead stitch variation

Slide several beads into place between knit stitches to create a decorative strand of beads between stitches. Stacking these strands in columns creates a glittery, lacy fabric that may need to be lined.

A third variation places the bead on the strand between stitches on reverse stockinette as you work the purl row.

Purl the stitch before the bead. Slide the bead against the completed stitch. Purl the next stitch. This technique can also be used to place a decorative strand of several beads between stitches.

RIBBON

Knitting with ribbon is interesting since it is broad and flat rather than round like yarn. Many of the knitting ribbons and tapes available are themselves knitted, and are more sinuous, fluid, and flexible than woven ribbon. When held and used the same way yarn is used, knitting causes twists in the flat structure, producing long coils of ribbon and a slinky, stretchy fabric. Most knitting ribbons on the market are used this way.

Traditional ribbon knitting emphasizes the flatness and sheen of ribbon. Folds catch the light, resulting in a rich, glossy fabric that in some stitches looks woven and in other patterns looks frothy. Reverse knitting (see page 85) aids this process. Simple stitches are the most dramatic in this medium, since the goal is to display the sheen of flat surfaces as much as possible. Once you are comfortable with the wrapping technique, ribbon knitting becomes a luxurious pastime. Even a small project is sure to be admired and treasured.

Cold blocking with water can spoil the finish or run the dyes on space-dyed ribbons. Dry block ribbon knitting with a dry iron and a press cloth, just as you press the ribbon for knitting.

MATERIALS are narrow ribbons of all kinds, and large needles. Beginning steps in ribbon knitting are easier when done with wood or bamboo needles, because slick ribbon stitches leap off needles at the least provocation. Use a needle with a diameter wider than the ribbon, to make stitches large enough to keep from compressing and distorting the ribbon as it passes through them in the next row. A size 11 (8 mm) or 13 (9 mm) needle is suitable for 7 mm ribbon. Larger needles may be even better.

Silk embroidery ribbon is soft and very flexible, and is excellent for both flat and frothy effects. It is wonderful for special gifts. You can practice on polyester or other synthetic craft ribbons, either in hanks or on spools. Heavy satin ribbons are beautiful in the woven patterns. One way to be sure you are not twisting the ribbon is to make a mark along one side (3 or 4 yards of ribbon should be enough for this experiment) and to knit the ribbon so that you do not see the mark.

WOVEN STITCHES are wrapped on the needle without twisting. Ribbon goes into a stitch flat and comes out of a stitch flat, so any twisting is confined to the ribbon below the needle; for each twist that would have been on a needle there is a twist in the working strand of ribbon. Slip a rubber band around the ribbon to secure it (ribbon slithers off spools and out of hanks, right before your eyes). Every few stitches, pick up the secured spool or hank of ribbon and let it twirl in the air to untwist. Any crease in the ribbon will throw off the evenness of the stitch and the fabric. It is always worth the effort to heat an iron and smooth out any creases. Test a few inches of ribbon with the iron to see which setting presses without damaging the ribbon, and use a press cloth if necessary. The iron setting should be dry, because steam will damage the finish of many ribbons.

FLAT STITCHES are highly directional. The width of ribbon causes stitches to slant out to the left or right like increases, rather than being simple columns of Vs. Alternating rows of regular and reverse knitting angle the smooth ribbon folds to the right and the left. When pressed, the angles flatten to form distinctive and intriguing woven-looking patterns. Wrap a length of ribbon around a knitting needle to see how it works. Hold the button of the needle in your right hand and wrap the ribbon clockwise around the needle. At the natural slant, ribbon lies flat against the needle. Hold the needle the same way and wrap the ribbon counterclockwise to slant the ribbon in the opposite direction. These angles are preserved or manipulated with the different types of knit and purl stitches.

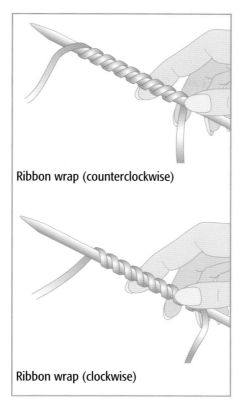

Ribbon wrap (counterclockwise)

Ribbon wrap (clockwise)

RIBBON CASTING-ON should have as few twists as possible. The primitive half-hitch cast-on is perfect here (see page 41). Make a single loop knot around your finger and slip it onto the needle. Lay the ribbon flat across the top of the needle. Pick up this "open loop" between your left thumb and index finger and rotate it clockwise, to make a loop like a 9. Slip the loop onto the needle. There should be no twist in the ribbon as it lies flat across the needle and drops below the horizontal ribbon strand below the needle. Do this for each stitch. When you work the first row, slip the first stitch and knit the second.

Another way to begin is to cast on with yarn, perhaps with the crocheted vanishing cast-on, and begin the ribbon knitting after this. When you pick out the cast-on, just run a length of ribbon through the loops to secure them, and stitch the ends of the ribbon. This will make a flat seam if you are going to sew the bottom of the piece for a pillow or bag.

RIBBON BINDING-OFF can be done by running a length of ribbon through the loops on the needle, leaving a flat edge for a seam or a drawstring. If

you are careful about wrapping the ribbon and lifting the stitches, a simple lifted bind-off makes a graceful scroll edge.

A row of garter stitch makes a wonderful ruffle. End the pattern on a knit row, then turn the work and work an over knit row (see below), binding-off as you go. If you end on a purl row, turn and work an over purl row (see below), binding-off as you go.

Knit stitches are worked through the back leg to avoid twisting the stitch on the needle.

UNDER AND OVER STITCHES Unlike yarn knitting, ribbon knitting makes a distinction between stitches wrapped under the needle and those wrapped over the needle. Different pattern stitches require that you know both varieties of knit and purl. We refer to them as Under and Over stitches. Each type uses a different amount of ribbon and slants a different way, making differences in the finished fabrics.

Over knit: insert the needle through the back leg of the stitch. Bring the ribbon up over the top of the needle and wrap it toward you, counterclockwise.

Under knit: insert the needle through the back leg of the stitch. Bring the ribbon up from under the needle and wrap it away from you, clockwise.

REVERSE KNITTING (see page 85) controls the amount of twist in knit stitches. Once you have learned the reverse technique you will find it useful in a number of situations. As in the knit stitches, wrapping the ribbon under or over makes a difference in the look of reverse knit and purl stitches. In the woven-looking patterns reverse knitting replaces purling.

Under reverse knit: insert the left (empty) needle into the stitch from front to back. Bring the ribbon up from beneath the needle and wrap it over the needle away from you, clockwise.

Over reverse knit: insert the left (empty) needle into the stitch from front to back. Bring the ribbon over the top of the needle and wrap it toward you, counterclockwise.

PURLING is used when there is a need for both knit and purl stitches in the same row. Under purling is theoretically possible. If you find a situation that requires it, feel free.

The stitches in the row immediately below the needle will be vertical and squeezed until the row above them is worked and they can relax to the right or left as needed in the pattern. After that, as the fabric forms use the needle point to pull and tweak a squeezed or twisted stitch into a smoother position.

Tension should be loose. It is tempting to cinch the ribbon down to keep it flat, but this has the opposite effect. Lay the ribbon across the needle and draw it through the stitches below with as much ease as you can, while keeping the stitches even. A stiff ribbon will resist being drawn too tightly; treat delicate silk ribbon exactly the same way.

TABBY-WEAVE is as elegant a ribbon pattern as you will find, and is pure simplicity to knit. It is an excellent introduction to the craft. This pattern works best with heavy ribbon. Do not crowd the stitches; size 11(8 mm) or 13(9 mm) needles work well with ¼" ribbon. Cast on any number of stitches.

Row 1: Under knit across the row. Do not turn the work.

Row 2: Reverse under knit across the row.

Repeat these 2 rows for the desired length.

FISH SCALE PATTERN uses two different sized needles to achieve the undulations of this fascinating pattern, worked over an odd number of stitches. A size 13 (9 mm) and size 11 (8 mm) needle work well for ¼" ribbon. Use the large needle for purl rows and the small needle for knit rows.

Row 1: * Under knit 2 stitches together through the back loop; drop only the first stitch from the source needle. * Repeat from * to * across the row until the last stitch remains. Under knit the last stitch by itself.

Row 2: Reverse under knit each stitch, across the row.

Repeat these 2 rows for the desired length.

INCREASES AND DECREASES are worked on edge stitches to avoid disrupting the pattern or slant of the stitches.

JOINING new lengths of ribbon is easiest if you sew the ribbons together at the seams to minimize slipping. Just a stitch will hold them together until you can fold them into the seam while finishing the garment. On an exposed edge clip the ribbon, fold the end under, and secure it with a few stitches on the back of the fabric.

FINISHING ribbon knits is quite different from finishing yarn knitting. Ribbon knits are pressed to flatten the fabric and accentuate the folds of the patterns, even on ruffled stitches. Heat the iron only as hot as the ribbon will stand, depending on whether you use silk or synthetic ribbons. Many ribbons are adversely affected by moisture, so test for color-fastness before pressing. If the color is fast, place the fabric on a well-padded ironing board and press on silk setting through a damp press cloth. Then set the iron to the lowest setting and press out the dampness in the piece. If the color runs, place the fabric on an old towel and use an old, dampened towel to press the fabric, and another old towel to press it dry. Do not stretch the fabric, but flatten it evenly to crease the folds you have so carefully made. For small pieces of ribbon work that will be used for purses, etc. consider using a fusible interlining when lining the finished piece to stabilize the stitches.

SEWING PIECES TOGETHER is just like dressmaking. The pieces should be basted together rather than pinned, to avoid marring the ribbon. Sew by hand for the most accurate and invisible seams.

TUBULAR KNITTING

TUBULAR KNITTING, DOUBLE KNITTING, REVERSIBLE KNITTING are techniques for simultaneously knitting two layers of fabric flat, rather than in the round. The layers can be either completely separate from each other (tubular) or interlocked (reversible), so glove fingers as well as reversible afghans are possible on 2 single-pointed needles. The fabrics of single color and 2-color fabrics differ slightly in their construction. This is also possible on double-pointed or circular needles, but there is little magic in that.

Use tubular (Kitchener) cast-on (see pages 40–41) as if you are casting on a K1, P1 ribbing. Both odd and even numbers will work, so long as you strictly alternate knit and purl stitches. This cast-on will produce an open-ended tube using the magic formula below.

SINGLE-COLOR TUBE requires that you suspend disbelief for a row or two. If you knit AND purl the stitches across the row it produces a single layer of ribbing. This is nothing new. The magic occurs when you treat knit and purl stitches differently.

The Magic: Knit ONLY the knit stitches. SLIP the purl stitches purlwise without working them. At the end of the row, turn the work. Work the same way on each row, knitting only the knit stitches, slipping only the purl stitches, turning the work at the end.

Slipping the purl stitches confines the working strand of yarn to the knit face of the fabric, linking the knit stitches side by side as they face you. After turning the work, knit stitches of the other side are linked. The fabric of each side will be normal stockinette fabric, one layer thick. It is a tube on one needle, connected to the other layer only at the row ends. Skeptics can slip the knit and purl stitches onto separate needles and look inside the tube. Slip them back onto one needle, alternating knit and purl.

REVERSIBLE PATTERNS use the tubular cast-on (see tubular cast-on, pages 40–41), for any number of stitches. This will produce a closed tube. For an open tube use the tubular cast-on twice, each time with half the stitches and one color. Then slip the cast-on stitches onto one needle, alternating colors. Alternately knit and purl with the colors, holding the strands in separate hands. Both strands of yarn must move to the back of the work for a knit stitch, both strands must move to the front of the fabric for each purl stitch, even though you work the stitch with only one strand. Otherwise the unused color will lie on the outside of the tube, spoiling the color pattern. Maintain the strict alternation of knit and purl stitches when switching color segments from side to side.

Working with only one strand at a time requires two passes down each row using a circular or double-pointed needle. On the first row knit the knit stitches with the first color and slip the stitches of the other color. At the end of the row, slide the work back to the end of the needle and work the second color stitches in the same direction. Then turn the work to knit the row on the other side in two passes.

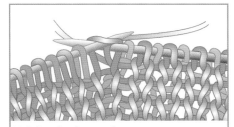

Knitting the front color

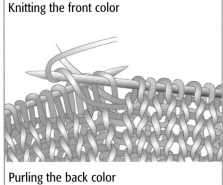

Purling the back color

STRANDED BROCADE is made by deliberately not moving the unused color to the front and back, letting the unused strand lie outside the knitted tube. Yes, we call it a mistake just above, but if you do a mistake systematically it becomes a design.

Stranded brocade can be worked on both sides of the fabric at the same time, but it is hard on the brain, thinking of the negative image of the side you are not seeing. Get used to the technique by working the front of the fabric while leaving the brocade strand to the back of the work as you knit with the main color. Any charted seed stitch or 2-color pattern will work for this.

MULTICOLOR PATTERNS can be worked in a 2-needle tube just as they are on circular needles, but it is inefficient and rather tedious. If you can knit a multicolor tube on 2 needles you can certainly do it on one circular needle, which we recommend.

Smooth edges are very easy if you leave a border of your favorite color on the edge of the second side. Do not change segments of the color pattern at the edge of either side or the yarns will be visibly twisted along the edge in a messy way. Work all the edge stitches of both sides with the same color. When working the first stitch of each row, lay the unused strand across the working needle, between the fabric and the working strand of yarn. Knit or purl with the working color, taking care not to catch up the unused color in the new stitch. Working around the unused strand twists the 2 colors together, joining the edges. Move both colors to work the second stitch and tug them to pull the strands firmly inside the seam. Continue knitting and purling alternate stitches.

FELTING AND FULLING

These two techniques compact and unify animal hair fibers into a less elastic and more dense strand or fabric. Dating back to perhaps 3000 B.C., felt was useful in cold, harsh climates to keep out the elements. Felt does not require skill in sewing, weaving, or shaping, since it does not fray at the edges. But knitted or woven fabrics can be felted for even warmer, more durable garments, so the technique was used in cultures with high or minimal textile-making skills. There are two kinds of felt, the kind made of fibers kneaded together with heat and moisture, and the kind made from yarn that has been woven or knitted, then kneaded into a more solid fabric. This is also called "fulling," and has been the finishing touch to many fine wool fabrics for centuries.

In its least desirable form, felt is a cashmere sweater that has gone through the washer and dryer and is now 8 sizes too small. But felting done deliberately produces beautiful hats, the fabric for both poodle skirts and housing for nomadic Mongolians, and garments that are dense and stretchy.

WOOL has exterior protein scales. Under warm, moist conditions the fibers can be pounded, kneaded, or agitated until the scales interlock. This forms the dense mat of fibers that is felt. If the original structure was yarn that has been knitted into a shape, the shape will be retained and the fibers that are already somewhat unified will interlock most in the areas that are adjacent. Knitted fabric will keep the structure of the stitches,

91

Felted baby booties, Pitter Patter project, page 111.

but the yarn fibers will mat with those beside, above, and below them, leaving a dense, somewhat stretchy fabric.

For any of these techniques use pure wool yarn, *not* the washable kind. Though woolen knit or Germantown type yarns are best for felting, a worsted can be used if that is all you can find. Brown Sheep Yarn Company's single ply worsted will felt better than a 3- or 4-ply. Wool roving from spinning supply houses, Icelandic Lopi yarn, or other very loosely twisted wools will also work very well. Pure kid mohair or angora (rabbit) yarns felt very well, but these luxury fibers are often plied with a binding thread that will not felt.

For home experimentation felt-making can be as simple as knitting a wool garment and throwing it into the washer. A little very hot water with lots of soap lubricates and softens the fibers, allowing them to interlock. Do not use fabric softener because it keeps the fibers slippery, preventing felting rather than aiding it. Add old bath towels or jeans to create friction and aid felting. Since dyes run, the friction fabrics will change color. Agitate the load on the most vigorous cycle there is. Take the wool garments out periodically to see if they have shrunk to the right size. This technique works for mittens, hats, and socks that will be slippers.

EMBROIDERY AND KNITTING

EMBROIDERY AND KNITTING go together. There is something about a soft piece of knitted fabric that invites beautiful threads and stitches. Felted fabrics have been decorated with embroidery for centuries in Scandinavia. The long winters gave a broad canvas for anything colorful, and warm clothing is warmer with gay flowers and bright designs.

CREWEL STITCHES are generally suitable for knitted fabric. Traditional stitches for this kind of work are satin stitch, herringbone stitch, stem stitch, and French and bullion knots. Couching stitches, cross stitches, silk ribbon, and all other manner of embroidery wait for the right garment. A felted vest with crewel flowers filled and

couched with gold would melt an iceberg. A silk bolero with a delicate spray of silk flowers on the shoulder embellishes a strapless gown on a chilly evening. Refer to *Donna Kooler's Encyclopedia of Needlework*, Leisure Arts, 2000.

Knitted fabric is stretchy and open. To work close stitches on anything other than felted knitting, use a reinforcing fabric behind the embroidery. Silk organza is a good choice. Lightweight, non-woven interfacing can also be used and carefully trimmed, especially if you use an outlining stitch afterwards. Draw the design onto the reinforcing fabric and stitch it securely in place on the knitting. A crewel needle is necessary to pierce the reinforcing fabric and yarn. Embroidering with one hand above the fabric and one hand below, passing the needle completely through the knitting, produces the best results.

CROSS STITCH adapts charted designs to the almost-square units of stockinette knitting. This is a wonderful way to indulge in cross stitch without having to thread tiny needles. The knit stitch is a natural for people used to counting 2 threads by 2 threads. When you look at the front of stockinette you can see that each stitch (a V, 2 threads wide) is connected to 2 threads above and below (the legs of the stitches above and below). Bring the needle up in the center of the threads between 2 rows and 2 columns of V stitches. From this position you can count 2 connecting threads in either direction and across a V stitch in either direction to insert the needle. Insert it under the V stitch and out the other side for the beginning of the second

To get the covering effect of cross stitch, both of the V threads and both of the between-stitch threads at the upper and lower edges of the V stitch must be crossed during stitching. Usually stitching begins from the lower left corner of the stitch, making on leg to the upper right corner of each stitch in the row, then crosses from lower right to upper left on the second pass across the row. Though it is not necessary to work from

left to right, whichever way you work the top crossing legs should lie in the same direction for visual harmony. If the 2 thread x 2 thread rule is followed, you can work designs horizontally or vertically along the rows of knitting, allowing adaptation of border designs for vertical stripes, etc.

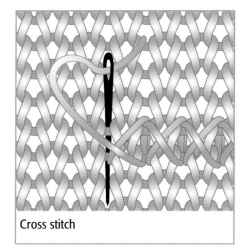

Cross stitch

Embroidery yarn of a similar diameter will cover the knitting best. For delicate or dressy effects, a shiny floss, reeled silk yarn, or even embroidery ribbons can be used. On the wrong side weave the ends into the embroidery material to hide it, knotting it around a similar strand or securing ribbon with a stitch or two of sewing thread.

DUPLICATE STITCH (SWISS DARNING) on stockinette addresses the practical reasons to embroider knitting. A strand of yarn replicates the stitches in a piece of knitting for mending, reinforcing, or just for the joy of color. Simple duplication of knit stitches is soothing and enjoyable work, and can turn a simple cardigan (even a commercially made one) into a designer original in one pleasant evening.

We describe the process from right to left, the direction most people knit, but it works equally well from left to right. The essential process follows the thread of one stitch over and under the neighboring threads.

Materials can be anything suitable for embroidery on the sweater. Persian needlepoint yarns provide the widest range of color if you are working on dry clean only wool knits. Use washable embroidery materials if you are working on a washable sweater. The embroidery strand should be large enough to cover the knitting yarn, and can even be somewhat larger for embossed effects. While it is easier to embroider with smooth strands, textured ones can produce exciting results, such as fuzzy angora bunnies or bouclé sheep. Start with about 18" of yarn. Delicate textured yarns may fray even at this length, so cut the embroidery strand when it starts to look frowsy, and begin a new one.

Use a tapestry or yarn needle with a generous eye. Knitting stretches to accommodate a needle, so make yourself and the embroidery yarn comfortable. Fold the yarn around the top of the needle and slide it down to the point, then take the flat fold of yarn and insert it through the eye.

Bring the embroidery strand up from the back of the work, leaving a 4" tail. The needle should emerge at the point of the V, beneath the back strand of the stitch below. Follow the yarn path up the right leg of the V. Slip the needle horizontally behind both legs of the stitch above. Stretch the knitting a little to avoid splitting the yarn as you sew. Follow the left leg of the V back down to the point. If you are working several stitches horizontally in a row, insert the needle under both strands of the neighboring lower stitch at the point of the V. These strands form an upside-down V. Bring the needle out at the point of the next stitch to be worked, and continue across the row, starting and ending each stitch at the point of the V.

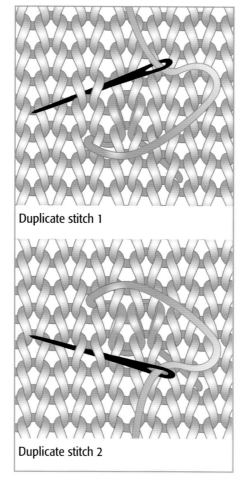

Duplicate stitch 1

Duplicate stitch 2

To work back: If you are comfortable working from left to right as in reverse knitting, work that way, or turn the work upside down to continue working from right to left on alternate rows. If working vertically, skip one vertical strand on the back of the work, then bring the needle up in the center of the preceding stitch. Pass the needle behind the 2 legs of the stitch above (or below). Complete the stitch by inserting the needle in the center of the beginning stitch.

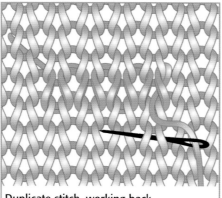

Duplicate stitch, working back

FINISHING TECHNIQUES

JOINS AND SEAMS allow you to create, preserve, and adjust knitted garments. Even garments knitted in the round may require some small seams or joins, and eventually most things need repair. We hope that since you always knit a gauge swatch before starting a project, altering knits is necessary only to satisfy the whims of fashion or to allow more people of varied sizes to wear one of your hand-knit creations.

SEAMS are necessary where edges are joined, whether at the sides, shoulders, or sleeves. Not all edges have the same requirements, but usually seams should be flexible and small. A spreading type of pattern, such as cables, is drawn in one row before the seam row, to eliminate excess bulk. Occasionally an external seam is used as a design feature. Shoulders have the weight of the garment hanging from them, and are aided by a firm seam. Armhole seams must be stretchy, strong, and unobtrusive. Side seams and sleeve seams should be minimal; sock toe seams should be undetectable. There is a seam for each need and each fabric, fine or bulky.

In flat knitted garments with edge shaping and decorative pattern stitches, an unpatterned selvage makes the difference between an unobtrusive seam and a difficult seam. To eliminate unnecessary seams, consider adapting patterns to knitting in the round. Sleeves can be knitted in the round in most instances, taking care that the finished dimensions match the bodice. Flat pattern garments can often be adapted to seamless knitting, even with side shaping, by marking where a seam would have been, and shaping on either side of it. False seams are sometimes added for fold lines without sewing.

Materials for seams are not necessarily the yarns used for the garments. Chunky, textured, and novelty yarns are not suitable for seams. Consider using embroidery floss, crochet or tatting threads, or Persian yarns to match the color while giving you a choice of thickness. Make sure the thread you choose is compatible with the cleaning required by the knitting yarn.

Knitting worsted, fingering yarn, sport weight yarn, and other smooth, well-twisted knitting yarns can be used for seams as they are, or split into a few plies for a finer thread. When using the knitting yarn for the seam, leave a long tail and wind it into a butterfly or ball to keep it out of the way until you need it for the seam. About 1½ to 2 times the length of the seam is enough thread to sew it. You can cut the strand into shorter sections for sewing.

Choose a blunt tapestry or yarn needle with a generous eye to avoid fraying the sewing yarn. When pairing the edges to be joined, use coil-less safety pins or baste the pieces together. Knitted fabric sheds straight pins. If you use pattern stitch rows to do your counting, pin and seam them from the right side of the garment to make sure the match is perfect, especially with stripes.

SEWN SEAMS give a precise edge. The smaller the seam, the neater and more comfortable the garment. This is especially true in chunky knits, where a single stitch can be a half inch wide. Sewn seams worked from the right side of the fabric allow you to see exactly what you are doing, especially on complex color or texture patterns. When working on the inside is necessary, check the outside of the seam frequently.

Picking up the eye of the stitch makes an invisible seam in full-fashioned or straight stockinette and reverse stockinette, and in ribbing. The row counts in the pieces being joined must be accurate within 3 rows. If you are joining pieces that are less accurate than that the seam is likely to be puckered, no matter how you do it. A single stitch chain selvage (see page 65) can be worked with this method of seaming only on the right side of stockinette fabric. The join is best with a plain stockinette edge. The eye of a stitch is the arch of the stitch below. On stockinette fabric it is found at the base of the V of a stitch. In this join the needle crosses from one piece to another, catching the eye of each edge stitch on each piece. The needle enters each stitch once and exits each stitch once.

The threads between columns of stitches are sometimes referred to as the eye of a stitch, but these horizontal "between" threads are not part of a stitch. A seam of "between" threads will be bulkier than one of edge stitches. Turning the knitting between rows loops an edge stitch around the outside leg of the stitch above; the eye of one stitch will be offset every 2nd row. It does not make a difference in the seam, however. Bring the needle up below the twist and insert it above the twist.

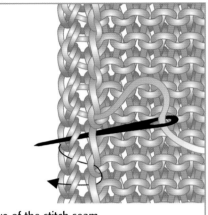

Eye of the stitch seam

STOCKINETTE SEAM

Lay side by side the two edges to be joined, right side up. Work with the right side of the fabric facing you,

Bring the needle up below the eye of the first stitch, one thread in from the edge.

Cross over to the first stitch of the opposite piece. Insert the needle in the center of the first stitch, front to back.

Bring the needle up above the eye of the stitch above, back to front.

Cross over and insert the needle in the hole it came from, front to back.

Bring the needle up above the eye of the stitch above, back to front.

Cross over and insert the needle in the hole it just came from, front to back.

Bring the needle up above the eye of the stitch above.

Continue crossing the fabric, inserting the needle in the hole it emerged from, then bring it up above the eye of the next stitch. Pull the working yarn firmly as you go up the seam, pulling the thread very tightly at top and bottom when you have finished the seam. Then stretch the seam vertically, to give a little ease.

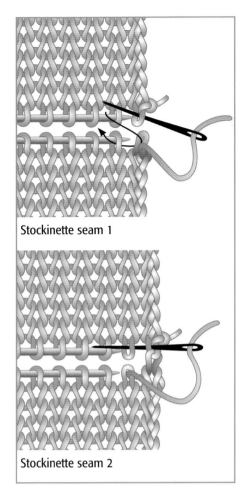

Stockinette seam 1

Stockinette seam 2

RIBBING SEAMS should maintain the ribbing pattern. A stockinette ribbing will have one stitch V on the outside of the seam. When working 1 x 1 ribbing, ending each edge with a Knit stitch will create 1 exterior V. For a 2 x 2 ribbing, end one piece with 1 knit stitch and its seam-mate with 2 knit stitches. The half stitch each donates to the seam will create 1 exterior V on the seam. To avoid this problem completely, use a crocheted vanishing cast-on (see page 41), knit the pieces without ribbing, and seam them. Then remove the vanishing cast-on, pick up the stitches on a circular needle, and knit the ribbing in one piece from the top down.

REVERSE STOCKINETTE without a selvage can be joined by this method on the wrong (knit) side of the fabric, producing an invisible seam without the curling edge problem. Put the right (purled) sides of the fabric face down. Work with the knit side facing you. The seam will form facing you, with the purled side of the fabric down.

Insert the needle into the center of the first stitch from knit side to purl side.

Cross to the opposite piece and insert the needle in the center of the first stitch from purl to knit side.

Bring the needle up on the purl side, above the eye of the stitch above.

Cross to the opposite piece and insert the needle in the hole it came from, front purl to knit side.

Bring the needle up above the eye of the stitch above, from knit to purl side.

Cross over and insert the needle in the hole it just came from, from purl to knit side.

Bring the needle up above the eye of the stitch above.

Continue crossing the fabric, inserting the needle in the hole it emerged from, then bring it up above the eye of the next stitch. Pull the working yarn firmly as you go up the seam, pulling the thread very tightly at top and bottom when you have finished the seam. Then stretch the seam from top and bottom to give a little vertical ease.

GARTER STITCH SEAM uses a simple running stitch to join butted edges without bulk, but there may be tiny gaps in the seam when stretched. Pulling the thread tight enough to completely eliminate this may gather the fabric of the seam. The bumpiness of garter stitch should conceal this adequately. You can also make a seam by picking up the eye of the stitch on alternate rows (the ones with Vs facing you), as you would with stockinette.

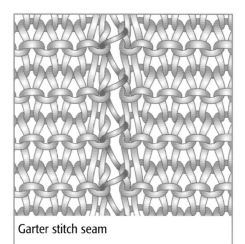

Garter stitch seam

KNITTED AND CROCHETED SEAMS are for people or projects that require something different.

JOINERY BIND-OFF joins two pieces and binds-off the resulting row as you go. It is excellent for shoulders or seams in garments knit wrist-to-wrist. One row before you are ready to bind-off, put the stitches on a holder to await assembly. If you have already worked the pieces and bound them off, when you want to make the seam undo the final stitches of each piece and rip out the bind-off row one stitch at a time. Put the stitches of both edges onto one needle, alternating one stitch from each piece. To work the join, knit or purl 2 stitches together each time (one from each piece), while using your preferred bind-off as if you were binding-off the last row of a single piece.

A variation of this is useful to set in sleeves, even though the edges are bound off. After the shoulder seam is worked, pin together the right sides of the sleeve cap and armhole. With a small (2.25 mm) needle, pick up 2 stitches (see page 94) through both layers, just inside the selvages. Knit these 2 stitches and lift-over bind-off one (see page 50). Pick up and knit another stitch and bind off one stitch. Continue around the armhole.

PIPED SEAM simultaneously makes a horizontal or vertical seam and covers the seam with I-cord. (See page 69.) Cast on 3 stitches, then pick up just the inner strands of the 2 edge stitches being joined. Knit the first 2 stitches. Knit together the 2 seam stitches and the 3rd stitch, lifting the 2 seam stitches off the point first, then the 3rd stitch. Working in this order keeps the seam stitches under the cord. Slide the stitches back down the needle and begin the new row.

SLIP STITCH SEAM is a crocheted seam that is quick to work, stretchy, and can be used when the two pieces do not have identical row counts. As if these advantages were not enough, it is easy to do. The joining yarn should be only about half the diameter of the knitting yarn, to eliminate bulk.

Lay the edges to be joined right sides together, and pin them with coil-less safety pins. Use a crochet hook the same

diameter as your knitting needles or a little smaller. Work through the selvage stitches if possible, or in the "between" threads beside the selvage. Make a slip knot and draw it up through both pieces. Insert the crochet hook through both pieces and draw a loop through both pieces and the loop on the hook. Repeat this once in each row or stitch. Do not draw the seam too tight as you work. To finish, draw up a final loop, cut the yarn, and draw the end through the last loop.

GRAFTING (Kitchener stitch) invisibly joins two horizontal edges, "live" or bound-off, and is used where no seam should exist, such as sock toes and heels, or mends. It is completely stretchy and identical to knitting. When you want the visual blending of grafting but the reinforcement of a seam, such as in shoulders, grafting over bound-off stitches permits both.

Grafting can be as annoying or as enjoyable as children's sewing cards. The needle follows the path of a knitted stitch, looping around the legs of the row above and through the arches of the stitches below. Same direction grafting is used for a horizontal mend, to add pockets, etc. Head-butting grafting occurs where the top of knitting meets the top of knitting, such as in shoulders and sock toes. The stitches are mirror images, and must be offset by half a stitch for grafting. This presents no real problem in stockinette or garter stitch, but ribbings, cables, and color patterns will not line up perfectly. Graft onto a stockinette row whenever possible because ribbings, cables, and color patterns will not line up perfectly.

Material is usually the knitting yarn used for the garment. If color contrast is desired, the same diameter yarn should be used. Because grafting pulls the entire length of yarn through each stitch, delicate or textured yarns will wear during the process. Use short lengths of such yarns if the graft is a very wide one, or choose a different method of joining.

Graft on or off the needles. Block pieces before grafting. You may prefer to graft sock toes on the needles. Work on a large, flat surface to support the fabric.

FLAT GRAFTING makes it easier to understand the mechanics. The grafting yarn passes through each stitch twice, imitating the knitted loop. It is a fascinating process. The needle exits a stitch, passes once through 2 more stitches, and then returns through the first hole from which it emerged. This is true for every stitch in the line of grafting. The difference between knit and purl stitches is the direction the yarn enters and exits a stitch, the front or back. This determines whether the grafting yarn connects stitches behind the stitch legs in front of them.

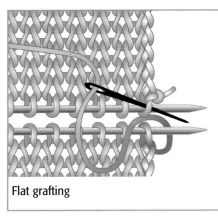

Flat grafting

STOCKINETTE GRAFTING loops pass behind the legs of stitches, creating smooth Vs on the front of the fabric. On the first pass through a stitch the needle always enters from back to front. The second pass of the needle is always from front to back. This is true for each stitch, top or bottom row alike.

Purl stitch loops pass in front of the legs of stitches, creating the purl bumps seen in reverse stockinette. The first pass of the needle through each stitch is always from front to back; the second pass is always from back to front. Each time the needle enters a stitch for the first time, it enters from the front; the second pass of the needle will enter from the back. This is true for each stitch, top or bottom row alike.

GARTER STITCH GRAFTING combines these two opposite techniques, one for the lower row and one for the higher row. For the bumpy stitches the first pass of the needle always enters stitches from the front. For the smooth stitches the first pass of the needle always enters stitches from the back.

ON THE NEEDLE STOCKINETTE GRAFTING is used for sock toes and other things you can't lay flat. Some people prefer this even for things you could lay flat. As with flat grafting, the grafting needle passes through each stitch twice. It exits a stitch, passes once through 2 more stitches, and then returns through the first hole from which it emerged. This is true for every stitch in the line of grafting. After you have worked the process done flat (see above), you will easily understand it on needles. A small verse will cement itself in your memory: Into the old stitch; out of the new.

When the grafting needle enters a stitch from the front (right side), it is entering that stitch for the second time. When the grafting needle emerges from the front of a stitch, that is the first pass of the needle. Wait until the second pass of the needle before you drop a stitch off. Draw the yarn around the edge of the knitting rather than across the top of the knitting needles.

To weave you through the first few stitches, hold two needles of knitting parallel, purl sides together. The right side of the front needle is facing you; the right side of the back needle is facing the opposite direction. Begin at the right side on the front needle. Do a preparatory stitch purlwise in the front stitch; take the needle around the right edge of the fabric and into the back stitch knitwise.

Front: Pass the needle knitwise through the first stitch. It is "into the old." Drop the stitch.

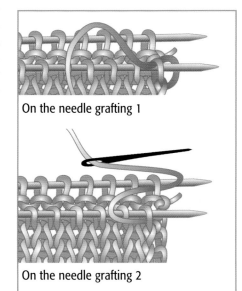

On the needle grafting 1

On the needle grafting 2

Front: Insert the needle purlwise in the second stitch. This is "out of the new." Leave the stitch on the needle.

Back: Pass the needle purlwise through the first stitch. This is "into the old." Drop the stitch.

Back: Insert the needle in the second stitch knitwise. This is "out of the new." Leave the stitch on the needle.

Repeat these 4 steps across the row. Remember that unless you are working a front stitch knitwise or a back stitch purlwise, it is not finished.

VERTICAL GRAFTING adds an extra column of stitches to make a smooth seam. Because it is worked over edges formed by flat knitting, it has the stability of grafting across a seam, but is seamless on the outside. This technique is ideal for work done flat that you would like to present seamless in the round. It requires a crochet hook of the same diameter as the knitting needles.

TECHNIQUE Pick up the eye of the stitch or the between thread as you would to sew a seam, but do not draw the sewing yarn taut. This creates a column of thread rungs exactly like a long run. Use a crochet hook the same diameter as the knitting needle to pick up the stitches as if fixing a dropped stitch (see page 47).

Reclaiming yarn is like washing your hair after a very unsuccessful set. It is useful if you need yarn for finishing an alteration, or to salvage yarn from abandoned projects. You can reclaim any yarn that can be washed, as well as some that say they can't be washed.

Any protein yarn can be washed, since the fibers are all processed with water in the yarn-making process, but the dyes may run. You can take the chance with water (since you scrapped the project), or you can make skeins and take them to a dry cleaner. Synthetics are usually water safe. Blended fiber yarns should be handled the same way they are laundered. Weird yarns may become more weird. If this is the second chance for the yarn, what do you have to lose?

Unravel the garment and wrap loose skeins from palm to elbow. Several small skeins are better than one big one. Tie together the yarn ends of each skein in a large, easy-to-find bow. ⊕

elegant beaded scarf

The appeal of pearl beads has never been more apparent than when surprisingly paired with luxurious alpaca yarn. Together they create an elegant accent that's perfect with a simple black dress or can become casually chic when worn with jeans and jacket.

DESIGN BY JANE DAVIS FOR BLUE SKY ALPACAS, INC.
Skill level: Intermediate
Finished project size: 8" x 52" (20 cm x 130 cm), excluding fringe

MATERIALS
Blue Sky Alpacas sport weight yarn 100% alpaca (2 ounces/57 grams, 134 yards/122.5 meters per skein): 4 skeins of Natural White (000)
Size 5 (3.75 mm) needles or size needed to obtain gauge
Size 6 pearl toned seed beads: 3½ ounces/96 grams
Size 11 pearl toned seed beads: 1 ounce/28 grams
DMC Perle cotton size 12 or beading thread size B or D
Beading needle, size 11 or 12

GAUGE
In seed st, 24 sts = 4" (10 cm)
Take time to check your gauge.

STITCH PATTERN
Begin this scarf at the center and knit in seed stitch to one end. Then slide pre-strung beads into a variation of plaited and twisted Stockinette stitch to create an elegant bead pattern. Pick up at the center of the scarf and repeat the pattern in the opposite direction. Add a delicate bead fringe and you will have created a fabulous bead knitted scarf.

NOTES

The number in parentheses after the row number is the number of beads required for that row. Slide that number of beads up near your knitting before beginning each row. About every four rows, it will be necessary to slide the remaining beads down the yarn in order to have enough yarn to knit with. To do this, keep the skein in a basket and slide about 4"–6" /10-15 cm at a time along the yarn until there is about 4'/1.2 meters of yarn without beads (except what is needed for the current) near your knitting. Be sure to make a gauge swatch, because if your gauge is too loose, the beads may not stay to the front of the work. To string the size 6 beads, thread the beading needle with 10"/25.5 cm length of perle cotton and tie to the end of a new skein of yarn. Be sure that the perle cotton is tied around the strand so that the yarn is folded in half, not knotted, or the beads will not slide onto the yarn. String the beads onto the yarn to measure 4'/1.2 meters meters or 630 beads.

ABBREVIATIONS

k = knit

p = purl

PB = purl a stitch, pushing bead into the stitch as it is made.

k tbl = knit through back loop–knit a stitch by inserting the needle into the back of the stitch and wrapping the yarn around the needle clockwise.

KB = same as knit through the back loop, pushing a bead into the stitch as it is made.

k2 tog tbl = knit two stitches together through the back loop as one.

p2 tog = purl two stitches together as one.

sl 1, p1, psso = slip next stitch purlwise, purl the next stitch, pass slipped stitch over the purled one.

sl 1, k1 tbl, psso = slip next stitch purlwise, knit the next st through the back loop, pass slipped stitch over the knitted one.

INSTRUCTIONS

FIRST END - CENTER

Cast on 48 stitches.

Row 1 (rs): (K1, p1) across.

Row 2: (P1, k1) across.

Continue to work in seed stitch until Center measures 17½"/ 44.5 cm; ending by working Row 2. Attach skein strung with beads.

BEAD ROWS

Row 1: (0) K3 tbl, (p1, k1) across to last 3 sts, k3 tbl.

Row 2: (4) P1, PB2, p2, k1, (p1, k1) across to last 6 sts, p3, PB2, p1.

Row 3: (4) K2 tbl, KB2 tbl, k2 tbl, (k1, p1) across to last 6 sts, k2 tbl, KB2 tbl, k2 tbl.

Row 4: (4) P3, PB2, p2, k1, (p1, k1) across to last 8 sts, p3, PB2, p3.

Row 5: (4) K4 tbl, KB2 tbl, k2 tbl, (k1, p1) across to last 8 sts, k2 tbl, KB2 tbl, k4 tbl.

Row 6: (4) P5, PB2, p2, k1, (p1, k1) across to last 10 sts, p3, PB2, p5.

Row 7: (4) K6 tbl, KB2 tbl, k2 tbl, (k1, p1) across to last 10 sts, k2 tbl, KB2, k6 tbl.

Row 8: (4) P7, PB2, p2, k1, (p1, k1) across to last 12 sts, p3, PB2, p7.

Row 9: (4) K8 tbl, KB2 tbl, k2 tbl,

(k1, p1) across to last 12 sts, k2 tbl, KB2 tbl, k8 tbl.

Row 10: (4) P9, PB2, p2, k1, (p1, k1) across to last 14 sts, p3, PB2, p9.

Row 11: (4) K 10 tbl, KB2, k2 tbl, (k1, p1) across to last 14 sts, k2 tbl, KB2, k 10 tbl.

Row 12: (8) P5, PB2, p4, PB2, p2, k1, (p1, k1) across to last 14 sts, p3, PB2, p4, PB2, p5.

Row 13: (14) K4 tbl, KB5, k3 tbl, KB2, k2 tbl, (k1, p1) 8 times, k2 tbl, KB2, k4 tbl, KB5, k3 tbl.

Row 14: (16) P3, PB6, p4, PB2, p2, k1, (p1, k1) 6 times, p3, PB2, p4, PB6, p3.

Row 15: (18) K3 tbl, KB7, k4 tbl, KB2, k2 tbl, (k1, p1) 6 times, k2 tbl, KB2, k4 tbl, KB7, k2 tbl.

Row 16: (14) P2, PB4, p3, PB1, p5, PB2, p2, k1, (p1, k1) 5 times, p3, PB2, p5, PB1, p3, PB4, p2.

Row 17: (12) K3 tbl, KB4, k9 tbl, KB2, k2 tbl, (k1, p1) 4 times, k2 tbl. KB2, k 10 tbl, KB4, k2 tbl.

Row 18: (12) P2, PB4, p 11, PB2, p2, k1, (p1, k1) twice, p3, PB2, p 11, PB4, p2.

Row 19: (18) K3 tbl, KB4, k5 tbl. KB3, k3 tbl, KB2, k2 tbl, (k1, p1) twice, k2 tbl, KB2, k4 tbl, KB3, k5 tbl, KB4, k2 tbl.

Row 20: (18) P3, PB3, p5, PB4, p4, PB2, p2, k1, p3, PB2, p4, PB4, p5, PB3, p3.

Row 21: (22) K4 tbl, KB4, k3 tbl, KB5, (k4 tbl, KB2) twice, k5 tbl, KB5, k3 tbl, KB4, k3 tbl.

Row 22: (16) P4, PB4, p3, PB2, p8, PB2, p2, PB2, p8, PB2, p3, PB4, p4.

Row 23: (18) K6 tbl, KB7, k9 tbl, KB4, k 10 tbl, KB7, k5 tbl.

Row 24: (20) P7, PB6, p4, PB3, p3, PB2, p3, PB3, p4, PB6, p7.

Row 25: (16) K 10 tbl, KB4, k3 tbl, KB4, k7 tbl, KB4, k3 tbl, KB4, k9 tbl.

Row 26: (30) P5, PB 10, p1, PB5, p6, PB5, p1, PB 10, p5.

Row 27: (20) K5 tbl, KB6, k3 tbl, KB2, k1 tbl, KB2, k 11 tbl, KB2, k1 tbl, KB2, k3 tbl, KB6, k4 tbl.

Row 28: (16) P4, PB4, p6, PB4, p 12, PB4, p6, PB4, p4.

Row 29: (14) K4 tbl, KB4, k8 tbl, KB3, k 11 tbl, KB3, k8 tbl, KB4, k3 tbl.

Row 30: (14) P4, PB4, p8, PB3, p10, PB3, p8, PB4, p4.

Row 31: (14) K4 tbl, KB5, k9 tbl, (KB2, k9 tbl) twice, KB5, k3 tbl.

Row 32: (20) P4, PB6, p1, PB3, p4, PB1, p 10, PB1, p4, PB3, p1, PB6, p4.

Row 33: (22) K5 tbl, KB5, k1 tbl, KB5, k3 tbl, KB1, k9 tbl, KB1, k3 tbl, KB5, k1 tbl, KB5, k4 tbl.

Row 34: (26) P1, PB2, p2, PB4, p1, PB6, p3, PB1, p8, PB1, p3, PB6, p1, PB4, p2, PB2, p1.

Row 35: (15) K2 tbl, KB2, k7 tbl, KB2, k3 tbl, KB2, k2 tbl, KB1, (k3 tbl, KB1) twice, k2 tbl, KB2, k3 tbl, KB2, k7 tbl, KB2, k2 tbl.

Row 36: (14) Sl 1, p1, psso, p1, (PB2, p5) twice, (PB1, p2) twice, PB2, (p2, PB1) twice,(p5, PB2) twice, p1, p2 tog—46 sts.

Row 37: (9) Sl 1, k1 tbl, psso, k1 tbl, KB2, k5 tbl, KB1, k 11 tbl, KB3, k 11 tbl, KB1, k4 tbl, KB2, k1 tbl, k2 tog tbl—44 sts.

Row 38: (10) Sl 1, p1, psso, p1, PB2, p4, PB1, p 10, PB4, p 10, PB1, p4, PB2, p1, p2 tog—42 sts.

Row 39: (15) Sl 1, k1 tbl, psso, k1 tbl, KB2, k 10 tbl, KB3, k1 tbl, KB5, k1 tbl, KB3, k 10 tbl, KB2, k1 tbl, k2 tog tbl—40 sts.

Row 40: (16) Sl 1, p1, psso, p1, PB2, p8, PB4, (p1, PB4) twice, p8, PB2, p1, p2 tog—38 sts.

Row 41: (17) Sl 1, k1 tbl, psso, k1 tbl, KB2, k7 tbl, KB5, k1 tbl, KB3, k1 tbl, KB5, k6 tbl, KB2, k1 tbl, k2 tog tbl—36 sts.

Row 42: (12) Sl 1, p1, psso, p1, PB2, p6, PB2, p2, PB1, p1, PB2, p1, PB1, p2, PB2, p6, PB2, P1, P2 tog—34 sts.

Row 43: (11) Sl 1, k1 tbl, psso, k1 tbl, KB2, k6 tbl, KB2, k2 tbl, (KB1, k1 tbl) twice, KB1, k2 tbl, KB2, k5 tbl, KB2, k1 tbl, k2 tog tbl—32 sts.

Row 44: (8) Sl 1, p1, psso, p1, PB2, p9, PB4, p9, PB2, p1, p2 tog—30 sts.

Row 45: (6) Sl 1, k1 tbl, psso, k1 tbl, KB2, k9 tbl, KB3, k8 tbl, KB2, k1 tbl, k2 tog tbl—28 sts.

Row 46: (6) Sl 1, p1, psso, p1, PB2, (p8, PB2) twice, p1, p2 tog—26 sts.

Row 47: (9) Sl 1, k1 tbl, psso, k1 tbl, KB2, k5 tbl, KB1, k1 tbl, KB3, k1 tbl, KB1, k4 tbl, KB2, k1 tbl, k2 tog tbl—24 sts.

Row 48: (10) Sl 1, p1, psso, p1, PB2, p4, PB6, p4, PB2, p1, p2 tog—22 sts.

Row 49: (5) Sl 1, k1 tbl, psso, k1 tbl, KB2, k6 tbl, KB1, k5 tbl, KB2, k1 tbl, k2 tog tbl—20 sts.

Row 50: (6) Sl 1, p1, psso, p1, PB2, (p4, PB2) twice, p1, p2 tog—18 sts.

Row 51: (5) Sl 1, k1 tbl, psso, k1 tbl, KB2, k4 tbl, KB1, k3 tbl, KB2, k1 tbl, k2 tog tbl—16 sts.

Row 52: (4) Sl 1, p1, psso, p1, PB2, p6, PB2, p1, p2 tog—14 sts.

Row 53: (4) Sl 1, k1 tbl, psso, k1 tbl, KB2, k4 tbl, KB2, k1 tbl, k2 tog tbl—12 sts.

Row 54: (4) Sl 1, p1, psso, p1, PB2, p2, PB2, p1, p2 tog—10 sts.

Row 55: (4) Sl 1, k1 tbl, psso, k1 tbl, KB4, k1 tbl, k2 tog tbl—8 sts.

Row 56: (2) Sl 1, p1, psso, p1, PB2, p1, p2 tog—6 sts.

Row 57: (0) Sl 1, k1 tbl, psso, k2 tbl, k2 tog tbl—4 sts.

Row 58: (0) Sl 1, p1, psso, p2 tog—2 sts.

Row 59: (0) K2 tog tbl.
Fashion off.

SECOND END
With new skein of yarn, pick up 48 sts along the first row of Center and repeat same as First End.

Weave in all yarn ends and block scarf.

FRINGE
Using the perle cotton and beading needle, attach the perle cotton at one edge of the "V" of the scarf. String 37 size 11 seed beads, one size 6 bead, and one size 11 bead. Skip the last size 11 bead and pass the needle through the large bead and the 37 small beads. Make a small knot through the edge of the scarf and bury the perle cotton in the yarn, coming out about 5/16"/8 mm away along the scarf edge. Make a small knot; repeat the process all along the scarf edge. Finish the opposite end in the same manner. ☸

Jane Davis designs for the Blue Sky Alpacas Company, who in turn design and distribute exquisite, exclusive alpaca and alpaca-blend yarns for handknitters. Jane's Elegant Beaded Scarf is one pattern in a series of patterns by Blue Sky Alpacas.

take it from the top pullover

This is a great project for those who like their knitting simple. Knit from the top down, all in one piece! The beginner/intermediate knitter will enjoy the simplicity of this no shaping, no seams, so easy sweater.

DESIGN BY DEB GEMMELL
Skill level: Intermediate
Finished project sizes: Small (Medium, Large, Extra Large); instructions are for smallest size with changes for larger sizes in parentheses
Finished measurements at bust: 42" (46", 50", 54"), 106.5 (117, 127, 137) cm
Cropped length: 24" (61 cm), Tunic length: 26–27" (66-68.75 cm)

MATERIALS

Naturally Landscape worsted weight yarn (95% merino wool, 5% poly binder)
(1¾ ounces/50 grams, 90 yards/83 meters per ball): 14(14, 16, 18) balls of Periwinkle
Size 8 (5 mm) circular needles, 16"(40 cm), 24" (60 cm), and 30" (80 cm) long or sizes needed to obtain gauge
Size 6 (4 mm) circular needles, 16" (40 cm) and 30" (80 cm) long
Size 6 (4 mm) double pointed needles
Markers
Yarn needle

GAUGE

With larger needles, 18 sts = 4" (10 cm)
Take time to check your gauge.

STITCH PATTERN

This sweater starts at the collar and in ONE PIECE works down the yoke, splits into the body and two sleeves. The sleeves are finished before the body so that you can vary the body length with assurance of enough yarn. The sleeves are knit down to the wrist, and as you progress, the sweater can be tried on, so that a perfect sleeve length can be achieved. For a more comfortable fit, the collar at the front of the sweater should be lower than at the back. This sweater has extra rows worked across the back of the neck and shoulders, raising the back of the neck and causing the front to be lower. After knitting the collar, follow the instructions and work part way around the circular needle from the front left shoulder around the back to the right front shoulder only, turn, leaving the neck front stitches unworked and purl back—2 extra rows across the back of the neck. After all the extra rows are worked, you will work a full round, knitting around all the stitches on the circular needle to complete the neck shaping.

ABBREVIATIONS

k = knit
Rnd = round
sl = slip
ssk (slip, slip, knit) = slip 2 stitches one at a time as if to knit, insert source needle into the front of these two slipped stitches from left to right and knit them together from this position.
double decrease = slip two stitches together as if to knit, k1, pass two slipped stitches over the end of the needle.
sts = stitches
Open m1 (with holes) = knit under the running thread between the stitch just worked and the next stitch without lifting or twisting it.
Closed m1 (no holes) = with the source needle, lift the running thread between the stitch just worked and the next stitch from back to front and knit in the resulting loop.

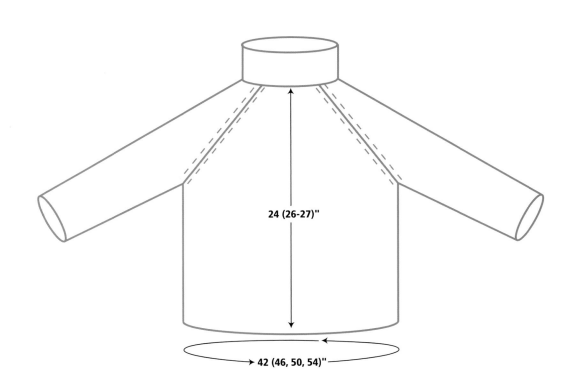

24 (26-27)"

42 (46, 50, 54)"

INSTRUCTIONS

ROLLED COLLAR

With 16" (40 cm) larger needle, cast on 84 stitches.

Join in the round being careful not to twist the stitches.

Place marker to mark beginning of round.

Change to the 16" (40 cm) smaller needle and knit each round until Collar measures 3" (7.5 cm) from cast on edge.

YOKE

Note: The raglan yoke is set up with 4 marked shapelines. An increase is worked before and after each of the 4 shapelines every other row. There are two choices of increases: one creates small holes and the other does not.

MARKER RND: Change to the 16" (40 cm) larger needle, k 11, place marker #2 (left back shoulder), k 31, place marker #3 (right back shoulder), k 11, place marker #4 (right front shoulder), k 31. You should be back at beginning of the round marker #1, which is at the left front shoulder.

NECK SHAPING

Note: Begin working in short rows. Change to longer needles when needed.

Row 1: With rs facing, m1 (see Abbreviations), slip marker #1, k1 (shapeline st), m1, k 10, m1, slip marker #2, k1 (shapeline st), m1, k 30, M1, slip marker #3, k1 (shapeline st), m1, k 10, m1, slip marker #4, k1 (shapeline st), m1, k2, TURN.

Row 2: Sl 1, purl to marker #1, p3, TURN.

Row 3: Sl 1, * knit to next marker, m1, slip marker, k1, m1; repeat from * three more times, knit 2 sts past where you ended last time, TURN.

Row 4: Sl 1, purl back around and purl 2 sts past where you ended last time, TURN.

Repeat Rows 3 and 4 until there are 40 sts between markers #2 and #3, ending by working Row 4.

Note: Both the Front and the Back should have 40 sts between the shapeline sts and each Sleeve should have 20 sts (do not count the 4 shapeline sts). Begin working in rounds.

Rnd 1: With rs facing, knit to marker #1, m1, slip marker, k1, m1, * knit to next marker, m1, slip marker, k1, m1; repeat from * two more times, knit across front neck stitches to marker #1.

Rnd 2: Knit around.

Rnd 3 (Increase Rnd): *m1, slip marker, k1, m1, knit to next marker; repeat from * 3 more times.

Repeat Rnds 2 and 3 until the Front and Back each have 90(94, 98, 102) stitches between shapeline sts ending by working Rnd 2 OR until the Yoke when measured vertically from the base of the Collar at the center Back neck to the knitting needle measures 10(10, 11, 11)"/25.5(25.5, 28, 28) cm.

Note #1: If you have increased to the number of stitches needed for your size and the Yoke does not measure 10(10, 11, 11)"/25.5(25.5, 28, 28) cm, repeat Rnd 2 until it does.

Note #2: If the Yoke is the length needed for your size, but you haven't reached the number of stitches required, separate the Body and Sleeves as in the instructions below. The extra stitches needed will be added at the underarm when working Body Rnd 1.

SEPARATE BODY AND SLEEVES

Note: The 4 shapeline sts belong to the Body.

Next Rnd: Starting at marker #1, k1 (shapeline st), knit across left sleeve to marker #2, with yarn needle and waste yarn, slip sleeve sts off needle and remove marker, knit across Back to marker #3, remove marker, k1 (shapeline st), knit across right sleeve to marker #4, with yarn needle and waste yarn, slip sleeve sts off needle and remove marker, knit across Front sts.

Note: The Front and Back should be on one needle, still unattached to each other, and have the same number of stitches. Both Sleeves should be on waste yarn.

BODY

Note: If you reached the length of the yoke before reaching the number of stitches stipulated for the yoke, cast on enough stitches at the underarm to make up the number of body stitches for your size.

Number of stitches for the Front plus the stitches cast on at the underarm: 94(104, 112, 122) sts. Back plus underarm sts is the same number.

JOIN THE BODY IN THE ROUND AS FOLLOWS:

Next Rnd: Cast on 2(8, 12, 18) sts or the number of stitches you need to make up the body stitches for your size, knit across the Back, cast on the same number of stitches as above at the underarm, knit across the Front to end of round – 188(208, 224, 244) sts.

Knit each rnd until you have used up the skein you are using. Leave the body stitches on the needle and start the sleeves.

Note: If you put the two ends of the circular needle for the body together and put a rubber band around them, you won't lose any stitches as you are working on the sleeves.

Once the sleeves are done you can vary the length of the sweater depending on how much yarn you have left.

SLEEVES

Note: At the underarm you will be picking up and knitting 1 stitch for each of the cast on underarm stitches of the body PLUS 1 extra stitch in the center for the seamline stitch. If you cast on an odd number of stitches at the underarm, when working the body, do not add an extra stitch as below, just use the center stitch of the odd number of stitches for the seamline stitch.

Rnd 1: With the 16" (40 cm) larger circular needle, slip all the stitches on the spare yarn onto the needle. Attach yarn at the center of the cast on stitches at the underarm, pick up and knit one stitch for each cast on stitch, knit around sleeve, pick up and knit one stitch for each cast on stitch to center of underarm, m1 (closed) in the center.

Mark the center stitch at the underarm as your seamline stitch. (You can stick a safety pin through this stitch and move the safety pin at every decrease.)

Rnds 2–5: Knit 4 rounds.

Decrease Rnd: Knit around to one stitch before the seamline stitch, slip 2 sts together as if to knit, k1, pass 2 slipped stitches over end of needle. (The seamline stitch is the middle stitch of the Double Decrease.)

Work Decrease Rnd on every 5th round until you have 57 sts.

Work straight until you have reached 2½" (6.5 cm) before desired length. For Sleeve length, measure a garment of the intended recipient or check the Wrist-to-Wrist Measurement (below). If you reach the Sleeve length for the cuff without decreasing to 57 sts, stop decreasing and work the Cuff.

WRIST-TO-WRIST MEASUREMENT:

Women's Small 58" (147.5 cm); Medium 60" (152.5 cm); Tall 62" (157.5 cm)

Men's Small 60" (152.5 cm); Regular 63" (160 cm); Tall 65" (165 cm)

Use Wrist-to-Wrist measurement as a guide for sleeve length OR measure a sweater you own. Measure the width of the body. Subtract that number from wrist to wrist measurement and divide by 2 = total Sleeve length; make an allowance for the cuff.

CUFF

Rnd 1: With the double pointed needles, knit and decrease evenly to 46 sts.

Knit around for 3" (7.5 cm). The roll at the end of the sleeve will use up approximately 1" (2.5 cm) of knitting.

Bind off.

Sew in the end so that it will not show when the sleeve rolls up.

Repeat for second Sleeve.

BODY

Continue now with the Body.

Knit around until 3" (7.5 cm) before desired length. Stop at 21" (53.5 cm) for the cropped length of 24" (61 cm) or stop at 23–24" (58.5–61 cm) for a longer finished length of 26–27" (66–68.5 cm).

Change to smaller circular needle and knit around for 4" (10 cm). The bottom roll will use up approximately 1" (2.5 cm) of knitting.

Sew in the end so that it will not show when the bottom rolls up. ⚜

Sisters Deb and Lynda Gemmell started their Cabin Fever knitting design company in 1997. Their "no sewing" sweater designs are worked in the round or made all in one piece, with the sleeves knitted from the shoulder down to the wrist for a perfect sleeve length. This led to knitting the entire sweater from the top down.

103

chameleon hat

Depending upon your mood, this fashionable hat can be worn many different ways.
The unusual stitch creates an interesting geometric pattern, which in turn frames the
face and is very flattering. It's a perfect project for the intermediate knitter.

DESIGN BY NICKY EPSTEIN
Skill Level: Intermediate
Finished size: One size fits average adult

MATERIALS

Mission Falls 1824 Wool, 100% Superwash Wool
(1¾ ounces/50 grams, 85 yards/78 meters per ball): 3 balls of 001 Natural
Size 8 (5 mm) straight needles for knitting rows or
Size 8 (5 mm) 16" (40.5 cm) circular knitting needles or double pointed knitting needles for knitting in rounds
Tapestry needle
Marker (for knitting in the round)

GAUGE

In pattern, 16 sts = 3" (7.5 cm)
30 rows/rnds = 4" (10 cm)
Take time to check your gauge.

ABBREVIATIONS

k = knit
p = purl
p2 tog = purl 2 stitches together
k2 tog = knit 2 stitches together
k3 tog = knit 3 stitches together
st(s) = stitch (es)
sl = slip
St st = Stockinette stitch

NOTES

Cast on 1 selvage stitch for seaming at very beginning and end of work if using straight needles; omit selvage stitches if knitting in the round.

Stitch counts in the directions include selvage stitches only as noted for working on straight needles.

STITCH PATTERN

Reversible Diagonal Rib (multiple of 8 sts)

Row/Rnd 1: *K1, p1, k1, p5; repeat from * across.

Row/Rnd 2 and every alt row/rnd: Knit the knit sts and purl the purl sts as they face you.

Row/Rnd 3: *K1, p1, k5, p1; repeat from * across.

Row/Rnd 5: *K1, p5, k1, p1; repeat from * across.

Row/Rnd 7: *K5, p1, k1, p1; repeat from * across.

Row/Rnd 9: P4, *k1, p1, k1, p5; repeat from * across to last 4 sts, (k1, p1) twice.

Row/Rnd 11: K3, p1, k1, p1, *k5, p1, k1, p1; repeat from * across to last 2 sts, k2.

Row/Rnd 13: P2, k1, p1, k1, *p5, k1, p1, k1; repeat from * across to last 3 sts, p3.

Row/Rnd 15: (K1, p1) twice, *k5, p1, k1, p1; repeat from * across to last 4 sts, k4.

Row/Rnd 16: Knit the knit sts and purl the purl sts as they face you.

Repeat Rows/Rnds 1–16 for pattern.

INSTRUCTIONS

HAT

FOR WORKING IN THE ROUND:

With circular knitting needles or double pointed knitting needles, cast on 104 sts.

FOR WORKING FLAT WITH A SEAM:

With straight knitting needles, cast on 106 sts (104 pattern sts + 2 sts for selvages).

Maintain selvage sts in St st.

Work in Reversible Diagonal Rib for 8½" (21.5 cm), ending with Row/Rnd 16.

CROWN

FOR STRAIGHT KNITTING NEEDLES:

Row 1: K1, *(k1, p1) twice, (k2 tog) twice; repeat from * across to last st, K1 – 80 sts.

Rows 2 & 4: Knit the knit sts and purl the purl sts as they face you.

Row 3: K1, (k1, p1) twice, *k3 tog, p1, k1, p1; repeat from * across to last 3 sts, k2 tog, K1 – 55 sts.

Rows 5–9: Work even in rib as established.

Row 10: P1, (p2 tog) across to last 4 sts, p3tog, p1 – 28 sts.

Row 11: K1, (k2 tog) across to last st, k1 – 12 sts.

Row 12: P2, (p2 tog) across to last st, p1 – 9 sts.

Leaving a long end cut yarn, weave yarn end through sts on last row and gather tightly; then sew back seam, reversing seam over first 4" (10 cm) from lower edge.

FOR CIRCULAR KNITTING:

Change to double-pointed needles as necessary.

Rnd 1: *(K1, p1) twice, (k2tog) twice; repeat from * across – 78 sts.

Rnds 2 & 4: Knit the knit sts and purl the purl sts as they face you.

Rnd 3: Remove marker, sl 1, place marker to reestablish beg of rnd, *p1, k1, p1, k3 tog; repeat from * across – 52 sts.

Rnds 5–9: Work even in rib as established.

Rnd 10: (K2tog) across – 26 sts.
Rnd 11: (K2tog) across – 13 sts.
Rnd 12: K1, (k2tog) across – 7 sts.

Leaving a long end cut yarn, weave yarn end through sts on last rnd and gather tightly, secure end.

FINISHING

Weave in all ends.

FOLDING

To shape basic fold hat, fold bottom edge up 3" (7.5 cm).

For Robin Hood, fold same as basic fold hat, then fold brim in half again toward crown while pulling down at center front to form the point.

For rolled-brim hat, simply roll bottom edge to desired length.

For cloche, place basic fold hat on the back of your head and pull fold down at back of neck.

For miller's hat, just wear the hat without any folds, letting the top flop over. ✤

Nicky Epstein's unique designs and pre-emptive techniques are admired and used by knitters, teachers, and designers everywhere. Her 4th book *Knitting for Barbie Doll* won the Independent Publisher's Award as "Craft Book of the Year" for 2002. For more of Nicky's designs see "Flower Power Patchwork" on page 120 and "Embossed Floral" on page 131.

baltic pillow sampler

These earthy accent pillows were knitted using an easy but intriguing braided pattern. The perfect project for all that left-over yarn you just can't bear to part with. Before you know it, you will be knitting pillows for every room and every friend.

DESIGN BY THE PHILOSOPHER'S WOOL COMPANY
Skill level: Intermediate
Finished project size: 10" x 12" (25.5 cm x 30.5 cm)

MATERIALS
Philosopher's Wool, worsted weight yarn, 100% wool or equivalent
(4 ounces/112 grams, 210 yards/192 meters per skein): Lt Green Heather, Dk Green Heather, Lt Blue Heather, Dk Blue Heather, Lt Purple Heather, Dk Purple Heather, Lt Grey, Wine, and Natural
16" (40.5 cm) circular needles, size 8 (5 mm) or size needed to obtain gauge
Polyester fiberfill
Yarn needle

GAUGE
20 sts = 4" (10 cm)
Take time to check your gauge.

STITCH PATTERN
This technique was developed in Latvia and Estonia as well as in the Baltic region of Europe. It is very easy to learn and can be used for edging a garment with a two-color braid or to create an entire piece of work as in this pillow sampler.

In this pillow, for almost every round of purl work that you see, there is a knitted round below giving the richly textured effect. The pillow measures approximately 10" x 12".

ABBREVIATIONS
k = knit
p = purl
st(s) = stitch(es)

INSTRUCTIONS
BRAIDED PILLOW
Cast on 100 sts, place a marker to mark beginning of round.

The next 6 rounds are used at the end of the work to create the edge. You may use either the ribbing edge or the moss stitch edge.

RIBBING EDGE
Knit 6 rounds of k1, p1, ribbing.

MOSS STITCH EDGING
Round 1: *K1, p1 * repeat from * to * around.

Round 2: *P1 k1 * repeat from * to * around.

Repeat Rounds 1 and 2, twice.

You will now start the multicolored textured work.

TO MAKE GARTER BANDS
Step 1: Knit one round in one color.

Step 2: Purl the next round in the same color or another color.

TO MAKE A SINGLE BRAID
\\\\\\\\\\\
Step 1: Work one round using two colors as follows: ** K1 in color one, k1 in color two**. Repeat from ** to ** to the end of the round.

Step 2: Bring both colors to the front as if to purl. P1 with color one, ** bring color two from the front under color one and up, p1, bring color one from the front under color two and up, p1 **. Repeat from ** to ** to the end of the round being careful to always twist in the same direction.

The yarn will be twisting in a counterclockwise direction with each stitch and will become twisted. Keep pushing the twist away from yourself.

Step 3: To complete a single braid, it is necessary to untwist the yarn. To do this, push the knitting well back from the needle points. Hold the work up and allow the work to dangle and spin until the twist is eliminated.

TO MAKE A DOUBLE BRAID
\\\\\\\\\\\\
////////////
Choose two new colors.

Step 1: Same as for Single Braid.
Step 2: Same as for Single Braid.

Step 3: P1 in color one. ** Bring color two from the back under color one (that is, in the opposite direction as in Step 2) and p1; bring color one from the back under color two and p1. ** Repeat from ** to ** to the end of the round, being careful to always twist in the same direction. The yarn will twist in a clockwise direction with each stitch and by the end of the round will completely untangle the twists created in Step 2.

We suggest that you start by making a garter band in one or two colors and then trying a single braid or two. Remember that when you change colors, you must do a knit round alternating the two new colors before twisting the purl round. It is very important to change colors almost every time you start a new braid. Our pillows were knit in pleasing color combinations to the middle [about 5½"(14 cm)] and then the color work was copied in mirror image to the outside edge where the first 6 rounds were repeated.

TO FINISH
Bind off loosely. Stuff the pillow and sew up the two ends. 🪡

Ann and Eugene Bourgeois of Philosopher's Wool Co. produce beautiful wool yarn at their farm near the shores of Lake Huron. They travel across North America teaching knitters how easily they can knit Fair Isle work without puckering or twisting their wool. Knitters love their Fair Isle kits and patterns. See "Sunshine Duo," a beautiful Fair Isle sweater design from Philosopher's Wool Co., on page 151.

illumination lace scarf

Enjoy the tactile pleasure of knitting a scarf, as light and delicate as an evening breeze. The decorative lace pattern creates a scarf of sheer elegance. This diaphanous accent will add a touch of elegance to any outfit.

DESIGN BY EVELYN A. CLARK
Skill level: Intermediate
Finished project size: 9" x 54" (23 cm x 137 cm)

MATERIALS

JaggerSpun Zephyr 2/18, super fine weight yarn (50% wool, 50% silk)
(2 ounces/57 grams, 630 yards/576 meters per skein): 1 skein of Vanilla
Size 5 (3.75 mm) knitting needles or size needed to obtain gauge
For scalloped picot edging: Crochet hook, size F (3.75 mm), 3 yards waste yarn, and safety pin
Split ring marker
Rustproof pins
Optional: blocking wires

GAUGE

Unblocked gauge: In garter st, 24 sts = 4" (10 cm)
Blocked gauge: In garter st, 22 sts = 4" (10 cm)
Take time to check your gauge.

NOTES

1) Scarf is knit from end to end with either plain ends or scalloped picot edgings.
2) For scalloped picot edging, begin with a provisional cast on. Wind 5 yards of main color into a small ball; do not break yarn. Secure this ball with a safety pin so that it will not unwind as you pick up sts. This ball will be used later for the edging on the first end.
To work the provisional cast on: with a smooth, contrasting color waste yarn and crochet hook, chain 55 sts. Using knitting needles and main color yarn with the small ball hanging as the tail, pick up 49 sts in back loops of the crochet chain. Later, when starting the picot cast off, undo the waste yarn beginning with the last chain stitch. The chain will "unzip," and the remaining sts can be put on the needles.
3) First stitch of every row is slipped purlwise with the yarn held in front of work.
4) It is helpful to hang a split ring marker at the beginning of odd number rows. Move marker up as scarf lengthens.
5) Lace will grow when blocked. If using other yarns, block a swatch or the beginning of the scarf to determine the number of pattern repeats needed for desired length.
6) To make a wider piece, add to the cast on a multiple of 24 sts and repeat center 24 sts between the first 13 sts and last 12 sts desired number of times. If the size of the scarf is changed, yarn needed will also change.
7) Lace can be knit from written instructions or charts.

ABBREVIATIONS

k = knit
k2 tog = knit 2 stitches together
sl = slip
ssk = slip 2 stitches one at a time as if to knit. Insert left needle through the front of these slipped stitches from left to right and knit together from this position.
sk2p = slip 1 stitch knitwise, k2 tog and pass the slipped stitch over the k2 tog stitch.
st = stitch
yo = yarn over
* = repeat instructions between *s.
( ) = repeat instructions between parentheses specified number of times.

CHART NOTES

1) See written instructions for cast on, beginning, ending, and bind off.
2) Read charts from bottom to top and from right to left.
3) Only odd numbered rows are charted. All even rows: Sl 1, knit across.
4) Lace is a 24 st repeat pattern worked over 16 rows.

INSTRUCTIONS

SCARF

PICOT EDGING: Using provisional cast on, cast on 49 sts (see Note 2).
Rows 1–4: Sl 1, knit across.
PLAIN EDGING: Cast on 49 sts.
Rows 1–5: Sl 1, knit across.

BODY

Preparation Row a (RS): Sl 1, k2, k2 tog, yo, k1, (k2 tog, yo) twice, k5, (yo, ssk) twice, k1, (yo, ssk) twice, k1, (k2 tog, yo) twice, k1, (k2 tog, yo) twice, k5, (yo, ssk) twice, k1, yo, ssk, k3.

Preparation Row b: Sl 1, knit across.
Row 2 and all even number rows: Sl 1, knit across.

Refer to page 23 for key to chart symbols.

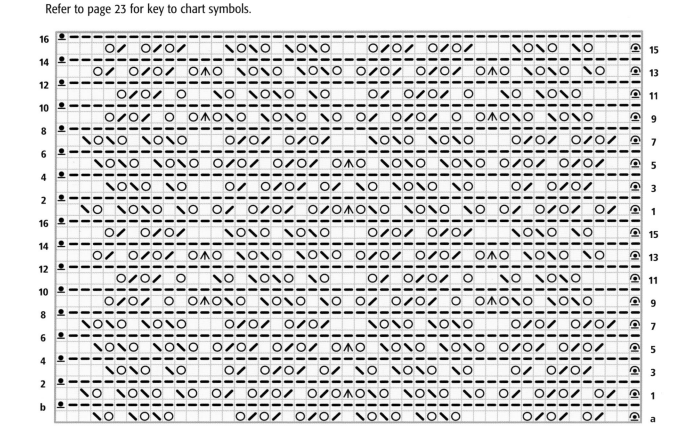

Row 1: Sl 1, k1, * k2 tog, yo, k1, (k2 tog, yo) twice, k1, k2 tog, yo, k1, yo, ssk, k1, (yo, ssk) twice, k1, yo, ssk *, yo, sk2p, yo, repeat between * to * once, k2.

Row 3: Sl 1, k3, * (k2 tog, yo) twice, k1, k2 tog, yo, k3, yo, ssk, k1, (yo, ssk) twice *, k1, yo, ssk, k1, k2 tog, yo, k1, repeat between * to * once, k4.

Row 5: Sl 1, k2, * (k2 tog, yo) twice, k1, (k2 tog, yo) twice, k1, (yo, ssk) twice, k1, (yo, ssk) twice *, k1, yo, sk2p, yo, k1, repeat between * to * once, k3.

Row 7: Sl 1, k1, * (k2 tog, yo) twice, k1, (k2 tog, yo) twice, k3, (yo, ssk) twice, k1, (yo, ssk) twice *, k3, repeat between * to * once, k2.

Row 9: Sl 1, k3, * (yo, ssk) twice, k1, yo, ssk, yo, sk2p, yo, k2 tog, yo, k1, (k2 tog, yo) twice *, k1, k2 tog, yo, k1, yo, ssk, k1, repeat between * to * once, k4.

Row 11: Sl 1, k4, * (yo, ssk) twice, k1, yo, ssk, k1, k2 tog, yo, k1, (k2 tog, yo) twice *, k1, k2 tog, yo, k3, yo, ssk, k1, repeat between * to * once, k5.

Row 13: Sl 1, k2, yo, ssk, * k1, (yo, ssk) twice, k1, yo, sk2p, yo, k1, (k2 tog, yo) twice, k1 *, (k2 tog, yo) twice, k1, (yo, ssk) twice, repeat between * to * once, k2 tog, yo, k3.

Row 15: Sl 1, k3, yo, ssk, k1, (yo, ssk) twice, k3, (k2 tog, yo) twice, k1, (k2 tog, yo) twice, k3, (yo, ssk) twice, k1, (yo, ssk) twice, k3, (k2 tog, yo) twice, k1, k2 tog, yo, k4.

Work Rows 1–16 , 25 times total or until scarf measures desired length (see Note 5, page 108).

PLAIN EDGING

Next 5 rows: Sl 1, knit across.

Bind off all sts loosely knitwise.

PICOT EDGING

Top End: Next 4 rows: Sl 1, knit across.

Note: To work knitted cast on: k into first st, do not let old st drop from needle, twist new st, and place on left needle.

Last row: Bind off one st, sl st back onto left needle; * using knitted cast on, cast on 2 sts, bind off 2 sts, knitting in front loop of the first st and in the back loop of next 2 sts (picot made), bind off 3 edge sts, sl st back onto left needle *; repeat between * to * across to last 3 sts, work last picot and bind off last 2 sts.

Bottom End: Slowly "Unzip" crochet chain (See Note 2) beginning with last chain. Put 49 sts onto needles and using small ball wound at beginning, work same as Top End.

FINISHING

Weave in all yarn ends.

BLOCKING: Soak the scarf in water for at least 20 minutes. Roll in a towel to remove excess moisture. If using blocking wires, thread through each st from the same direction along both sides and picot scallops on each end and pin wires in place. If not using wires, spread out on a flat surface, smooth into shape, and pin. Leave in place until thoroughly dry. ✺

Evelyn A. Clark is a Seattle native who has been knitting since she was eight years old. She is a writer, photographer, and designer whose knitting patterns have been published in knitting books and magazines. Her knitting passion is lace. She has taught lace knitting and design classes, as well as beginning knitting for children, with the Helping Hands volunteer program.

pitter patter

These felted Mary Jane's are sure to become treasured keepsakes for the newest member of the family. Remember to tuck a special message in the toe before presenting your handmade gift of love.

DESIGN BY BEV GALESKAS
Skill level: Intermediate
Finished length: Approximately 4" (10 cm) to 4½" (11.5 cm) long

Sizes: This is a one-size pattern, but shown in two yarns. In Nature Spun the finished length will be about 4" long and in Lamb's Pride about 4½". Exact finished size is controlled by the amount of felting.
Caution: These shoes are not intended for children old enough to be standing or walking.
They can be very slippery unless some sort of non-slip sole is added.

MATERIALS

For smaller shoes: Brown Sheep Co. Nature Spun worsted weight, 100% wool, (245 yards/224 meters per skein): 70 yards/64 meters of Purple Splendor (N60)

For larger shoes: Brown Sheep Co. Lamb's Pride worsted weight, 85% wool, 15% mohair, (190 yards/173.5 meters per skein): 80 yards/73 meters of Supreme Purple (M100)

Caution: Do not use a "super wash" wool. All yarns felt differently so it is important to test felt a sample if substituting yarns.

Size 10 (6 mm) needles for Nature Spun or size 10½ (6.5 mm) for Lamb's Pride

Mild detergent, soap, or Woolmix wool-wash

Beading elastic

Sewing needle

Button

GAUGE BEFORE FELTING

In Garter st,

in Nature Spun 15 sts = 4" (10 cm)

in Lamb's Pride 14 sts = 4" (10 cm).

Take time to check your gauge.

ABBREVIATIONS AND TERMS

Garter Stitch in Rows = knit all rows. Two rows make one ridge.

k = knit

k2tog = knit two stitches together as one

m1 (make one) = insert source needle from front to back under the thread between next stitch on the source needle and the stitch just worked forming a loop on needle. Knit this loop through the back to form a new stitch.

ssk (slip, slip, knit) = slip 2 stitches one at a time as if to knit. Insert left needle through the front loops of these slipped stitches from left to right and knit them together from this position.

st = stitch

W&T (Wrap & Turn) = slip next stitch to right needle as if to purl. Bring the yarn between the needles to the front. Put the slipped stitch back on the left needle. Turn to work in the other direction.

INSTRUCTIONS

Loosely cast on 31 sts.

Row 1: Knit across.

Row 2: K1, (m1, k14, m1, k1) twice – 35 sts.

Row 3: Begin working in short rows as follows: k26, W&T, k8, m1, k1, m1, k8, W&T, knit to end – 37 sts.

Row 4: K1, m1, k16, m1, k3, m1, k16, m1, k1 – 41 sts.

Row 5: Knit across.

Row 6: K1, m1, k17, m1, k5, m1, k17, m1, k1 – 45 sts.

Rows 7–11: Knit 5 rows even in garter stitch.

TOE SHAPING

Row 12: K17, ssk, k7, k2tog, k17 – 43 sts.

Row 13: Knit across.

Row 14: K17, ssk, k5, k2tog, k17 – 41 sts.

Row 15: Knit across.

Row 16: K17, ssk, k3, k2tog, k17 – 39 sts.

Row 17: Knit across.

Row 18: K17, ssk, k1, k2tog, k17 – 37 sts.

Row 19: K10, firmly bind off the center 17 sts. Put the last st back onto the left needle and cast on 11 sts for strap; knit across the cast on sts, then across the remaining 10 sts of shoe.

Next Row: K21, turn.

Bind off all sts loosely, knitwise.

With rs facing, join yarn at front edge of rem 10 sts and knit one row.

Bind off all sts loosely, knitwise.

Make second shoe the same.

Before sewing sole and back seam, turn one shoe inside out so that there is a right and left shoe.

Sew sole and center back seam using an overcast stitch, just bringing the edges together. If the seam is kept flat and is the same thickness as knitting, it will not be visible after felting.

Work in all yarn ends.

Follow the General Felting Instructions on page 113.

BUTTON LOOP

To attach an elastic loop to the end of strap, cut a 6" length of elastic and thread into a sharp needle. Start on the wrong side of the strap about ½" from the end and run the needle through the center of the strap coming out the end. Put the needle back into the end next to where it came out and come back out next to where you started. Adjust length so a very small loop of elastic remains on the end of the strap. Tie in a square knot. Bury ends in felt and trim excess.

Sew button to side of shoe.

Repeat for second shoe.

Care: Hand wash in cool water and avoid excess agitation. Shape and air-dry away from heat and sunlight. ✿

Beverly Galeskas is a renowned authority on felting and the owner of Fiber Trends, the largest knitting pattern company in the U.S. She has developed a national reputation as the "queen of felting." Her patterns are known for their accuracy, style, and comfort. She has authored a book containing many of her patterns as well as complete instructions covering everything a knitter needs to know about the felting process. Bev also designed the felted hat and sheep projects on pages 114–119.

GENERAL FELTING INSTRUCTIONS

FELTING TIPS

1. Agitation is the key to felting. To help increase the agitation, you may wish to add an old pair of jeans to the wash. Be careful not to add anything like towels, as lint may get caught up in your felt.

2. Hot water is used to soften the wool and speed the felting process, but extremely hot or boiling water is not needed. It will make little difference in the felting time and makes it difficult to handle your shoes during the process.

3. Detergent or soap works with the hot water to soften the wool and speed felting. We use less than a tablespoon of Woolmix woolwash.

4. To protect your washer from excess lint, place the shoes in a zippered pillow protector, or at the very least, a fine mesh bag.

5. The most important step in felting is to check on the progress regularly. That is the only way that you will be able to stop when the size is right.

6. Do not use your washer's spin and rinse cycle as it may set permanent creases in your felt.

FELTING INSTRUCTIONS

TO BEGIN FELTING, set washer for hot wash, low water level, and maximum agitation. Add a small amount of a mild detergent or Woolmix. Place the bag with the shoes in the washer.

After about 5 minutes, check on the progress. Check again every 3 to 5 minutes. Every time you check on the progress, remove the knitted item(s) from the bag and change the way they are folded before returning to the washer. Reset the washer to continue agitating if necessary. Do not let it drain and spin. Just keep agitating and checking on them, until they are down to size and firm enough to hold their shape. Smaller items (such as baby shoes) may take quite awhile to felt. When the items appear to be the right size, remove and rinse by hand in cool water. Use a towel to remove some water and check the fit.

If they are still too large, return to the washer and continue agitating. When you are happy with the size, remove and rinse by hand. Machine rinsing is not recommended, as it is impossible to control the amount of additional shrinkage that may occur. *Note:* Rinsing is not needed if Woolmix is used. Use towels to remove as much water as possible, and then shape and air-dry. Shoes may be stuffed with soft fabric or paper towels to shape them while drying.

color me pretty

What's twice the fun of getting dressed up in a pretty hat—having a twin sister to share the pleasure. Knitting one or more of these colorful hats is an opportunity to explore the exciting knitting specialty of felting. Who wouldn't love to wear such a popular fashion statement?

DESIGN BY BEV GALESKAS
Skill level: Intermediate
Finished project size: To fit most children's head sizes up to approximately 20"
Note: The amount of felting and how the hat is blocked will determine the exact finished size.

MATERIALS
Baabajoes Wool Co. Wool Pak 14 ply bulky yarn, 100% pure New Zealand Wool (9 ounces/250 grams, 310 yards/283.5 meters per hank): 1 hank of Teal or Lavender

Caution: All wools react differently when felted. This pattern is designed specifically for the Wool Pak 14 ply Yarn. Using other yarns may give different results.

Size 11 (8 mm) 24" (61 cm) circular needle

Size 11 (8 mm) double pointed needles

Pins or colored thread for marking stitches

Mild detergent, soap, or Woolmix woolwash

GAUGE BEFORE FELTING
In St st, approx. 3 sts = 1" (2.5 cm)

Note: Knitting must be loose to felt properly.

Take time to check your gauge.

ABBREVIATIONS
k = knit

k2tog = knit two stitches together as one

m1 (make one) = insert source needle from front to back under the thread between next stitch on the source needle and the stitch just worked forming a loop on needle. Knit this loop through the back to form a new stitch.

ssk (slip, slip, knit) = slip 2 stitches one at a time as if to knit. Insert left needle through the front loops of these slipped stitches from left to right and knit them together from this position.

st = stitch

St st = Stockinette stitch

( ) = repeat instructions between parentheses specified number of times.

INSTRUCTIONS
BRIM
With circular needle, cast on 107 sts; mark beginning of rnd.

Join into rnd, being careful that sts are not twisted on the needle.

Purl 2 rnds.

Knit 8 rnds.

Next Rnd: (K10, k2tog) around to last 11 sts, k9, k2tog – 98 sts.

Knit 8 rnds.

CROWN
Rnd 1: (K2tog 3 times, k1) around – 56 sts.

Rnds 2 and 3: Knit around.

Rnd 4: (K4, m1) around – 70 sts.

Knit 22 rnds even.

SHAPING
Note: Change to double pointed needles when necessary.

Rnd 1: (K8, k2tog) around – 63 sts.

Rnd 2 and all remaining even numbered rounds: Knit around.

Rnd 3: (K7, ssk) around – 56 sts.

Rnd 5: (K6, k2tog) around – 49 sts.

Rnd 7: (K5, ssk) around – 42 sts.

Rnd 9: (K4, k2tog) around – 35 sts.

Rnd 11: (K3, ssk) around – 28 sts.

Rnd 13: (K2, k2tog) around – 21 sts.

Rnd 15: (K1, ssk) around – 14 sts.

Rnd 17: K2tog around; cut yarn – 7 sts.

With a tapestry needle, thread yarn through the remaining 7 sts and pull together. Fasten off.

Work in all yarn ends.

FELTING INSTRUCTIONS
Follow instructions on page 113 carefully, as this wool tends to felt very quickly.

BLOCKING & FINISHING
Blocking is important for a nicely finished hat. Do not dry in the dryer as this will cause more shrinkage and result in a limp and poorly shaped hat.

To block, use a hat form or find a bowl or ball that is slightly larger than head size. Stretch the finished, wet hat over the form and leave until completely dry. Brush to remove any clumps of wool.

If you need to reshape the hat, rinsing in cool water and reblocking obtain best results. ◉

See Bev's other felting projects on pages 111 and 116.

INSTRUCTIONS
BODY

With main color, loosely cast on 17 sts.

Row 1 (WS): Knit across.

Row 2: K6, (m1, k1) 5 times, m1, W&T, k11, W&T, (k2, m1) twice, k3, m1, k2, m1, k8 – 27 sts.

Row 3: Knit across.

Row 4: K9, (m1, k2) twice, m1, k1, m1, (k2, m1) twice, k4, W&T, k23, W&T, k4, (m1, k3) 5 times, m1, k9 – 39 sts.

Row 5: Knit across.

Row 6: K15, (m1, k2) twice, m1, k1, m1, (k2, m1) twice, k11, W&T, k37, W&T, k14, (m1, k3) 3 times, m1, k18 – 49 sts.

Row 7: Knit across.

Row 8: K21, m1, k3, m1, k1, m1, k3, m1, k15, W&T, k41, W&T, k19, m1, k3, m1, k17, W&T, k39, W&T, k47 – 55 sts.

Row 9 (WS): Knit across.

Mark center stitch on the right side of work for tail placement.

Row 10: K44, W&T, k33, W&T, k30, W&T, k27, W&T, k24, W&T, k21, W&T, k18, W&T, k15, W&T, k12, W&T, k9, W&T, k6, W&T, k3, W&T, k29 – 55 sts.

Row 11 (WS): Knit across.

Rows 12 and 13: Bind off 7 sts at the beginning of each row, knit to end – 41 sts.

Rows 14–27: Knit across.

Rows 28 and 29: Cast on 7 sts at beginning of each row, knit to end – 55 sts.

Row 30: K51, W&T, k47, W&T, k51 – 55 sts.

Row 31 (WS): Knit across.

Row 32: K23, slip sts just worked onto st holder, bind off 9 sts for neck opening, knit across – 23 sts.

LEFT SIDE

Row 33 (WS): Knit across.

Row 34: K1, ssk, k17, W&T, k19 – 22 sts.

Row 35 (RS): K1, ssk, k19 – 21 sts.

Rows 36–39: Knit.

Row 40 (WS): Bind off 7 sts, knit to end – 14 sts.

Row 41: K11, k2tog, k1 – 13 sts.

Row 42: Knit across.

Row 43: K10, k2tog, k1 – 12 sts.

Row 44: Knit.

Row 45: K9, k2tog, k1. Mark the last stitch of this row with a pin or thread.

Row 46: Bind off remaining 11 sts; cut yarn and fasten off.

RIGHT SIDE

Slip sts from st holder onto needle.

Join yarn with ws facing.

Row 33 (WS): Knit across.

Row 34: K20, k2tog, k1 – 22 sts.

Row 35: K19, W&T, k16, k2tog, k1 – 21 sts.

Rows 36–38: Knit across.

Row 39 (RS): Bind off 7 sts, knit to end – 14 sts.

Row 40: Knit across.

Row 41: K1, ssk, k11 – 13 sts.

Row 42: Knit across.

Row 43: K1, ssk, k10 – 12 sts.

Row 44: Knit across.

Row 45: K1, ssk, k9. Mark first stitch of this row with a pin or thread.

Row 46: Bind off remaining 11 sts; cut yarn and fasten off.

HEAD

With RS facing, join main color at edge of neck opening. Pick up and knit a total of 27 sts around neck opening.

Row 1: K5, inc in each of next 8 sts, k1, inc in each of next 8 sts, k5 – 43 sts.

Row 2: K39, W&T, k35, W&T, k33, W&T, k31, W&T, k29, W&T, k27, W&T, k25, W&T, k23, W&T, k21, W&T, k19, W&T, k17, W&T, k15, W&T, k13, W&T, k11, W&T, k9, W&T, k7, W&T, k5, W&T, k3, W&T, k23 – 43 sts.

Row 3: Knit across.

NOSE

Change to black.

Row 4: K1, (k2tog) 10 times, k1, (ssk) 10 times, k1 – 23 sts.

Row 5 (WS) and all remaining WS rows: Purl across.

Row 6: K4, k2tog, k2, k2tog, k3, ssk, k2, ssk, k4 – 19 sts.

Row 8: K6, k2tog, k3, ssk, k6 – 17 sts.

Row 10: K4, (k2tog) twice, k1, (ssk) twice, k4 – 13 sts.

Row 12: K4, k2tog, k1, ssk, k4 – 11 sts.

Row 14: K1, (k2tog) twice, k1, (ssk) twice, k1; cut yarn leaving a long tail – 7 sts.

Note About Seams: Always use the same yarn for sewing as was used for knitting. Sew flat seams, just catching the edges together and keep tension loose. The seams should not be visible after felting.

With a tapestry needle, thread yarn through remaining 7 sts and pull together tightly. With same yarn, sew seam in nose to the end of contrast color. With main color, continue sewing the seam in neck down to the marked stitches.

INNER LEGS AND TUMMY

With main color, loosely cast on 17 sts.

Row 1 (WS): Knit across.

Row 2: K7, W&T, k7.

Row 3: (RS) Knit across.

Row 4: K7, W&T, k7.

Row 5 (WS): Knit across.

Row 6: (RS) K8, m1, k1, m1, k8 – 19 sts.

Row 7: Knit across.

Row 8: K7, W&T, k7.

Row 9 (RS): K9, m1, k1, m1, k9 – 21 sts.

Row 10: K7, W&T, k7.

Row 11 (WS): Knit across.

Rows 12 and 13: Bind off 7 sts at the beginning of each row, knit to end – 7 sts.

Rows 14–17: Knit across.

Row 18 (RS): K2, m1, k3, m1, k2 – 9 sts.

Rows 19–26: Knit across.

Row 27 (WS): K2, k2tog, k1, ssk, k2 – 7 sts.

Rows 28 and 29: Cast on 7 sts at the beginning of each row, knit to end – 21 sts.

Row 30: K9, W&T, k9.

Row 31 (RS): Knit across.

Row 32: K9, W&T, k9.

Row 33 (WS): Knit across.

Rows 34–37: Repeat rows 30-33.

Rows 38 and 39: Bind off 7 sts at the beginning of each row, knit to end – 7 sts.

Row 40: Ssk, k3, k2tog – 5 sts.

Row 41: Knit across.

Row 42: Ssk, k1, k2tog – 3 sts.

Row 43: Knit across.

Row 44: Sl 1, k2tog, psso; cut yarn and fasten off.

Position point of this section at the marked stitches of body and sew down each side of chest and the fronts of the legs. Do not sew across bottom of legs.

FRONT HOOVES

Open front legs flat. With RS facing, use black to pick up and knit 12 sts along bottom edge of front leg.

Row 1: Knit across.

Row 2: K1, (ssk) twice, k2, (k2tog) twice, k1 – 8 sts.

Row 3: Bind off while working the following: k2tog, (k1, k2tog) twice; cut yarn and fasten off.

Repeat for other front leg.

With black, sew seam in hoof. With main color, sew seams from back of front legs, across tummy and down the fronts of back legs.

BACK HOOVES

Open back legs flat. With RS facing, use black to pick up and knit 14 sts along bottom edge of back leg.

Row 1: Knit across.

Row 2: K1, ssk, k1, ssk, k2, k2tog, k1, k2tog, k1 – 10 sts.

Row 3: Bind off while working the following: k2tog, k2, k2tog, k2, k2tog; cut yarn and fasten off.

Repeat for other back leg.

With black, sew seams in hooves, then use main color to sew about 1" at each end of leg seam, leaving center open for stuffing.

EARS (MAKE 2)

With black or main color, cast on 3 stitches.

Row 1: Purl across.

Row 2: K1, m1, k1, m1, k1 – 5 sts.

Row 3: Purl across.

Row 4: Ssk, k1, k2tog – 3 sts.

Row 5: Purl across.

Row 6: Slip 1, k2tog, psso; cut yarn and fasten off.

Pin ears to head so the purl side faces forward and slightly down. Adjust position to your liking and sew cast on edge of each ear to head.

TAIL

With main color or black, cast on 5 sts.

Beginning with a purl row, work 3 rows of Stockinette stitch.

Row 4: Ssk, k1, k2tog – 3 sts.

Row 5: Purl across.

Row 6: Slip 1, k2tog, psso; cut yarn and fasten off.

Fold tail in half lengthwise and sew the edges together from cast on to point. Position tail just below marked stitch and sew to body.

PREPARE FOR FELTING

Work in all yarn ends loosely on wrong side. Check for any holes and stitch them loosely together if necessary.

With a colorfast cotton waste yarn, baste the opening closed on inner leg.

Follow instructions on page 113 carefully, as this wool tends to felt very quickly.

SHAPING

For the best shape, stuff firmly with a temporary stuffing until dry. Ears should be molded into desired shape while drying.

FINISHING

When completely dry, attach eyes if desired, then re-stuff to desired firmness.

Use matching wool and lace the opening together as invisibly as possible. To make the seam all but disappear, brush over the seam with a stiff brush. Pearl cotton or wool may be used to add a mouth, if desired.

If desired, thread bell on a cord and tie around lamb's neck. ✺

See Bev's other felting projects on pages 111 and 114.

✺

STUFFED ANIMALS AND SMALL CHILDREN

Because all fibers shed some, these animals should not be given to small babies to handle or sleep with. For children under three years of age, do not use any attached eyes or other decorations.

flower power patchwork

One word describes this great afghan—colorful! Splashed across the surface are appliquéd flowers in a glorious array of autumn hues. Enjoy creating this wool tweed bouquet, knowing that when the temperature drops, you will be snug and warm in your lovely knitted flower garden.

DESIGN BY NICKY EPSTEIN
Skill Level: Experienced
Finished Project Size: 40" x 54" (101.5 cm x 137 cm) including fringe

MATERIALS

Reynolds Turnberry Tweed 100% wool (3½ ounces/100 grams, 220 yards/201 meters per skein):

2 skeins each of Blue (#32), Purple (#33), Pink (#66), Dark Red (#81), Red (#64), Yellow (#30), Dark Green (#87), and Green (#67)

Sizes 6 (4 mm) and 7 (4.5 mm) knitting needles or size needed to obtain gauge

Size 6 (4 mm) 24" (61 cm) circular needle

Coordinating sewing thread; sewing needle; tapestry needle

GAUGE

In St st, with larger needles, 18 sts and 28 rows = 4" (10 cm)

Take time to check your gauge.

NOTES

Cable Cast-on Method: Cast on two stitches. Insert the working needle between the two stitches on the source needle. Wrap the yarn as if to knit. Draw the yarn through to complete the stitch, and slip the new stitch onto the source needle (see diagram on page 40).

ABBREVIATIONS

k = knit
p = purl
st(s) = stitch(es)
St st = Stockinette stitch
rem = remaining
RS = Right Side
WS = Wrong Side

INSTRUCTIONS

PANEL 1

With Pink and larger needles, cast on 29 sts.

Work St st for 44 rows, ending with a WS row; piece should measure about 6¼" (16 cm) square. Change to Red and work St st for 44 rows.

Change to Green and knit 1 (RS) row, then work rev St st (purl on RS, knit on WS) for 44 rows (45 rows total).

Continue working 44 rows of St st and 45 rows of rev St st in this manner in the following sequence: Purple in St st, Yellow in St st, Dark Red in St st, Dark Green in rev St st, and Blue in St st – 8 color blocks. Mark first color block as bottom edge of panel.

Bind off all sts.

PANELS 2–6

Work same as Panel 1 in the following color sequences:

Panel 2: Dark Red in rev St st, Yellow in St st, Blue in St st, Red in rev St st, Dark Green in St st, Green in St st, Purple in St st, Pink in rev St st.

Panel 3: Green in St st, Purple in rev St st, Pink in St st, Dark Red in St st, Blue in St st, Red in rev St st, Yellow in St st, Dark Green in St st.

Panel 4: Blue in St st, Red in St st, Green in rev St st, Yellow in St st, Purple in rev St st, Dark Green in St st, Pink in St st, Dark Red in St st.

Panel 5: Yellow in rev St st, Dark Red in St st, Dark Green in St st, Blue in rev St st, Pink in St st, Purple in St st, Green in St st, Red in rev St st.

Panel 6: Dark Green in St st, Pink in rev St st, Purple in St st, Green in St st, Red in St st, Yellow in rev St st, Blue in St st, Pink in St st.

FLOWER

Make 48 as follows: 8 Blue, 6 Purple, 5 Pink, 4 Dark Red, 7 Red, 8 Yellow, 4 Dark Green, and 6 Green.

With smaller straight needles, cast on 12 sts.

Rows 1 and 2: Knit across.

Row 3: Bind off 10 sts, k1 – 2 sts.

Row 4: K2, turn; cast on 10 sts using Cable Method Cast On – 12 sts.

Repeat Rows 1–4 six times more – 7 petals.

Bind off all sts.

Break yarn; thread tail through tapestry needle and sew last 2 sts of bound off edge to first 2 sts of cast on edge, forming a ring.

FINISHING

Refer to photo below for color placement. With RS facing, bottom edges together, and corresponding yarn, sew panels together. With RS facing and using matching sewing thread and needle, sew one flower to center of each color block.

RIGHT BORDER

With Green, circular needle, and RS facing, pick up and knit 35 sts along edge of Pink block, join Purple and pick up and knit 35 sts along edge of Red block, join Yellow and pick up and knit 35 sts along Green block, join Dark Green and pick up and knit 35 sts along Purple block, join Dark Red and pick up and knit 35 sts along Yellow block, join Blue and pick up and knit 35 sts along Dark Red block, join Pink and pick up and knit 35 sts along Dark Green block, join Red and pick up and knit 35 sts along Blue block – 280 sts total.

Do not join. Keeping colors as established and twisting yarns at color changes, work garter st for 9 rows [about 1½" (3.8 cm)]. Bind off all sts.

LEFT BORDER

Work as for Right Border, picking up and knitting 35 sts in each block with the following colors: Green, Dark Red, Pink, Dark Green, Yellow, Red, Blue, Purple.

TOP FRINGE

With Pink and smaller needles, cast on 12 sts.

Work as for Flowers until a total of 11 petals have been worked, ending with Row 3.

Change to Green, P2, Cable Cast On 10 sts, and continue working as established until a total of 9 petals have been worked.

Change to Purple, P2, Cable Cast On 10 sts, and continue in this manner, working 9 petals each in Purple, Yellow, and Dark Red.

Change to Blue and work 11 petals. Bind off all sts.

With sewing thread and needle, sew fringe to top edge of blanket.

BOTTOM FRINGE

Work as for Top Fringe in the following color sequence: Pink, Green, Purple, Yellow, Red, Blue. Weave in loose ends. Block lightly. ✺

Nicky Epstein is one of America's leading knitwear designers and authors. Her work has been featured in the nation's top magazines, in yarn manufacturer's catalogues, in best-selling books, on television, and in museums. For more of Nicky's designs see "Chameleon Hat" on page 104 and "Embossed Floral" on page 131.

classic vest

With its timeless styling, this vest is the perfect gift for every man in your life! The Entrelac pattern, paired with his alma mater colors, creates a favorite sweater to be treasured for many years.

DESIGN BY
KATHLEEN POWER JOHNSON

Skill level: Intermediate
Finished project sizes: Small (Medium, Large). Model is size Large. Instructions are for smallest size with changes for larger sizes in parentheses.
Finished chest measurements: 40"(45", 50")/101.5 (114.5,127) cm
Back length: 25¾" (27", 29½") /65.5 (68.5,75) cm

MATERIALS

Plymouth Yarn's Cleckheaton Country 8-Ply, 100% Superwash wool yarn (1¾ ounces/50 grams, 106 yards/97 meters per skein): 9(10, 11) skeins of Dark Blue (#1812) for MC; 3 skeins of Red (#1823) for CC
Sizes 3 (3 mm) and 5 (3.75 mm) straight knitting needles or size needed to obtain gauge
Size 3 (3 mm) 16" (40.5 cm) circular knitting needle
Tapestry needle

GAUGE

With larger needles, in St st, 22 sts, and 28 rows = 4" (10 cm)
Diagonal Measurement of 1 block 1¼" (3 cm)
Take time to check your gauge.

NOTE: It is a good idea to check the diagonal measurement of your blocks from time to time so you can adjust your needle size if necessary.

STITCH PATTERN

The Entrelac graph indicates the arrangement of Tiers along with the direction of the stitches in each Tier. Once you get the rhythm of the construction of the two basic Tiers, you'll be able to use this graph as your pattern. If you get lost, match the direction of the stitches in your work with the arrow in the corresponding Tier.

ABBREVIATIONS AND NOTE

k = knit

p = purl

sl = slip

rem = remaining

p2 tog = purl 2 stitches together

k2tog = knit 2 stitches together

psso = pass slipped stitch over

dec = decrease

MC = Main Color

CC = Contrasting Color

m1 (make one) = with the source needle, lift the running thread between the stitch just worked and the next stitch from back to front and knit in the resulting loop.

RS = right side

WS = wrong side

ssk = slip 2 sts one at a time as if to knit. Insert source needle into the front of these two slipped stitches from left to right and knit them together from this position.

Note: slip all stitches as they present themselves; slip knit stitches knitwise and purl stitches purlwise.

ENTRELAC BLOCKS

Note: Turn work after every row and after every Tier unless otherwise indicated.

TRIANGLES

BASE TRIANGLE (BT)

Row 1: K1.

Row 2 and all even numbered rows: Purl across.

Row 3: Sl 1, k1.

Row 5: Sl 1, k2.

Row 7: Sl 1, k3.

Row 9: Sl 1, k4.

Do not turn.

RIGHT SELVAGE TRIANGLE (T1)

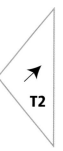

Row 1: With WS facing, p1.

Row 2: Knit into front and back of stitch.

Row 3: P1, p2 tog (1 stitch of each color).

Row 4: K1, m1, k1.

Row 5: P2, p2 tog.

Row 6: K2, m1, k1.

Row 7: P3, p2 tog.

Row 8: K3, m1, k1.

Row 9: P4, p2 tog.

Do not turn.

LEFT SELVAGE TRIANGLE (T2)

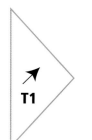

Row 1: Along the edge of the next triangle or rectangle, pick up and purl 5 sts.

Row 2 and all even-numbered rows: Knit across.

Row 3: Sl 1, p2, p2 tog.

Row 5: Sl 1, p1, p2 tog.

Row 7: Sl 1, p2 tog.

Row 9: P2 tog. Rem stitch becomes the first picked up stitch on the next Tier.

TRIANGLE 3 (T3)

Row 1: With RS facing, pick up and knit 5 sts. Slip last picked-up stitch to left hand needle and ssk.

Row 2 and all even-numbered rows: Purl across.

Row 3: K2 tog, k2, ssk.

Row 5: K2 tog, k1, ssk.

Row 7: K2 tog, ssk.

Row 9: Sl 1, ssk, psso. Rem st counts as first st of next triangle or rectangle.

Do not turn.

TRIANGLE 4 (T4)

Row 1: Along the edge of the next rectangle, pick up and knit 5 sts.

Row 2 and all even-numbered rows: Purl across.

Row 3: Sl 1, k2, k2 tog.

Row 5: Sl 1, k1, k2 tog.

Row 7: Sl 1, k2 tog.

Row 9: K2tog. Rem stitch becomes the first picked up stitch on the next Tier.

TRIANGLE 5 (T5)

Row 1: K1.

Row 2: Purl into front and back of stitch.

Row 3: K1, k2 tog (1 stitch of each color).

Row 4: P1, m1, p1.

Row 5: K2, k2 tog.

Row 6: P2, m1, p1.

Row 7: K3, k2 tog.

Row 8: P3, m1, p1.

Row 9: K4, k2 tog.

Do not turn.

RECTANGLES
RECTANGLE 1 (R1)

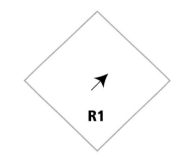

Row 1: With WS facing, pick up and purl 5 sts. Slip last picked-up stitch to source needle and p2 tog (1 st of each color).

Row 2 and all even-numbered rows: K5.

Row 3 and all odd-numbered rows through Row 9: Sl 1, p3, p2 tog.

Do not turn.

RECTANGLE 2 (R2)

Row 1: With RS facing, pick up and knit 5 sts. Slip last picked-up stitch to source needle and ssk (1 st of each color).

Row 2 and all even-numbered rows: P5.

Row 3 and all odd-numbered rows through Row 9: Sl 1, k3, ssk.

Do not turn.

INSTRUCTIONS
FRONT

With smaller needles and MC, cast on 100(112, 124) sts.

Work in k1, p1 ribbing for 2" (5 cm), ending with a RS row.

Change to larger needles.

Purl across dec 20(22, 24) sts evenly across row – 80(90, 100 sts).

TIER 1 (MC): Work 16(18, 20) BT.

Turn work.

TIER 2 (CC): Work T1 once, R1 15(17, 19) times, ending T2.

TIER 3 (MC): Transfer rem st to empty needle. Work R2 16(18, 20) times.

TIERS 4 THROUGH 18(20, 24): Work Tiers 2 and 3, 9(10,12) times.

ARMHOLE AND NECK SHAPING
TIER 19(21, 25) (MC):

For Size L: Work T3 once.

For all sizes: Work R2 8(9, 9) times; bind off the final row of the last R2.

Rem st becomes first picked up st of next rectangle. Work R2 8(9, 9) more times.

For Size L only: Bind off final row of the last R2. Rem st becomes first picked up st of next triangle. Work T3 once.

Fasten off.

Turn work.

RIGHT ARMHOLE AND NECKLINE (WORKED SEPARATELY)
TIER 20(22, 26) (CC):

For Sizes S and M: Work T1 once.

For Size L: Join yarn to top of last R1 of Tier 24.(see diagram)

For all sizes: Work R1 7(8, 8) times, binding off last row of last rectangle.

Fasten off.

TIER 21(23, 27) (MC): Join yarn to top of last R1.

Work R2 7 times.

For Size M: Work T3 once.

Fasten off.

TIER 22(24, 28) (CC):

For Sizes S and L: Work T1 once.

For Size M: Join yarn to top of last R2 completed.

For all sizes: Work R1 6 times.

TIER 23(25, 29) (MC): Work T5 once, R2 5(5, 6) times.

For Size S: Work T3 once.

Fasten off.

TIER 24(26, 30) (CC):

For Size S: Join yarn to top of last R2 completed.

For Sizes M and L: Work T1 once.

For all sizes: Work R1 5(5, 6) times, binding off last row of last R1.

Fasten off.

TIER 25(27, 31) (MC): Join yarn to top of last R1, work R2 4(5, 6) times.

TIER 26(28, 32) (CC): Work T1 once, R1 3(4, 5) times, T2 once.

TIER 27(29, 33) (MC): Work R2 4(5, 6) times

TIER 28(30, 34) (CC): Work T1 once, R1 5 times.

TIER 29(31, 35) (MC): Work T5 once, R2 3(4, 5) times.

TIER 30(32, 36) (CC): Work T1 once, R1 3(4, 5) times, binding off last row of last R1.

Fasten off.

TIER 31(33, 37) (MC): Join yarn to top of last R1, work R2 3(4, 5) times.

TIER 32(34, 38) (CC): Work T1 once, R1 2(3, 4) times, T2 once.

TIER 33(35, 39) (MC): Work R2 3(4, 5) times.

TIER 34(36, 40) (CC): Work T1 once, R1 2(3, 4) times.

TIER 35(37, 41) (MC): Work T5 once, R2 2(3, 4) times.

TIER 36(38, 42) (CC): Work T1 once, R1 2(3, 4) times, binding of last row of last R1.
Fasten off.

TIER 37(39, 43) (MC): Join yarn to top of last R1, work R2 2(3, 4) times.

TIER 38(40, 44) (CC): Work T1 once, R1 1(2, 3) times, T2 once.

TIER 39(41, 45) (MC): Work T3 2(3, 4) times.
Fasten off.

LEFT ARMHOLE AND NECKLINE

TIER 20(22, 26) (CC): WS facing, attach yarn to top of last R2 worked on neck edge of Left Front.
Work R1 7(8, 8) times.
For Sizes S and M: Work T2 once.
For Size L: bind off last row of last R1.
Fasten off.

TIER 21(23, 27) (MC):
For Size M: Work T3 once.
For Size L: Join yarn to top of last R1.
For all sizes: Work R2 7 times, binding off last row of last R2.
Fasten off.

TIER 22(24, 28) (CC): Join yarn to top of last R2, work R1 6 times.
For Sizes S and L: Work T2 once.
For Size M: Bind off last row of last R1.
Fasten off.

TIER 23(25, 29) (MC):
For Size S: Work T3 once.
For Size M: Join yarn to top of last R1.
For all sizes: Work R2 5(5, 6) times, T4 once.

TIER 24(26, 30) (CC): Work R1 5(5, 6) times.
For Size S: Bind off last row of last R1.
Fasten off.
For Sizes M and L: Work T2 once.

TIER 25(27, 31) (MC):
For Size S: Join yarn to top of last R1.
For all sizes: Work R2 4(5, 6) times.

TIER 26(28, 32) (CC): Work T1 once, R1 4(5, 5) times, T2 once.

TIER 27(29, 33) (MC): Work R2 4(5, 6) times, binding off last row of last R2.
Fasten off.

TIER 28(30, 34) (CC): Join yarn to top of last R2, work R1 3(4, 5) times, T2 once.

TIER 29(31, 35) (MC): Work R2 3(4, 5) times, T4 once.

TIER 30(32, 36) (CC): Work R1 3(4, 5) times, T2 once.

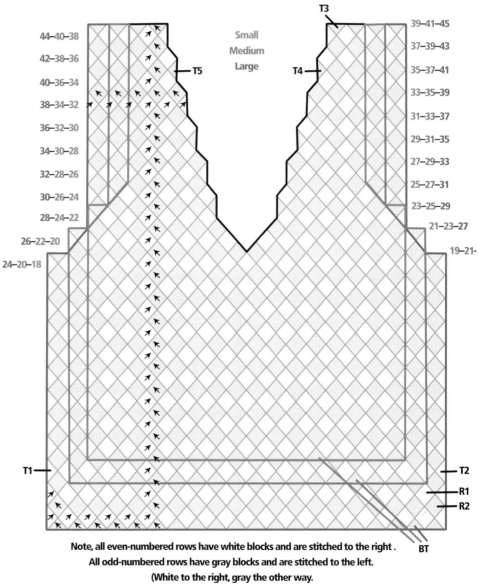

Note, all even-numbered rows have white blocks and are stitched to the right .
All odd-numbered rows have gray blocks and are stitched to the left.
(White to the right, gray the other way.
It seems less intimidating than trying to figure out all the arrows.)

TIER 31(33, 37) (MC): Work R2 3(4, 5) times.

TIER 32(34, 38) (CC): Work T1 once, R1 2(3, 4) times, T2 once.

TIER 33(35, 39) (MC): Repeat Tier 31, binding off last row of last R2. Fasten off.

TIER 34(36, 40) (CC): Join yarn to top of last R2, work R1 2(3, 4) times. T2 once.

TIER 35(37, 41) (MC): Work R2 2(3, 4) times, T4 once.

TIER 36(38, 42) (CC): Work R1 2(3, 4) times, T2 once.

TIER 37(39, 43) (MC): Work R2 2(3, 4) times.

TIER 38(40, 44) (CC): Work T1 once, R1 1(2, 3) times, T2 once.

TIER 39(41, 45) (MC): Work T3 2(3, 4) times.
Fasten off.

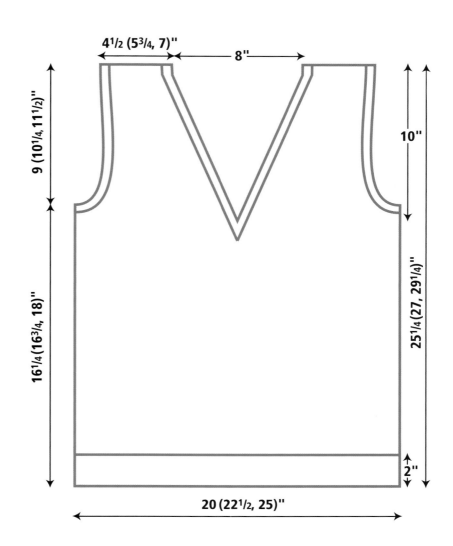

BACK

Work ribbing as for Front. Change to larger needles and work in St st with MC, inc 10(12, 14) sts evenly across the first row – 110(124, 138) sts.

ARMHOLE SHAPING: When Back measures the same as Front to armhole, bind off 7 sts at the beginning of the next 2 rows, then 3 sts at the beginning of the next 6 rows, then dec 1 st at the beg of the next 2 rows– 82(96, 110) sts. Work even until Back measures 8¾(10, 11¼)"/22(25.5, 28.5) cm from beg of armhole shaping, ending with a WS row.

BACK NECK SHAPING

Work across 27(34, 41) sts, bind off 28 sts, finish row.

Working each side separately, at each neckline edge, bind off 4 sts once and 3 sts three times.

When Back measures the same as Front, bind off 14(21, 28) shoulder sts.

FINISHING

Sew shoulder seams together. Sew side seams.

NECKBAND

With circular needle and rs facing, starting at the right shoulder seam pick up 67 sts across the back neck, 89 sts along left neck edge, M1 for center st in running thread connecting two blocks and pick up 91 sts along right neck edge—245 sts.

Place a marker for the end of the rnd.

Rnd 1: Work k1, p1 ribbing until two sts before center st, ssk, k center st, k2tog, complete rnd in p1, k1 ribbing.

Rnd 2: Work k1, p1 ribbing until two sts before center st, p2 tog, k center st, p2 tog, complete rnd in ribbing as established. Repeat Rnd 1 and 2 until

band measures 1" (2.5 cm). Bind off in ribbing, working dec as usual.

ARMBANDS

With circular needle and RS facing, starting at the underarm seam, pick up 148 (168, 186) sts around armhole; mark end of rnd. Work in k1, p1 ribbing for 1" (2.5 cm).

Bind off in ribbing.
Block. 🌣

Kathleen Power Johnson is a self-taught crochet and knit designer whose designs and articles have appeared in most of the well-known crochet and knitting magazines on the market.

kaleidoscope

An interesting Entrelac pattern makes the experience of knitting with rich multicolored silk-blend yarn even more enjoyable. Create this luxurious wrap using jewel-tone colors as beguiling as the colors in a kaleidoscope!

DESIGN BY LISA DANIELS
Skill level: Intermediate
Finished project size: 10" x 68" (25.5 cm x 172.5 cm)

MATERIALS

Noro, 45% Silk/45% Kid Mohair/10% Lambs Wool yarn
(1¾ ounces/50 grams, 110 yards/100 meters per skein): 4 skeins of Silk Garden (#22)
Size 8 (5 mm) knitting needles or size needed to obtain gauge

GAUGE

In Entrelac Pattern, 30 sts = 10" (25.5 cm)
Take time to check gauge.

STITCH PATTERN

Entrelac (meaning interlacing) fabric mimics the look of basketweave. It is worked in such a way that each square is constructed, one at a time, moving across the knit side of the fabric, then working back across the purl side of the fabric. The fabric begins with base triangles and ends again with triangles

The expression turn or turn the work means to physically turn the piece of knitting in your hands to the opposite side (if the knit side is facing you, turn the knitting so that the purl side is facing).

ABBREVIATIONS AND TERMS

St st = knit the right side rows and purl the wrong side rows.
Purlwise increase = purl through the front of the st as usual, then leaving the st on the left hand needle purl through the same st again, but through the back loop. Makes 2 sts.
p2tog = purl 2 sts together.
skp = slip the next st as if to knit, knit the next st, pass the slipped st over the st just knitted. 1 st remains.
st(s) = stitch(es)
psso = pass the slipped st over.

SCARF

Cast on 30 sts.

BEGIN WORKING THE BASE TRIANGLES AS FOLLOWS:

*Knit first 2 sts, turn the work, purl the same 2 sts. Turn the work. Knit 3 sts (the same 2 plus 1), turn the work. Purl 3 sts. Turn the work. Continue working in this way adding one st more each knit row, until knit 10 sts are on the right hand needle. Do not turn the work. * Now, leaving these 10 sts on the right hand needle, repeat from * to * twice more. 3 Base triangles are completed (see Diagram 1). Turn the work.

Note: Once you get going with the series of Entrelac squares, you are essentially working the 10 sts at any one time.

Diagram 1

← **direction of knitting**

This is what gives the appearance of lots of little squares sewn together.

WORK ACROSS THE PURL SIDE AS FOLLOWS:

The first step on the purl side of the work is to construct an edge triangle. The triangle will create a straight edge to work. With the purl side facing, begin by working a purlwise increase in the first st, then p2 tog (3 sts). Turn the work and knit these 3 sts. Turn the work. Work a purlwise increase in the first st, p1, p2 tog. Turn the work and knit 4 sts. Continue in this way until you have 10 purl sts on the right hand needle. *With these 10 sts on the right hand needle, pick up and purl 10 sts (insert your needle from the knit side through to the purl side in approx. every other row) down the side of the same base triangle. Once all 10 sts have been picked up, slip the last picked-up st back to the left hand needle and p2 tog. Turn the work. Knit these 10 sts. Turn the work. Purl 9 sts, purl the last st of these 10 sts together with the first st of the base triangle. Turn the work and knit these 10 sts. Continue to work in this way until all 10 sts of the second base triangle have been worked. * Repeat from * to * once more.

Work an edge triangle (to square-off the fabric) by picking up and purling as above until just 9 sts have been picked up down to the edge of the last side of

Using the Entrelac pattern and multicolored yarn allows you to create a colorful patchwork look without changing yarns for each section.

the last or third-base triangle. Turn the work. Knit 9 sts. Turn the work. Purl 7 sts then p2 tog. Turn the work. Knit 8 sts. Continue working back and forth, in this same way until 1 purl st remains. At this point the purl side of the fabric has been worked and all sts are on one needle (see Diagram 2). Turn the work.

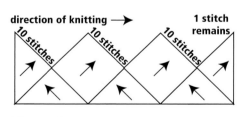

Diagram 2

NEXT, WORK THE KNIT SIDE OF THE WORK AS FOLLOWS:

+Knit the one st left from the previous row, then pick-up and knit 9 sts down the edge triangle. Before turning the work, knit the first st of the next 10 sts on the left hand needle, that form a rectangle, then pass the 9th picked up st over it. Turn the work and purl 10+

*Turn the work. Knit 9, slip the 10th st as if to knit, knit the next st on the left hand needle (or the next st of the full rectangle), pass the slipped st over (psso). Turn the work and purl 10 sts. * Repeat from * to * until all 10 sts of the full rectangle have been worked and do not turn the work to purl back. To begin the next new rectangle, pick up and knit 10 sts down the edge of the next full rectangle. Knit the first st of the next rectangle and pass the 10th st picked up over it. Turn and purl 10 sts. Continue as above from * to *. Pick up and work a third and final rectangle as given. These steps complete the knit side of the work (see Diagram 3).

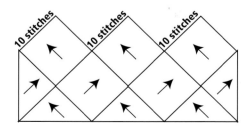

Diagram 3

As mentioned earlier, the technique that forms "Entrelac" is working across the knit side of the work and then returning across the purl side of the work. So, continue in the above manner until most of your yarn has been used and you have just finished working across the purl side of the work.

The next step is to bind off the Entrelac with the knit side of the fabric facing. Begin working the knit side of the fabric as above (portion from + to +) until the first turn and purl 10 sts. Next row, skp, work to the last st as in the directions above (portion from * to *) and work skp, as before. Continue in this manner until all sts have been decreased but one. Begin picking up the next set of 10 sts and bind off the remaining single st at the same time. Continue to work in this way finishing off all the remaining sts (see Diagram 4). ✺

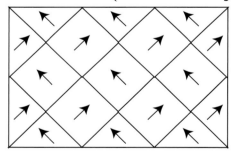

Diagram 4

Lisa Daniels is a talented and enthusiastic instructor specializing in designing hand-knits for her clientele and yarn companies. Lisa is the owner of the Big Sky Studio, which stocks yarns and kits from the finest companies. It is a unique environment catering to the needs of the adventurous and creative knitter—skill level not important.

LEAF (MAKE 6)

Cast on 5 sts.

Row 1 (RS): K2, yo, k1, yo, k2 – 7 sts.

Row 2 and all WS rows: Purl across.

Row 3: K3, yo, k1, yo, k3 – 9 sts.

Row 5: K4, yo, k1, yo, k4 – 11 sts.

Row 7: Ssk, k7, k2 tog – 9 sts.

Row 9: Ssk, k5, k2 tog – 7 sts.

Row 11: Ssk, k3, k2 tog – 5 sts.

Row 13: Ssk, k1, k2 tog – 3 sts.

Row 15: Sk2p.

Fasten off.

DOUBLE-KNITTED TASSELS (MAKE 4)

With larger needles, cast on 20 sts.

Work in garter st for 24 rows.

Bind off 12 sts.

Fasten off. Slip rem 8 sts onto st holder.

Sew seam, gather, and pull tightly at top edge. *Insert one large cotton ball. Gather at base of ball and tie securely. Repeat from * once more.

Remove st holder, unravel 8 sts for fringe.

Cut and trim fringe evenly.

BANDS (MAKE 8)

With larger needles, cast on 13 sts.

Bind off 13 sts.

Sew bands at base of each cotton ball.

FINISHING

Sew large and small flowers, half-flowers, and leaves to one block for Front (see photo on page 131 for placement).

Tie one bobble to center of larger flower.

Tie three bobbles on either side of floral arrangement.

With Front and Back together with Front facing and working through both pieces, join yarn with slip st in any st, ch1, sc evenly around working 3 sc in each corner and inserting pillow form before closing; join with slip st to first sc. Fasten off.

Sew one tassel to each corner.

Nicky Epstein is one of America's leading and most prolific knitwear designers and authors. Her work has been featured in the nation's top magazines, in yarn manufacturer's catalogues, in best-selling books, on television, and in museums. Nicky's 4th book *Knitting for Barbie Doll* won the Independent Publisher's Award as "Craft Book of the Year" for 2002. For more of Nicky's designs see "Chameleon Hat" on page 104 and "Flower Power Patchwork" on page 120.

best-dressed

When the leaves fall and temperature drops, this bright woolen dog sweater will keep your pooch toasty warm. Wearing your matching socks in the same pattern is sure to turn heads when stepping out for a brisk autumn walk. Learn sampler style color work while knitting these charming garments.

DESIGN BY JOANNE CLARK
Skill level: Experienced
Finished project size: Medium chest size 30" (76 cm)

dog coat

MATERIALS
Dale of Norway FALK Sport Weight Yarn, 100% Superwash New Wool yarn (1¾ ounces/50 grams, 118 yards/108 meters per skein): 2 skeins each of Purple (5036), and Red (3727); 1 skein each of White (0017), Navy (5563), Gold (2427), Sky Blue (5813), Green (9155), and Turquoise (8426)
Size 2 (2.75 mm) 16-inch circular needles or size needed to obtain gauge
2 stitch holders

GAUGE
6 sts = 1" (2.5 cm)
Take time to check your gauge.

NOTE: Pattern can be sized up or down in increments of 8 sts. Increase chest piece to the distance between the dog's front legs.

INSTRUCTIONS
NECK
Using Purple, loosely cast on 160 sts.

Knit 13 rows of k1, p1 ribbing in the following color stripe pattern: 3 rows Purple, 2 rows Red, 3 rows Purple, 2 rows Red, 3 rows Purple.

Row 14: With Purple, knit across.

BODY
Note: Rows 17, 48, 68, 79 and 91 are purl on the right side or knit on the wrong side to form garter ridge.

Bind off 5 sts, k 20 and place 21 sts on a holder, bind off 4 sts. Using remaining sts [130 sts, 16 repeats plus 2 edge sts (extra sts worked in last color at end or beginning of row)], beginning with a purl row, work in Stockinette stitch following color chart Rows 1–104 on page 136.

BODY SHAPING
After Row 80 or 4" (10 cm) short of desired length, decrease one stitch on each side every other row 6 times and then decrease every row 6 times, keeping pattern correct on middle part and decreasing into patterns as necessary. Place remaining 106 sts on holder.

BODY HEM
With Navy and starting at neck edge, pick up 3 sts for every 4 rows down the side of the body and pick up 1 stitch for every row in decrease area. Knit across sts on holder. Knit 1 stitch for every row in decrease area and pick up 3 sts for every 4 rows up the side of the body. (You should have 84+106+84 sts.)

Row 1 and all other odd numbered rows (WS): Purl across.

Row 2: Knit across.
Row 4: Knit across.
Row 6: Purl across.
Row 8: Knit across.
Row 10: Knit across.
After working in ends, either bind off loosely or sew hem down with live sts. Attach hem ends to neck at previous bind off.

CHEST PIECE
Slip 21 sts from holder onto a needle.

PATTERN STITCH (4 row repeat)
Row 1 and all odd numbered rows (RS): Knit across.
Row 2: P2, k1, (p1, k1) across to last 2 sts, p2.
Row 4: P1, (k1, p1) across.

Work this pattern in the following color stripe pattern: 4 rows Purple, 2 rows Red. Carry colors loosely down the side. At the same time, increase each side every 4th row to 35 sts. Knit straight to 10½" (26.5 cm) or desired chest length less one inch. Continuing in color stripe pattern, knit 1" (2.5 cm) of k1, P1 ribbing.

Try sweater on dog and mark front leg openings. Sew chest to back, leaving openings as marked for front legs.

Work in ends and block.

(See pattern on next page.)

DOG COAT CHART

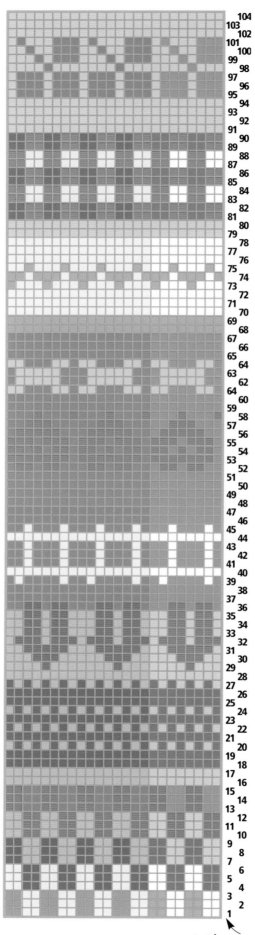

start here

socks

Skill level: Experienced
Finished project size: Women's Medium;
Women's Large numbers in parentheses

MATERIALS

Dale of Norway FALK Sport Weight Yarn, 100%
Superwash New Wool yarn
(1¾ ounces/50 grams, 118 yards/108 meters per
skein): 1 skein each of White (0017), Navy
(5563), Gold (2427), Purple (5036), Sky Blue
(5813), Green (9155), Red (3727), and
Turquoise (8426)
Size 2 (2.75 mm) double pointed needles or
size needed to obtain gauge

GAUGE

6 sts = 1" (2.5 cm)
Take time to check your gauge.

ABBREVIATIONS

cm = centimeters
k = knit
k2 tog = knit 2 sts together.
mm = millimeters
p = purl
p2 tog = purl 2 sts together.
Rnd(s) = round(s)
RS = right side
ssk = slip, slip, knit
WS = wrong side

SOCKS CHART

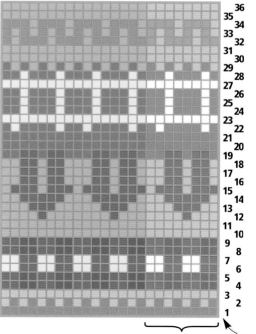

start here

INSTRUCTIONS

CUFF

Using Purple, loosely cast on 48 (56) sts. Divide onto three double pointed needles.

Rnds 1–3: K1, p1 around.

Rnds 4 and 5: With Red, k1, p1 around.

Rnds 6–8: With Purple, k1, p1 around.

Rnds 9 and 10: With Red, k1, p1 around.

Rnds 11–13: With Purple, k1, p1 around.

Rnd 14: Knit around.

LEG

Follow sock chart (page opposite), knitting all rounds. Cut and join colors as needed.

HEEL

Divide sts onto two needles, with first 25 (29) sts on the Heel needle and 23 (27) sts on the Instep needle.

Row 1 (RS): With Purple, knit across.

Row 2: P2, k1, (p1, k1) across to last 2 sts, p2.

Row 3: Knit across.

Row 4: P1, (k1, p1) across.

Row 5: With Red, knit across.

Row 6: P2, k1, (p1, k1) across to last 2 sts, p2.

Row 7: With Purple, knit across.

Row 8: P1, (k1, p1) across.

Row 9: Knit across.

Row 10: P2, k1, (p1, k1) across to last 2 sts, p2.

Row 11: With Red, knit across.

Row 12: P1, (k1, p1) across.

Row 13: With Purple, knit across.

Row 14: P2, k1, (p1, k1) across to last 2 sts, p2.

Row 15: Knit across.

Row 16: P1, (k1, p1) across.

Row 17: With Red, knit across.

Row 18: P1, (k1, p1) across.

Row 19: With Purple, knit across.

Row 20: P1, (k1, p1) across.

Row 21: Knit across.

Row 22: P2, k1, (p1, k1) across to last 2 sts, p2; cut yarn.

Row 23: With Red, knit across.

Row 24: P1, (k1, p1) across; cut yarn.

Row 25: With Navy and WS facing, purl across.

TURN HEEL

Row 1 (RS): K14 (16), ssk, k1, turn.

Row 2: Slip 1, p4, p2 tog, p1, turn.

Row 3: Slip 1, k5, ssk, k1, turn.

Row 4: Slip 1, p6, p2 tog, p1, turn.

Continue in this manner, working one more stitch before decreasing each row.

Last row, being a purl row, should have 15 (17) sts.

INSTEP SET-UP ROUND

K7 (8) to center Heel.

Needle 1: K8 (9), pick up 14 sts on the side of the Heel and 3 sts from the Instep needle— 25 (26) sts.

Needle 2: Knit to the last 3 sts on the Instep needle – 17 (21) sts.

Needle 3: Knit the last 3 sts on the Instep needle and pick up 14 sts down the other side of the Heel. Knit 7 (8) sts off the Heel needle – 24 (25) sts

(Middle of Heel is the beginning of the round)

Color Note: Use the following color stripe pattern while working the Instep Shaping and Foot: 7 rounds of Navy, 5 rounds of Sky Blue, 4 rounds of Red, 6 rounds of Green, 3 rounds of Yellow, 9 rounds of Purple, 2 rounds of White, (2 rounds of Turquoise, 2 rounds of White), twice. Adjust stripe pattern to desired length of foot and colors can be adjusted for color availability (if using leftovers from the dog coat project).

INSTEP SHAPING

RND 1:

Needle 1: Knit to last 4 sts, k2 tog, k2.

Needle 2: Knit across.

Needle 3: K2, ssk, knit across.

RND 2: Knit around.

Repeat rnds 1 and 2 until you have 48 (56) sts.

FOOT

Continue stripe color pattern, knit to desired Foot length less 2½" (6.5 cm).

TOE SHAPING

Rnd 1: With Red, knit around.

Rnd 2: (P6, p2 tog) around – 45 (49) sts.

Rnds 3–7: With Purple, knit around.

Rnd 8: With Red, knit around.

Rnd 9: (P5, p2 tog) around – 36 (42) sts.

Rnds 10–13: With Purple, knit around.

Rnd 14: With Red, knit around.

Rnd 15: (P4, p2 tog) around.

Rnds 16–18: With Purple, knit around.

Rnd 19: With Red, knit around.

Rnd 20: (P3, p2 tog) around.

Rnds 21–22: With Purple, knit around.

Rnd 23: With Red, knit around.

Rnd 24: (P2, p2 tog) around.

Rnd 25: With Purple, knit around.

Rnd 26: With Red, knit around.

Rnd 27: (P1, p2 tog) around.

Rnd 28: Knit around.

Rnd 29: K2 tog around.

FINISHING

Cut yarn. Using a tapestry needle, thread yarn through the remaining sts. Pull together firmly and secure. Work in all ends carefully and block. ✺

Joanne Clark has been knitting since her first baby needed a sweater. Now, many sweaters later, she enjoys teaching sweater construction and technique classes in Northwest Washington and British Columbia, Canada. Several of her designs have been published by Fiber Trends, and for several years she was partners with Beverly Galeskas in a Bellingham, Washington, yarn shop called "Fibers."

quiet reflection

The color of nature, captured in "soft as silk" cashmere and paired with exquisite shaping, creates a sweater of understated exceptional beauty. Once you've worn a garment designed by Lily Chin, you won't leave home without it.

DESIGN BY LILY CHIN
Skill level: Intermediate
Finished chest measurement: 35" (38", 41", 44")/ 89(96.5, 104, 112) cm
Instructions for smallest size with changes for larger sizes in parentheses
Finished length = 21½" (22", 22½", 23")/54.5(56, 57, 58.5) cm

MATERIALS
Karabella "Margrite" 80% extra fine merino wool, 20% cashmere
(1¾ ounces/50 grams, 154 yards/141 meters per skein): 7 (8, 8, 9) skeins of Sage (#23)
Sizes 5 (3.75 mm) and 7 (4.5 mm) knitting needles or sizes needed to obtain gauge
Size 5 (3.75 mm) 16" (40.5 cm) circular needle
Stitch marker
Stitch holder

GAUGE
With larger needles, in St st, 20 sts and 28 rows = 4" (10 cm)
Take time to check your gauge.

ABBREVIATIONS AND TERMS
increase = knit into the front, then into the back of the same stitch.
k = knit
k2 tog = knit two stitches together as one.
LH = left hand
p = purl
p2 tog = purl two stitches together as one.
RH = right hand
RS = right side

ssk (slip, slip, knit) = slip 2 stitches one at a time as if to knit. Insert left needle through the front of these slipped stitches from left to right and knit them together from this position.
ssp (slip, slip, purl) = slip 2 stitches one at a time as if to knit. Insert the left needle into the back of both stitches from back to front and purl them together from this position.
st = stitch
St st = Stockinette stitch
tbl = through back loop
W&T (Wrap & Turn) = slip next stitch to right needle as if to purl. Bring the yarn between the needles to the front. Put the stitch back on the left needle. Turn and work in the other direction.
WS = wrong side.
[ ] = repeat instructions between brackets specified number of times.

SPECIAL STITCHES
Twisted 1 x 1 Rib (worked over an odd number of sts)
    Row 1 (WS): P 1, [k1 tbl, p1] across.
    Row 2 (RS): K 1 tbl, [p1, k1 tbl] across.
    Repeat Rows 1 and 2 for pattern.

INSTRUCTIONS
BACK
RIBBING
With smaller needles, cast on 89(97, 105, 113) sts.
    BEG TWISTED 1 X 1 RIB PATTERN AS FOLLOWS:
    Row 1 (WS): P2, k1 tbl, [p1, k1 tbl] across to last 2 sts, p2.
    Row 2 (RS): K1, [k1 tbl, p1] across to last 2 sts, k1 tbl, k1.
    Repeat Rows 1 and 2 for pattern until piece measures 5" (12.5 cm).

BODY
Change to larger needles. Work in St st until piece measures 14" (35.5 cm) or 9" (23 cm) above ribbing, ending with a WS row.
    SHAPE ARMHOLES:
    Bind off 1(2, 3, 4) sts beginning next 2 rows—87(93, 99, 105) sts.
    Decrease on next row [a RS row] and every other row, 16 (18, 18, 20) times as follows:
    K2, k2 tog, knit across to last 4 sts, ssk, k2—55 (57, 63, 65) sts.
    Decrease every row, 13(13, 15, 15) times as follows:

(WS) P2, ssp, purl across to last 4 sts, p2 tog, p2.

(RS) Dec is same as before.

Bind off remaining 29(31, 33, 35) sts.

FRONT

Work as for Back to Armhole Shaping.

SHAPE ARMHOLES:

Bind off 1(2, 3, 4) sts beginning next 2 rows: 87(93, 99, 105) sts.

Work even in St st until piece measures 3¼"(3¾", 4¼", 4¾")/8.5 (9.5, 11, 12) cm from beginning of Armhole Shaping, ending with a WS row.

SHAPE FRONT NECK WITH SHORT ROWS:

* Knit across the first 33(35, 37, 39) sts only; do not work across remaining sts, wrap and turn (W&T) by slipping next st unknit st from LH to RH needle, bring yarn to the front of the work, slip this unknit st back onto LH needle, turn work. Bring yarn to front of work and purl back. Notice that there is a "wrap" or loop around first unworked st.

K across the first 27(29, 31, 32) sts only; do not work across remaining sts, W&T, purl back.

K across the first 22(24, 25, 26) sts only; do not work across remaining sts, W&T, purl back.

K across the first 18(20, 20, 21) sts only; do not work across remaining sts, W&T, purl back.

K across the first 15(16, 16, 17) sts only; do not work across remaining sts, W&T, purl back.

K across the first 13(13, 13, 14) sts only; do not work across remaining sts, W&T, purl back.

K across the first 11 sts only; do not work across remaining sts, W&T, purl back.

K across the first 9 sts only; do not work across remaining sts, W&T, purl back.

K across the first 7 sts only; do not work across remaining sts, W&T, purl back.

K across the first 5 sts only; do not work across remaining sts, W&T, purl back.

K across the first 3 sts only; do not work across remaining sts, W&T, purl back.

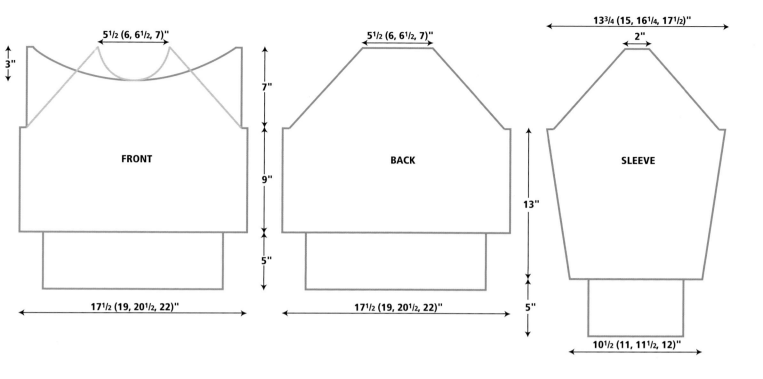

K across all sts on next row hiding or closing up the 11 wrapped sts as follows: go upward into the wrapped loop from below with RH needle in a knitwise fashion, go into actual st itself also with RH needle, k both wrap and st together.

On next WS row, begin short row process again from * except work in purl instead of knit st and wrap by bringing yarn to the back of the work after slipping st, then bring yarn to back of work after turning to knit.

After completing last 3-st sequence, purl across all sts on next row, hiding or closing up the 11 wrapped sts as follows: lift wrap loop with RH needle from behind up and onto LH needle, purl both wrap, and st together.

On next RS row, k3 tog across, place remaining 29(31, 33, 35) sts onto st holder.

SLEEVE (MAKE 2)

With smaller needles, cast on 55(57, 59, 61) sts.

Work Twisted 1 x 1 Rib pattern as for Back until piece measures 5" (12.5 cm), ending with a RS row.

Change to larger needles and begin St st beginning with a purl row. At same time, increase on RS rows as follows:

K2, increase, knit across to last 2 sts, increase, k2. Increase every 8th (8th, 6th, 6th) row, 10(10, 7, 14) times, then every 0(0, 8th, 0) row, 5 times.

Work even on 71(77, 83, 89) sts until Sleeve measures approx. 18" (45.5 cm) total or 13" (33 cm) above ribbing, ending with a WS row.

SHAPE CAP:

Bind off 1(2, 3, 4) sts beginning next 2 rows – 69(73, 77, 81) sts.

Decrease on next row [a RS row] and every other row, 16 (18, 18, 20) times as follows:

K2, k2 tog, knit across to last 4 sts, ssk, k2 – 37(37, 41, 41) sts.

Decrease every row, 13(13, 15, 15) times as follows:

(WS) P2, ssp, purl across to last 4 sts, p2 tog, p2.

(RS) decrease is same as before.

Bind off remaining 11 sts.

FINISHING

Block pieces to measurement.

Sew Sleeves to Body. Sew side and sleeve seams.

TURTLENECK

With RS facing and circular needle, pick up and knit 27(29, 31, 33) sts across Back Neck, pick up and knit 9 sts from Left Sleeve, knit across Front Neck 29(31, 33, 35) sts from st holder, pick up and knit 9 sts from Right Sleeve— 74(78, 82, 86) sts.

Place st marker to mark beginning/ end of rnds.

Work Twisted 1 x 1 rib pattern as follows:

Rnd 1: [K1 tbl, p1] around.
Rnd 2: [K1, p1 tbl] around.

Repeat rnds 1 and 2 for pattern.

Work until turtleneck measures 6" (15 cm).

Bind off very loosely. 🏵

Named a Master Knitter by Vogue Knitting, this NYC native has been involved in some aspect of the fashion industry since age 13. Lily designs for magazines and yarn companies and does fabric development and samples for Seventh Ave, from the Gap to Diane von Furstenburg. See Lily's knit shawl project "Reversible Wrap" on page 142.

reversible wrap

Wrap yourself in volumes of luxurious blended Mohair and wait for the compliments to begin. The experienced knitter will love Lily Chin's reverse cable pattern where both front and back appear the same as if by magic.

DESIGN BY LILY CHIN
Skill level: Experienced
Finished project size: 24" x 66" (61 cm x 167.5 cm)

MATERIALS

Trendsetter/Lane Borgosesia "Mohair", 50% Mohair, 50% Acrylic

(1¾ ounces/50 grams, 164 yards/150 meters per skein): 8 skeins of Taupe (#68)

Size 7 needles or size needed to obtain gauge

Cable needle

Stitch markers

GAUGE

In Garter st, 20 sts and 26 rows = 4" (10 cm)

48-st OXO Center Panel = 7" (18 cm)

12-st Lattice (either right or left) = 2" (5 cm)

24-st Braid (either right or left) = 3½" (9 cm)

32 rows of any of these patterns = 5¼" (13.5 cm)

These are STEAM BLOCKED gauges.
Take time to check your gauge.

NOTE: Slip markers as you work.

ABBREVIATIONS

beg = begin

cn = cable needle

C4Frib = Cable 4 Front in 1 x 1 ribbing (worked over 4 sts). Place next 2 sts onto cn and hold in front of work, [k1, p1] next 2 sts, [k1, p1] 2 sts from cn.

C4Brib = Cable 4 Back in 1 x 1 ribbing (worked over 4 sts). Place next 2 sts onto cn and hold in back of work, [k1, p1] next 2 sts, [k1, p1] 2 sts from cn.

C16Frib = Cable 16 Front in 2 x 2 ribbing (worked over 16 sts). Place next 8 sts onto cm and hold in front of work, [k2, p2] twice next 8 sts, [k2, p2] twice 8 sts from cn.

C16Brib = Cable 16 Back in 2 x 2 ribbing (worked over 16 sts). Place next 8 sts onto cm and hold in back of work, [k2, p2] twice next 8 sts, [k2, p2] twice 8 sts from cn.

C8Fgarter-rib = Cable 8 Front (worked over 8 sts). Place next 4 garter sts onto cn and hold in front of work, [k1, p1] twice next 4 sts, knit 4 sts from cn.

C8Bgarter-rib = Cable 8 Back (worked over 8 sts). Place next 4 garter sts onto cn and hold in back of work, [k1, p1] twice next 4 sts, knit 4 sts from cn.

C8Frib-garter = Cable 8 Back (worked over 8 sts). Place next 4 rib sts onto cn and hold in front of work, k next 4 sts, [k1, p1] twice 4 sts from cn.

C8Brib-garter = Cable 8 Back (worked over 8 sts). Place next 4 rib sts onto cn and hold in back of work, k next 4 sts, [k1, p1] twice 4 sts from cn.

k = knit

patt = pattern

p = purl

pm = place marker

rep = repeat

[ ] = repeat instructions between brackets specified number of times.

STITCH PATTERNS

Garter St = K all rows.

1 x 1 Rib = [k1, p1] across. On subsequent rows, k the k sts and p the p sts.

LATTICE RIGHT – worked over 12 sts (4 row rep)

Row 1: [C4Brib] 3 times.

Rows 2 and 4: [K1, p1] 6 times.

Row 3: K1, p1, [C4Frib] twice, k1, p1.

Repeat Rows 1–4 for pattern.

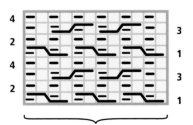

Lattice Right

LATTICE LEFT – worked over 12 sts (4 row rep)

Row 1: [C4Frib] 3 times.
Rows 2 and 4: [K1, p1] 6 times,
Row 3: K1, p1, [C4Brib] twice, k1, p1.
Repeat Rows 1-4 for pattern.

BRAID RIGHT – worked over 24 sts (32 row rep)

Rows 1-8: [K2, p2] 6 times.
Row 9: C16Brib, [k2, p2] twice.
Rows 10–24: [K2, p2] 6 times.
Row 25: [K2, p2] twice, C16Frib.
Rows 26–32: [K2, p2] 6 times.
Repeat Rows 1–32 for pattern.

BRAID LEFT – worked over 24 sts (32 row rep)

Rows 1-8: [K2, p2] 6 times.
Row 9: [K2, p2] twice, C16Frib.
Rows 10-24: [K2, p2] 6 times.
Row 25: C16Brib, [k2, p2] twice.
Rows 26-32: [K2, p2] 6 times.
Repeat Rows 1–32 for pattern.

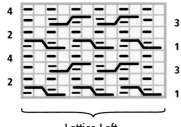

Lattice Left

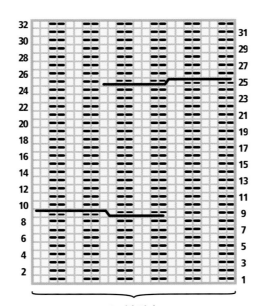

Braid Right

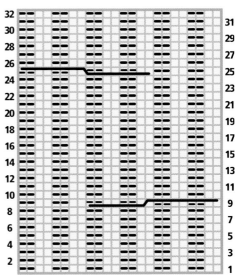

Braid Left

STITCH GUIDE

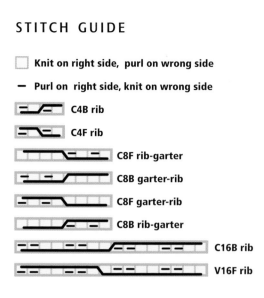

☐ Knit on right side, purl on wrong side

— Purl on right side, knit on wrong side

C4B rib

C4F rib

C8F rib-garter

C8B garter-rib

C8F garter-rib

C8B rib-garter

C16B rib

V16F rib

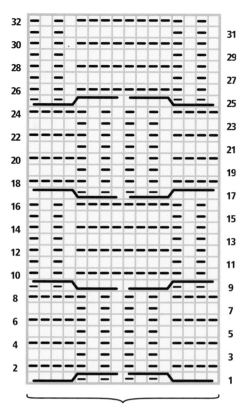

Garter XOX

GARTER XOX – worked over 16 sts (32 row rep)

Row 1: C8Frib-garter, C8Bgarter-rib.

Rows 2–8: K4, [k1, p1] 4 times, k4.

Row 9: C8Bgarter-rib, C8Frib-garter.

Rows 10–16: [K1, p1] twice, k8, [k1, p1] twice.

Row 17: C8Brib-garter, C8Fgarter-rib.

Rows 18–24: Rep Rows 2-8.

Row 25: C8Fgarter-rib, C8Brib-garter.

Rows 26–32: Rep Rows 10-16.
Repeat Rows 1–32 for pattern.

OXO – worked over 16 sts (32 row rep)

Row 1: C8Brib-garter, C8Fgarter rib.

Rows 2–8: K4, [k1, p1] 4 times, k4.

Row 9: C8Fgarter-rib, C8Brib-garter.

Rows 10–16: [K1, p1] twice, k8, [k1, p1] twice.

Row 17: C8Frib-garter, C8Bgarter rib.

Rows 18–24: Rep Rows 2-8.

Row 25: C8Bgarter-rib, C8Frib-garter.

Rows 26–32: Rep Rows 10-16.
Repeat Rows 1–32 for pattern.

STOLE

BOTTOM TRIM

Cast on 144 sts.

Row 1: K4, [k1, p1] 6 times, k4, [k2, p2] 6 times, k4, [k1, p1] twice, k8, * [k1, p1] 4 times, k8, rep from * once more, [k1, p1] twice, k4, [k2, p2] 6 times, k4, [k1, p1] 6 times, k4.

Note: In order to create a smooth chain-selvage, slip first st as if to knit on each row from this point on.

Repeat Row 1 until work measures approximately 1"(2.5 cm).

BODY

Row 1 (RS): Slip first st, k3, pm, beg Lattice Right patt over next 12 sts, pm, k4 (garter), pm, beg Braid Right over next 24 sts, pm, k4 (garter), pm, beg XOX over next 16 sts, pm, beg OXO over next 16 sts, pm, beg XOX over next

16 sts, pm, k4 (garter), pm, beg Braid Left over next 24 sts, pm, k4 (garter), pm, beg Lattice Left over next 12 sts, pm, k4 (garter).

Work in established patts until work measures approximately 65" (165 cm), ending with Row 9 of any of the XOX or Braid patts.

TOP TRIM

Work as for Bottom Trim for 1" (2.5 cm).

Bind off.

FINISHING

Block to finished measurement.

Master knitter Lily Chin's pattern line for both knitting and crochet, the Lily Chin collection, is put out by Fiber Trends. She has appeared on cable TV's "Handmade by Design" on Lifetime, HGTV, and on CNN. She was officially named the fastest crocheter in the world in 2002 international competition. See Lily's sweater project, "Quiet Reflections," on page 138.

beaded objects d'art

Lustrous beads of many colors, sizes, and types are used to fashion these exquisite knitted purses. An experienced knitter will enjoy the challenge of creating one or more of these tiny treasures. They are sure to become your favorite fashion accessories.

DESIGNS BY COY ROBERTS
Skill level: Experienced
Finished project sizes: Peacock Coin Purse 3" x 3½" (7.5 cm x 8.75 cm);
Ivory Opera Purse 3" x 6" (7.5 cm x 15 cm) ; Confetti Miniature Purse, 2" x 2" (5 cm x 5 cm)

peacock coin purse

Please read all of the instructions before beginning.

MATERIALS
2 hanks size 9 – 3-cut beads, color
    Peacock
2 cards [22 yards(20 meters each)] YLI
    1000 denier silk thread, (color #29)
1 pair size 0000 (1.25 cm) knitting needles
Tapestry needle size 24
Beading needle and beading thread
Scroll Delight Coin Purse Frame
Silk lining and trim, if desired

ABBREVIATIONS
k = knit
st(s) = stitch(es)
inc = increase one st (knit in the front
    & then the back of the same st).
dec = knit 2 sts together.
Sl 1 B = slip 1 bead up to the right
    needle before knitting the next
    stitch. The bead will be between
    the sts after knitting the st.

PREPARING THE BEADS AND THREAD FOR BEAD KNITTING

Do not untie the bead strands. They are tied in such a way as to be able to pull gently on a strand and it will release from the hank. Pull gently on a thread close to the knot. Release only one end of the strand and continue as below:

Unwind approximately 15 yards (13.5 meters) of the silk thread, [approximately 21 yards (20 meters) are on each card]. Following the diagram below, tie on one strand of beads. After tying the bead strand to the silk thread, slide the beads onto the silk thread. Push the beads along the 15 yards of thread. *[Load 6 strands of beads onto the 1st card of thread and 4 strands onto the 2nd card of thread]. Begin winding the thread and beads onto the card of thread. Keep the beads spread out. Leave about a yard of unbeaded thread with which to begin bead knitting. You are now ready to begin knitting.

*These bead strand amounts are approximate. They may vary, depending upon how you knit. When you tie on a new card of thread, always do so at the beginning of a row.

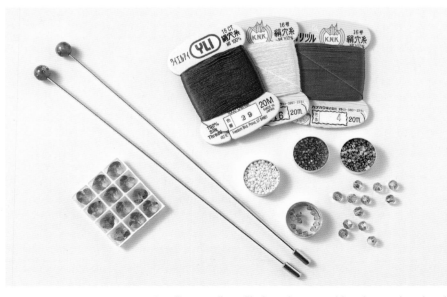

CLOCKWISE, FROM TOP LEFT: Beading needles, silk thread, assorted beads, teardrop beads.

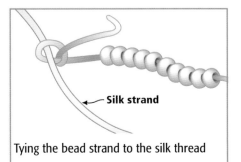

Tying the bead strand to the silk thread

INSTRUCTIONS

PURSE BODY

Knit 2 of the following:

Cast on 23 sts.

Rows 1–6: Knit across.

Rows 7–22: K3, (Sl 1 B, k1) 17 times, Sl 1B, k3. (16 rows)

Row 23: Inc, K1, (Sl 1 B, k1) 19 times, Sl 1 B, k1, inc – 25 sts.

Row 24: K3, (Sl 1 B, K 1) 19 times, Sl 1 B, k3.

Row 25: Inc, K1, (Sl 1 B, k1) 21 times, Sl 1 B, k1, inc – 27 sts.

Row 26: K3, (Sl 1 B, K 1) 21 times, Sl 1 B, k3.

Row 27: Inc, K1, (Sl 1 B, k1) 23 times, Sl 1 B, k1, inc – 29 sts.

Rows 28–30: K3, (Sl 1 B, k1) 23 times, Sl 1 B, k3. (3 rows)

Place a marker at the beginning and end of the next row.

Row 31: Inc, K1, (Sl 1 B, k1) 25 times, Sl 1 B, k1, inc – 31 sts.

Rows 32–56: K3, (Sl 1 B, k1) 25 times, Sl 1 B, k3. (25 rows)

Row 57: Dec, k2, (Sl 1 B, k1) 23 times, Sl 1 B, k2, dec – 29 sts.

Row 58: K 3, (Sl 1 B, k1) 23 times, Sl 1B, k3.

Row 59: Dec, k2, (Sl 1 B, k1) 21 times, Sl 1 B, k2, dec – 27 sts.

Row 60: All even numbered rows through Row 78, repeat Row 58.

There will be 2 less sts and 2 less beads Slipped on each of these rows as you progress. Row 78 will have 9 sts on the needle and a total of 4 beads slipped.

Row 61: Dec, k2, (Sl 1 B, k1) 19 times, Sl 1 B, k2, dec – 25 sts.

Row 63: Dec, k2, (Sl 1 B, k1) 17 times, Sl 1 B, k2, dec – 23 sts.

Row 65: Dec, k2, (Sl 1 B, k1) 15 times, Sl 1 B, k2, dec – 21 sts.

Row 67: Dec, k2, (Sl 1 B, k1) 13 times, Sl 1 B, k2, dec – 19 sts.

Row 69: Dec, k2, (Sl 1 B, k1) 11 times, Sl 1 B, k2, dec – 17 sts.

Row 71: Dec, k2, (Sl 1 B, k1) 9 times, Sl 1 B, k2, dec – 15 sts.

Row 73: Dec, k2, (Sl 1 B, k1) 7 times, Sl 1 B, k2, dec – 13 sts.

Row 75: Dec, k2, (Sl 1 B, k1) 5 times, Sl 1 B, k2, dec – 11 sts.

Row 77: Dec, k2, (Sl 1 B, k1) 3 times, Sl 1 B, k2, dec – 9 sts.

Row 79: Dec, k2, Sl 1 B, k1, Sl 1 B, k2, dec – 7 sts.

Row 80: K3, Sl 1 B, k1, Sl 1 B, k3.

Row 81: Dec, k3, dec – 5 sts.

Row 82: Dec, k1, dec – 3 sts.

Row 83: K3.

Cast off.

FINISHING

If you would like to line the coin purse, place the purse on top of the lining before you sew the purse together. Draw around the coin purse allowing ½" (12 mm) for seams. Sew the lining pieces together.

Sew the 2 sides of the coin purse together beginning at the marker at Row 31 and continuing around the coin purse to the marker on the opposite side. Knot off and dab the knot with FrayCheck.

Attach the coin purse to the frame as follows: Line up the center top edge of the purse with the center of the Scroll Delight coin purse frame. Using the silk thread that you used to knit the coin purse, sew using the backstitch method. Bring the needle up through the center hole, then down one hole to the right, then up one hole left of center. Continue the backstitch method sewing left until the left half of the coin purse is sewn to the left side of the frame. Knot off and dab the knot with FrayCheck. Now attach the right half in the same manner. Attach the opposite side of the coin purse to the frame in the same way. Ease the knitting in as you go, if necessary. Knot off and dab the knot with FrayCheck.

Sew in the lining by stitching it along the top of the knitting. If you would like, sew a pretty ribbon trim along the top edge.

ivory opera purse

Please read all of the instructions before beginning.

MATERIALS

2 hanks size 11 seed beads, color Ivory

3 cards [22 yards (20 meters each)] YLI 1000 denier silk thread (color #16)

1 pair size 0000 (1.25 cm) knitting needles

Tapestry needle size 24

Beading needle & beading thread

Scroll Delight Purse Frame

10–12 inches of chain

2 jump rings

Twenty-four 4 mm bi-cone Swarovski crystals

Twelve 6 mm round Swarovski crystals

Twelve 10 x 10.3 mm Swarovski crystal hearts

Twenty-four 5 mm bead caps

Silk lining and trim if desired

ABBREVIATIONS

See page 146.

PREPARING THE BEADS AND THREAD FOR BEAD KNITTING

Do not untie the bead strand. The hank of beads is tied in such a way as to be able to pull gently on a strand and it will release from the hank. Pull gently on a thread close to the knot to achieve this. Release only one end of the strand & continue as below:

Unwind approximately 15 yards (13.5 meters) of the silk thread, [approximately 21 yards (20 meters) are on each card]. Following the diagram on page 146, tie on one strand of beads. After tying the bead strand to the silk thread, slide the beads onto the silk thread. Push the beads along the 15 yards (13.5 meters) of thread, *[load 10 strands of beads onto the 1st card of thread, 10 strands onto the 2nd card and 2 strands onto the 3rd card of thread]. Keep the beads spread out. Leave about a yard of unbeaded thread with which to begin bead knitting. If at anytime you need more beads on the thread, unwind the remainder of the thread and add more beads from the other end of the thread. You are now ready to begin bead knitting.

*These bead strand amounts are approximate. They may vary, depending upon how you knit. When you tie on a new card of thread, always do so at the beginning of a row.

Sew in lining after attaching purse to frame. Add ribbon trim for finishing touch.

INSTRUCTIONS

PURSE BODY

Cast on 26.

Rows 1–6: Knit across.

Rows 7 and 8: K4, (Sl 1 B, k2) 9 times, Sl 1 B, k4.

Rows 9 and 10: K3, (Sl 1 B, k2) 10 times, Sl 1 B, k3.

Rows 11–22: Repeat Rows 7–10; 3 times. (12 rows)

Rows 23–24: K3, (Sl 1 B, k2) 10 times, Sl 1 B, k3.

Rows 25–28: K3, (Sl 2 B, k2) 10 times, Sl 2 B, k3.

Place a marker at the beginning and end of the next row.

Rows 29–32: K3, (Sl 3 B, k2) 10 times, Sl 3 B, k3. (4 rows)

Rows 33–92: K3, (Sl 4 B, k1, Sl 1 B, k1) 10 times, Sl 4 B, k3. (60 rows)

Rows 93 and 94: K3, (Sl 4 B, k2) 10 times, Sl 4 B, k3. Rows 93 and 94 are the lower edge of the purse.

Rows 94–186: Repeat Rows 92–1. Bind off.

FINISHING

If you would like to line the purse, place the purse on top of the lining before you sew the purse together. Draw around the purse allowing ½" (12 mm) for seams. Sew the pieces together.

FRINGE

The fringes will be sewn on the lower edge of the purse. There will be 12 fringes attached in the "knit 2" areas of Rows 93 and 94. When sewing the fringes at the ends of the row, do so close to the beads to allow enough room to sew the side seams. Using a beading needle and beading thread, begin on either the right or left side, slip beads onto the needle in the following order, 3 seed beads, one 4 mm crystal, 1 seed bead, 1 bead cap, one 6 mm round crystal, 1 bead cap, 1 seed bead, one 4 mm crystal, 4 seed beads, one 10 x 10.3 mm crystal heart, 3 seed beads. Now pass the needle up through 1 seed bead, one 4 mm crystal, 1 seed bead, 1 bead cap, one 6 mm round crystal, 1 bead cap, 1 seed bead, one 4 mm crystal and 3 seed beads, through the knitted thread to the inside of the purse. Pull up all the slack in the beading thread, secure with a knot and dab the knot with FrayCheck. Progress across the row until all 12 fringes have been made.

Sew the side seams from the lower edge of the purse up to the marker between Rows 28 and 29, using the silk thread and a tapestry needle.

Attach the purse to the frame as follows: Line up the center top of the purse with the center of the Scroll Delight purse frame. Using the silk thread that you used to knit the purse, sew using the backstitch method. Bring the needle up through the center hole, then down one hole to the right, then up one hole left of center. Continue the backstitch method sewing left until the left half of the purse is sewn to the left side of the frame. Knot off, and dab the knot with FrayCheck. Now attach the right half in the same manner. Attach the opposite side of the purse to the frame in the same way. Ease the knitting in as you stitch if necessary.

Sew in the lining by stitching it along the top of the knitting. If you would like, sew a pretty ribbon trim along the top edge.

Attach the chain and jump rings.

confetti
miniature purse

Please read all of the instructions before beginning.

MATERIALS

1 hank size 11 seed beads, multicolor
1 card [22 yards (20 meters)] YLI 1000 denier silk thread (color 4)
1 pair size 0000 (1.25 cm) knitting needles
Silk lining and trim if desired
Tapestry needle size 24
Beading needle & beading thread
Doll Delight Purse Frame
3–4 inches of chain
Jump ring
Four 4 mm bi-cone Swarovski crystals
Four 9 x 6 mm Millefiori drops

ABBREVIATIONS

See page 146.

PREPARING THE BEADS AND THREAD FOR BEAD KNITTING

Do not untie the bead strands. They are tied in such a way as to be able to pull gently on a strand and it will release from the hank Pull gently on a thread close to the knot. Release only one end of the strand and continue as below:

Unwind approximately 15 yards (13.5 meters) of the silk thread, [approximately 21 yards (20 meters) are on each card]. Following the diagram on page 146, tie on one strand of beads. After tying the bead strand to the silk thread, slide the beads onto the thread. Push the beads along the 15 yards (13.5 meters) of thread. Keep the beads spread out. Leave about a yard of unbeaded thread

with which to begin bead knitting. You are now ready to begin knitting.

INSTRUCTIONS

PURSE BODY

Cast on 14 sts.

Rows 1–3: Knit across.

Rows 4 and 5: K3, (Sl 1 B, k1) 8 times, Sl 1 B, k3.

Rows 6–9: K2, (Sl 1 B, k1; 10 times), Sl 1 B, k2. (4 rows)

In the following rows, 10–33, you will begin slipping 2 beads increasing to 13 beads in the 3 "swag" sections of the purse.

Rows 10 and 11: K2, (Sl 1 B, k1) 2 times, *Sl 2 B, k1, (Sl 1 B, k1) 2 times*, repeat from* to *, Sl 2 B, k1, Sl 1 B, k1, Sl 1 B, k2.

Place a marker at the beginning and end of the next row.

Rows 12–33: Repeat Rows 10 and 11, 10 times. Except, inc. 1 bead in each "swag" section every 2 rows. When you knit Rows 32 and 33, you will be slipping 13 beads in each "swag." (22 rows) The following 2 rows make the lower edge of the purse.

Rows 34 and 35: K4, *Sl 14 B, k3*, repeat from * to * once, Sl 14 B, K4.

In the following rows, 36–57, you will begin slipping 13 beads decreasing to 2 beads in the 3 "swag" sections of the purse.

Rows 36 and 37: K2, *(Sl 1 B, k1) 2 times, Sl 13 B, k1*, repeat from * to * 2 times, Sl 1 B, k1, Sl 1 B, k2.

Rows 38–59: Repeat Rows 36 and 37, 10 times. Except, dec. 1 bead in each "swag" section every 2 rows. When you knit Rows 58 and 59, you will be slipping 2 beads in each "swag." (22 rows)

Rows 60–63: K2, (Sl 1 B, k1; 10 times), Sl 1 B, k2. (4 rows)

Rows 64 and 65: K3, (Sl 1 B, k1; 8 times), Sl 1 B, k3.

Rows 66–68: Knit across. (3 rows)
Bind off.

FINISHING

If you would like to line the doll purse, place the purse on top of the lining before you sew the purse together. Draw around the purse allowing ½" (12 mm) for seams. Sew the lining pieces together.

Sew the 2 sides of the coin purse together beginning at the marker at Row 31 and continuing around the coin purse to the marker on the opposite side. Knot off and dab the knot with FrayCheck.

FRINGE

The fringes will be sewn on the lower edge of the purse. There will be 4 fringes attached in the "knit 2" areas of Rows 34 and 35. When sewing the fringes at the ends of the row, do so close to the beads to allow enough room to sew the side seams. Using beading needle and beading thread, begin on either the right or left side, slip beads onto the needle in the following order *if using millefiori drops, or any drop with a lengthwise drilled hole, 1 seed bead, one 4 mm crystal, 1 seed bead, 1 millefiori drop, 1 seed bead. Now pass the needle up through the millefiori drop, 1 seed bead, one 4 mm crystal, 1 seed bead, through the knitted thread to the inside of the purse.

Pull up all the slack in the beading thread, secure with a knot and dab the knot with FrayCheck. Progress across the row until completing all 4 fringes.

Sew the side seams from the lower edge of the purse up to the marker between Rows 11 and 12, using the silk thread and a tapestry needle.

Attach the purse to the frame as follows: Line up the center top of the purse with the center of the Doll Delight purse frame. Using the silk thread, which you used to knit the purse, sew using the backstitch method. Bring the needle up through the center hole, then down one hole to the right, then up one hole left of center. Continue the backstitch method, sewing left until the left half of the purse is sewn to the left side of the frame. Knot off and dab the knot with FrayCheck. Now attach the right half in the same manner. Attach the opposite side of the purse to the frame in the same way. Ease the knitting in as you stitch, if necessary.

Attach the chain and jump ring. ❧

Coy Roberts is a beaded knitting designer specializing in beaded knitted purses. Her designs have been published in *Vogue Knitting* Fall 2000, *Interweave Knits* Fall 2001, and *Salon Magazine* 2002.

sunshine duo

BY PHILOSOPHER'S WOOL CO.

sunshine duo

Mother and daughter will be warm and comfortable while frolicking outdoors in their beautiful Fair Isle worsted wool sweaters. The knowledgeable knitter is in for a challenging and enjoyable experience creating these extraordinary sweaters.

DESIGN BY THE PHILOSOPHER'S WOOL CO.
Skill level: Intermediate/Advanced
Finished project sizes: Adult Small (Medium, Large, Extra Large)/ Child's Small (Medium, Large).
Instructions are for the smallest size with changes for the larger sizes in parentheses.
Finished chest size: 41" (46", 50", 55") / 30" (34", 41") for ages 1–4, 5–8, 9–11, approximately.
Finished length: 26" (27", 29", 30") / 16½" (18", 21")

DESIGNER'S NOTES

Philosopher's Wool Fair Isle cardigans are knit using the same method that weavers and knitters have used all over the world for over a century. It is only since the Industrial Revolution that sweaters have been knit in pieces and then sewn or stitched together, a methodology that mimics the work of knitting machines. Each sweater is made from knitted tubes, two for the sleeves and one for the body. The body tube is knit with steeks (vertical columns of one purl stitch each), which show you where to make the opening for the sleeves and button bands. Using this method, you cut your work open at the front, and as if by magic, the sweater is ready to wear. In reality, you are knitting tubular fabric, which is machine stitched to stabilize the steeks, and then cut. Discovering how well steeking works will empower you to simplify many of the sweaters you will knit in the future—and maybe even adjust some you have knit in the past!

MATERIALS

Philosopher's Wool 2-ply 100% wool, worsted weight or equivalent
(4 ounces/112 grams, 210 yards/192 meters): 14 skeins for an adult and child's sweater (4 Yellow, 2 each of Dark Purple and Light Maroon, 1 each of Light Raspberry, Special Raspberry, Koolaid Orange, Light Green, Periwinkle, Light Purple)

Size 8 (5 mm) circular needles, 16" (40 cm) for sleeves and 32" (80 cm) for Fair Isle work on adult body, 24" (60 cm) for child's body, or size needed to obtain gauge.
Size 4 (3.5 mm) circular needles, 32" (80 cm) for ribbing.
Stitch holders
Sewing machine and thread to match yarn
Buttons

GAUGE

With larger needle over Fair Isle, knit in the round 21 sts = 4" (10 cm).

Take time to check your gauge, using your sleeves as your tension swatch.

HELPFUL HINTS

Carry the 2nd color loosely on the back of the work over 2, 3, or 4 stitches. A flatter Fair Isle is achieved by weaving in each stitch—one over, one under. "Weave in" new colors over 6 stitches before they are used, and "weave out" old colors in the 6 stitches after they are finished. Always work the sleeves first; this ensures that both sleeves will match.

INSTRUCTIONS

SLEEVES

The ribbing can be multicolored, using 2 row stripes of your colors in this order: cast on in Dark Purple and work 2 rows each of Dark Purple, Light Purple, Periwinkle, Light Green, Yellow, Koolaid Orange, Special Raspberry, Light Raspberry, Light Maroon and Dark Purple.

Cast on 48(52,56,60) / 36(36,42) sts and work K1, P1 ribbing for 4" for adult's / 2½" for child's.

Work your ribbing flat and then sew together for the cuff.

Change to 16" (40 cm) size 8 (5 mm) circular needle and knit one round in background color, increasing evenly to 60(72,72,84) / 40(44,48) sts.

Follow the graph on page 154, increasing 2 sts, one at the beginning and one at the end of every fourth round for adult's / third round for child's, until the sleeve measures 9"(9", 9 1/2", 10") / 5½"(6", 7½") across [or 18" (18", 19", 20") / 11"(12½", 14") around].

Continue to follow the graph. Remember also to end with Band "A." Finished sleeve length is 18"(19", 19 ½", 20") / 11"(12½", 14"), or desired length. Bind off loosely.

BODY

Cast on 156(176, 200, 224) / 140(162, 200) sts and work k1, p1 ribbing for about 4" for adult's / 2½" for child's to match the colors of the cuffs.

Change to larger needle and knit one round in background color, increasing evenly to 216(240, 264, 288) / 156(180, 216) sts.

Follow the graph on page 154.
Note: Make the middle stitch a purl stitch to mark the center of the body

Inside pocket

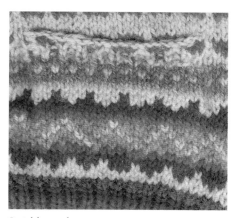

Outside pocket

"tube." As you continue to work in the round, work this purl stitch using both colors of yarn held together. This purl stitch marks what will eventually become the front opening. It is your front "steek." Make your color changes at the beginning of the rounds, i.e., at the side of the sweater under the arm.

Knit until the body measures 5" for adult's / 3" for child's from the top of the ribbing.

POCKETS

Knit 2 pocket squares (leaving them on the needles): 29 sts wide by 5" deep for adult's and 20 sts wide by 3" deep for child's. When the body of the sweater measures 5"/3" from the top of the ribbing, position the pocket patches so that they are appropriately placed (in about the middle of each side) and knit across them leaving the corresponding main body stitches on a holder. Later, complete the stitches on the holder with 2 to 4 rows of ribbing with your Fair Isle needle. With a darning needle, sew the bottom of the pocket patch to the top of the ribbing and sew the pocket and ribbing into place.

Continue to knit the body of the sweater until it measures approximately 16½"(17½", 18", 18½") / 10½"(11½", 13") and you are at the end of a Fair Isle band. Make sure the pattern is centered before continuing.

SIDE SEAMS

Check that you have the same number of stitches for the front and the back halves. Now at each "side seam" as you continue the body, make one purl stitch

every round using both colors of yarn held together. These purl stitches mark what will eventually become the armhole openings. (They are your armhole steeks). These purl stitches may be one of your pattern stitches or they may be an extra stitch you have created. You will continue to Fair Isle until your body tube is the desired finished length.

FINISHING THE BODY

Machine stitch 2 straight rows on either side of the purl sts at center front and at each armhole. Cut armholes open between machine stitching (along the purl "side seam") and bind off the shoulders together using a 3-needle bind off. Use one third of the stitches for each shoulder and the remaining third becomes the width of the neck opening.

For the neck opening, mark the center front approximately 3" lower and baste or sketch an arc from one shoulder edge to the other shoulder edge through this mark. Machine stitch this arc, using a zigzag or stretch stitch if available on

your machine, or 2 rows of fairly fine straight stitches.

With smaller size needle, pick up 86(90, 100, 106) / 80(82, 84) sts for neck band on the body side of the front stitches and across the back. Knit back and forth. Use the same colors as in the other ribbing.

Rib 3½" / 2½".

Bind off loosely and cut away excess fabric. Turn neck rib under and slip stitch into place.

Sew sleeves in place.

FRONT BANDS

At center front pick up and knit a 24-stitch trial mini-band to test tension and buttonhole size. Use smaller size needles and check the look of the band and buttonhole size. If needed, adjust needle size to get a flat, well-fitted band. Take out your trial band. Pick up one stitch from each round on the body side of the machine stitching at center front. Knit front bands to match ribbed bands on sleeves, creating evenly spaced buttonholes, by binding off 2 stitches on the row before the middle and casting them on again on the next row.

Hint: When making buttonholes on button band, sew up the extra buttonholes with the buttons. This will ensure that your buttons and buttonholes match perfectly as well as making your cardigan suitable for either adult men or women and boys or girls.

Sew buttons in place and cut open the center steek between machine stitching (see photo on page 68). Your sweater is now ready to wear. ❀

Detail of sleeve pattern

knitting
pattern gallery

There are few things more enjoyable than knitting. As soon as you have mastered the basics you'll be tempted by the virtual reality of our stitch gallery—all you could imagine and more from the simple use of yarn and needles. If you had one project in mind when you started turning these pages it may easily blossom into several projects. But be careful: that sampler scarf may morph into an afghan for two if you include all the wonderful stitches that catch your fancy, and why not? Knitting your fancies as you snuggle under them is a fine way to become better acquainted with the world of knitting.

How could the simple knit stitch, coupled with the equally simple purl stitch, become page after page of texture, color, cable, and lace? It's simple, with a yarn over here, a decrease there, careful charts, and impeccable instructions. We have chosen the most unusual, most useful, most elegant stitches we could find from centuries of knitting lore. Some have not been published for years, while others produce the sweaters that are passed lovingly from mother to daughter or from father to son. Tradition is at hand.

Stride into the boardroom in classic herringbone, or trot out cables as crisp and snappy as the first fall apple. Whimsical jacquard and Fair Isle combinations will soon have you longing to be "stranded" with nothing but your needles and a treasure chest of yarn. Whatever is beautiful, imaginative, festive, or just plain perfect is what we have in store.

Here you will find the delicate stitches perfect for baby's first layette or a bridal shower showpiece. Want something absolutely simple and devastatingly chic? Try jazzy, knit-and-purl geometrics, ribs of all kinds, or utterly understated brocades. And you thought knitting was sedate…

Just turn the page and step into inspiration.

This section on simple combinations includes brocades, ribs, increases and decreases, and patterns with an occasional yarn over.

Brocades are fabrics that alternate knit and purl stitches in decorative patterns. Moss stitch, which alternates knit and purl every stitch, is the simplest of the brocade stitches. There are infinite combinations that can make up brocades. Only a few are shown here.

Rib stitches are stitches that stack knit and purl stitches in lines with short repeats. Lines of alternating knit and purl stitches produce fabrics with extra stretch perpendicular to the lines. Classic ribs form vertical lines with horizontal stretch. Diagonal ribs produce fabrics with a bias stretch. Horizontal ribs are called welt and have vertical stretch.

Patterns using simple increases and decreases are also included here. When making fabric with increases and decreases, the two types of stitches are paired. That is, each increase is matched with a decrease so that the number of stitches remains the same. Increases and decreases cause stitches to curve out of the traditional vertical and horizontal lines.

158

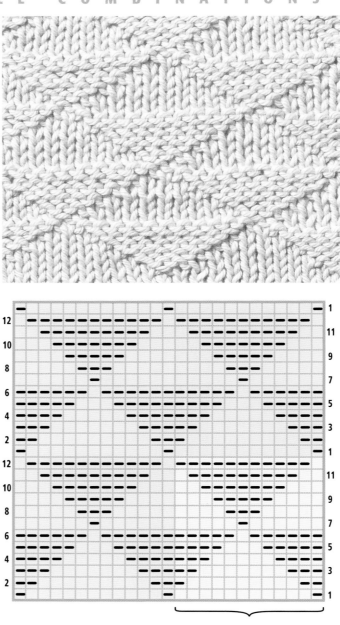

Multiple of 12 stitches + 1.

Rows 1 and 12: *P1, k11; repeat from * ending with p1.
Rows 2 and 11: K2, *p9, k3; repeat from * ending with k2.
Rows 3 and 10: P3, *k7, p5; repeat from * ending with p3.
Rows 4 and 9: K4, *p5, k7; repeat from * ending with k4.
Rows 5 and 8: P5, *k3, p9; repeat from * ending with p5.
Rows 6 and 7: K6, *p1, k11; repeat from * ending with k6.
Repeat rows 1–12.

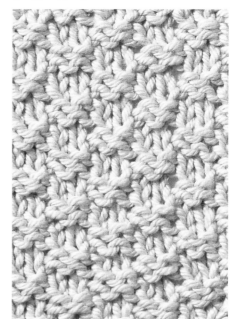

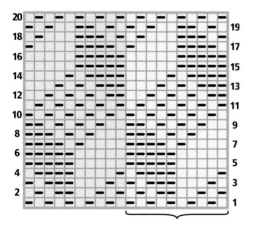

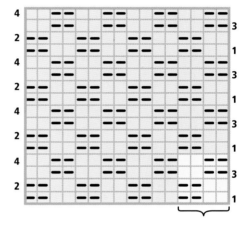

159

STACKED BLOCKS

INSTRUCTIONS
Multiple of 10 stitches.

Row 1: *K1, p1; repeat from * to end of row.

Row 2: P1, k1, p1, *k2, p2, (k1, p1) 3 times; repeat from * ending with k1, p1, k1.

Row 3: K1, p1, *k3, p3, (k1, p1) 2 times; repeat from * ending with k1, p1.

Row 4: *P1, k4, p4, k1; repeat from * to end of row.

Rows 5 and 6: *K5, p5; repeat from * to end of row.

Row 7: *K4, p1, k1, p4; repeat from * to end of row.

Row 8: *K3, (p1, k1) 2 times, p3; repeat from * to end of row.

Row 9: *K1, (k1, p1) 4 times, p1; repeat from * to end of row.

Row 10: *K1, p1; repeat from * to end of row.

Row 11: *P1, k1; repeat from * to end of row.

Row 12: *P1, (p1, k1) 4 times, k1; repeat from * to end of row.

Row 13: *P3, (k1, p1) 2 times, k3; repeat from * to end of row.

Row 14: *P4, k1, p1, k4; repeat from * to end of row.

Rows 15 and 16: *P5, k5; repeat from * to end of row.

Row 17: *K1, p4, k4, p1; repeat from * to end of row.

Row 18: P1, k1, *p3, k3, (p1, k1) 2 times; repeat from * ending with p1, k1.

Row 19: K1, p1, k1, *p2, k2, (p1, k1) 3 times; repeat from * ending with p1, k1, p1.

Row 20: *P1, k1; repeat from * to end of row.

Repeat rows 1–20.

DOUBLE MOSS STITCH
Other Names: Double Seed Stitch, Double Rice Stitch

INSTRUCTIONS
Multiple of 4 stitches.

Rows 1 and 2: *K2, p2; repeat from * to end of row.

Rows 3 and 4: *P2, k2; repeat from * to end of row.

Repeat rows 1–4.

VARIATIONS
Moss Stitch – All rows: K1, p1.
Sand Stitch – Row 1: K1, p1; Row 2: Knit.

knitting pattern gallery

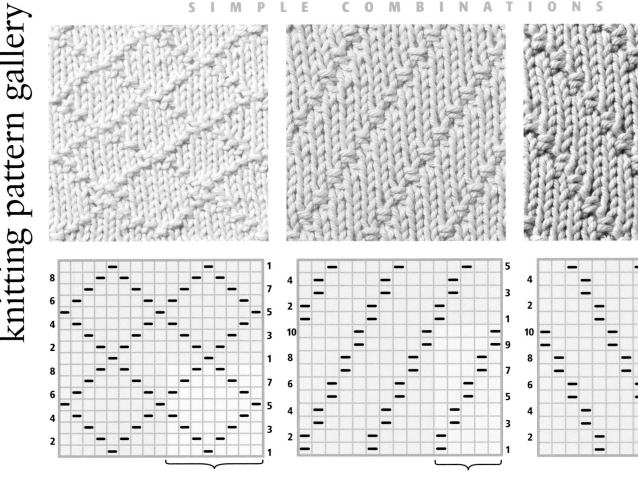

160

DIAMOND BROCADE

INSTRUCTIONS
Multiple of 8 stitches + 1.

Row 1: K4, *p1, k7; repeat from * ending with p1, k4.
Row 2: P3, *k1, p1, k1, p5; repeat from * ending with k1, p1, k1, p3.
Row 3: K2, *p1, k3; repeat from * ending with p1, k2.
Row 4: P1, *k1, p5, k1, p1; repeat from * to end of row.
Row 5: *P1, k7; repeat from * ending with p1.
Row 6: Same as Row 4.
Row 7: Same as Row 3.
Row 8: Same as Row 2.
Repeat rows 1–8.

VARIATIONS
Any simple geometric pattern can be used.

RIGHT DIAGONAL BROCADE

NOTE
Diagonal patterns can be worked as mirror images. See Left Diagonal Brocade.

INSTRUCTIONS
Multiple of 5 stitches.

Row 1: *K4, p1; repeat from * to end of row.
Row 2 and all even rows: knit in the knit stitches and purl in the purl stitches.
Row 3: *K3, p1, k1; repeat from * to end of row.
Row 5: *K2, p1, k2; repeat from * to end of row.
Row 7: *K1, p1, k3; repeat from * to end of row.
Row 9: *P1, k4; repeat from * to end of row.
Row 10: Same as row 2.
Repeat rows 1–10 ending on any row.

LEFT DIAGONAL BROCADE

INSTRUCTIONS
Multiple of 5 stitches.

Row 1: *P1, k4; repeat from * to end of row.
Row 2 and all even rows: knit in the knit stitches and purl in the purl stitches.
Row 3: *K1, p1, k3; repeat from * to end of row.
Row 5: *K2, p1, k2; repeat from * to end of row.
Row 7: *K3, p1, k1; repeat from * to end of row.
Row 9: *K4, p1; repeat from * to end of row.
Row 10: Same as row 2.
Repeat rows 1–10 ending on any row.

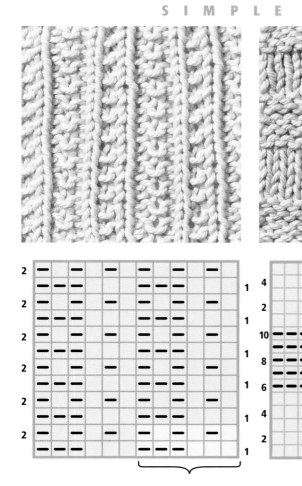

BEADED RIB

NOTE
This rib is not elastic.

INSTRUCTIONS
Multiple of 6 stitches.

Row 1: *K3, p3; repeat from * ending with p1.
Row 2: *K1, p1; repeat from * ending with k1.
Repeat rows 1–2.

5 X 5 BASKETWEAVE

INSTRUCTIONS
Multiple of 10 stitches + 5.

Row 1: *K5, p5; repeat from * ending with k5.
Rows 2–5: Knit the knit stitches, purl the purl stitches.
Row 6: Same as Row 1.
Rows 7–10: Knit the knit stitches, purl the purl stitches.
Repeat rows 1–10 ending with either row 5 or row 10.

VARIATIONS
You can use any number of stitches for each block such as a 4 x 4 Basketweave or 3 x 7 Basketweave. Use moss stitch block or garter stitch block instead of purl block.

HERRINGBONE

NOTES
V **inc** – with point of working needle to back, insert needle from top to bottom through the purl bump of the stitch below the next stitch, knit this purl bump, knit the next stitch.

INSTRUCTIONS
Multiple of 10 stitches + 4.

Row 1: *K4, (with point of working needle to back, insert needle from top to bottom through purl bump of st below next st, k purl bump, k next st), k4, k2tog; repeat from * ending with k4.
Row 2: Purl.
Repeat rows 1–2.

knitting pattern gallery

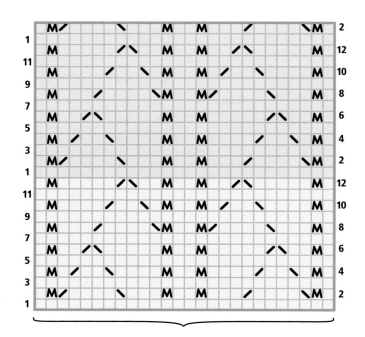

DRAGON SKIN

INSTRUCTIONS
Multiple of 26 stitches.
Begin on wrong side.

Row 1 and all odd rows: Purl.
Row 2: K1, *m1, skp, k4, k2tog, k3, m1, k2, m1, k3, skp, k4, k2tog, m1, k2; repeat from * ending with k1 instead of k2.
Row 4: K1, *m1, k1, skp, k2, k2tog, k4, m1, k2, m1, k4, skp, k2, k2tog, k1, m1, k2; repeat from * ending with k1 instead of k2.
Row 6: K1, *m1, k2, skp, k2tog, k5, m1, k2, m1, k5, skp, k2tog, k2, m1, k2; repeat from * ending with k1 instead of k2.
Row 8: K1, *m1, k3, skp, k4, k2tog, m1, k2, m1, skp, k4, k2tog, k3, m1, k2; repeat from * ending with k1 instead of k2.
Row 10: K1, * m1, k4, skp, k2, k2tog, k1, m1, k2, m1, k1, skp, k2, k2tog, k4, m1, k2; repeat from * ending with k1 instead of k2.
Row 12: K1, *m1, k5, skp, k2tog, (k2, m1) 2 times, k2, skp, k2tog, k5, m1, k2; repeat from * ending with k1 instead of k2.
Repeat rows 1–12.

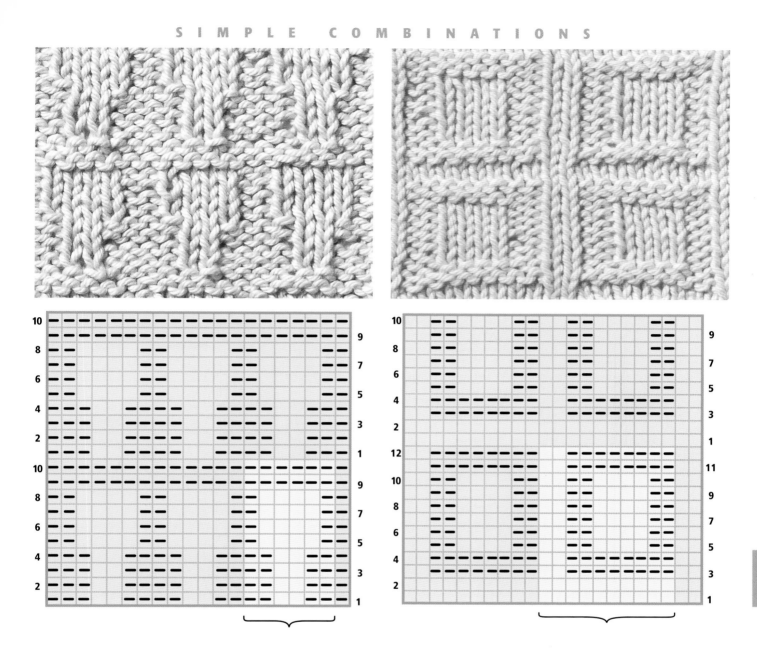

GOBLETS

INSTRUCTIONS
Multiple of 6 stitches + 2.

Row 1: P3, k2, *p4, k2; repeat from * ending with p3.
Row 2: K3, p2, * k4, p2; repeat from * ending with k3.
Row 3: Same as Row 1.
Row 4: Same as Row 2.
Row 5: P2, *k4, p2; repeat from * to end of row.
Row 6: K2, *p4, k2; repeat from * to end of row.
Row 7: Same as Row 5.
Row 8: Same as Row 6.
Row 9: Purl.
Row 10: Knit.
Repeat rows 1–10.

SQUARED CHECKS

INSTRUCTIONS
Multitple of 10 stitches + 2.

Row 1: Knit.
Row 2: Purl.
Row 3: K2, *p8, k2; repeat from * to end of row.
Row 4: P2, *k8, p2; repeat from * to end of row.
Row 5: K2, *p2, k4, p2, k2; repeat from * to end of row.
Row 6: P2, *k2, p4, k2, p2; repeat from * to end of row.
Rows 7 and 8: Same as Rows 5 and 6.
Rows 9 and 10: Same as Rows 5 and 6.
Rows 11 and 12: Same as Rows 3 and 4.
Repeat rows 1–12.

163

knitting pattern gallery

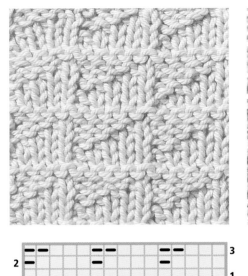

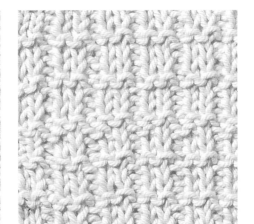

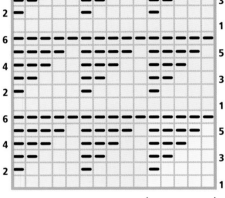

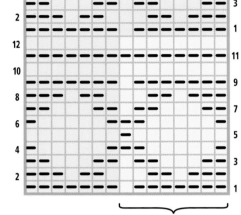

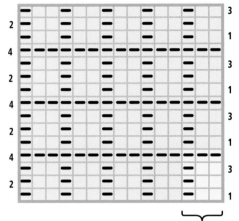

PENNANTS

INSTRUCTIONS
Multiple of 5 stitches.

Row 1: Knit.
Row 2: *K1, p4; repeat from * to end of row.
Row 3: *K3, p2; repeat from * to end of row.
Row 4: *K3, p2; repeat from * to end of row.
Row 5: *K1, p4; repeat from * to end of row.
Row 6: Knit.
Repeat rows 1–6.

RIDGE & DIAMOND STRIPES

INSTRUCTIONS
Multiple of 8 stitches + 7.

Row 1: P7, *k1, p7; repeat from * to end of row.
Row 2: K3, p1, *k2, p3, k2, p1; repeat from * ending with k3.
Row 3: P2, k3, p2, *k1, p2, k3, p2; repeat from * to end of row.
Row 4: K1, p5, *k3, p5; repeat from * ending with k1.
Row 5: K7, *p1, k7; repeat from * to end of row.
Row 6: Same as Row 4.
Row 7: Same as Row 3.
Row 8: Same as Row 2.
Row 9: Same as Row 1.
Rows 10–12: Purl.
Repeat rows 1–12.

WAFFLED SQUARES

INSTRUCTIONS
Multiple of 3 stitches.

Row 1: *K2, p1; repeat from * to end of row.
Row 2: *K1, p2; repeat from * to end of row.
Row 3: Same as Row 1.
Row 4: Knit.
Repeat rows 1–4.

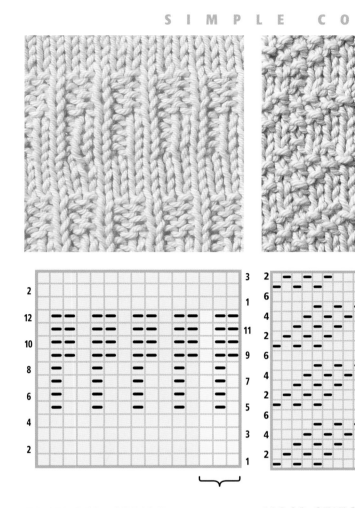

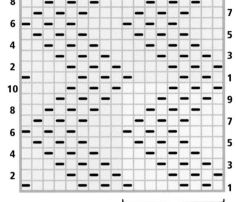

TEXTURED STRIPE

INSTRUCTIONS
Multiple of 3 stitches.

Rows 1 and 3: Knit.
Rows 2 and 4: Purl.
Rows 5 and 7: *K1, p1, k1; repeat from * to end of row.
Rows 6 and 8: *P1, k1, p1; repeat from * to end of row.
Rows 9 and 11: *P2, k1; repeat from * to end of row.
Rows 10 and 12: *P1, k2; repeat from * to end of row.
Repeat rows 1–12.

MOSS STITCH PARALLELOGRAMS

INSTRUCTIONS
Multiple of 10 stitches.

Row 1: *K5, (p1, k1) twice, p1; repeat from * to end of row.
Row 2: *(P1, k1) 3 times, p4; repeat from * to end of row.
Row 3: *K3, (p1, k1) 3 times, k1; repeat from * to end of row.
Row 4: *P3, (k1, p1) 3 times, p1; repeat from * to end of row.
Row 5: *(K1, p1) 3 times, k4; repeat fro * to end of row.
Row 6: Purl.
Repeat rows 1–6.

MOSS STITCH ZIGZAG

INSTRUCTIONS
Multiple of 9 stitches.

Row 1: *(K1, p1) 2 times, k4, p1, repeat from * to end of row.
Row 2: *P4, (k1, p1) 2 times, k1; repeat from * to end of row.
Row 3: *(k1, p1) 3 times, k3; repeat from * to end of row.
Row 4: *P2, (k1, p1) 2 times, k1, P2; repeat from * to end of row.
Row 5: *K3, (p1, k1) 3 times; repeat from * to end of row.
Row 6: *(K1, p1) 2 times, k1, p4; repeat from * to end of row.
Row 7: Same as Row 5.
Row 8: Same as Row 4.
Row 9: Same as Row 3.
Row 10: Same as Row 2.
Repeat rows 1–10.

165

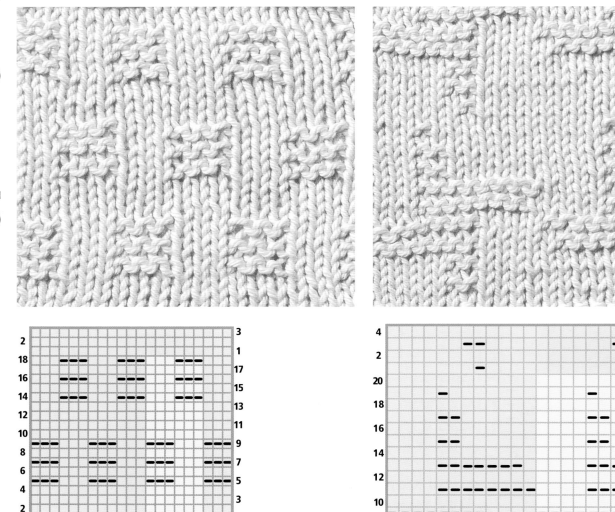

LIZARD LATTICE

INSTRUCTIONS
Multiple of 6 stitches + 3.

Row 1: Knit.
Row 2: Purl.
Rows 3 and 4: Same as Rows 1 and 2.
Row 5: P3, *k3, p3; repeat from * to end of row.
Row 6: Purl.
Rows 7 and 8: Same as Rows 5 and 6.
Row 9: Same as Row 5.
Rows 10–13: Same as Rows 1–4.
Row 14: P3, *k3, p3; repeat from * to end of row.
Row 15: Knit.
Rows 16 and 17: Same as Rows 14 and 15.
Row 18: Same as Row 14.
Repeat rows 1–18.

ART DECO

INSTRUCTIONS
Multiple of 12 stitches.

Row 1: K4, p1, *k11, p1; repeat from * ending k7.
Row 2 and all even rows: Purl.
Rows 3 and 5: K4, p2, *k10, p2; repeat from * ending with k6.
Row 7: K4, p7, *k5, p7; repeat from * ending with k1.
Row 9: *K4, p8; repeat from * to end of row.
Row 11: K1, p7, *k5, p7; repeat from * ending with k4.
Row 13: *P8, k4; repeat from * to end of row.
Rows 15 and 17: K6, p2, *k10, p2; repeat from * ending with k4.
Row 19: K7, p1, *k11, p1; repeat from * ending with k4.
Row 20: Purl.
Repeat rows 1–20.

knitting pattern gallery

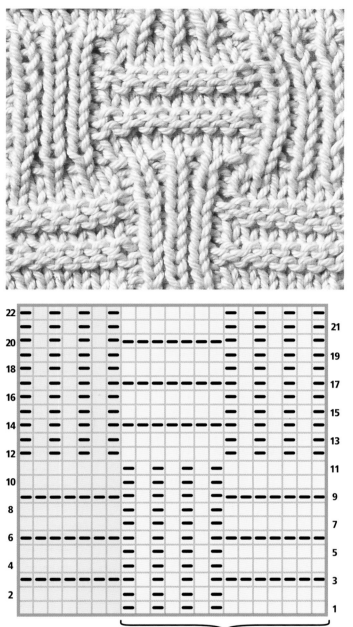

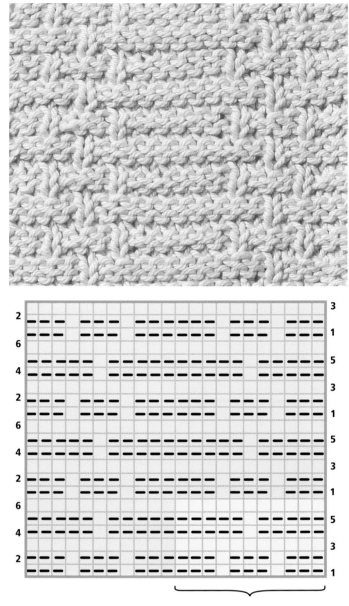

EXPANDED BASKETWEAVE

INSTRUCTIONS
Multiple of 14 stitches + 7.

Rows 1, 5, 7, and 11: *K7, (p1, k1) 3 times, p1; repeat from * ending with k7.

Rows 2, 4, 8, and 10: *P7, (k1, p1) 3 times, k1; repeat from * ending with p7.

Rows 3 and 9: *P7, (p1, k1) 3 times, p1; repeat from * ending with p7.

Row 6: *K7, (k1, p1) 3 times, k1; repeat from * ending with k7.

Rows 12, 16, 18, and 22: *(K1, p1) 3 times, k1, p7; repeat from * ending with (k1, p1) 3 times, k1.

Rows 13, 15, 19, and 21: *(P1, k1) 3 times, p1, k7; repeat from ending with (p1, k1) 3 times, p1.

Rows 14 and 20: *(K1, p1) 3 times, k8; repeat from * ending with (k1, p1) 3 times, k1.

FENCE POSTS

INSTRUCTIONS
Multiple of 11 stitches.

Row 1: *P3, (k1, p3) 2 times; repeat from * to end of row.

Row 2: *K3, (p1, k3) 2 times; repeat from * to end of row.

Row 3: Knit.

Row 4: *K5, p1, k5; repeat from *to end of row.

Row 5: *P5, k1, p5; repeat from *to end of row.

Row 6: Purl.

Repeat rows 1–6.

Row 17: *(P1, k1) 3 times, p8; repeat from * ending with (p1, k1) 3 times, p1.

Repeat rows 1–22.

knitting pattern gallery

KNOTS, BOBBLES, AND EMBOSSED STITCHES

Knots, bobbles, and embossed stitches use increase stitches to create raised textures. Knots are made by working multiple stitches into one stitch and then treating the multiple stitches as one in the next row. Bobbles work increase stitches and the corresponding decrease stitches in one stitch. Embossed stitches work increase and decrease stitches over a few stitches.

TRINITY STITCH

INSTRUCTIONS
Multiple of 4 stitches.

Row 1: *(K1, p1, k1) in same st, p3tog; repeat from * to end of row.
Row 2: Purl.
Row 3: *P3tog, in next st (k1, p1, k1); repeat from * to end of row.
Row 4: Purl.
Repeat rows 1–4 ending with row 2 or 4.

VARIATION
Use (k1, k1 tbl, k1) in place of (k1, p1, k1).

PURL TWIST KNOT

NOTE
● **knot** – p2tog leaving stitches on needle, insert working needle from back between stitches just purled together and purl the first stitch again, slip both stitches from needle.

INSTRUCTIONS
Multiple of 4 stitches.
Begin on wrong side.

Row 1: Purl.
Row 2: *K2, knot; repeat from * to end of row.
Row 3: Purl.
Row 4: *Knot, k2; repeat from * to end of row.
Repeat rows 1–4 ending with row 1 or 3.

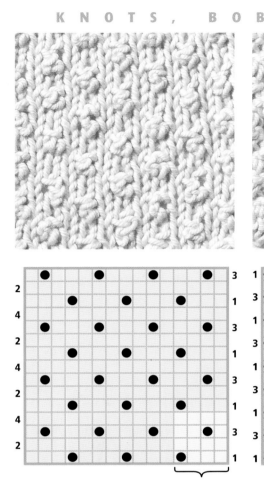

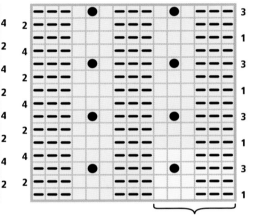

169

PEPPERCORN

NOTES

The peppercorn stitch is a chain of 3 stitches.

● **peppercorn** – K1, (slip the stitch just knit back onto holding needle and knit it again through the back loop) 3 times.

INSTRUCTIONS

Multiple of 4 stitches + 3.

Row 1: *K3, peppercorn; repeat from * ending with k3.
Row 2: Purl.
Row 3: K1, *peppercorn, k3; repeat from * ending with k1.
Row 4: Purl.
Repeat rows 1–4 ending with row 2 or 4.

BLACKBERRY STITCH

NOTES

● **bobble** – in next st (k1, p1, k1, p1, k1).

INSTRUCTIONS

Multiple of 6 stitches + 2.
Begin on wrong side.

Row 1: K1, *p5tog, bobble; repeat from * ending with k1.
Row 2: Purl.
Row 3: K1, *bobble, p5tog; repeat from * ending with k1.
Row 4: Purl.
Repeat rows 1–4 ending with row 2 or 4.

BERRY RIB

NOTES

● **bobble** – (k1, yo, k1, yo, k1) in base stitch, turn, k5, turn, k5, one at a time pass each stitch over first stitch.

You can work this bobble faster and without turning if you knit the second row of the bobble left handed (from left to right).

INSTRUCTIONS

Multiple of 6 stitches + 3.

Row 1: *P3, k3; repeat from * ending with p3.
Row 2: *K3, p3; repeat from * ending with k3.
Row 3: *P3, k1, bobble, k1; repeat from * ending p3.
Row 4: Same as Row 2.
Repeat rows 1–4 ending with row 2 or 4.

knitting pattern gallery

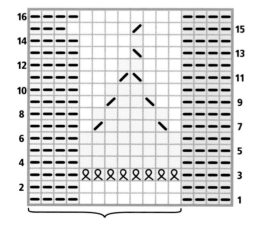

BELL INSERTION

NOTE
Use half hitch cast on.

INSTRUCTIONS
Multiple of 4 stitches + 4.

Row 1: Purl.
Row 2: Knit.
Row 3: P4, *co8, p4; repeat from * to end of row.
Row 4: *K4, p8; repeat from * ending with k4.
Row 5: P4, *k8, p4; repeat from * to end of row.
Row 6: Same as Row 4.
Row 7: P4, *skp, k4, k2tog, p4; repeat from * to end of row.
Row 8: *K4, p6; repeat from * ending with k4.
Row 9: P4, *skp, k2, k2tog, p4; repeat from * to end of row.
Row 10: *K4, p4; repeat from * ending with k4.
Row 11: P4, *skp, k2tog, p4; repeat from * to end of row.
Row 12: *K4, p2; repeat from * ending with k4.
Row 13: P4, *skp, p4; repeat from * to end of row.
Row 14: *K4, p1; repeat from * ending with k4.
Row 15: P4, *k2tog, p3; repeat from * to end of row.
Row 16: Knit.
Repeat rows 1–16.

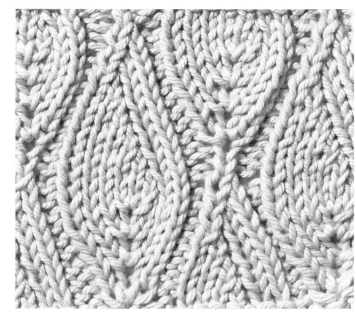

CANDLE FLAME

INSTRUCTIONS

Multiple of 12 stitches + 2.

Row 1: *P2, in next st (k1, yo, k1), p2, k2, k2tog, k3; repeat from * ending with p2.

Row 2: K2, *p6, k2, p3, k2; repeat from * to end of row.

Row 3: *P2, k1, in next st (k1, yo, k1), k1, p2, k2, k2tog, k2; repeat from * ending with p2.

Row 4: K2, *p5, k2; repeat from * to end of row.

Row 5: *P2, k2, in next st (k1, yo, k1) k2, p2, k2, k2tog, k1; repeat from * ending with p2.

Row 6: K2, *p4, k2, p7, k2; repeat from * to end of row.

Row 7: *P2, k3, in next st (k1, yo, k1), k3, p2, k2, k2tog; repeat from * ending with p2.

Row 8: K2, *p3, k2, p9, k2; repeat from * to end of row.

Row 9: *P2, k8, p2, k1, k2tog; repeat from * ending with p2.

Row 10: K2, *p2, k2, p8, k2; repeat from * to end of row.

Row 11: *P2, k2, k2tog, k4, p2, k2tog; repeat from * ending with p2.

Row 12: K2, *p1, k2, p7, k2; repeat from * to end of row.

Row 13: *P2, k2, k2tog, k3, p2, in next st (k1, yo, k1); repeat from * ending with p2.

Row 14: K2, *p3, k2, p6, k2; repeat from * to end of row.

Row 15: *P2, k2, k2tog, k2, p2, k1, in next st (k1, yo, k1), k1; repeat from * ending with p2.

Row 16: K2, * p5, k2; repeat from * to end of row.

Row 17: *P2, k2, k2tog, k1, p2, k2, in next st (k1, yo, k1), k2; repeat from * ending with p2.

Row 18: K2, * p7, k2, p4, k2; repeat from * to end of row.

Row 19: *P2, k2, k2tog, p2, k3, in next st (k1, yo, k1), k3; repeat from * ending with p2.

Row 20: K2, * p9, k2, p3, k2; repeat from * to end of row.

Row 21: *P2, k1, k2tog, p2, k2, k2tog, k5; repeat from * ending with p2.

Row 22: K2, *p8, k2, p2, k2; repeat from * to end of row.

Row 23: *P2, k2tog, p2, k2, k2tog, k4; repeat from * ending with p2.

Row 24: K2, *p7, k2, p1, k2; repeat from * to end of row.

Repeat rows 1–24 ending with row 12 or 24.

VARIATION

Replace (k, yo, k) of leaf vein with (yo, k1, yo).

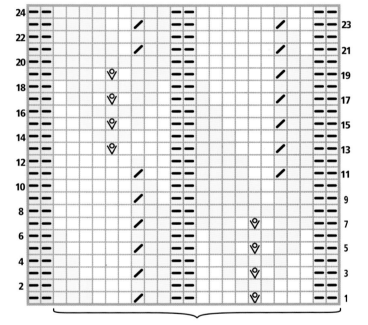

knitting pattern gallery

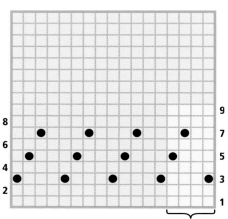

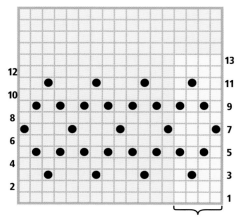

KNOB ROPE INSERTION

NOTES

● **knob – Row 1:** Into base stitch (wyif k1 kwise, yo, k1, yo, k1), drop base stitch. 6 sts made.
Row 2: Turn, p6.
Row 3: Turn, sl 1, k5.
Row 4: Turn, sl 1, p5.
Row 5: Turn, sl 1, k5.
Row 6: Turn, (p2tog) 3 times.
Row 7: Turn, sk2p.

You can work this bobble faster and without turning by knitting the purl stitches in rows 2, 4, and 6 left handed (from left to right).

INSTRUCTIONS

Multiple of 4 stitches.
All even rows: Purl.

Row 1: Knit.
Row 2 and all even rows: Purl.
Row 3: *Knob, k3; repeat from * ending with knob.
Row 5: *K3, knob; repeat from * ending with k1.
Row 7: K2,*knob, k3; repeat from * ending with k2.
Row 9: Knit.

CHENILLE TUFT INSERTION

NOTE

● **tuft** – knit next stitch but do not drop base stitch from source needle; slip new stitch back onto source needle and knit new stitch, which transfers new stitch to working needle; repeat three more times working into base stitch each time. Drop base stitch from source needle. With holding needle lift second, third, and fourth stitches on working needle over the first stitch.

INSTRUCTIONS

Multiple of 4 stitches + 1.

Row 1: Knit.
Row 2 and all even rows: Purl.
Row 3: K2, *tuft, k3; repeat from * ending with k2.
Row 5: *K1, tuft; repeat from * ending with k1.
Row 7: *Tuft, k3; repeat from * ending with tuft.
Row 9: Same as Row 5.
Row 11: Same as Row 3.
Row 13: Same as Row 1.

CROSSED STITCHES, CABLES, AND THREADED STITCHES

Decorative patterns can be produced by having stitches swap places in the knitted fabric.

Crossed stitches are produced when the points of the knitting needles are used to swap the places of one or two stitches. Other books often refer to these as twisted stitches because the second stitch on the needle is worked through the back loop (a twist stitch) and then the first two stitches on the needle are worked together.

Cables are crossed stitches that move substantial distances across the fabric. They require the stitches being moved to be placed on a temporary holder, a cable needle, to store them for later use.

Threaded stitches have one stitch passing through the middle of another stitch as the stitches are being swapped.

Simple crossed and twisted stitches are usually worked as a ground. Cable stitches can be worked as a ground but are also worked as accents and are often combined with other cables and stitches such as eyelets and bobbles.

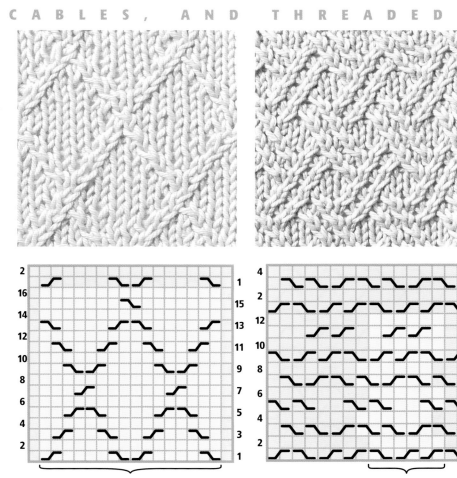

173

TRELLIS STITCH

INSTRUCTIONS
Multiple of 16 stitches + 2.

Row 1: K1, *lc, k4, rc; repeat from * ending with k1.
Row 2 and all even rows: Purl.
Row 3: K2, *lc, k2, rc; repeat from * to end of row.
Row 5: K3, *lc, rc, k4; repeat from * ending with k3.
Row 7: K4, *rc, k6; repeat from * ending with k4.
Row 9: K3, *rc, lc, k4; repeat from * ending wit k3.
Row 11: K2, *rc, k2, lc, k2; repeat from * to end of row.
Row 13: K1, *rc, k4, lc; repeat from * ending with k1.
Row 15: K8, *lc, k6; repeat from * ending with k2.
Row 16: Purl.
Repeat rows 1–16.

DOUBLE LATTICE

INSTRUCTIONS
Multiple of 6 stitches + 4.

Row 1: *Lc, (rc) 2 times; repeat from * ending with lc, rc.
Row 2 and all even rows: Purl.
Row 3: K1, lc, *rc, (lc) 2 times; repeat from * ending with k1.
Row 5: Lc, *lc, k2, lc; repeat from * ending with lc.
Row 7: K1, lc, *lc, rc, lc; repeat from * ending with k1.
Row 9: Rc, *lc, (rc) 2 times; repeat from * ending with lc.
Row 11: K3, *(rc) 2 times, k2; repeat from * ending with (rc) 2 times, k3.
Row 12: Purl.
Repeat rows 1–12.

knitting pattern gallery

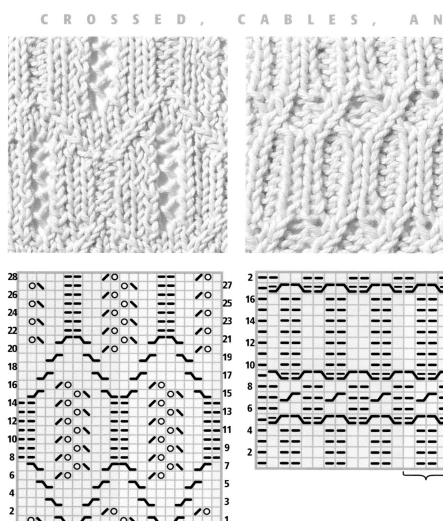

TWISTED CHAINS

NOTE

rckp – right slanting cross: knit, purl – knit second stitch on source needle, purl first stitch, slip both stitches from source needle.

lcpk – left slanting cross: purl, knit – working behind first stitch on source needle, purl into back of second stitch, knit first stitch, slip both stitches from source needle.

INSTRUCTIONS
Multiple of 4 stitches + 2.

Row 1: P1, k1, p2, *k2, p2; repeat from * ending with k1, p1.

Row 2: K1, p1, k2, *p2, k2; repeat from * ending with p1, k1.

Rows 3 and 4: Repeat Rows 1 and 2.

Row 5: P1, *lcpk, rckp; repeat from * ending with p1.

Row 6: K2, *p2, k2; repeat from * to end of row.

Row 7: P2, *rc, p2; repeat from * to end of row.

Row 8: K2, *p2, k2; repeat from * to end of row.

Row 9: P1, *rckp, lcpk; repeat from * ending with p1.

Row 10: Same as Row 2.

Rows 11–16: Repeat Rows 1 and 2 three times.

Repeat rows 5–16.

GABLE PATTERN

INSTRUCTIONS
Multiple of 10 stitches + 2.

Row 1: K4, *rc, lc, k1, ssk, yo, K3; repeat from * ending with k1.

Row 2: P9,* p2tog, yo, p8; repeat from * ending with p2tog, yo, p1.

Row 3: K3, *rc, k2, lc, k4; repeat from * ending with k3.

Row 4: Purl.

Row 5: K2, *rc, k4, lc, k2; repeat from * to end of row.

Row 6: P4, *p2tog, yo, p8; repeat from * ending with p2tog, yo, p6.

Row 7: K1, *rc, k1, ssk, yo, k3, lc; repeat from * ending with k1.

Rows 8, 10, 12, and 14: K2, *p2, p2tog, yo, p4, k2; repeat from * to end of row.

Rows 9, 11, and 13: P2, *k2, ssk, yo, k4, p2; repeat from * to end of row.

Row 15: K1, *lc, k1, ssk, yo, k3, rc; repeat from * ending with k1.

Row 16: Same as Row 6.

Row 17: K2, *lc, k4, rc, k2; repeat from * to end of row.

Row 18: Same as Row 4.

Row 19: K3, *lc, k2, rc, k4; repeat from * ending with k3.

Row 20: Same as Row 2.

Row 21: K4, *lc, rc, k1, ssk, yo, k3; repeat from * ending with k1.

Rows 22, 24, 26, and 28: P5, *k2, p2, p2tog, yo, p4; repeat from * ending with p1.

Rows 23, 25, and 27: K5, *p2, k2, ssk, yo, k4; repeat from * ending with k1.

Repeat rows 1–28.

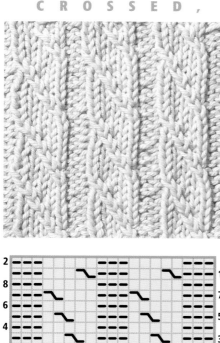

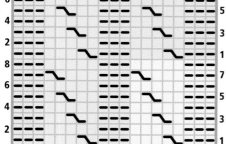

DIAGONAL CROSS RIB

INSTRUCTIONS
Multiple of 8 stitches + 3.

Row 1: *P3, lc, k3; repeat from * ending with p3.
Row 2 and all even rows: *K3, p5; repeat from * ending with k3.
Row 3: *P3, k1, lc, k2; repeat from * ending with p3.
Row 5: *P3, k2, lc, k1; repeat from * ending with p3.
Row 7: *P3, k3, lc; repeat from * ending with p3.
Row 8: Same as Row 2.
Repeat rows 1–8.

VARIATION
Use rc instead of lc for a right slanting cable.

WAFFLE STITCH

INSTRUCTIONS
Multiple of 4 stitches + 2.

Row 1: K1, yo, *skp, k2tog, (yo) 2 times; repeat from * ending with skp, k2tog, yo, k1.
Row 2: K2, p2, *k 1st yo tbl, k 2nd yo, p2; repeat from * ending with k2.
Row 3: K1, *p1, rc, p1; repeat from * ending with k1.
Row 4: K1, *k1, p2, k1; repeat from * ending with k1.
Row 5: K1, *k2tog, (yo) 2 times, skp; repeat from * ending with k1.
Row 6: K1, *p1, k 1st yo tbl, k 2nd yo, p1; repeat from * ending with k1.
Row 7: K2, *p2, rc; repeat from * ending with p2, k2.
Row 8: K1, p1, k2, *p2, k2; repeat from * ending with p1, k1.
Repeat rows 1–8.

AUSTRIAN BLOCK PATTERN

INSTRUCTIONS
Multiple of 10 stitches + 1.
Begin on wrong side.

Rows 1, 3, 5, 7, and 9: P1, *k2, p5, k2, p1; repeat from * to end of row.
Rows 2, 4, 6, 8, and 10: K1 tbl, *p2, rc, k1, lc, p2, k1 tbl; repeat from * to end of row.
Rows 11, 13, 15, 17, and 19: P3, *k2, p1, k2, p5; repeat from * ending with p3.
Rows 12, 14, 16, 18, and 20: K1, *lc, p2, k1 tbl, p2, rc, k1; repeat from * to end of row.
Repeat rows 1–20.

177

knitting pattern gallery

178

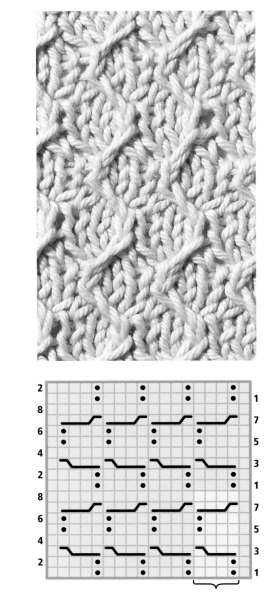

HERRINGBONE CABLE

TREE OF LIFE

NOTES

⌐‾L on wrong side **rckp** – right slanting cross: knit, purl – working behind first stitch on source needle, purl second stitch, knit skipped stitch, slip both stitches from source needle.

⌐F on wrong side **lcpk** – left slanting cross: purl, knit – working in front of first stitch on source needle, knit second stitch, purl skipped stitch, slip both stitches from source needle.

● **bobble** – in next stitch (k1, p1, k1, p1), turn, p4, turn, (p2tog) 2 times, turn, k2tog. You can eliminate the turns by knitting every other row left handed.

INSTRUCTIONS
Panel of 16 stitches.

Row 1: P6, rc, lc, p6.
Row 2: K5, rckp, p2, lcpk, k5.
Row 3: P4, (rc) 2 times, (lc) 2 times, p4.
Row 4: K3, rckp, p6, lcpk, k3.
Row 5: P2, rc, p1, rc, k2, lc, p1, lc, p2.
Row 6: K2, p1, k2, p1, k1, p2, k1, p1, k2, p1, k2.
Row 7: P2, bobble, p1, rc, p1, k2, p1, lc, p1, bobble, p2.
Row 8: K4, p1, k2, p2, k2, p1, k4.
Row 9: P4, bobble, p2, k2, p2, bobble, p4.
Row 10: K7, p2, k7.
Repeat rows 1–10.

VARIATION
No bobble or your favorite bobble can be substituted for bobble given.

HERRINGBONE CABLE

INSTRUCTIONS
Multiple of 4 stitches +2.

Row 1: K1, * sl 1 kwise, k3; repeat from * ending with k1.
Row 2: P1, *p3, sl 1 kwise; repeat from * ending with p1.
Row 3: K1, *sl 1 st onto cn and hold at front, k3, k1 from cn; repeat from * ending with k1.
Row 4: Purl.
Row 5: K1, *k3, sl 1 kwise; repeat from * ending with k1.
Row 6: P1, *sl 1 kwise, p3; repeat from * ending with p1.
Row 7: K1, *sl 3 sts onto cn and hold at back, k1, k3 from cn; repeat from * ending with k1.
Row 8: Purl.
Repeat rows 1–8.

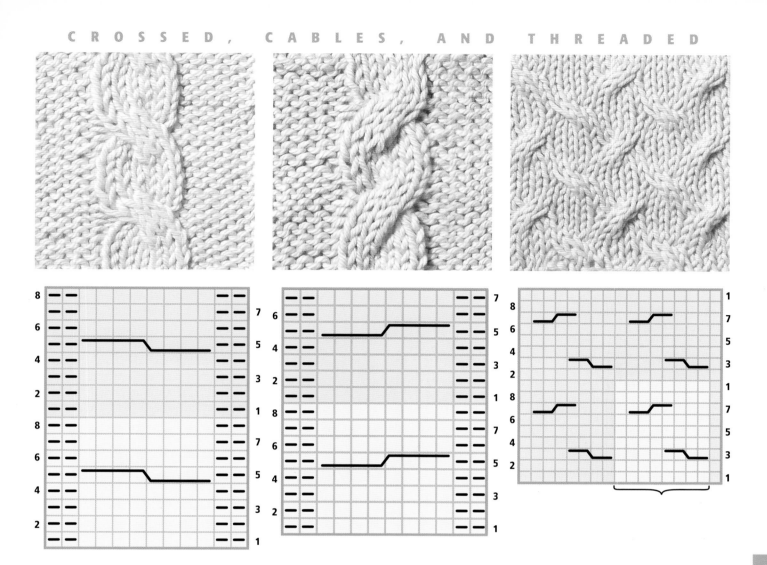

CLASSIC LEFT CABLE

NOTE
Work on reverse stockinette ground.

INSTRUCTIONS
Panel of 12 stitches.

Rows 1 and 3: P2, k8, p2.
Row 2 and all even rows: K2, p8, k2.
Row 5: P2, sl 4 sts onto cn and hold at front, k4, k4 from cn, p2.
Row 7: Same as Row 1.
Row 8: Same as Row 2.
Repeat rows 1–8.

CLASSIC RIGHT CABLE

NOTE
Work on reverse stockinette ground.

INSTRUCTIONS
Panel of 12 stitches.

Rows 1 and 3: P2, k8, p2.
Row 2 and all even rows: K2, p8, k2.
Row 5: P2, sl 4 sts onto cn and hold at back, k4, k4 from cn, p2.
Row 7: Same as Row 1.
Row 8: Same as Row 2.
Repeat rows 1–8.

SHADOW CABLE

INSTRUCTIONS
Multiple of 8 stitches + 1.

Row 1: Knit.
Row 2 and all even rows: Purl.
Row 3: K1, *sl 2 sts onto cn and hold at front, k2, k2 from cn, k4; repeat from * to end of row.
Row 5: Knit.
Row 7: K4, sl 2 sts onto cn and hold at back, k2, k2 from cn, *k4, sl 2 sts onto cn and hold at back, k2, k2 from cn; repeat from * ending with k1.
Row 8: Purl.
Repeat rows 1–8.

knitting pattern gallery

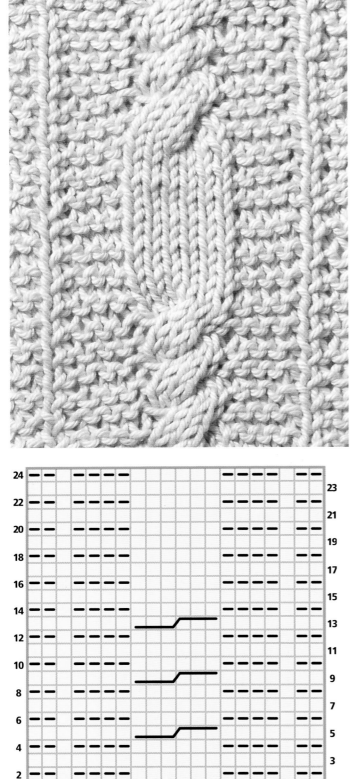

180

CORKSCREW CABLE

NOTE
Worked on reverse stockinette ground.

INSTRUCTIONS
Panel of 20 stitches.

Rows 1: Knit.
Row 2 and all even rows: K2, p1, k4, p6, k4, p1, k2.
Row 3: Knit.
Row 5: K7, sl 3 sts onto cn and hold at back, k3, k3 from cn ending with k7.
Rows 7: Knit.
Row 9: K7, sl 3 sts onto cn and hold at back, k3, k3 from cn ending with k7.
Row 11: Knit.
Row 13: K7, sl 3 sts onto cn and hold at back, k3, k3 from cn ending with k7.
Row 15: Knit.
Row 17: Knit.
Row 19: Knit.
Row 21: Knit.
Row 23: Knit.
Row 24: Knit.
Repeat rows 1–24.

VARIATION
Substitute left slanting cable for right slanting cable by holding stitches on cable needle to front instead of to back.

SAXON BRAID

NOTE
Work on reverse stockinette ground.

INSTRUCTIONS
Panel of 26 stitches.
Begin on wrong side.

Row 1: K3, (p4, k4) 2 times, p4, k3.
Row 2: P3, (sl 2 sts onto cn and hold at back, k2, k2 from cn, p4) 2 times, sl 2 sts onto cn and hold at back, k2, k2 from cn, p3.
Row 3: Same as Row 1.
Row 4: P2, sl 1 st onto cn and hold at back, k2, p1 from cn, (s1 2 sts onto cn and hold at front, p2, k2, from cn sl 2 sts onto cn and hold at back, k2, p2 from cn) 2 times, sl 2 onto cn and hold at front, p1, k2 from cn, p2.
Row 5: K2, p2, k3, p4, k4, p4, k3, p2, k2.
Row 6: P1, sl 1 st onto cn and hold at back, k2, p1 from cn, p3, sl 2 sts onto cn and hold at front, k2, k2 from cn, p4, sl 2 sts onto cn and hold at back , k2, k2 from cn, p3, sl 2 sts onto cn and hold at front, p1, k2 from cn, p1.
Row 7: K1, p2, (k4, p4) 2 times, k4, p2, k1.
Row 8: P1, k2, p3, sl 1 st onto cn and hold at back, k2, p1 from cn, sl 2 sts onto cn and hold at front, p2, k2 from cn, sl 2 sts onto cn and hold at back, k2, p2 from cn, sl 2 sts onto cn and hold at front, p1, k2 from cn, p3, k2, p1.
Row 9: K1, (p2, k3) 2 times, p4, (k3, p2) 2 times, k1.
Row 10: P1, (k2, p3) 2 times, sl 2 sts onto cn and hold at back, k2, k2 from cn, (p3, k2) 2 times, p1.
Row 11: Same as Row 9.
Row 12: P1, k2, p3, sl 2 sts onto cn and hold at front, p1, k2 from cn, sl 2 sts onto cn and hold at back, k2, p2 from cn, sl 2 sts onto cn and hold at front, p2, k2 from cn, sl 1 st onto cn and hold at back, k2, p1 from cn, p3, k2, p1.
Row 13: Same as Row 7.
Row 14: P1, sl 2 sts onto cn and hold at front, p1, k2 from cn, p3, sl 2 sts onto cn and hold at front, k2, k2 from cn, p4, sl 2 sts onto cn and hold at back, k2, k2 from cn, p3, sl 1 st onto cn and hold at back, k2, p1 from cn, p1.
Row 15: Same as Row 5.
Row 16: P2, sl 2 sts onto cn and hold at front, p1, k2 from cn, (sl 2 sts onto cn and hold at back k2, p2 from cn, sl 2 sts onto cn and hold at front, p2, k2 from cn) 2 times, sl 1 st onto cn and hold at back k2, p1 from cn, p2.
Repeat rows 1–16.

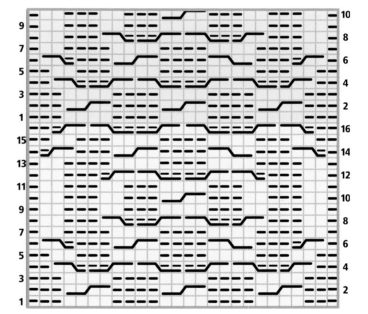

181

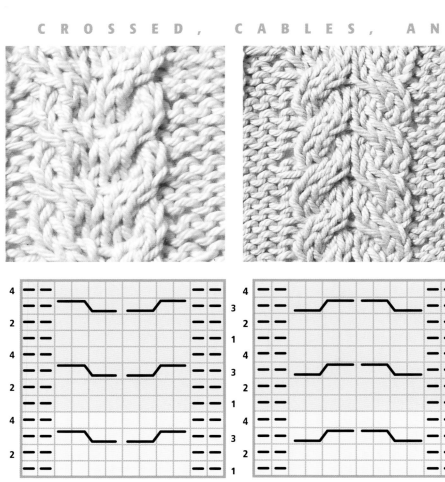

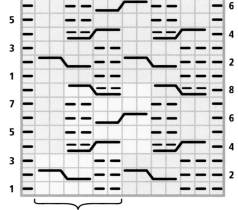

EXPANDING WHEATEAR

NOTE
Work on a reverse stockinette ground.

INSTRUCTIONS
Panel of 12 stitches.

Row 1: P2, k8, p2.
Row 2: K2, p8, k2.
Row 3: P2, sl 2 sts onto cn and hold at back, k2, k2 from cn, sl 2 sts onto cn and hold at front, k2, k2 from cn, p2.
Row 4: Same as Row 2.
Repeat rows 1–4.

CONVERGING WHEATEAR

NOTE
Work on a reverse stockinette ground.

INSTRUCTIONS
Panel of 12 stitches.

Row 1: P2, k8, p2.
Row 2: K2, p8, k2.
Row 3: P2, sl 2 sts onto cn and hold at front, k2, k2 from cn, sl 2 sts onto cn and hold at back, k2, k2 from cn, p2.
Row 4: Same as Row 2.
Repeat rows 1–4.

OPEN WOVEN LATTICE

INSTRUCTIONS
Multiple of 6 stitches + 2.
Begin on wrong side.

Row 1: K1, *p4, k2; repeat from * ending with k1.
Row 2: P1, *p2, sl 2 sts onto cn and hold at front, k2, k2 from cn; repeat from * ending with p1.
Row 3: Same as Row 1.
Row 4: P1, *sl 2 sts onto cn and hold at back, k2, p2 from cn, k2; repeat from * ending with p1.
Row 5: K1, p2, k2, *p4, k2; repeat from * ending with p2, k1.
Row 6: P1, k2, *p2, sl 2 sts onto cn and hold at back, k2, k2 from cn; repeat from * ending with p2, k2, p1.
Row 7: Same as row 5.
Row 8: P1, *sl 2 sts onto cn and hold at front, p2, k2 from cn, k2; repeat from * ending with p1.
Repeat rows 1–8.

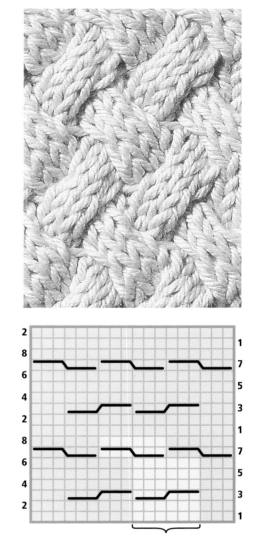

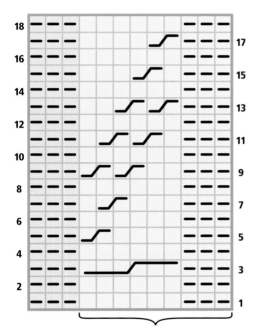

183

TWISTS AND CABLES

NOTE
Work on reverse stockinette ground.

INSTRUCTIONS
Multiple of 9 stitches + 3.

Row 1: *P3, k6; repeat from * ending with p3.

Row 2 and all even rows: *K3, p6; repeat from * ending with k3.

Row 3: *P3, sl 3 sts onto cn and hold at back, k3, k3 from cn; repeat from * ending with p3.

Row 5: *P3, k4, rc; repeat from * ending with p3.

Row 7: *P3, k3, rc, k1; repeat from * ending with p3.

Row 9: *P3, k2, (rc) 2 times; repeat from * ending with p3.

Row 11: *P3, k1, (rc) 2 times, k1; repeat from * ending with p3.

Row 13: *P3, (rc) 2 times, k2; repeat from * ending with p3.

Row 15: *P3, k1, rc, k3; repeat from * ending with p3.

Row 17: *P3, rc, k4; repeat from * ending with p3.

Row 18: Same as Row 2.
Repeat rows 1–18.

SOLID WOVEN LATTICE

INSTRUCTIONS
Multiple of 6 stitches.

Row 1: Knit.

Row 2 and all even rows: Purl.

Row 3: K3, *sl 3 sts onto cn and hold at back, k3, k3 from cn; repeat from * ending with k3.

Row 5: Knit.

Row 7: *Sl 3 sts onto cn and hold at front, k3, k3 from cn; repeat from * to end.

Row 8: Purl.

Repeat rows 1–8.

knitting pattern gallery

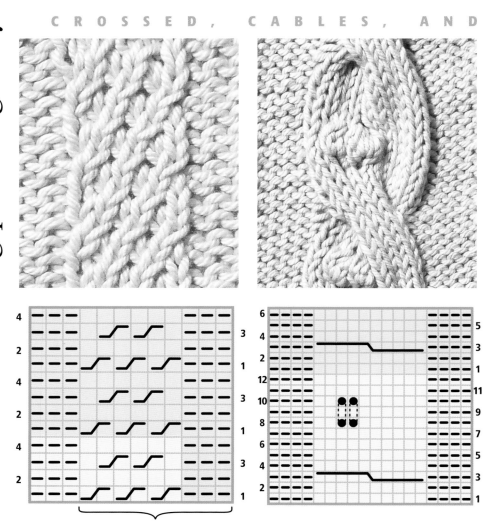

184

HERRINGBONE RIB

INSTRUCTIONS
Multiple of 9 stitches + 3.

Row 1: P3, *(rc) 3 times, p3; repeat from * to end of row.

Row 2: K3, *p6, k3; repeat from * to end of row.

Row 3: P3, *k1, (rc) 2 times, k1, p3; repeat from * to end of row.

Row 4: Same as Row 2.

Repeat rows 1–4.

VARIATION
Use lc in place of rc for a left slanting cable.

CABLE WITH BOBBLES

NOTES
Work on reverse stockinette ground.

bobble worked over 3 rows. Beginning on wrong side row, **Row 1:** In next st (p1, k1, p1, k1, p1). **Row 2:** Knit. **Row 3:** P5tog.

INSTRUCTIONS
Panel of 18 stitches.

Rows 1, 5, 7, and 11: P4, k10, p4.

Rows 2, 4, and 6: K4, p10, k4.

Row 3: P4, sl 5 sts onto cn and hold at front, k5, k5 from cn, p4.

Row 8: K4, p2, {begin bobble in next st (p1, k1, p1, k1, p1)} 2 times, p6, k4.

Row 9: P4, k18 (10 of these stitches are in the bobbles), p4.

Row 10: K4, p2, (p5tog) 2 times, p6, k4.

Row 12: Same as Row 2.

Repeat rows 1–12.

Push bobbles to right side.

HONEYCOMB TRELLIS

INSTRUCTIONS
Multiple of 6 stitches + 2.

Row 1: *K2, p4; repeat from * ending with k2.

Row 2: *P2, k4; repeat from * ending with p2.

Row 3: K1, *sl 1 st onto cn and hold at front, p2, k1 from cn, sl 2 sts onto cn and hold at back, k1, p2 from cn; repeat from * ending with k1.

Row 4: K3, *p2, k4; repeat from * ending with k3.

Row 5: P3, *k2, p4; repeat from * ending with p3.

Row 6: Same as Row 4.

Row 7: K1, *sl 2 sts onto cn and hold at back, k1, p2 from cn, sl 1 st onto cn and hold at front, p2, k1 from cn; repeat from * ending with k1.

Row 8: Same as Row 2.

Repeat rows 1–8.

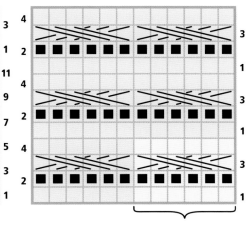

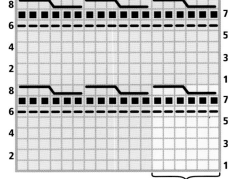

HONEYCOMB CABLE

INSTRUCTIONS
Multiple of 8 stitches.

Rows 1, 5, 7, and 11: Knit.
Row 2 and all even rows: Purl.
Row 3: *Sl 2 sts onto cn and hold at front, k2, k2 from cn, sl 2 sts onto cn and hold at back, k2, k2 from cn; repeat from * to end of row.
Row 9: *Sl 2 sts onto cn and hold at back, k2, k2 from cn, sl 2 sts onto cn and hold at front, k2, k2 from cn; repeat from * to end of row.
Row 12: Purl.
Repeat rows 1–12.

MULTIPLE THREADED STITCH

NOTE
■ On wrong side (yo 3 times, p1) in each stitch.

INSTRUCTIONS
Multiple of 6 stitches.

Row 1: Knit.
Row 2: P1, *(yo 3 times, p1) in each st; repeat from * to end of row.
Row 3: *(sl 6 sts onto working needle dropping yos, pass 3rd, 2nd, and 1st stitches over 6th, 5th, 4th onto source needle in that order, k3, k3 tbl; repeat from * to end of row.
Row 4: Purl.
Repeat rows 1–4.

CROSSED STITCH CABLE

NOTE
■ (Yo 2 times, k1) in each stitch.

INSTRUCTIONS
Multiple of 6 stitches.

Rows 1, 3, 5, and 6: Knit.
Rows 2 and 4: Purl.
Row 7: *(Yo 2 times, k1) in each st; repeat from * to end of row.
Row 8: *Sl 3 sts onto cn dropping yos and hold at front, k3 dropping yos, k3 from cn; repeat from * to end of row.
Repeat rows 1–8.

185

knitting pattern gallery

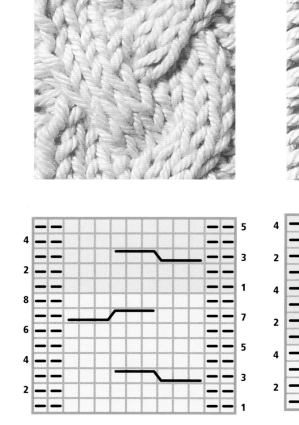

PLAIT CABLE

NOTE
Work on reverse stockinette ground.

INSTRUCTIONS
Panel of 13 stitches.

Row 1: P2, k9, p2.
Row 2 and all even rows: K the knit sts and p the purl sts.
Row 3: P2, sl 3 sts onto cn and hold at front, k3, k3 from cn, k3, p2.
Row 5: Same as Row 1.
Row 7: P2, k3, sl 3 sts onto cn and hold at back, k3, k3 from cn, p2.
Row 8: Same as Row 2.
Repeat rows 1–8.

ARAN BRAID

NOTE
Work on reverse stockinette ground.

INSTRUCTIONS
Panel of 12 stitches.

Row 1: P2, (sl 2 sts onto cn and hold at back, k2, k2 from cn) 2 times, p2.
Rows 2: K2, p8, k2.
Row 3: P2, k2, sl 2 sts onto cn and hold at front, k2, k2 from cn, k2, p2.
Rows 4: K2, p8, k2.
Repeat rows 1–4.

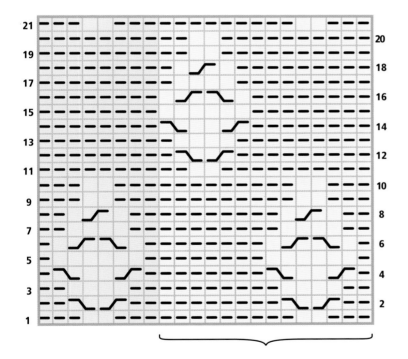

PALM LEAF BROCADE

INSTRUCTIONS

Multiple of 14 stitches + 8.
Begin on wrong side.

Row 1: K3, *p2, k12; repeat from * ending with p2, k3.

Row 2: P2, *rc, lc, p10; repeat from * ending with rc, lc, p2.

Row 3: K2, *p4, k10; repeat from * ending with p4, k2.

Row 4: P1, *rc, k2, lc, p8; repeat from * ending with rc, k2, lc, p1.

Row 5: K1, *p6, k8; repeat from * ending with p6, k1.

Row 6: P1, *k1, lc, rc, k1, p8; repeat from * ending with k1, rc, lc, k1, p1.

Row 7: Same as Row 3.

Row 8: P2, *k1, rc, k1, p10; repeat from * ending with k1, p2.

Row 9: Same as Row 1.

Row 10: P3, *k2, p12; repeat from * ending with k2, p3.

Row 11: K10, *p2, k12; repeat from * ending with k10.

Row 12: P9, * rc, lc, p10; repeat from * ending with p9.

Row 13: K9, *p4, k10; repeat from * ending with k9.

Row 14: P8, *rc, k2, lc, p8; repeat from * to end of row.

Row 15: K8, *p6, k8; repeat from * to end of row.

Row 16: P8, *k1, lc, rc, k1, p8; repeat from * to end of row.

Row 17: Same as Row 13.

Row 18: P9, *k1, rc, k1, p10; repeat from * ending with p9.

Row 19: Same as Row 11.

Row 20: P10, *k2, p12; repeat from * ending with p10.

Repeat rows 1–20.

187

knitting pattern gallery

SLIP STITCHES

Slip stitches produce patterns with elongated stitches. On the right side, the knit loop covers two rows in height. On the wrong side, the purl bump spans two stitches widthwise. Often the slip stitch is worked with the yarn in front so that the elongated purl bump is on the right side of the fabric.

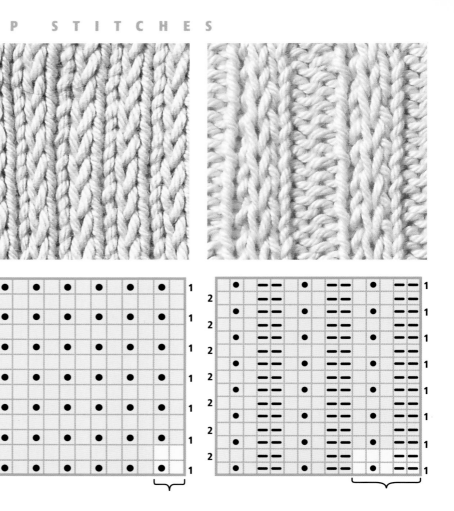

STOCKING HEEL STITCH

NOTE
Often used for sock heels being elastic and withstanding heavy wear.

INSTRUCTIONS
Multiple of 2 stitches + 1.

Row 1: *K1, wyib sl 1 kwise; repeat from * ending with k1.
Row 2: Purl.
Repeat rows 1–2.

CENTER SLIP STITCH RIB

INSTRUCTIONS
Multiple of 5.

Row 1: *P2, k1, wyib sl 1 kwise, k1; repeat from * to end of row.
Row 2: *P3, k2; repeat from * to end of row.
Repeat rows 1–2.

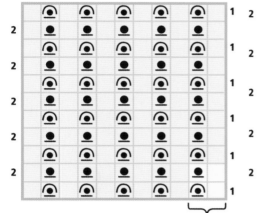

LINEN STITCH

INSTRUCTIONS
Multiple of 2 stitches + 1.

Row 1: *K1, wyif sl 1 pwise; repeat from
* ending with k1.
Row 2: P2, wyib sl 1 pwise * P1 wyib S1
pwise; repeat from * to last 2 sts, P2.
Repeat rows 1–2.

DOUBLE BARRED RIBBING

INSTRUCTIONS
Multiple of 4 stitches + 2.

Row 1: *P2, wyif sl 2 pwise; repeat from
* ending with p2.
Row 2: *K2, p2; repeat from * ending
with k2.
Repeat rows 1–2.

WOVEN STITCH

INSTRUCTIONS
Multiple of 4 stitches + 2.

Row 1: K3, *ywif sl 2 pwise, k2; repeat
from * ending with k3.
Row 2: Purl.
Row 3: K1, *ywif sl 2 pwise, k2; repeat
from * ending with k1.
Row 4: Purl.
Repeat rows 1–4.

VARIATION
Stitches in Row 3 can be offset by one
stitch to make a diagonal pattern.

189

knitting pattern gallery

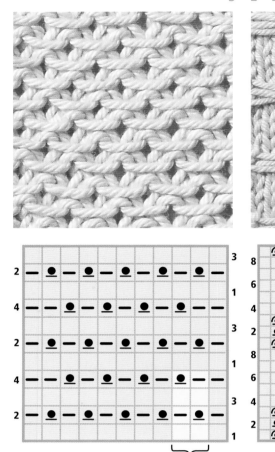

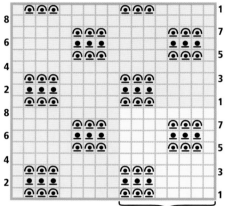

STAMEN STITCH

NOTE
Use large needles for a more open pattern.

INSTRUCTIONS
Multiple of 2 stitches + 1.

Row 1: Knit.
Row 2: *K1, wyib sl 1 pwise; repeat from * ending with k1.
Row 3: Knit.
Row 4: K2, *wyib sl 1 pwise, k1; repeat from * ending with k2.
Repeat rows 1–4.

SLIP STITCH LADDER

INSTRUCTIONS
Multiple of 8 stitches + 1.

Rows 1 and 3: *K5, wyif sl 3 pwise; repeat from * ending with k1.
Row 2: P1, *wyib sl 3 pwise, p5; repeat from * to end of row.
Rows 4: Purl.
Rows 5 and 7: K1, *wyif sl 3 pwise, k5; repeat from * to end of row.
Row 6: *P5, wyib sl 3 pwise; repeat from * ending with p1.
Row 8: Purl.
Repeat rows 1–8.

WOVEN DIAMOND

INSTRUCTIONS
Multiple of 16 stitches + 9.

Row 1: *K3, wyif sl 3 pwise, k3, wyif sl 2 pwise, k3, wyif sl 2 pwise; repeat from * ending with k3, wyif sl 3 pwise, k3.
Row 2 and all even rows: Purl.
Row 3: K2, *wyif sl 2 pwise, k1, wyif sl 2 pwise, k3, ; repeat from * ending with k2.
Row 5: K1, *wyif sl 2 pwise, k3, wyif sl 2 pwise, k3, wyif sl 3 pwise, k3; repeat from * ending with k1.
Row 7: *Wyif sl 2 pwise, k5, wyif sl 2 pwise, k7; repeat from * ending with wyif sl 2 pwise.
Row 9: Same as Row 5.
Row 11: Same as Row 3.
Row 13: Same as Row 1.
Row 15: *Wyif sl 1 pwise, k7, wyif sl 2 pwise, k5, wyif sl 2 pwise; repeat from * ending with wyif sl 1 pwise.
Row 16: Purl.
Repeat rows 1–16.

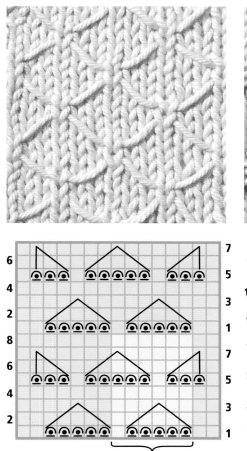

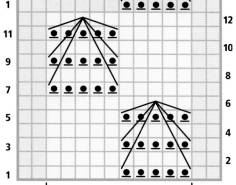

QUILTED LATTICE

INSTRUCTIONS

Multiple of 6 stitches + 3.

Row 1: K2, *wyif sl 5 pwise, k1; repeat from * ending with k1.
Row 2 and all even rows: Purl.
Row 3: K4, *insert working needle under slipped strand 2 rows below and knit in next st, k5; repeat from * ending with k4.
Row 5: K1, wyif sl 3 pwise, *k1, wyif sl 5 pwise; repeat from * ending with wyif sl 3 pwise, k1.
Row 7: K1, *insert working needle under slipped strand 2 rows below and knit in next st pulling loop around strand, k5; repeat from * ending with k1.
Row 8: Purl.
Repeat rows 1–8.

BUTTERFLY STITCH

INSTRUCTIONS

Multiple of 10 stitches + 4.
Begin on wrong side.

Rows 1, 3, and 5: P2, *p5, wyib sl 5 pwise; repeat from * ending with p2.
Rows 2, 4, 8, and 10: Knit.
Row 6: K2, *k2, insert working needle under 3 slipped strands below and knit in next st pulling loop around strands, k7; repeat from * ending with k2.
Rows 7, 9, and 11: P2, *wyib sl 5 pwise, p5; repeat from * ending with p2.
Row 12: K2, *k7, insert working needle under 3 slipped strands below and knit in next st pulling loop around strands, k2; repeat from * ending with k2.
Repeat rows 1–12.

BEE STITCH

INSTRUCTIONS

Multiple of 2 stitches + 1.
Begin on wrong side.

Rows 1: Knit.
Row 2: *K1 in next st through st below, k1; repeat from * ending with k1 in next st through st below.
Row 3: Knit.
Row 4: *K1, k1 in next st through st below; repeat from * ending with k1.
Repeat rows 1–4.

191

knitting pattern gallery

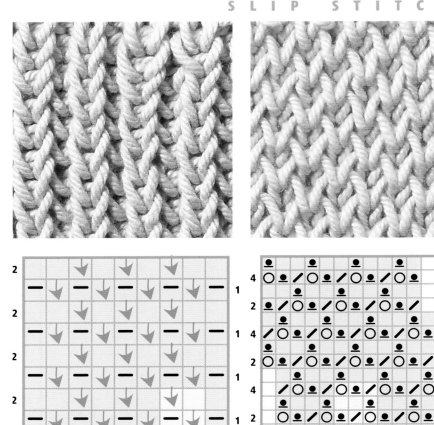

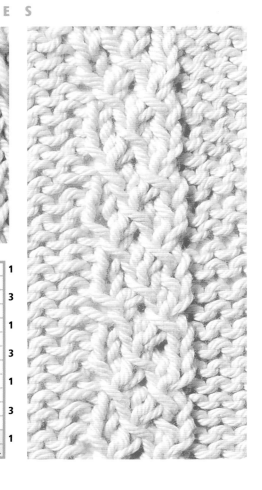

192

FISHERMAN'S RIB

NOTE
This pattern requires a preparation row of purl.

INSTRUCTIONS
Multiple of 2 stitches + 1.
Preparation row (wrong side): Purl.

Row 1: *P1, k in next st through st below; repeat from * ending with p1.

Row 2: P2, *k in next st through st below, p1; repeat from * ending with p1.

Repeat rows 1–2.

THREE-DIMENSIONAL HONEYCOMB

NOTES
This pattern requires a preparation row of (k1, yo, wyib s1 pwise).

INSTRUCTIONS
Multiple of 2 stitches.
Preparation row (wrong side): *K1, yo, wyib sl 1 pwise; repeat from * to end of row.

Row 1: K1, *wyib sl 1 pwise (the yarn over stitch), k2; repeat from * ending with k1.

Row 2: *Yo, wyib sl 1 pwise, k2tog (the slipped stitch and the next stitch); repeat from * to end of row.

Row 3: *K2, *wyib sl 1 pwise (the yarn over stitch); repeat from * to end of row.

Row 4: *K2tog (the slipped stitch and the next stitch), yo, wyib sl 1 pwise; repeat from * to end of row.

Repeat rows 1–4.

FASCINE BRAID

NOTE
Written instructions only.

INSTRUCTIONS
Multiple of 8 stitches + 4.
Begin on wrong side.

Rows 1 and 3: K4, *p4, k4; repeat from * to end of row.

Row 2: P4, *(wyib sl 1 kwise, k1, yo, psso) 2 times, p4; repeat from * to end of row.

Row 4: P4, *k1, wyib sl 1 kwise, k1, yo, psso, k1, p4; repeat from * to end of row.

Repeat rows 1–4.

PULLED AND WRAPPED STITCHES

Pulled and wrapped stitches are stitches that encircle a group of stitches. They look similar to the floats of decorative slip stitches. The difference is that pulled and wrapped stitches wrap around both the front and back of a group of stitches whereas floats are only on one side of the fabric. Pulled and wrapped stitches are usually worked tightly around the group of stitches to pinch or gather the stitches in the group together.

There are four methods to work pulled or wrapped stitches. In the first, one or more stitches previously formed are pulled over a group of stitches. In the second, a loop is drawn up between previous stitches and left on the working needle. It is knitted with another stitch on the next row. In the third, a loop of yarn is pulled between stitches on the holding needle, the intermediate stitches worked, and half of the loop slipped over the intermediate stitches. In the fourth, stitches are transferred to a cable needle, yarn wrapped around them, and the stitches returned to the original needle.

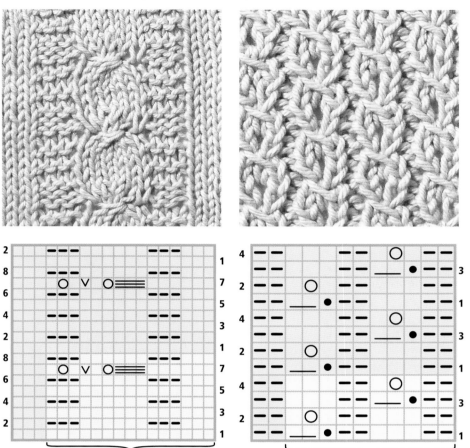

PULLED CABLE

NOTES

— **yo** – the yarn overs are formed by bringing the yarn forward, over the top of the needle, and then knitting the next stitch. On source needle pass 4th, 5th, and 6th sts over 1st, 2nd, and 3rd sts.

INSTRUCTIONS

Multiple of 15 stitches + 3.

Rows 1, 3, and 5: Knit.
Rows 2, 4, 6: *P3, k3, p6, k3; repeat ending with p3.
Row 7: *K6 , on the source needle pass the 4th, 5th, and 6th stitches knitted over 1st, 2nd, and 3rd sts, yo, k1, inc 1, k1, yo, k1; repeat from * ending with k3.
Row 8: Same as Row 2.
Repeat rows 1–8.

YARN OVER CABLE

INSTRUCTIONS

Multiple of 8 stitches + 2.

Row 1: *P2, k3, p2, wyib sl 1 kwise, k2, psso the 2 knitted stitches; repeat from * ending with p2.
Row 2: *K2, p1, yo, p1, k2, p3; repeat from * ending with k2.
Row 3: *P2, wyib sl 1 kwise, k2, psso over the 2 knitted stitches, p2, k3; repeat from * ending with p2.
Row 4: *K2, p3, k2, p1, yo, p1; repeat from * ending with p2.
Repeat rows 1–4.

193

knitting pattern gallery

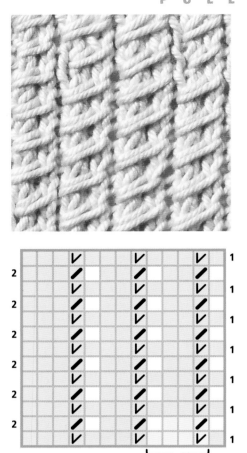

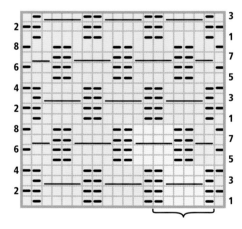

BLISTER COUCHING STITCH

NOTE
∨ **inc** – pull up a loop between 2nd and 3rd stitches of holding needle and place on working needle.

INSTRUCTIONS
Multiple of 3 stitches + 1.

Row 1: K1, *pull up a loop between 2nd and 3rd stitches of holding needle and place on working needle, k3; repeat from * to end of row.

Row 2: P1, *p2, p2tog (pulled loop and next stitch); repeat from * to end of row.

Repeat rows 1–2.

WHEAT STITCH

NOTE
— **wyib** pull up a loop between 4th and 5th stitches (2nd and 3rd for edge stitches) of holding needle and place on working needle, k4 (k2 for edge stitches), sl loop over stitches just knit.

INSTRUCTIONS
Multiple of 6 stitches + 1.

Row 1: K1, p1, *k4, p2; repeat from * ending with k4, p1, k1.

Rows 2 and 4: K2, *p4, k2; repeat from * to end of row.

Row 3: K1, p1, *wyib pull up a loop between 4th and 5th stitches of holding needle and place on working needle, k4, sl loop over 4 sts just knit, p2; repeat from * ending last repeat with p1, k1.

Row 5: K3, *p2, k4, repeat from * ending with p2, k3.

Row 6: K1, p2, *k2, p4; repeat from * ending with k2, p2, k1.

Row 7: K1, *wyib pull up a loop between 2nd and 3rd stitches of source needle and place on working needle, k2, sl loop over 2 sts just knit, p2, wyib pull up a loop between 4th and 5th stitches of source needle and place on working needle, k4, sl loop over 4 sts just knit, p2; repeat from * ending with wyib pull up a loop between 2nd and 3rd stitches of source needle and place on working needle, k2, sl loop over 2 sts just knit, k1.

Row 8: Same as Row 6.

Repeat rows 1–8.

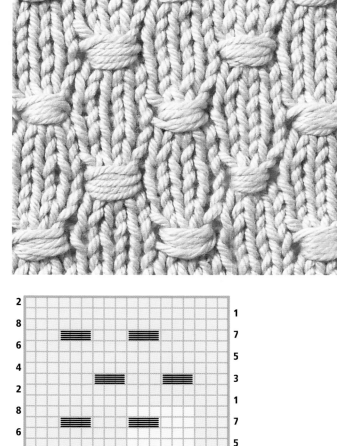

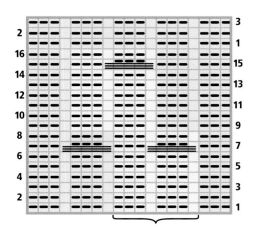

SMOCKED STITCH

NOTE

k1, p3, k1, sl last 5 sts worked onto cn, wrap yarn counterclockwise around these 5 sts 3 times, sl sts back onto working needle.

INSTRUCTIONS

Multiple of 8 stitches + 3.

Row 1: *P3, k1; repeat from * ending with p3.
Row 2 and all even rows: K3, *p1, k3; repeat from* to end of row.
Rows 3 and 5: Same as Row 1.
Row 7: *P3, k1, p3, k1, sl last 5 sts worked onto cn, wrap yarn counterclockwise around these 5 sts 3 times, sl sts back onto working needle; repeat from * ending with p3.
Rows 9, 11, and 13: Same as Row 1.
Row 15: P3, k1, p3, *k1, p3, k1, sl last 5 sts worked onto cn, wrap yarn counterclockwise around these 5 sts 3 times, sl sts back onto working needle, p3; repeat from * ending with k1, p3.
Row 16: Same as Row 2.
Repeat rows 1–16.

WRAPPED EYELET

NOTE

sl last 3 sts worked onto cn, wrap yarn counterclockwise around these 3 sts 5 times, sl sts back onto working needle.

INSTRUCTIONS

Multiple of 6 stitches + 3.

Rows 1 and 5: Knit.
Row 2 and all even rows: Purl.
Row 3: *K6, sl last 3 sts worked onto cn, wrap yarn counterclockwise around these 3 sts 5 times, sl sts back onto working needle; repeat from * ending with k6.
Row 7: K9, *sl last 3 sts worked onto cn, wrap yarn counterclockwise around these 3 sts 5 times, sl sts back onto working needle, k6; repeat from * ending with k3.
Row 8: Purl.
Repeat rows 1–8.

knitting pattern gallery

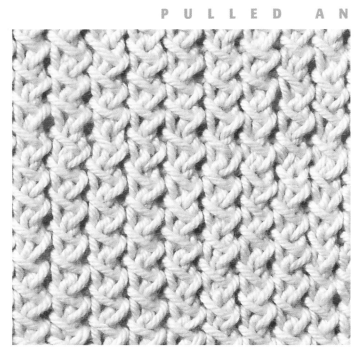

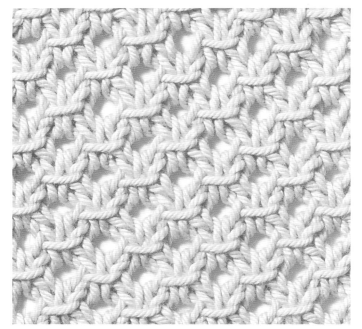

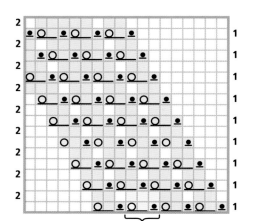

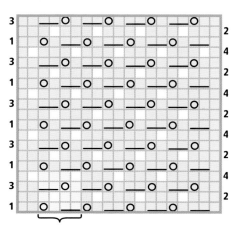

TWEEDED MOCK RIBBING

INSTRUCTIONS
Multiple of 2 stitches.

Row 1: *Wyib sl 1 pwise, k1, yo, psso;
   repeat from * to end of row.
Row 2: Purl.
Repeat rows 1–2.

STAR STITCH

INSTRUCTIONS
Multiple of 3 stitches.
Begin on wrong side.

Row 1: P2, *yo, p3, pass first of these 3
   stitches over the other 2 sts; repeat
   from * ending with p1.
Row 2: Knit.
Row 3: P1, *p3, pass first of these 3
   stitches over the other 2 sts, yo;
   repeat from * ending with p2.
Row 4: Knit.
Repeat rows 1–4.

DROP STITCHES

Drop stitch patterns are formed by purposefully dropping stitches from the holding needle. Horizontal patterns are usually formed by forming multiple yarn overs in one row and then dropping all but one in the next row. Vertical ladders are formed beginning with a make 1 stitch. In subsequent rows, the make 1 is worked as a normal stitch. Then, some rows later, the stitch above the make 1 is dropped and allowed to ravel. It will stop raveling at the make 1.

SPOT DROP STITCH

INSTRUCTIONS
Multiple of 8 stitches + 4.

Row 1: K1, *p2, k1, yo, k1, p2, k2; repeat from * ending with p2, k1.

Rows 2 and 4: P1, *k2, p3, k2, p2; repeat from * ending with k2, p1.

Rows 3 and 5: K1, *p2, k3, p2, k2, p2; repeat from * ending with p2, k1.

Row 6: P1, *k2, p1, drop next stitch unraveling it down to the yo, p1, k2, p2; repeat from * ending with k2. p1.

Row 7: K1, *p2, k2, p2, k1, yo, k1; repeat from * ending with p2, k1.

Rows 8 and 10: P1, *k2, p2, k2, p3; repeat from * ending with k2, p1.

Rows 9 and 11: K1, *p2, k2, p2, k3, p2; repeat from * ending with p2, k1.

Row 12: P1, *k2, p2, k2, p1, drop next stitch unraveling it down to the yo, p1; repeat from * ending with k2, p1.

Repeat rows 1–12.

BUTTERFLY DROP STITCH

NOTE

Butterfly stitch – insert holding needle in stitch 6 rows below next stitch, unravel next stitch down to needle, position 5 raveled strands on top of holding needle and knit stitch from below around strands.

INSTRUCTIONS
Multiple of 7 stitches.

Rows 1, 3, and 5: P2, *k3, p4; repeat from * ending with p2.

Rows 2, 4, and 6: K2, *p3, k4; repeat from * ending with k2.

Row 7: P2, *k1, insert holding needle in stitch 6 rows below next stitch, unravel next stitch down to needle, position 5 raveled strands on top of holding needle and knit stitch from below around strands, k1, p4; repeat from * ending with p2.

Row 8: Same as Row 2.

Repeat rows 1–8.

197

LACE

Lace patterns are most often formed using a combination of yarn overs and decreases to make holes. And often the holes are displaced on the bias to arrange the holes.

Other methods of lace making such as pairing a yarn over with a slip stitch or using pulled and wrapped stitches to bundle stitches leaving gaps also produce lace patterns, but are covered in other sections.

MERMAID'S MESH

INSTRUCTIONS

Multiple of 9 stitches + 4.
Begin on wrong side.

Row 1 and all odd rows: Purl except (k1, p1) in double yarn overs.

Row 2: K1, yo, *(ssk, yo) 3 times, k3tog, yo2; repeat from * ending with ssk, k1.

Row 4: *K2tog, yo2, (ssk, yo) 2 times, k3tog, yo; repeat from * ending with k2tog, yo, k2.

Row 6: K1, *k2tog, yo2, ssk, yo, k3tog, yo, k2tog, yo; repeat from * ending with k2tog, yo, k1.

Row 8: K2tog, yo, *k2tog, yo2, sk2p, (yo, k2tog) 2 times, yo; repeat from * ending with k2.

Row 10: K1, k2tog, yo, *k2tog, yo2, sk2p, (yo, k2tog) 2 times, yo; repeat from * ending with k1.

Row 12: K2tog, yo, *k2tog, yo2, ssk, yo, sk2p, yo, k2tog, yo; repeat from * ending with k2.

Row 14: K1, k2tog, *yo2, (ssk, yo) 2 times, sk2p, yo, k2tog; repeat from * ending with yo, k1.

Row 16: K2tog, *yo2, (ssk, yo) 3 times, k3tog; repeat from * ending with yo2, ssk.

Repeat rows: 1–16.

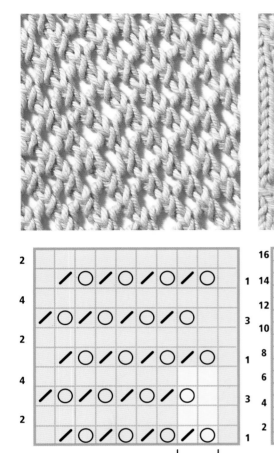

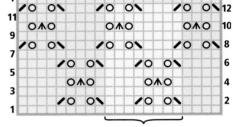

LACE NET

INSTRUCTIONS
Multiple of 2 stitches.

Row 1: K1, *yo, k2tog; repeat from * ending with k1.
Row 2: Purl.
Row 3: K2, *yo, k2tog; repeat from * to end.
Row 4: Purl.
Repeat rows 1–4.

DIAMOND EYELET

INSTRUCTIONS
Multiple of 8 stitches.

Row 1: Knit.
Row 2 and all even rows: Purl.
Row 3: K3, *yo, ssk, k6; repeat from * ending with k3.
Row 5: K1, *k2tog, yo, k1, yo, ssk, k3; repeat from * ending with k2.
Row 7: Same as Row 3.
Row 9: Knit.
Row 11: K7, *yo, ssk, k6; repeat from * ending with k1.
Row 13: K5, *k2tog, yo, k1, yo, ssk; repeat from * ending with k3.
Row 15: Same as Row 11.
Row 16: Purl.
Repeat rows 1–16.

SNOWFLAKES

INSTRUCTIONS
Multiple of 8 stitches + 5.
Begin on wrong side.

Row 1 and all odd rows: Purl.
Row 2: K4, *ssk, yo, k1, yo, k2tog, k3; repeat from * ending with k1.
Row 4: K5, *yo, (sl 2 kwise, k1, p2sso), yo, k5; repeat from * to end of row.
Row 6: Same as Row 2.
Row 8: Ssk, yo, k1, yo, k2tog, *k3, yo, k1, yo, k2tog; repeat from * to end of row.
Row 10: K1, *yo, (sl 2 kwise, k1, p2sso), yo, k5; repeat from * ending with k1.
Row 12: Same as Row 8.
Repeat rows 1–12.

199

knitting pattern gallery

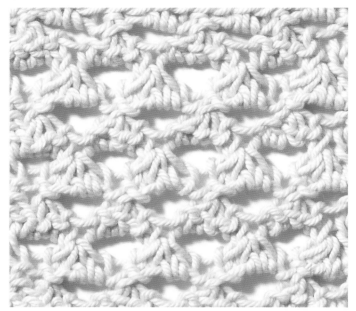

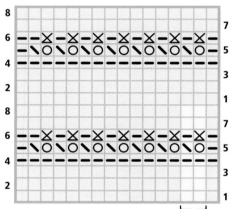

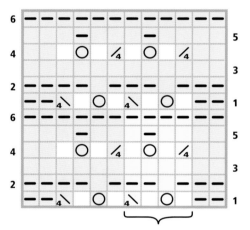

RIBBON EYELET

INSTRUCTIONS
Multiple of 2 stitches +2.

Rows 1: Knit.
Row 2: Purl.
Rows 3 and 4: Knit.
Row 5: P1, *yo, p2tog; repeat from *
    ending with p1.
Row 6: K2, *k1 tbl, k1; repeat from * to
    end of row.
Row 7: Knit.
Row 8: Purl.
Repeat rows 1–8.

GRAND EYELET

NOTES
This pattern is easier to work from the
written instructions than from the chart.
Use larger needles in rows 3 and 6.

INSTRUCTIONS
Multiple of 4 stitches.

Rows 1 and 4: P2, *yo, p4tog; repeat
    from * ending with p2.
Rows 2 and 5: K2, *k1 in p4tog, (k1,
    p1, k1) in yo; repeat from * ending
    with k2.
Rows 3 and 6: Knit.
Repeat rows 1–6.

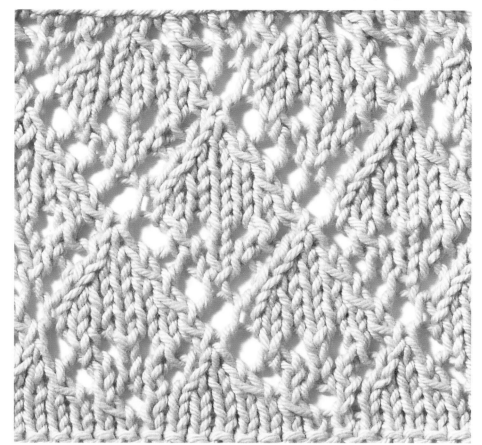

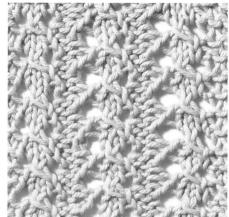

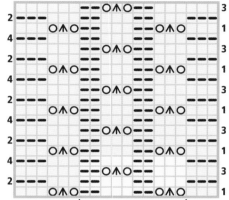

SNOWDROPS

INSTRUCTIONS
Multiple of 10 stitches + 9.

Row 1: K3, *yo, sk2p, yo, p2, k3, p2; repeat from * ending with yo, sk2p, yo, k3.

Row 2: K3, *p3, k2; repeat from * ending with p3, k3.

Row 3: K6, *p2, yo, slip 1, K2 tog, psso, yo, p2 K3; repeat from * ending with k6.

Row 4: K3, *p3, k2; repeat from * ending with p3, k3.

Repeat rows 1–4.

EYELET DIAMONDS

NOTE
\ k2tog tbl

INSTRUCTIONS
Multiple of 8 stitches.

Row 1: *Yo, k2tog tbl, k6; repeat from * to end of row.

Row 2 and all even rows: Purl.

Row 3: *K1, yo, k2tog tbl, k3, k2tog, yo; repeat from * to end of row.

Row 5: K2, *yo, k2tog tbl, k1, k2tog, yo, k3; repeat from * ending with yo, k2tog tbl, k1, k2tog, yo, k1.

Row 7: *K1, yo, k2tog, yo, k3tog, yo, k2tog tbl, yo; repeat from * to end of row.

Row 9: K4, *yo, k2tog tbl, k6; repeat from * ending with yo, k2tog, k2.

Row 11: K2, *k2tog, yo, k1, yo, k2tog tbl, k3; repeat from * ending with k2tog, yo, k2tog tbl, k1.

Row 13: *K1, k2tog, yo, k3, yo, k2tog tbl; repeat from * to end of row.

Row 15: K2tog, *yo, k2tog tbl, yo, k1, yo, k2tog tbl, yo, k3tog; repeat from * ending with yo, k2tog tbl, yo, k1, yo, k2tog tbl, yo.

Row 16: Purl.
Repeat rows 1–16.

201

knitting pattern gallery

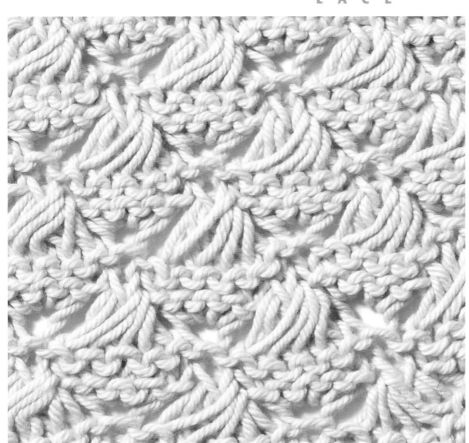

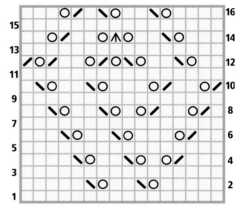

PURL SHELL

NOTE
Written instructions only.

INSTRUCTIONS
Multiple of 6 stitches + 3.

Rows 1 and 2: Knit.
Row 3: K1, (k1, yo, k1) in next st, *(k1, yo2) 5 times, (K1, yo, k1, yo, k1) in next st; repeat from * ending with (k1, yo, k1) in next to last st, k1.
Row 4: K4, *wyif sl 5 dropping extra wraps, insert source needle back into these 5 sts and p5tog, k5; repeat from * ending with k4.
Rows 5 and 6: Knit.

Row 7: K1, (k1, yo2) 3 times, *(k1, yo, k1, yo, k1) in next st, (k1, yo2) 5 times; repeat from * ending with (k1, yo2) 3 times, k1.
Row 8: K1, wyif sl 3 dropping extra wraps, insert source needle back into these 3 sts and p3tog, *k5, sl 5 dropping extra wraps, insert source needle back into these 5 sts and p5tog; repeat from * ending with k5, wyif sl 3 dropping extra wraps, insert source needle back into these 3 sts and p3tog, k1.

Repeat rows 1–8.

DIAMOND CHAIN LACE

NOTES
Work on a background of stockinette stitch.

INSTRUCTIONS
Panel of 16 stitches.
Begin on wrong side.

Row 1 and all odd rows: Purl.
Row 2: K5, yo, ssk, k2, yo, ssk, k5.
Row 4: K3, k2tog, yo, k1, yo, ssk, k2, yo, ssk, k4.
Row 6: K2, k2tog, yo, k3, yo, ssk, k2, yo, ssk, k3.
Row 8: K1, k2tog, yo, k2, k2tog, yo, k1, (yo, ssk, k2) 2 times.
Row 10: K2tog, yo, k2, k2tog, yo, k3, yo, ssk, k2, yo, ssk, k1.
Row 12: (K2, yo, ssk) 2 times, yo, k2tog, yo, k2, k2tog, yo, k2tog.
Row 14: K3, yo, ssk, k2, yo, sk2p, yo, k2, k2tog, yo, k2.
Row 16: K4, yo, ssk, k2, yo, ssk, k1, k2tog, yo, k3.
Repeat rows 1–16.

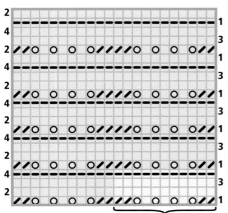

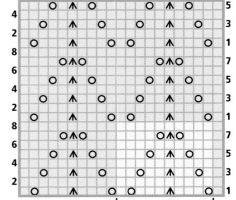

OLD SHALE

INSTRUCTIONS
Multiple of 11 stitches.

Row 1: (K2tog) 2 times, *(yo, k1) 3 times, yo, (k2tog) 2 times; repeat from * to end of row.
Row 2: Purl.
Row 3: Knit.
Row 4: Knit.
Repeat rows 1–4.

VARIATIONS
This version of Old Shale is composed of 4 paired increases and decreases. The number of paired increases and decreases can be varied at will. Likewise, the number of intervening knit rows can be varied.

FEATHER AND FAN

INSTRUCTIONS
Multiple of 12 stitches.

Row 1: Knit.
Row 2: Purl.
Row 3: (P2tog) 2 times, *(yo, k1) 4 times, (p2tog) 4 times; repeat from * to end of row.
Row 4: Purl.
Repeat rows 1–4.

HORSESHOES

INSTRUCTIONS
Multiple of 10 stitches + 1.

Row 1: K1, *yo, k3, sk2p, k3, yo. k1; repeat from * to end of row.
Row 2 and all even rows: Purl.
Row 3: K1, *k1, yo, k2, sk2p, k2, yo, k2; repeat from * to end of row.
Row 5: K1, *k2, yo, k1, sk2p, k1, yo, k3; repeat from * to end of row.
Row 7: K1,*k3, yo, sk2p, yo, k4; repeat from * to end of row.
Row 8: Purl.
Repeat rows 1–8.

203

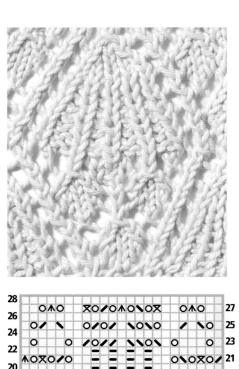

BELL LACE

NOTES
The number of stitches in a repeat varies from 18 to 22.

INSTRUCTIONS
Multiple of 18 stitches + 1.

Row 1: K1, * (p2, k1) 2 times, yo, k2tog, yo, k1, yo, ssk, yo, (k1, p2) 2 times, k1; repeat from * to end of row.

Row 2: *(P1, k2) 2 times, p9, k2, p1, k2; repeat from * ending with p1.

Row 3: K1, *(p2, k1) 2 times, yo, k2tog, yo, k3, yo, ssk, yo, (k1, p2) 2 times, k1; repeat from * to end of row.

Row 4: *(P1, k2) 2 times, p11, k2, p1, k2; repeat from * ending with p1.

Row 5: K1, *(p2tog, k1) 2 times, yo, k2tog, yo, ssk, k1, k2tog, yo, ssk, yo, (k1, p2tog) 2 times, k1; repeat from * to end of row.

Row 6: *(P1, k1) 2 times, p11, k1, p1, k1; repeat from * ending with p1.

Row 7: K1, *(p1, k1) 2 times, yo, k2tog, yo, k1 tbl, yo, sk2p, yo, k1 tbl, yo, ssk, yo, (k1, p1) 2 times, k1; repeat from * to end of row.

Row 8: *(P1, k1) 2 times, p13, k1, p1, k1; repeat from * ending with p1.

Row 9: K1, *(k2tog) 2 times, yo, k2tog, yo, k3, yo, k1, yo, k3, yo, ssk, yo, (ssk) 2 times, k1; repeat from * to end of row.

Rows 10, 12, and 14: Purl.

Row 11: K1, *(k2tog, yo) 2 times, ssk, k1, k2tog, yo, k1, yo, ssk, k1, k2tog, (yo, ssk) 2 times, k1; repeat from * to end of row.

Row 13: K2tog, *yo, k2tog, yo, k1 tbl, yo, sk2p, yo, k3, yo, sk2p, yo, k1 tbl, yo, ssk, yo, sk2p; repeat from * ending with ssk instead of sk2p.

Row 15: K1, *yo, ssk, yo, (k1, p2) 4 times, k1, yo, k2tog, yo, k1; repeat from * to end of row.

Row 16: P5, *(k2, p1) 3 times, k2, p9; repeat from * ending with p5.

Row 17: K2, *yo, ssk, yo, (k1, p2) 4 times, k1, yo, k2tog, yo, k3; repeat from * ending with k2.

Row 18: P6, *(k2, p1) 3 times, k2, p11; repeat from * ending with p6.

Row 19: K1, *k2tog, yo, ssk, yo, (k1, p2tog) 4 times, k1, yo, k2tog, yo, ssk, k1; repeat from * to end of row.

Row 20: P6, *(k1, p1) 3 times, k1, p11; repeat from * ending with p6.

Row 21: K2tog, *yo, k1 tbl, yo, ssk, yo, (k1, p1) 4 times, k1, yo, k2tog, yo, k1 tbl, yo, sk2p; repeat from * ending with ssk instead of sk2p.

Row 22: P7, *(k1, p1) 3 times, k1, p13; repeat from * ending with p7.

Row 23: K1, *yo, k3, yo, ssk, yo, (ssk) 2 times, k1, (k2tog) 2 times, yo, k2tog, yo, k3, yo, k1; repeat from * to end of row.

Rows 24 and 26: Purl.

Row 25: K1, *yo, ssk, k1, k2tog, (yo, ssk) 2 times, k1, (k2tog, yo) 2 times, ssk, k1, k2tog, yo, k1; repeat from * to end of row.

Row 27: K2, *yo, sk2p, yo, k1 tbl, yo, ssk, yo, sk2p, yo, k2tog, yo, k1 tbl, yo, sk2p, yo, k3; repeat from * ending with k2.

Row 28: Purl.

Repeat rows 1–28.

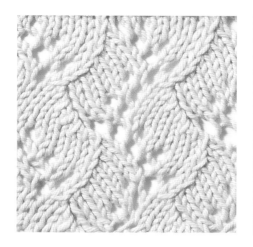

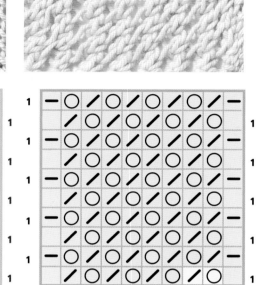

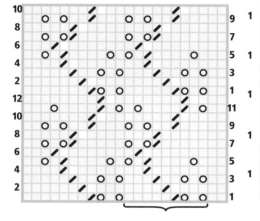

FERN LACE

INSTRUCTIONS
Multiple of 8 stitches + 4.

Row 1: K2, *yo, k1, yo, k2tog, k5; repeat from * ending with k2.

Row 2: P2, *p4, p2tog, p3; repeat from * ending with p2.

Row 3: K2, *yo, k1, yo, k2, k2tog, k3; repeat from * ending with k2.

Row 4: P2, *p2, p2tog, p5; repeat from * ending with k2.

Row 5: K2, *k1, yo, k4, k2tog, k1, yo; repeat from * ending with k2.

Row 6: P2, *p1, p2tog, p6; repeat from * ending with p2.

Row 7: K2, *k5, k2tog, yo, k1, yo; repeat from * ending with k2.

Row 8: P2, *p3, p2tog, p4; repeat from * ending with p2.

Row 9: K2, *k3, k2tog, k2, yo, k1, yo; repeat from * ending with k2.

Row 10: P2, *p5, p2tog, p2; repeat from * ending with p2.

Row 11: K2, *yo, k1, k2tog, k4, yo, k1; repeat from * ending with k2.

FAGOT STITCH
Other name: purse stitch

INSTRUCTIONS
Multiple of 2 stitches + 2.

Row 1: K1,*yo, p2tog; repeat from * ending with k1.
Repeat Row 1 for desired length.

Row 12: P2, *p6, p2tog, p1; repeat from * ending with p2.
Repeat rows 1–12.

WITCHES' LADDER

INSTRUCTIONS
Any number of stitches.

Row 1: K1,*yo, k2tog; repeat from * ending with k1.
Repeat Row 1 for desired length.

knitting pattern gallery

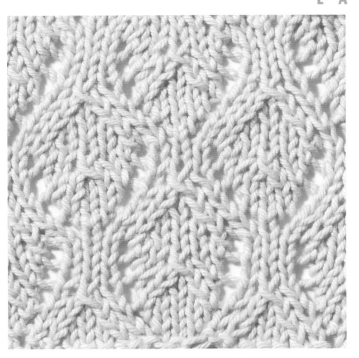

206

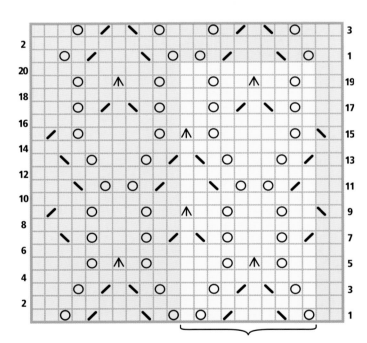

CHALICE

INSTRUCTIONS
Multiple of 10 stitches + 3.

Row 1: K2, *yo, k1, skp, k3, k2tog, k1, yo, k1; repeat from * ending with k2.
Row 2 and all even rows: Purl.
Row 3: K2, *k1, yo, k1, skp, k1, k2tog, k1, yo, k2; repeat from * ending with k1.
Row 5: K2, *k2, yo, k1, sk2p, k1, yo, k3; repeat from * ending with k1.
Row 7: K2, *k2tog, k1, yo, k3, yo, k1, skp, k1; repeat from * ending with k1.
Row 9: K1, skp, *k2, yo, k3, yo, k2, sk2p; repeat from * ending with k2tog, k1.
Row 11: K2, *k1, k2tog, (k1, yo) 2 times, k1, skp, k2; repeat from * ending with k1.
Row 13: K2, *k2tog, k1, yo, k3, yo, k1, skp, k1; repeat from * ending with k1.
Row 15: K1, skp, *k1, yo, k5, yo, k1, sk2p; repeat from * ending with k2tog, k1.
Row 17: K2, *k1, yo, k1, skp, k1, k2tog, k1, yo, k2; repeat from * ending with k1.
Row 19: K2, *k1, yo, k2, sk2p, k2, yo, k2; repeat from * ending with k1.
Row 20: Purl.
Repeat rows 1–20.

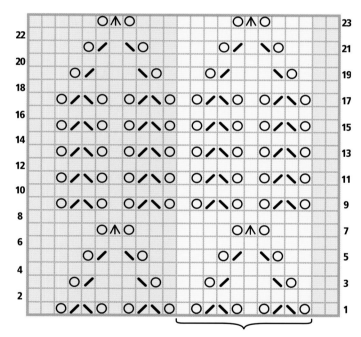

ARROWHEAD

INSTRUCTIONS
Multiple of 10 stitches + 3.

Rows 1: K2, *yo, skp, k2tog, yo, k1; repeat from * ending with k1.

Row 2 and all even rows: Purl.

Row 3: K3, *yo, skp, k3, k2tog, yo, k3; repeat from * to end of row.

Row 5: K4, * yo, skp, k1, k2tog, yo, k5; repeat from * ending with k4.

Row 7: K5, *yo, sk2p, yo, k7; repeat from * ending with k5.

Row 9: K2, *yo, skp, k2tog, yo, k1; repeat from * ending with k1.

Row 11: Same as Row 9.

Row 13: Same as Row 9.

Row 15: Same as Row 9.

Row 17: Same as Row 9.

Row 19: K3, *yo, skp, k3, k2tog, yo, k3; repeat from * to end of row.

Row 21: K4, *yo, skp, k1, k2tog, yo, k5; repeat from * ending with k4.

Row 23: K5, *yo, sk2p, yo, k7; repeat from * ending with k5.

Row 24: Purl.

Repeat rows 9–24.

207

RIBBINGS, EDGINGS, AND FRINGES

Ribbings, edgings, and fringes are all used as edge finishes. They can be knitted directly onto an item or they can be made separately and sewn on. In addition to the patterns in this section, a few rows of many other patterns can be used for an edging.

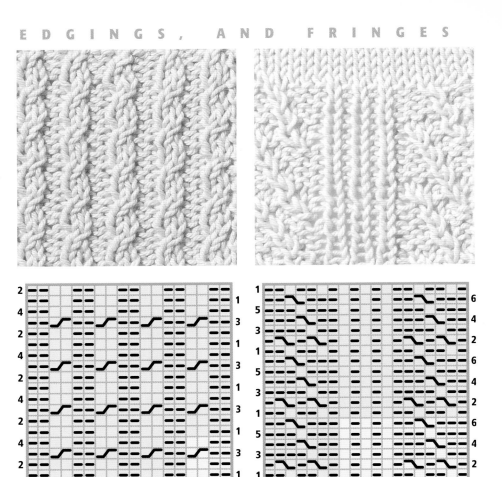

CABLE RIB

NOTE
For an edging, cast on and then repeat rows 1–4 four times.

INSTRUCTIONS
Multiple of 4 stitches + 2.

Row 1: *P2, k2; repeat from * ending with p2.
Row 2: Knit the knits and purl the purls.
Row 3: *P2, rc; repeat from * ending with p2.
Row 4: Same as Row 2.
Repeat rows 1–4.

TWIST RIB

INSTRUCTIONS
Multiple of 12 stitches + 7.
Begin on wrong side.

Row 1: (K2, p1) 2 times, *(k1, p1) 3 times. (k2, p1) 2 times; repeat from * ending with k1.
Row 2: P1, (lc, p1) 2 times, *(k1, p1) 3 times, (lc, p1) 2 times; repeat from * to end of row.
Row 3: K4, p1, k2, *p1, (k1, p1) 2 times, k4, p1, k2; repeat from * to end of row.
Row 4: *P2, lc, p3, (k1, p1) 2 times, k1; repeat from * ending with p2, lc, p3.
Row 5: *(K3, p1) 2 times, (k1, p1) 2 times; repeat from * ending with k3, p1, k3.
Row 6: *P3, lc, p2, (k1, p1) 2 times, k1; repeat from * ending with p3, lc, p2.
Repeat rows 1–6.

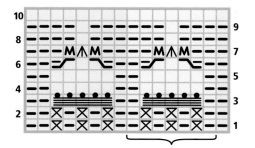

TASSEL RIB

NOTES

For edging, begin with a cast on row then repeat rows 1 and 2 to desired length of tassel skirt.

INSTRUCTIONS

Multiple of 7 stitches + 2.

Row 1: P2, *(k1 tbl, p1) 3 times, p1; repeat from * to end of row.

Row 2: K2, *(p1 tbl, k1) 3 times, k1; repeat from * to end of row.

Repeat Rows 1 and 2 for desired length of tassel skirt.

Row 3: P2, *sl next 5 sts onto cn, wrap yarn counterclockwise around these sts 4 times, sl sts onto working needle, p2; repeat from * to end of row.

Row 4: K2, *p5, k2; repeat from * to end of row.

Row 5: P2, *k5, p2; repeat from * to end of row.

Row 6: K2, *rckp, p1, lcpk, k2; repeat from * to end of row.

Row 7: P3 , *m1, sl 2 kwise, k1, p2sso, m1, p2; repeat from * ending with p1.

Row 8: K4, *p1, k6; repeat from * ending with k4.

Row 9: P4, *k1, p6; repeat from * ending with p4.

Row 10: Begin ground pattern.

SUGAR SCALLOPS

NOTE

Written instructions only.

Rows within the pattern repeat vary in length from 5–11 stitches. Eleven stitches are cast on for each repeat. When edging is completed, seven stitches remain to begin body of work.

INSTRUCTIONS

Cast on 11 stitches for each repeat + 2.

Row 1: Purl.

Row 2: K2, *k1 and sl st back onto source needle, pass next 8 sts over this st and off needle, yo 2 times, knit first st again, k2; repeat from * to end of row. 5 sts + 2.

Row 3: K1, *p2tog, drop one yo, in next loop (k1, p1, k1, p1, k1), p1; repeat from * ending with k1. 7 sts + 2.

209

SEA SCALLOP

NOTES
Rows within the pattern repeat vary in length from 21–26 stitches.

≡ sl these 4 sts onto cn, wrap yarn clockwise around these 4 sts 3 times

INSTRUCTIONS
Multiple of 21 stitches + 3.
Begin on wrong side.

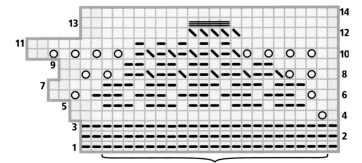

Row 1: Knit.
Row 2: Purl.
Row 3: Knit.
Row 4: K1, *yo, k21; repeat from * ending with k23.
Row 5: P2, *(p1, k3) 5 times, p2; repeat from * ending with p1.
Row 6: K1, *k1, yo, k1, (p3, k1) 5 times, yo; repeat from * ending with k2.
Row 7: P2, *p3, (k3, p1) 5 times, p1; repeat from * ending with p1.
Row 8: K1, *(k1, yo) 2 times, (ssk, p2) 5 times, (k1, yo) 2 times; repeat from * ending with k2. 23 sts.
Row 9: P2, *p4, (k2, p1) 5 times, p4; repeat from * ending with p5.

Row 10: K1, *(k1, yo) 4 times, (ssk, p1) 5 times, (k1, yo) 4 times; repeat from * ending with k2. 26 sts.
Row 11: P2, *p8, (k1, p1) 5 times, p8; repeat from * ending with p9.
Row 12: K1, *k8, ssk 5 times, k8; repeat from * ending with k10. 21 sts.
Row 13: P2, *p8, p4, sl these 4 sts onto cn, wrap yarn clockwise around these 4 sts 3 times, sl sts onto working needle, p9; repeat from * ending with p10.
Row 14: Knit.

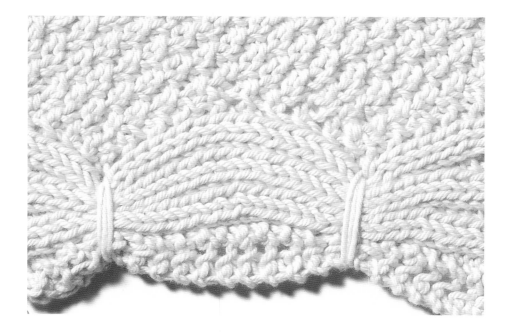

JOANIE'S JUBILEE

NOTES

Edging is worked across the width to any desired length. Rows within the pattern repeat vary in length from 22–27 stitches. Twenty two stitches are cast on.

≡ wrap yarn clockwise around 16 sts on source needle 3 times

INSTRUCTIONS

Cast on 22 stitches.

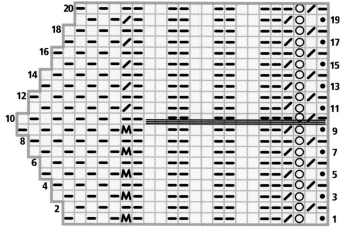

Row 1: Sl 1 kwise, k1, yo, k2tog, (p2, k2) 3 times, p1, m1, (p1, k1) 2 times, p1. 23 sts.

Rows 2 and 18: (P1, k1) 3 times, k1, (p2, k2) 3 times, k1, yo, k2tog, k1.

Row 3: Sl 1 kwise, k1, yo, k2tog, (p2, k2) 3 times, p1, m1, (p1, k1) 3 times. 24 sts.

Rows 4 and 16: (K1, p1) 3 times, k2, (p2, k2) 3 times, k1, yo, k2tog, k1.

Row 5: Sl 1 kwise, k1, yo, k2tog, (p2, k2) 3 times, p1, m1, (p1, k1) 3 times, p1. 25 sts.

Rows 6 and 14: (P1, k1) 4 times, k1, (p2, k2) 3 times, k1, yo, k2tog, k1.

Row 7: Sl 1 kwise, k1, yo, k2tog, (p2, k2) 3 times, p1, m1, (p1, k1) 4 times. 26 sts.

Rows 8 and 12: (K1, p1) 4 times, k2, (p2, k2) 3 times, k1, yo, k2tog, k1.

Row 9: Sl 1 kwise, k1, yo, k2tog, (p2, k2) 3 times, p1, m1, (p1, k1) 4 times, p1. 27 sts.

Row 10: (P1, k1) 5 times, k1, yarn forward, wrap yarn clockwise around 16 sts on source needle 3 times, work these 16 sts as follows (p2, k2) 3 times, k1, yo, k2tog, k1.

Row 11: Sl 1 kwise, k1, yo, k2tog, (p2, k2) 3 times, p1, k2tog, (p1, k1) 4 times. 26 sts.

Row 13: Sl 1 kwise, k1, yo, k2tog, (p2, k2) 3 times, p1, k2tog, (p1, k1) 3 times, p1. 25 sts.

Row 15: Sl 1 kwise, k1, yo, k2tog, (p2, k2) 3 times, p1, k2tog, (p1, k1) 3 times. 24 sts.

Row 17: Sl 1 kwise, k1, yo, k2tog, (p2, k2) 3 times, p1, k2tog, (p1, k1) 2 times, p1. 23 sts.

Row 19: Sl 1 kwise, k1, yo, k2tog, (p2, k2) 3 times, p1, k2tog, (p1, k1) 2 times, p1. 22 sts.

Row 20: (K1, p1) 2 times, k2, (p2, k2) 3 times, k1, yo, k2tog, k1.

Repeat rows 1–20 for desired length.

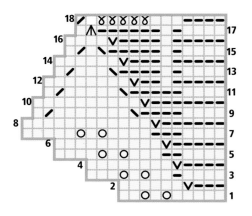

LEAF EDGING

NOTES

Edging is worked across the width to any desired length. Rows within the pattern repeat vary in length from 8–20 stitches. Eight stitches are cast on.

INSTRUCTIONS

Cast on 8 stitches.

Row 1: K5, yo, k1, yo, k2. 10 sts.
Row 2: P6, inc 1, k3. 11 sts.
Row 3: K4, p1, k2, yo, k1, yo, k3. 13 sts.
Row 4: P8, inc 1, k4. 14 sts.
Row 5: K4, p2, k3, yo, k1, yo, k4. 16 sts.
Row 6: P10, inc 1, k5. 17 sts.
Row 7: K4, p3, k4, yo, k1, yo, k5. 19 sts.
Row 8: P12, inc 1, k6. 20 sts.
Row 9: K4, p4, ssk, k7, k2tog, k1. 18 sts.
Row 10: P10, inc 1, k7. 19 sts.
Row 11: K4, p5, ssk, k5, k2tog, k1. 17 sts.
Row 12: P8, inc 1, k2, p1, k5. 18 sts.
Row 13: K4, p1, k1, p4, ssk, k3, k2tog, k1. 16 sts.
Row 14: P6, inc 1, k3, p1, k5. 17 sts.
Row 15: K4, p1, k1, p5, ssk, k1, k2tog, k1. 15 sts.
Row 16: P4, inc 1, k4, p1, k5.
Row 17: K4, p1, k1, p6, sk2p, k1. 14 sts
Row 18: P2tog, bo5, p3, k4. 8 sts.
Repeat rows 1–18 for desired length.

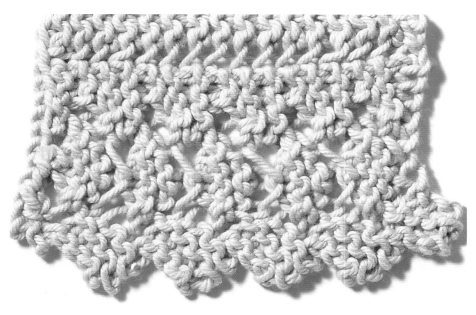

LOOP EDGING

NOTE
Written instructions only.

Loop – to make loop, k1 and leave st on source needle, yarn forward, wrap yarn clockwise around left thumb (right thumb for left handed knitter) to form loop, yarn back. k1 in back of same st.

INSTRUCTIONS
Multiple of 2 stitches + 1.

Row 1: K1, *make loop, k1; repeat from * to end of row.
Row 2: P1, *p2tog, p1; repeat from * to end of row.
Row 3: K2, *make loop, k1; repeat from * ending with k2.
Row 4: P2, *p2tog, p1; repeat from* ending with p2.
Repeat rows 1–4 for desired length.

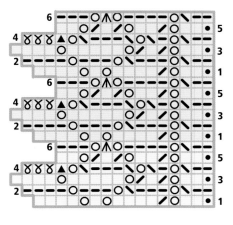

FORGET ME KNOT EDGING

INSTRUCTIONS
Cast on 14 stitches.

Row 1: Sl 1 kwise, k2, yo, k2tog, k4, yo, k1, yo, k4.
Row 2: K4, yo, k3, yo, k2tog, k3, yo, k2tog, k2.
Row 3: Sl 1 kwise, k2, yo, k2tog, k1, k2tog, yo, k5, yo, k4.
Row 4: Bo3, yo, k2tog, k3, k2tog, yo, k2tog, k1, yo, k2tog, k2.
Row 5: Sl 1 kwise, (k2, yo, k2tog) 2 times, k1, k2tog, yo, k2.
Row 6: K3, yo, sk2p, yo, k4, yo, k2tog, k2.
Repeat rows 1–6 for desired length.

213

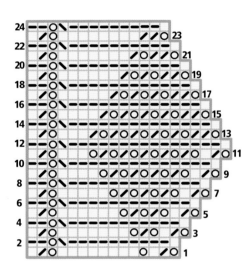

COCKLESHELL EDGING

NOTES
Edging is worked across the width to any desired length. Rows within the pattern repeat vary in length from 14–20 stitches. Fourteen stitches are cast on.

INSTRUCTIONS
Row 1: Yo, k2tog, k1, yo, k8, yo, k2tog, k1.

Row 2 and all even rows: K2, yo, k2tog, knit across to last st ending with p1.

Row 3: Yo, k2tog, k1, yo, k2tog, yo, k7, yo, k2tog, k1.

Row 5: Yo, k2tog, k1, (yo, k2tog) 2 times, yo, k6, yo, k2tog, k1.

Row 7: Yo, k2tog, k1, (yo, k2tog) 3 times, yo, k5, yo, k2tog, k1.

Row 9: Yo, k2tog, k1, (yo, k2tog) 4 times, yo, k4, yo, k2tog, k1.

Row 11: Yo, k2tog, k1, (yo, k2tog) 5 times, yo, k3, yo, k2tog, k1.

Row 13: Yo, (k2tog) 2 times, (yo, k2tog) 5 times, k3, yo, k2tog, k1.

Row 15: Yo, (k2tog) 2 times, (yo, k2tog) 4 times, k4, yo, k2tog, k1.

Row 17: Yo, (k2tog) 2 times, (yo, k2tog) 3 times, k5, yo, k2tog, k1.

Row 19: Yo, (k2tog) 2 times, (yo, k2tog) 2 times, k6, yo, k2tog, k1.

Row 21: Yo, (k2tog) 2 times, yo k2tog, k7, yo, k2tog, k1.

Row 23: Yo, (k2tog) 2 times, k8, yo, k2tog, k1.

Row 24: Same as Row 2.

Repeat rows 1–24 for desired length.

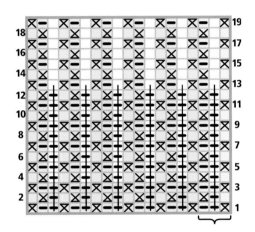

GOSSAMER FRINGE

INSTRUCTIONS
Multiple of 3 stitches + 1.

Rows 1: K1 tbl, *p2, k1 tbl; repeat from * to end of row.
Rows 2: P1, *k1 tbl, k1, p1; repeat from * to end of row.
Rows 3–12: Rows 1 and 2 (repeat 5 times).
Row 13: K1 tbl, *drop next st off needle and unravel to co st, p1, k1 tbl; repeat from * to end of row.
Rows 14: P1, * k1 tbl, p1; repeat from * to end of row.
Rows 15: K1 tbl, *p1, k1 tbl; repeat from * to end of row.
Rows 16–19: Rows 14 and 15 (repeat 2 times).

FRISEUR FRINGE

NOTE
Use cable cast on.

INSTRUCTIONS
Cast on 23 stitches.

Rows 1 and 2: Knit.
Row 3: Bo 19 sts, k3.
Row 4: K4, co 19 sts.
Repeat rows 1–4 for desired length.

215

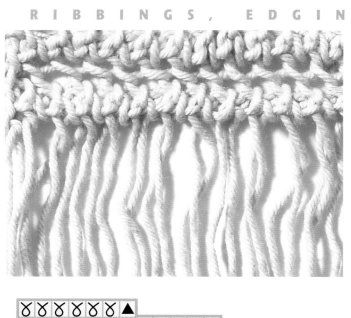

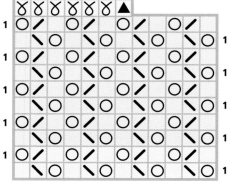

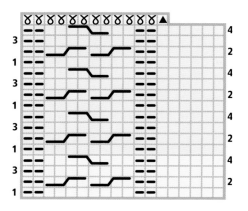

216

MOUNTMELLICK KNITTED EDGE

NOTES

For a thicker fringe, work with 4 or more strands of yarn held together.

Do not cut loops apart.

INSTRUCTIONS

Cast on 12 stitches.

Row 1: (Yo, k2tog, k1) 4 times.

Repeat Row 1 to desired length then bo 6 stitches, break yarn, pull yarn through last stitch on working needle. Drop all 5 stitches from source needle and unravel.

PLAITED FRINGE

NOTES

For a thicker fringe, work with 4 or more strands of yarn held together.

Do not cut loops apart.

INSTRUCTIONS

Cast on 18 stitches.

Begin on wrong side.

Row 1: K2, p8, k2, p6.

Row 2: K6, p2, (sl 2 sts onto cn and hold at back, k2, k2 from cn) 2 times, p2.

Row 3: K2, p8, k2, p6.

Row 4: K6, p2, k2, sl 2 sts onto cn and hold at front, k2, k2 from cn, k2, p2.

Repeat rows 1–4 to desired length ending with row 2 or 4. Then with wrong side facing, bo 13 stitches, break yarn, pull yarn through last stitch on working needle. Drop rem stitches from source needle and unravel.

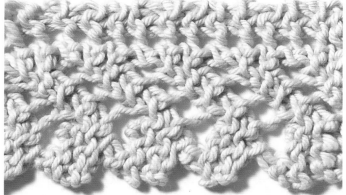

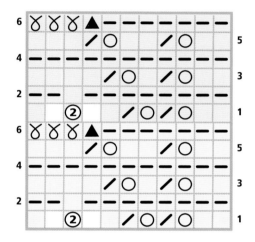

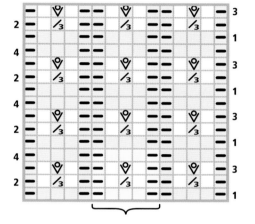

ENGLISH GADROON LACE

INSTRUCTIONS
Cast on 8 stitches.

Row 1: K2, (yo, k2tog) 2 times, k1, (yo2), k1.
Row 2: K1, drop one yo, in remaining yo (k1,p1, k1), k 7.
Row 3: K2, yo, k2tog, k1, yo, k2tog, k4.
Row 4: K11.
Row 5: K2, yo, k2tog, k2, yo, k2tog, k3.
Row 6: Bind off 3, k7.
Repeat rows 1–6 for desired length.

RIB V-STITCH

INSTRUCTIONS
Multiple of 5 stitches.

Row 1: *P1, k3, p1; repeat from * to end of row.
Row 2: *K1, p3tog, k1; repeat from * to end of row.
Row 3: *P1, in next st (k1, yo, k1), p1; repeat from * to end
of row.
Row 4: *K1, p3, k1; repeat from * to end of row.
Repeat rows 1–4.

217

knitting pattern gallery

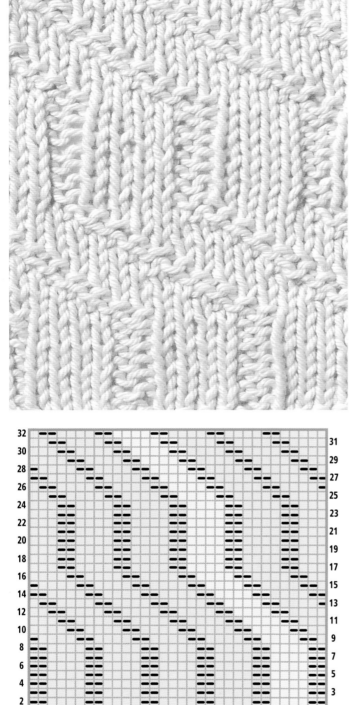

STAGGERED RIBS

INSTRUCTIONS
Multiple of 6 stitches + 2.

Row 1: P2, *k4, p2; repeat from * to end of row.

Row 2: K2, *p4, k2; repeat from * to end of row.

Rows 3–8: Repeat Rows 1 and 2 three times.

Row 9: K1, *p2, k4; repeat from * ending with p1.

Row 10: *P4, k2; repeat from * ending with p2.

Row 11: K3, p2, *k4, p2; repeat from * ending with k3.

Row 12: P2, *k2, p4; repeat from * to end of row.

Row 13: P1, *k4, p2; repeat from * ending with k1.

Row 14: Same as Row 8.

Row 15: Same as Row 9.

Row 16: Same as Row 10.

Row 17: Same as Row 11.

Row 18: P3, k2, *p4, k2; repeat from ending with p3.

Rows 19–24: Repeat Rows 17 and 18 three times.

Row 25: *K4, p2; repeat from * ending with k2.

Row 26: P1, *k2, p4; repeat from * ending with k1.

Row 27: Same as Row 1.

Row 28: K1, *p4, k2; repeat from * ending with p1.

Row 29: K2, *p2, k4; repeat from * to end of row.

Row 30: P3, k2, *p4, k2; repeat from * ending with p3.

Row 31: *K4, p2; repeat from *ending with k2.

Row 32: Same as Row 26.

Repeat rows 1–32.

COLOR CHANGES BY ROW

Color changes by row use one color of yarn for an entire row, sometimes multiple rows, before changing to another color. Although the patterns are often the same ones used when knitting with a single color, multiple colors are apt to make the patterns look dramatically different.

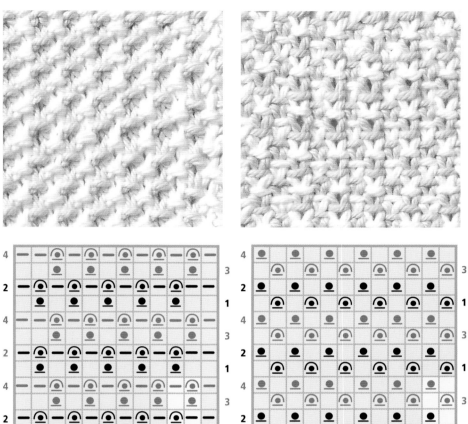

TWO COLOR SEED STITCH

INSTRUCTIONS
Multiple of 2 stitches.

Row 1: With color A – k1, *k1, sl 1 pwise; repeat from * ending with k1.
Row 2: With color A – k1, *wyif sl 1 pwise, wyib k1; repeat from * ending with k1.
Row 3: With color B – k1, *sl 1 pwise, k1; repeat from * ending with k1.
Row 4: With color B – k1, *k1, wyif sl 1 pwise, wyib k1; repeat from * ending with k1.
Repeat rows 1–4.

TWO COLOR LINEN STITCH

INSTRUCTIONS
Multiple of 2 stitches.

Row 1: With color A – *wyif sl 1 pwise, wyib k1; repeat from * to end of row.
Row 2: With color A – *wyib sl 1 pwise, wyif p1; repeat from * to end of row.
Row 3: With color B – *wyif sl 1 pwise, wyib k1; repeat from * to end of row.
Row 4: With color B – *wyib sl 1 pwise, wyif p1, yarn back; repeat from * to end of row.
Repeat rows 1–4.

219

knitting pattern gallery

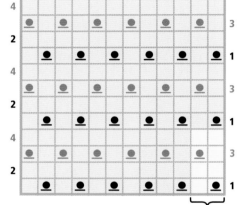

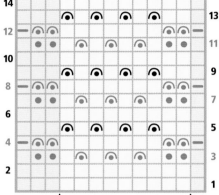

TWO COLOR CROSSED STITCH

NOTE
Written instructions only.

INSTRUCTIONS
Multiple of 3 stitches + 1.

Row 1: With color A – knit.
Row 2: With color B – p1, *with source needle, lift horizontal bar between stitches, twist bar and knit 1 stitch into it, p2; repeat from * ending with p1.
Row 3: With color A – *k3, pass 1st of these 3 stitches over the other 2; repeat from * to end of row.
Row 4: With color B – *p2, with source needle, lift horizontal bar between stitches, twist bar and knit 1 stitch into it; repeat from * ending with p2.
Row 5: With color B – k1, *k3, pass 1st of these 3 stitches over the other 2; repeat from * ending with k1.
Repeat rows 2–5.

PARTRIDGE EYE

INSTRUCTIONS
Multiple of 2 stitches.

Row 1: With color A – *sl 1 pwise, k1; repeat from * to end of row.
Row 2: With color A – purl.
Row 3: With color B – *k1, sl 1 pwise; repeat from * to end of row.
Row 4: With color B – purl.
Repeat rows 1–4.

WOVEN BLOCK STITCH

INSTRUCTIONS
Multiple of 9 stitches + 4.

Row 1: With color A – knit.
Row 2: With color A – purl.
Rows 3: With color B – k1, *wyib sl 2 pwise, k1, (wyif sl 1 pwise, k1) 3 times; repeat from * ending with wyib sl 2 pwise, k1.
Rows 4: With color B – K1, * wyif sl 2 pwise, p7; repeat from * ending with wyif sl 2 pwise, k1.
Rows 5: With color A – k3, * wyif sl 1 pwise, (k1, wyif sl 1 pwise) 3 times, k2; repeat from * ending with k1.
Rows 6: With color A – purl.
Rows 7–14: Repeat Rows 3–6 twice more.
Repeat rows 1–14.

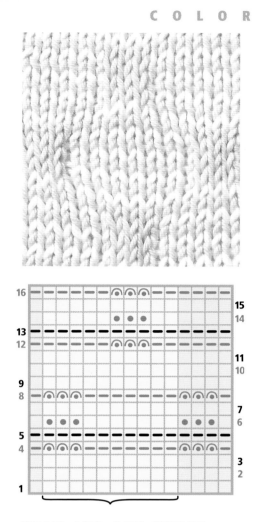

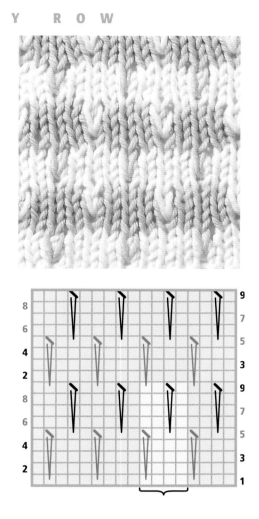

WAVE AND BOX STITCH

NOTE

Use double pointed needles. The work is turned after every odd numbered row. After every even numbered row, slide stitches to the opposite end of the needle, do not turn.

INSTRUCTIONS

Multiple of 10 stitches + 5.
Begin on wrong side.

Row 1: With color A – purl, turn.
Row 2: With color B – Knit, slide sts to other end of needle.
Row 3: With color A – Knit, turn.
Row 4: With color B – p1, *wyif sl 3 pwise, p7; repeat from * ending with wyif sl 3 pwise, p1, slide sts to other end of needle.
Row 5: With color A – purl, turn.
Row 6: With color B – k1, *wyib sl 3 pwise, k7; repeat from * ending with wyib sl 3 pwise, k1, slide sts to other end of needle.

Row 7: With color A – knit, turn.
Row 8: With color B – repeat Row 4, slide sts to other end of needle.
Rows 9, 10, and 11: Repeat Rows 1, 2, and 3.
Row 12: With color B – p6, *wyif sl 3 pwise, p7; repeat from * ending with wyif sl 3 pwise, p6, slide sts to other end of needle.
Row 13: With color A – purl.
Row 14: With color B – k6, *wyib sl 3 pwise, k7; repeat from * ending with wyib sl 3 pwise, k6, slide sts to other end of needle.
Row 15: With color A – knit.
Row 16: Same as Row 12.
Repeat rows 1–16.

FEZ PATTERN

NOTE

V draw up a loop in stitch 3 rows below, k1, pass loop over this stitch.

INSTRUCTIONS

Multiple of 4 stitches + 1.

Rows 1 and 3: With color A – knit.
Rows 2 and 4: With color A – purl.
Row 5: With color B – *k3, draw up a loop in stitch 3 rows below, k1, pass loop over this stitch; repeat from * ending with k1.
Rows 6 and 8: With color B – purl.
Row 7: With color B – knit.
Row 9: With color A – k1, * draw up a loop in stitch 3 rows below, k1, pass loop over this stitch, k3; repeat from * ending with k3.
Repeat rows 2–9.

221

knitting pattern gallery

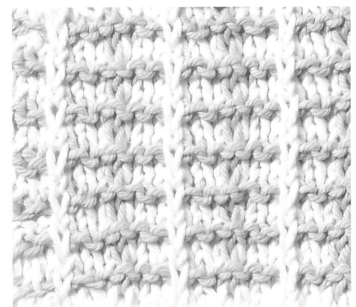

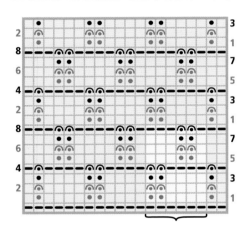

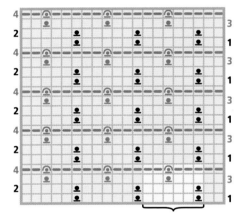

222

TWO COLOR LATTICE

INSTRUCTIONS
Multiple of 6 stitches + 2.
Cast on Color A and knit 1 row.

Row 1: With color B – k1, wyib sl 1 pwise, *k4, wyib sl 2 pwise; repeat from * ending with wyib sl 1 pwise, k1.
Row 2: With color B – p1, wyif sl 1 pwise, *p4, wyif sl 2 pwise; repeat from * ending with wyif sl 1 pwise, p1.
Row 3: With color A – k1, wyib sl 1 pwise, *k4, wyib sl 2 pwise; repeat from * ending with wyib sl 1 pwise, k1.
Row 4: With color A – k1, wyif sl 1 pwise, *k4, wyif sl 2 pwise; repeat from * ending with wyif sl 1 pwise, k1.
Row 5: With color B – k3, *wyib sl 2 pwise, k4; repeat from * ending with wyib sl 2 pwise, k3.
Row 6: With color B – p3, *wyif sl 2 pwise, p4; repeat from * ending with wyif sl 2 pwise, p3.
Row 7: With color A – k3, *wyib sl 2 pwise, k4; repeat from * ending with wyib sl 2 pwise, k3.
Row 8: With color A – k3, *wyif sl 2 pwise, k4; repeat from * ending with wyif sl 2 pwise, k3.
Repeat rows 1–8.

PLAID LADDERS

INSTRUCTIONS
Multiple of 6 stitches + 2.

Row 1: With color A – k2, *sl 1 pwise, k5; repeat from * to end of row.
Row 2: With color A – p5, *sl 1 pwise, p5; repeat from * ending with sl 1 pwise, p2.
Row 3: With color B – *k5, sl 1 pwise; repeat from * ending with k2.
Row 4: With Color B – k2, *wyif sl 1 pwise, wyib k5; repeat from * to end of row.
Repeat rows 1–4.

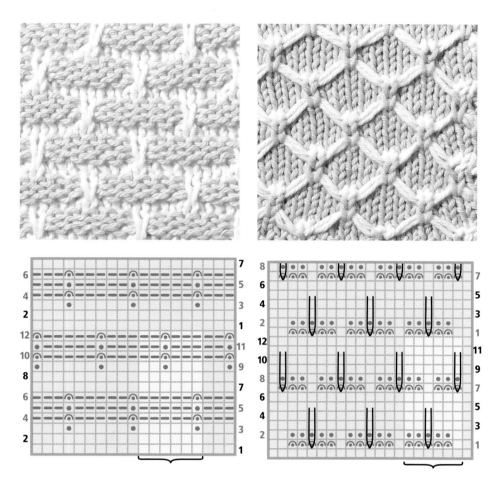

BRICK PATTERN

NOTE
Work Row 2 loosely.

INSTRUCTIONS
Multiple of 6 stitches + 1.

Rows 1 and 7: With color A – knit.

Rows 2 and 8: With color A – purl loosely.

Row 3: With color B – k3, *sl 1 pwise, k5; repeat from * ending with sl 1 pwise, k3.

Rows 4 and 6: With color B – k3, *wyif sl 1 pwise (same stitch slipped in previous row), wyib k5; repeat from * ending with wyif sl 1 pwise, wyib k3.

Row 5: With color B – p3, sl 1 pwise (same stitch slipped in previous row), p5; repeat from * ending with sl 1 pwise, p3.

Row 7: With color A – knit.

Row 8: With color A – purl.

Row 9: With color B – *sl 1 pwise, k5; repeat from * ending with s1 pwise.

Rows 10 and 12: With color B – *wyif sl 1 pwise (same stitch slipped in previous row), wyib k5; repeat from * ending with sl 1 pwise.

Row 11: With color B – *sl 1 pwise, p5; repeat from * ending with sl 1 pwise.

Repeat rows 1–12.

BUTTERFLY QUILTING

NOTE
Keep color B strands loose as they are carried across the front of the work.

INSTRUCTIONS
Multiple of 6 stitches + 3.
Cast on with color A and purl one row.

Row 1: With color B – k2, *wyif sl 5 pwise, k1; repeat from * ending with k1.

Row 2: With color B – p2,*wyib sl 5 pwise, p1; repeat from * ending with p1.

Row 3: With color A – knit.

Row 4: With color A – purl.

Row 5: With color A – k4, *insert working needle under the 2 loose strand of color B, k1 catching both strands of color B behind the stitch as it is knitted, k5; repeat from * ending with k4.

Row 6: With color A – purl.

Row 7: With color B – k1, wyif sl 3 pwise, *k1, wyif sl 5 pwise; repeat from * ending with k1, wyif sl 3 pwise, k1.

Row 8: With color B – p1, wyib sl 3 pwise, *p1, wyib sl 5 pwise; repeat from * ending with p1, wyib sl 3 pwise, p1.

Rows 9 and 10: With color A – repeat Rows 3 and 4.

Row 11: With color A – k1, *insert working needle under the 2 loose strand of color B, k1 catching both strands of color B behind the stitch as it is knitted, k5; repeat from * ending with k1.

Row 12: With color A – purl.

Repeat rows 1–12.

223

knitting pattern gallery

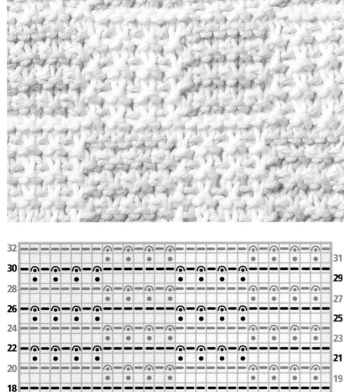

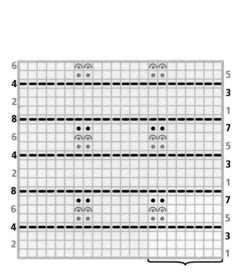

224

CHESSBOARD

INSTRUCTIONS
Multiple of 14 stitches + 2.

Rows 1 and 2: With color A – knit.
Rows 3, 7, 11, and 15: With color B – k1, *k7, (wyib sl 1 pwise, k1) 3 times, wyib sl 1 pwise; repeat from * ending with k1.
Row 4 and all even rows: With same color as previous row – knit the stitches that are the same color, wyif sl the other colors pwise (there are no slip stitches in rows 2 and 18).
Rows 5, 9, and 13: With color A – k1, *(wyib sl 1 pwise, k1) 3 times, wyib sl 1 pwise, k7; repeat from * ending with k1.
Rows 17 and 18: With color A – knit.
Rows 19, 23, 27, and 31: With color B – k1, *(ywib sl 1 pwise, k1) 3 times, wyib sl 1 pwise, k7; repeat from * ending with k1.
Rows 21, 25, and 29: With color A – k1, *k7, (wyib sl 1 pwise, k1) 3 times, wyib sl 1 pwise; repeat from * ending with k1.
Row 32: Same as Row 4.
Repeat rows 1–32.

OVAL CHAIN

INSTRUCTIONS
Multiple of 8 stitches + 6.

Row 1: With color A – knit.
Row 2: With color A – purl.
Rows 3 and 4: With color B – knit.
Row 5: With color A – k6, *wyib sl 2 pwise, k6; repeat from * to end of row.
Row 6: With color A – p6, *wyif sl 2 pwise, p6; repeat from * to end of row.
Row 7: With color B – k6, *wyib sl 2 pwise, k6; repeat from * to end of row.
Row 8: With color B – knit.
Repeat rows 1–8.

COLOR—STRANDING AND WEAVING

Color stranding uses two or more colors of yarn in one row, switching colors every few stitches. Carrying an extra strand of yarn across the back produces a thick, insulating fabric, so color stranding is often used to make warm winter sweaters and mittens.

When yarn colors are more or less in blocks, small amounts of different colors are wrapped on bobbins. Each color is worked from its bobbin. Colors are twisted together where they meet. There is no stranding or weaving. Stockinette stitch is normally used.

Charted designs for other types of needlework can be used for color knitting. If worked in stockinette stitch the patterns can be used directly because stockinette stitch produces a stitch that is about the same height as width.

Two-color charts can also be used for double knitting and bead knitting.

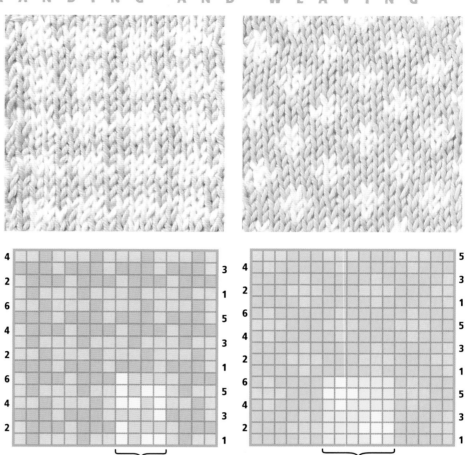

HOUNDSTOOTH CHECK

NOTE
Work on stockinette ground.

INSTRUCTIONS
Multiple of 4 stitches.

FLEUR DE LIS

NOTE
Work on stockinette ground.

INSTRUCTIONS
Multiple of 6 stitches + 3.

225

knitting pattern gallery

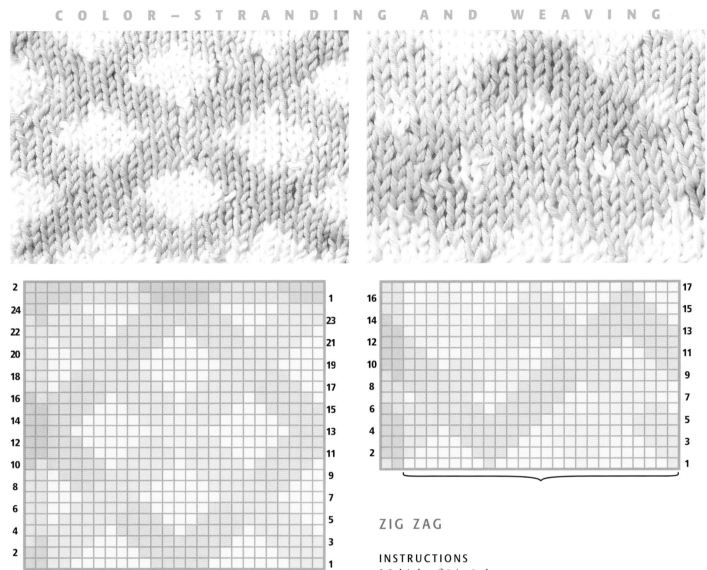

FAIR ISLE ARGYLL

INSTRUCTIONS
Multiple of 24 stitches + 1.
Multiple of 24 rows + 1.

ZIG ZAG

INSTRUCTIONS
Multiple of 24 stitches.

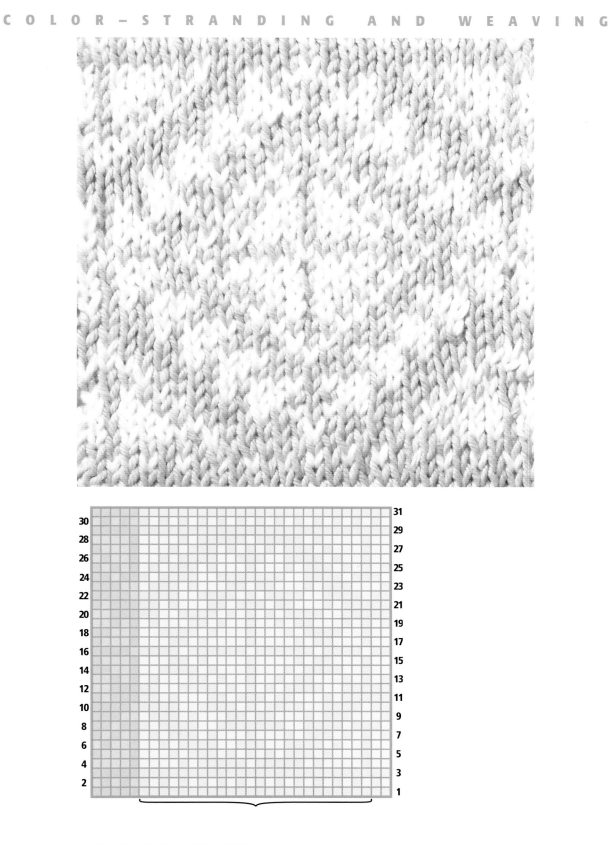

31
30
29
28
27
26
25
24
23
22
21
20
19
18
17
16
15
14
13
12
11
10
9
8
7
6
5
4
3
2
1

227

FAIR ISLE DIAMOND

INSTRUCTIONS
Multiple of 24 stitches + 1.

knitting pattern gallery

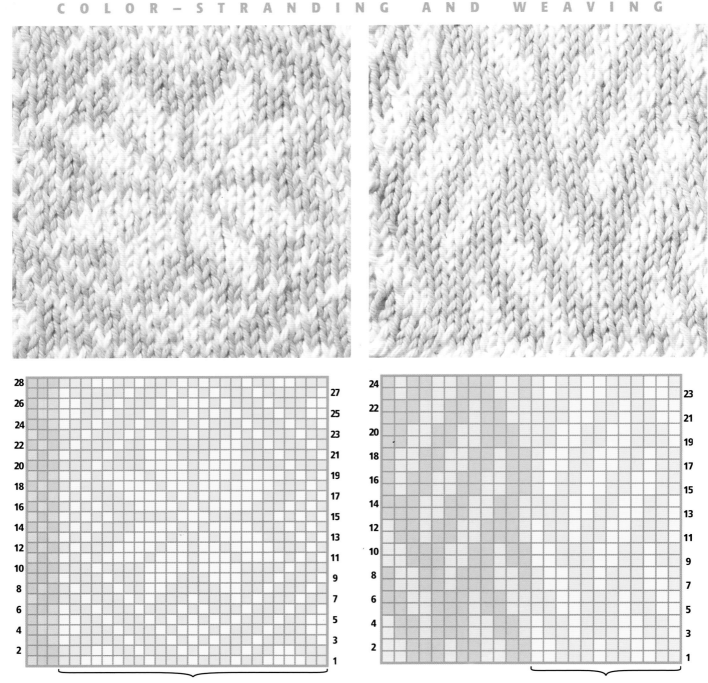

NORWEGIAN STAR

INSTRUCTIONS
Multiple of 25 stitches.

STRIPED DIAMONDS

INSTRUCTIONS
Multiple of 12 stitches + 1.
Multiple of 24 rows.

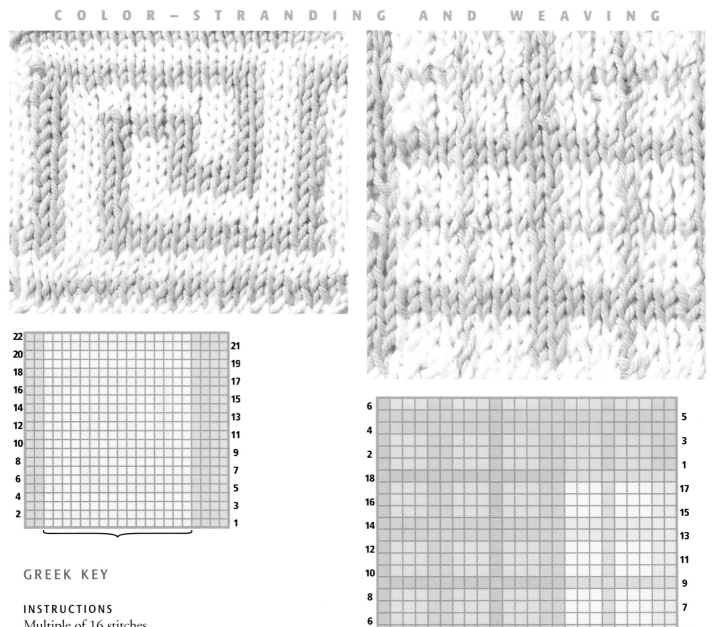

GREEK KEY

INSTRUCTIONS
Multiple of 16 stitches.

TARTAN PLAID

INSTRUCTIONS
Multiple of 9 stitches + 2.
Multiple of 18 rows + 1.

229

knitting pattern gallery

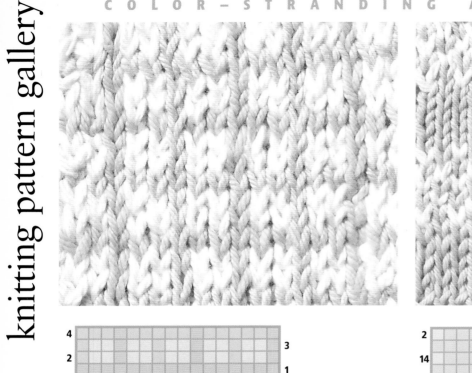

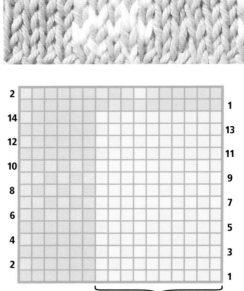

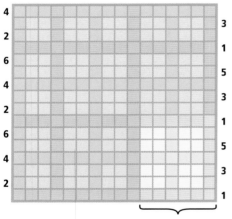

FAIR ISLE PLAID

INSTRUCTIONS
Multiple of 6 stitches + 1.
Multiple of 6 +1 rows.

FAIR ISLE CHECK

INSTRUCTIONS
Multiple of 10 stitches + 5.
Multiple of 14 rows.

INTARSIA ARGYLL

INSTRUCTIONS
Multiple of 16 stitches + 1.
Multiple of 32 rows + 2.

knitting pattern gallery

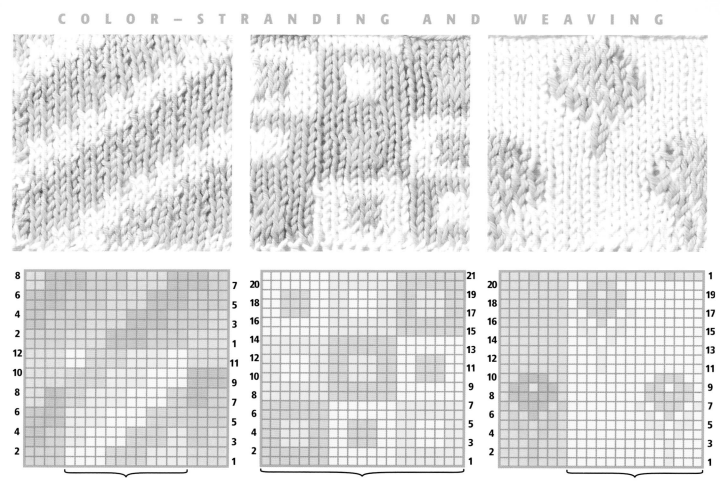

DIAGONAL STRIPES

INSTRUCTIONS
Multiple of 12 stitches.
Multiple of 12 rows.

COLOR BLOCKS

INSTRUCTIONS
Multiple of 7 stitches (21 stitches for all
    three colors).
Multiple of 7 rows (21 rows for all three
    colors).

FLOWERS

INSTRUCTIONS
Multiple of 14 stitches + 7.
Multiple of 20 rows.

232

resources and suppliers

bibliography

Big Sky Studio and Gallery (yarns, materials)
961 'C' Moraga Road
Lafayette, CA 94549
Phone: 925-284-1020
Fax: 925-284-2624
E-mail: bigskys@pacbell.net
Website: www.bigskystudio.com

Blue Sky Alpacas (alpaca yarn)
P.O. Box 387
St. Francis, MN 55070
Phone: 763-753-5815
Website: www.blueskyalpacas.com

Bryson Distributors (kits, yarns, materials)
(Fiber Trends, Brittany, Clover, Susan
Bates, Boyle)
4065 W. 11th Ave. #39
Eugene, OR 97402
Phone: 800-544-8992
Fax: 541-334-6489
Website: www.brysonknits.com

Cabin Fever (kits)
111 Nottawasago Street
Orillia, Ontario
L3V 3J7 Canada
Phone: 800-671-9112
E-mail: infor@cabinfever.ca
Website: www.cabinfever.ca

Coats & Clark (yarns)
Consumer Services
P.O. Box 12229
Greenville, SC 29612-0229
Phone: 800-648-1479
Website: www.coatsandclark.com

Coy (beads, silk threads, bead knitting kits,
needles, purse findings)
Coy Roberts
Phone: 949-475-7601
E-mail: Coysdelight@aol.com
Website: www.coysdelight.com

Creative Castle (beads)
2321 Michael Drive
Newbury Park, CA 91320-3233
Phone: 805-499-1377
Fax: 805-499-7923
E-mail: ctripp@creativecastle.com

Fiber Trends (kits, patterns, felting materials)
P.O. Box 2634
Bellingham, WA 98226
Phone: 888-733-5991
E-mail: ftknits@aol.com
Website: www.fibertrends.com

The Knitting Guild of America
(TKGA) (National Organization)
1100-H Brandywine Blvd.
Zanesville, OH 43702-3388
Phone: 800-274-6034
Fax: 740-452-2552
E-mail: tkga@tkga.com
Website: www.tkga.com

Lion Brand Yarn (yarns)
34 15th Street
New York, NY 10011
Phone: 800-258-9276
Website: www.lionbrand.com

Philosopher's Wool Co. (wool yarn and kits)
Inverhuron, Ontario
N0G 2T0 Canada
Phone: 519-368-5354
E-mail: philosophers88@magma.ca
Website: www.philosoperswool.com

NOTES FOR THE HISTORY OF KNITTING
(PAGES 10–19)

1. Do not lose any sleep over this. Even with knitted stockings, wars might have lasted just as long because of the knights' irritation over runs in their stockings.

2. Payne, Blanche, *History of Costume: from the Ancient Egyptians to the Twentieth Century*, Harper and Row, NY, 1965, pp. 107–108.

3. Piecework.

4. Rutt, Richard, *A History of Hand Knitting*, Interweave Press, Loveland, CO, 1987, p. 147.

5. Barber, E.J.W., *Prehistoric Textiles*, Princeton University Press, Princeton, NJ, 1992, p. 154.

6. Rutt, Richard, p. 32–33, and Mary Thomas, p. 91.

7. Hsia Nai, ed.; *New Archaeological Finds in China: Discoveries During the Cultural Revolution*; Foreign Language Press, Peking, China, 1975, pp. 53–4. Chinese were exporting silk to the West by the 3rd century B.C.

8. Rutt, op.cit., p. 41.

9. Regions of Spain were Muslim until the last Moorish stronghold was overthrown by King Ferdinand and Queen Isabella in 1491.

10. Rutt, op.cit., p. 56.

11. Ibid.

12. Paraphrase from Chairman Mao T'se-T'ung, Hsia Nai, op.cit., p. 26.

13. Rutt, op.cit., p. 46.

14. Though Constantinople, the capital of the Byzantine Empire, finally fell to Turkish armies in 1453, teams of Byzantine mosaic artisans were living in Sicily and decorating the churches more than 300 years earlier.

15. Vatne, Dr. Diane, private correspondence.

16. Rutt, op.cit., pp. 60–1.

17. Rutt, op.cit., p. 58.

18. Rutt, op.cit., p. 58.

19. Rutt, op.cit., p. 73.

234

20. Nicholson, Heather, *The Loving Stitch: a History of Knitting and Spinning in New Zealand*, Auckland University Press, Auckland, NZ, 1998, p. 15.

21. Payne, op.cit., p. 261.

22. Payne, op.cit., p. 261.

23. Payne, op.cit., p. 265.

24. Payne, op.cit., p. 262.

25. Payne, op.cit., p. 276.

26. Lambert, Miss, *Miss Lambert's Complete Guide to Needlework*, T.B. Peterson, Philadelphia, PA, 1857, pp. 184–5.

27. Payne, op.cit., p. 276

28. Ibid.

29. Payne, op.cit., p. 276

30. Rutt, op.cit., p. 73.

31. Rutt's insistence the spread of knitting in England waited on the technology to draw steel wire (op.cit., p. 62) bears some discussion. Fine needles were made of brass and iron, even in the 18th century. Split bamboo and brass needles in 2.25 mm are available even now, though there is not much demand for such small sizes. Drawn metal is helpful for a smooth needle, but certainly not essential. Medieval chain mail metalsmiths were skilled enough to make rods which could be smoothed into a thin needle. Even bone can be worked into needles small enough for fine gloves and stockings. Had knitting been in great demand earlier, needles would have been made or imported to meet the need.

32. MacDonald, Anne L., *No Idle Hands: the Social History of American Knitting*, Ballantine Books, New York, NY, 1988, p. 5.

33. Lambert, op.cit., p. 186

34. Rutt, op.cit., p. 83.

35. Ibid, p. 85.

36. Payne, op.cit., p. 452.

37. Nicholson, op.cit., p. 19.

38. Lane, Rose Wilder, *The Woman's Day Book of American Needlework*, Simon and Schuster, New York, NY, 1963, p. 166.

39. Rutt, op.cit., pp. 80–1.

40. MacDonald, op.cit., p. 3.

41. MacDonald, op.cit., p. 13.

42. Lambert, op.cit., pp. 186–7

43. Nicholson, op.cit., p. 21. The middle class arrived later, seeking real estate which at home was in the hands of the upper class.

44. Nicholson, op.cit., p. 57. This leads to the interesting situation that there were people who had never seen knitting at the beginning of World War I, and who had to learn to knit to join the war effort.

45. Nicholson, op.cit., p. 57.

46. Nicholson, op.cit., p. 30.

47. Scott, Shirley A., *Canada Knits*, McGraw-Hill Ryerson, Toronto, Ontario, Canada, 1990, pp. 5, 26.

48. Stephens, Ann S., *Ladies' Complete Guide to Crochet and Fancy Knitting*, Garrett & Co., New York, NY, 1854, p. 10, rudely comments on "one of the most distinguished literary ladies of this century" who loved to knit. "Our friend is only singular in the homeliness of her taste in knitting useful stockings, instead of pretty ornaments."

49. Nicholson, op.cit., p. 19.

50. *The Ladies' Work-table Book*, Philadelphia, PA, T.B. Peterson and Brothers, 1864, p. 99. May be because so many noble families exported their own black sheep to the colonies.

51. Stephens, Mrs. Ann S., *Ladies' Complete Guide to Crochet and Fancy Knitting*, Garrett & Co., New York, NY, 1854, p. 8.

52. *The Ladies' Work-table Book*, op.cit, p. 99.

53. The last Russian empress, Alexandra Feodorovna, Queen Victoria's granddaughter, attempted to get the notoriously pleasure-loving Russian nobility to knit three garments for charity each year, as she herself did. They refused! Massey, Robert K., *Nicholas and Alexandra*, Atheneum Books, New York, NY, 1967, p. 73.

54. Though Miss Lambert (op.cit.) introduced the wire gauge as a way of measuring the size of a needle, without a stitch and row gauge knowing what size needle to use is only half the battle.

55. Nicholson, op.cit., p. 67.

56. Lambert, op.cit., p. 190.

57. Lambert, op.cit., p. 221.

58. *The Ladies' Work-table Book*, (op.cit.), Miss Lambert, op.cit., p. 221, and others encouraged women to hold needles in the German

(Continental) way, with the yarn coming over the left fingers. This method is both practical and had not been associated with peasant knitting in Britain, so it was not threatening to the nouveau riche. Another occasional reason for this technical preference is that some American books shamelessly cribbed everything, including illustrations, from English books, since copyrights did not extend across the oceans.

59. Stephens, op.cit., p. 10.

60. Susannah Caulfeild tactlessly comments that "stocking knitting is chiefly the work of the ladies of England and the peasants of the Shetland Isles and Scotland." Caulfeild, S.F.A. and Blanche C. Saward, *The Dictionary of Needlework*, (reprint of the 1882 publication); Arno Press, New York, NY, 1972, p. 304.

61. In cold climates, like Scandinavia, traditional knitting went on without interruption because being warm was more important than being a non-peasant. We are still borrowing useful techniques from them.

62. Frost, S. Anne, *The Ladies' Guide to Needlework, Embroidery, Etc.*, Henry T. Williams, New York, NY, 1877, p. 73.

63. Nicholson, op.cit., pp. 54–55.

64. Nicholson, op.cit., p. 55.

65. Payne, op.cit., p. 453. For a while at the beginning of the 19th century, gentlemen wore tight double-knitted trousers, but since they were usually corseted, to look good in these, there was no advantage except at the knees.

66. Caulfeild, op.cit., pp. 277–8.

67. Nicholson, op.cit., p. 67

68. Nicholson, op.cit., p. 67.

69. Nicholson, op.cit., pp. 59–60.

70. Nicholson, op.cit., p. 61.

71. Nicholson, op.cit., p. 71. In the 1960s, at my own school in Sydney, we still wore woven underwear, tunics, shirts, and ties when playing hockey.

72. Nicholson, op.cit., p. 93.

73. Nicholson, op.cit., p. 94.

74. Nicholson, op.cit., p. 94.

75. Nicholson, op.cit., p. 94.

Abbey, Barbara. *The Complete Book of Knitting*. The Viking Press, New York, NY, 1971.

Allen, Pam. *Knitting For Dummies*. Hungry Minds Inc., New York, NY, 2002.

An American Lady, A Winter Gift for Ladies. G. B. Zeiber, Philadelphia, PA, 1847.

Barber, E.J.W. *Prehistoric Textiles*. Princeton University Press, Princeton, NJ, 1992.

Barsaloux, Elsa. *Utopia Yarn Book*. Henry E. Frankenberg Co., New York, NY, 1913.

____, *Edgings. J. & P. Coats and Clark's Book 162, 4th Edition*, The Spool Cotton Company, Charlotte, NC, 1941.

Buss, Katharina. *Big Book Of Knitting*. Sterling Publications Co., Inc., New York, NY, 1999.

Bourgeois, Ann and Eugene. *Fair Isle Sweaters Simplified*. Martingale & Company, Woodinville, WA, 2000.

Caulfeild, S. F. A. and Blanche C. Saward. *The Dictionary of Needlework*, (reprint of the 1882 publication). Arno Press, New York, NY, 1972.

Dandanell, Birgitta and Ulla Danielsson. *Twined Knitting*. Interweave Press, Loveland, CO, 1989.

Don, Sarah. *Art of Shetland Lace*. Lacis, Berkeley, CA, 1991.

Epstein, Nicky. *Nicky Epstein's Knitted Embellishments*. Interweave Press, Loveland, CO, 1999.

____. *The Knit Hat Book*. Taunton Press, Newton CT, 1997.

Frost, S. Anne. *The Ladies' Guide to Needle Work, Embroidery, Etc.* Henry T. Williams, New York, NY, 1877.

Gibson-Roberts, Priscilla. *Knitting in the Old Way*. Interweave Press, Loveland, CO, 1985.

Goldberg, Rhoda Ochser. *The New Knitting Dictionary*. Crown, New York, NY, 1984.

Harmony Guides. *Harmony Guide To Knitting Stitches, Vol. 1*. Lyric Books Limited, London, NW7, UK, 1983.

Harmony Guide. *Harmony Guide To Knitting Stitches, Vol. 2*. Lyric Books Limited, London, NW7, UK, 1987.

Hiatt, June Hemmons. *The Principles of Knitting*. Simon and Schuster, New York, NY, 1988.

Hsia, Nai, ed. *New Archaeological Finds in China: Discoveries During the Cultural Revolution*. Foreign Language Press, Peking, China, 1974.

The Ladies' Work-table Book. T. B. Peterson and Brothers, G. B. Zeiber & Co., Philadelphia, PA, 1864.

Lambert, Miss (Frances). *Miss Lambert's Complete Guide to Needlework and Embroidery*. T. B. Peterson, Philadelphia, PA, 1857.

Lane, Rose Wilder. *The Woman's Day Book of American Needlework*. Simon and Schuster, New York, NY, 1963.

Lavold, Elsebeth. *Viking Patterns for Knitting*. Trafalgar Square, North Pomfret, UK, 2000.

Leisure Arts. *99 Knit Stitches*. Leisure Arts, Little Rock, AR, 1997.

____. *I Can't Believe I'm Knitting*, Leisure Arts, Little Rock, AR, 1997.

Lewis, Susanna E. *Knitting Lace*. Taunton Press, Newtown, CT, 1992.

MacDonald, Anne L. *No Idle Hands: the Social History of American Knitting*. Ballantine Books, New York, NY, 1988.

Massey, Robert K. *Nicholas and Alexandra*. Atheneum Books, New York, NY, 1967.

Mon Tricot Knitting Dictionary, 900 Stitch Patterns, English Translation. R. Cartier, Paris, France, 1963.

Nicholson, Heather. *The Loving Stitch: a History of Knitting and Spinning in New Zealand*. Auckland University Press, Auckland, NZ, 1998.

Parry-Jones, Maria. *The Knitting Stitch Bible*. Krause Publications, Iola, WI, 2002.

Payne, Blanche. *History of Costume: from the Ancient Egyptians to the Twentieth Century*. Harper and Row, New York, NY, 1965.

Phillips, Mary Walker. *Knitting Counterpanes*. Taunton Press, Newtown, CT, 1989.

Reader's Digest. *Reader's Digest Complete Guide To Needlework*. The Reader's Digest Association, Inc., Pleasantville NY, 1979.

Rosen, Evie. *The All New Teach Yourself To Knit*. Leisure Arts, Little Rock, AR, 1992.

Royce, Beverly. *Notes on Double Knitting*. Schoolhouse Press, Pittsville, WI, 1994.

Rutt, Richard. A *History of Hand Knitting*. Interweave Press, Loveland, CO, 1987.

Scott, Shirley. *Canada Knits*, McGraw-Hill Ryerson, Toronto, Ontario, Canada, 1990.

Stanfield, Lesley. *The New Knitting Stitch Library*. Lark Books, Asheville, NC, 1998.

Stanfield, Lesley, and Melody Griffiths. *The Encyclopedia of Knitting*. Quarto Publishing, London, UK, 2000.

Stanley, Montse. *Knitter's Handbook*. Reader's Digest, New York, NY, 1993.

Starmore, Alice. *Tudor Roses*. Broad Bay Co., Fort Bragg, CA, 1998.

Stephens, Ann S. *Ladies' Complete Guide to Crochet and Fancy Knitting*. Garrett & Co., New York, NY, 1854.

Thomas, Mary. *Mary Thomas's Book of Knitting Patterns*, Macmillan Co., New York, NY, 1941.

____. *Mary Thomas's Knitting Book*, Dover, New York, NY, 1972.

Threads Magazine. *Hand-knitting Techniques*. Taunton Press, Newtown, CT, 1991.

____. *Knitting Around the World*. Taunton Press, Newtown, CT, 1993.

Vogue (editors). *Vogue Knitting Book*. Vogue, Sixth & Spring Books, New York, NY, 2002.

Walker, Barbara G. *A Second Treasury of Knitting Patterns*, Charles Scribner's Sons, New York, NY, 1970.

Westfall, Fran. *Encyclopedia of Knitting and Crochet Stitches*, Bonanza Books, New York, NY, 1971.

Zimmermann, Elizabeth. *Knitting Without Tears*, Simon and Schuster, New York, NY, 1995.

235

index

For a complete list of knitting patterns see the Pattern Index on page 240.

index

pattern index